BEYBLADE

Vol. 4

Tyson vs. the White Tigers

Beyblade
Vol. 4
Tyson vs. the White Tigers

Story and Art by Takao Aoki

English Adaptation/Fred Burke
Translation/Akira Watanabe
Touch-up Art & Lettering/Dave Lanphear
Cover & Interior Design/Andrea Rice
Editor/Ian Robertson

Managing Editor/Annette Roman
Director of Production/Noboru Watanabe
Editorial Director/Alvin Lu
Sr. Director of Acquisitions/Rika Inouye
Vice President of Sales & Marketing/Liza Coppola
Executive Vice President/Hyoe Narita
Publisher/Seiji Horibuchi

Published by VIZ, LLC
P.O. Box 77010
San Francisco, CA 94107

10 9 8 7 6 5 4 3 2 1
First printing, June 2005

PARENTAL ADVISORY
BEYBLADE is rated A for All Ages.

store.viz.com

www.viz.com

story thus far

Tyson is an Elementary School student who loves Beyblades. He enjoys a good fight, but he cares for his friends and has their trust. In the Super Battle Tournament it is revealed that Max's Beyblade, Draciel, is the legendary third Beyblade, and Ray's Beyblade, Driger, is the fourth legendary Beyblade. Tyson narrowly defeats Ray with the help of the new Dragoon Beyblade developed by the Chief and unleashes a new type of attack.

In the final battle Tyson is victorious. During this battle Kai reveals that he wants revenge not against Tyson but against all Beyblades, because Kai's father abandoned him to pursue a career in Beyblade development. Kai's ambition was to use the four legendary Beyblades to destroy all the Beyblades in the world. In the end he gives up this idea to pursue a new goal: to defeat Tyson. Tyson also learns that the identity of the masked stranger Jin, is none other than his older brother Hitoshi, who had left years ago to help their father excavate ruins in China.

After the tournament, Hitoshi takes Tyson, Max, The Chief, and Kai to China, where they meet up with Ray. They proceed to the excavation site, which turns out to be an ancient Beyblade shrine. Once there, the spirit contained within each of their Beyblades is released and awakens the Beyblading ambitions of millions of Beybladers all over the world.

Also while in China they meet a group called the White Tigers, which is the tribe of Beybladers that Ray is from. One of the members of the White Tigers holds a terrible grudge against Ray. Now Ray must confront his past, but at what cost?

Tyson: an energetic youth with a passionate Beyblader spirit!

Max: Tyson's American-born Beyblading pal!

The Chief: Tyson's best friend, Kenny, loves science more than battling.

Ray: a skilled Beyblader from China.

Lee: an intense Beyblader from the Chinese Beyblade team, the White Tigers

Hitoshi: Tyson's older brother who was masquerading as Jin

Kai Hiwatari: Kai will do anything to get Tyson's Dragoon!

Contents

Chapter 1: Tyson vs. the White Tigers
7

Chapter 2: Demolition Boys
66

Special Section: Introducing USA's Ace Michael
155

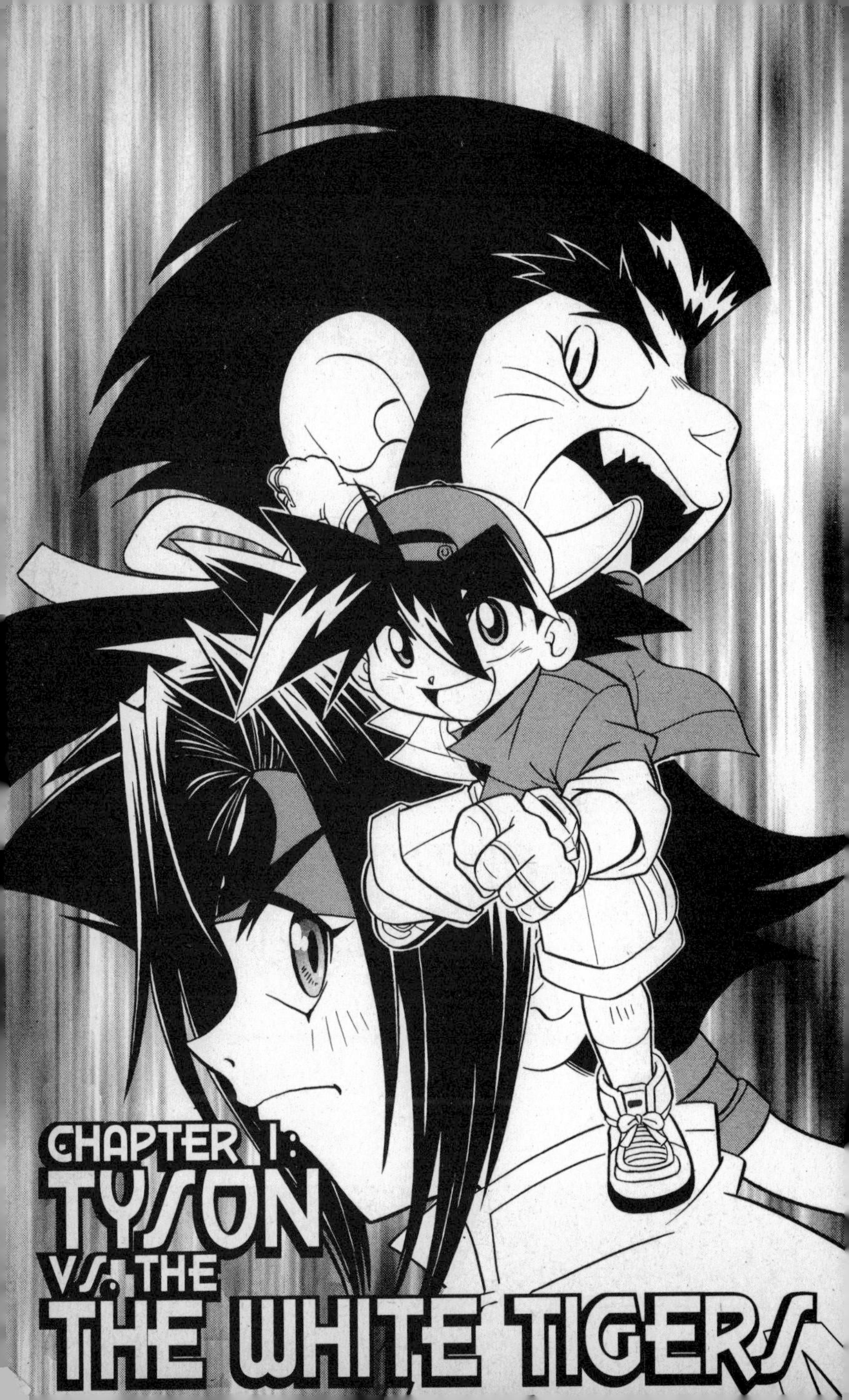
CHAPTER 1:
TYSON
VS. THE
THE WHITE TIGERS

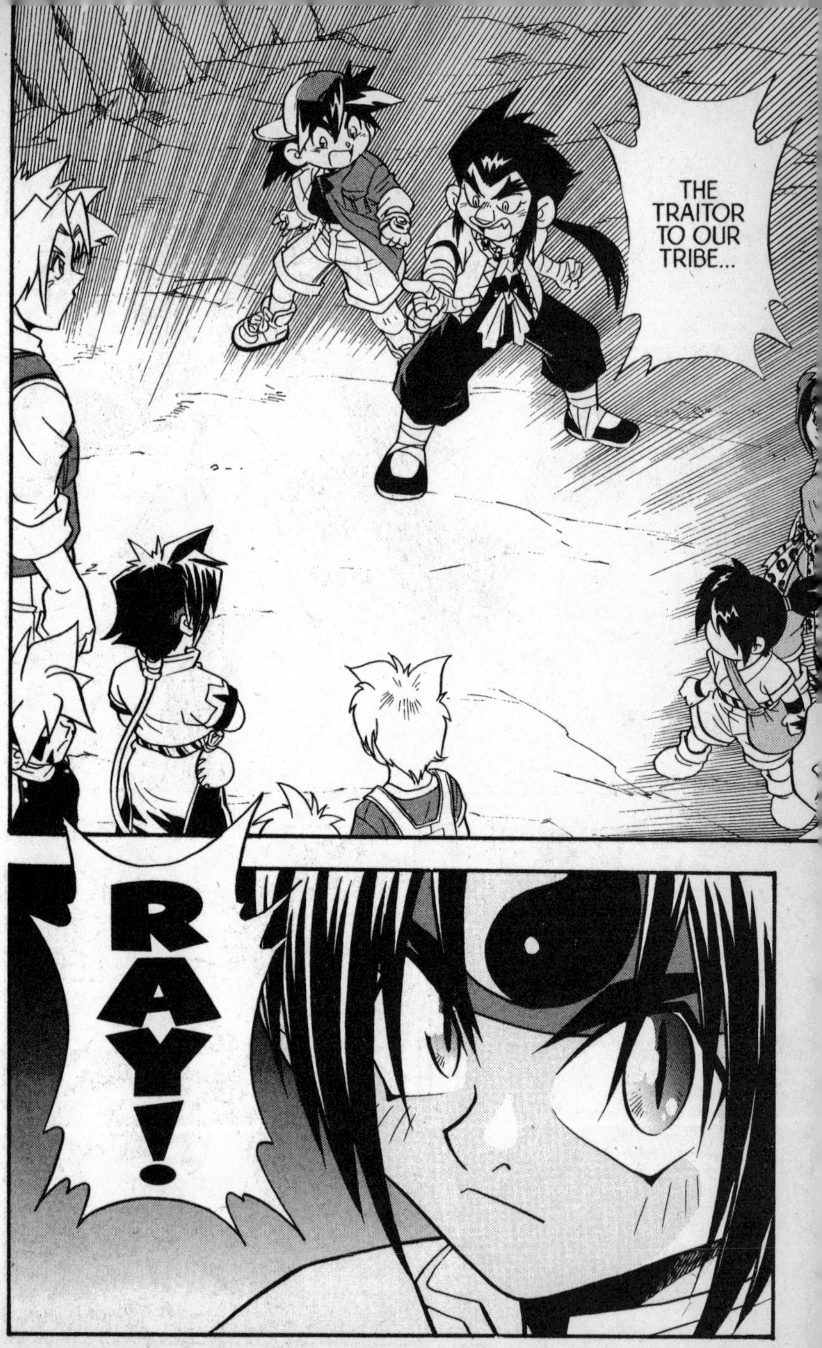
THE TRAITOR TO OUR TRIBE...
RAY!

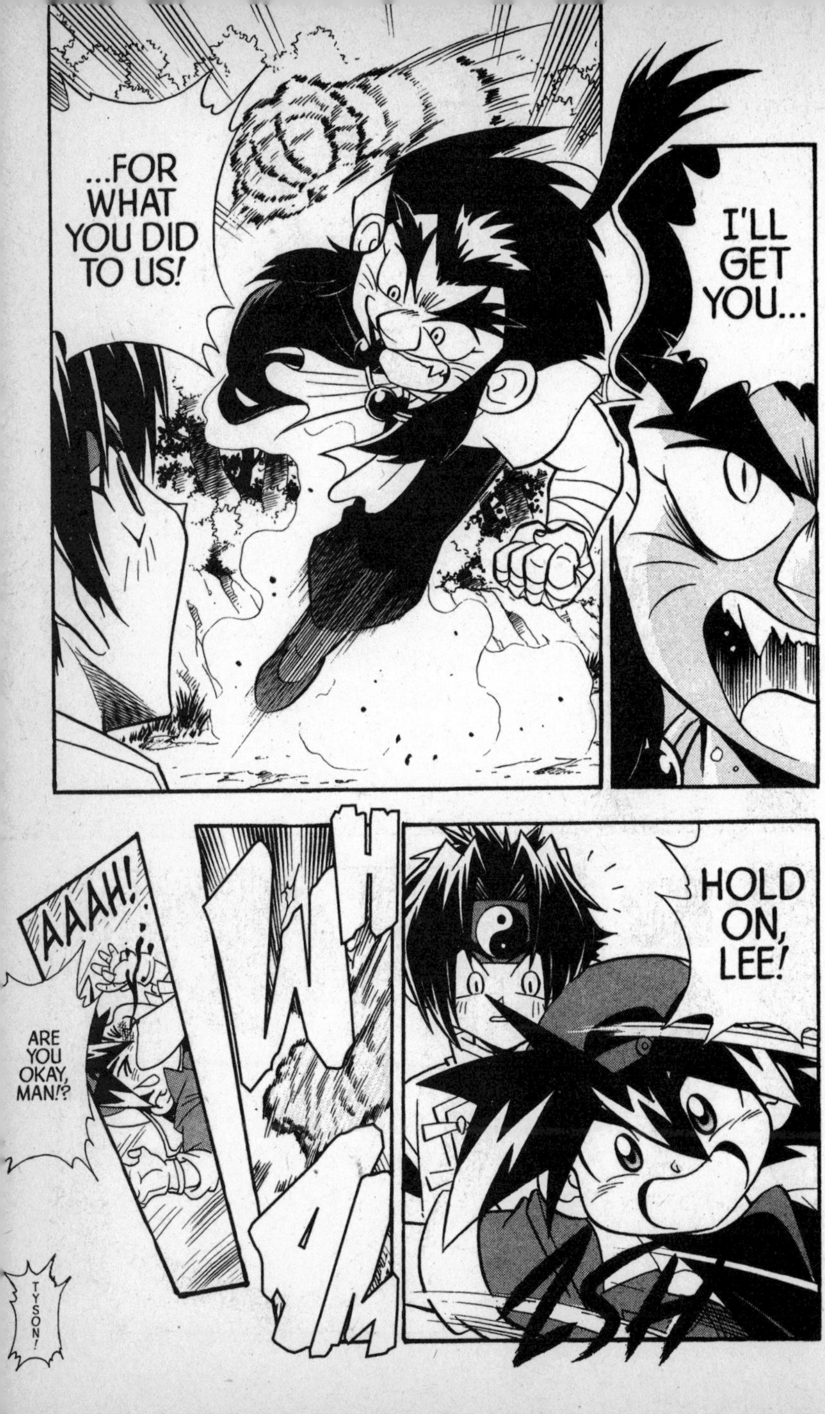
I'LL GET YOU...
...FOR WHAT YOU DID TO US!
HOLD ON, LEE!
AAAH!
ARE YOU OKAY, MAN!?
TYSON!

TYSON! UP AND AT 'EM!

WAKE UP!

UNNGH...

vip!

!!

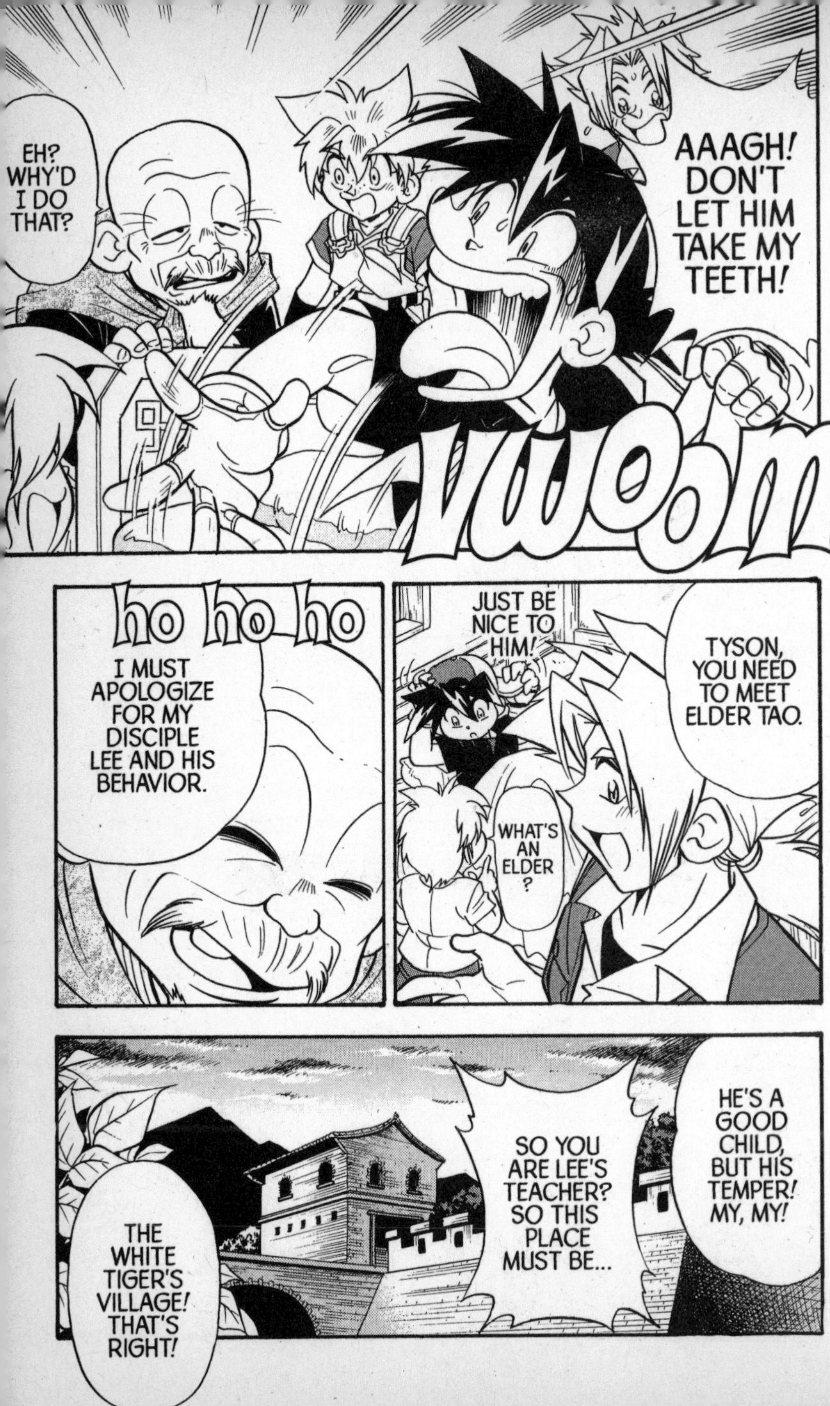
AAAGH! DON'T LET HIM TAKE MY TEETH!
VWOOM
EH? WHY'D I DO THAT?
TYSON, YOU NEED TO MEET ELDER TAO.
JUST BE NICE TO HIM!
WHAT'S AN ELDER?
ho ho ho
I MUST APOLOGIZE FOR MY DISCIPLE LEE AND HIS BEHAVIOR.
HE'S A GOOD CHILD, BUT HIS TEMPER! MY, MY!
SO YOU ARE LEE'S TEACHER? SO THIS PLACE MUST BE...
THE WHITE TIGER'S VILLAGE! THAT'S RIGHT!

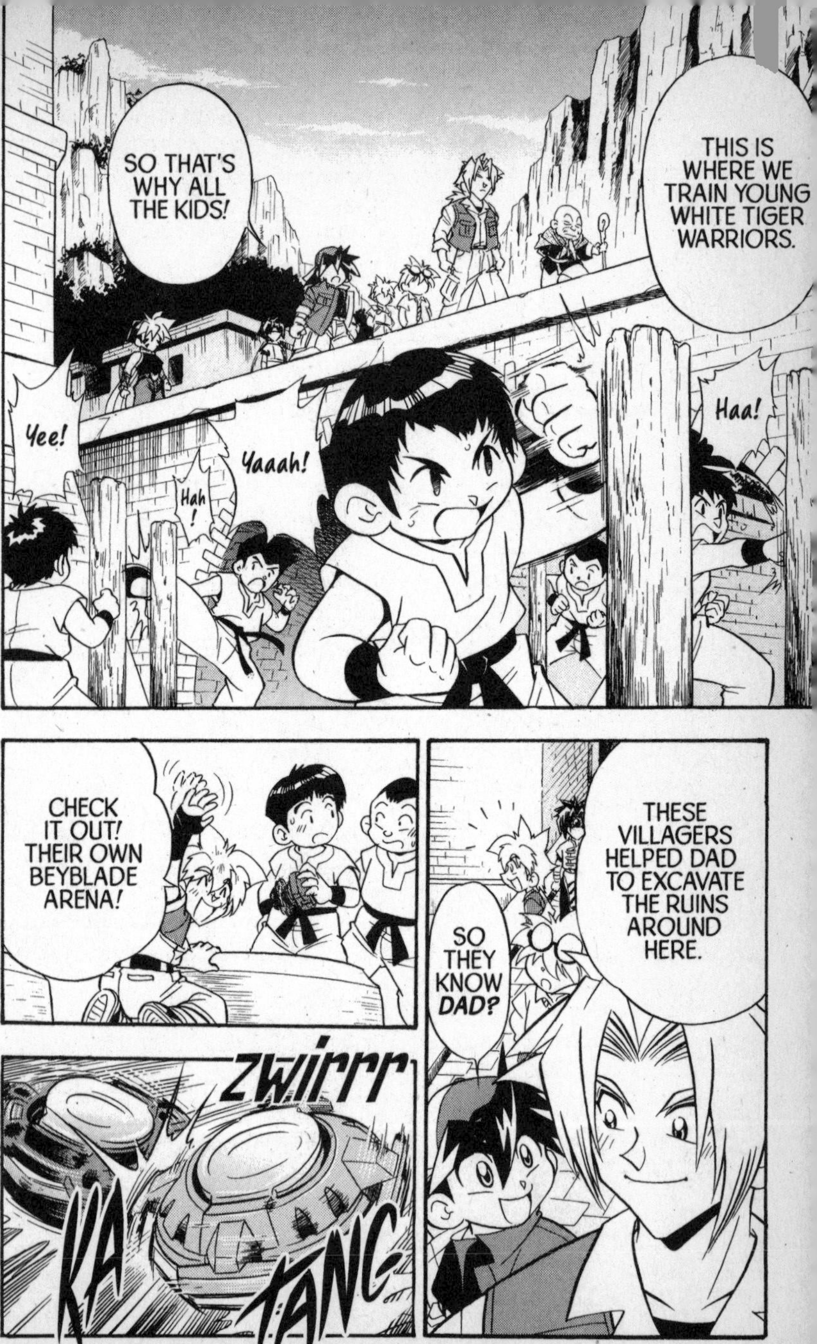
THIS IS WHERE WE TRAIN YOUNG WHITE TIGER WARRIORS.
SO THAT'S WHY ALL THE KIDS!
Haa!
Yaaah!
Hah!
Yee!
THESE VILLAGERS HELPED DAD TO EXCAVATE THE RUINS AROUND HERE.
SO THEY KNOW *DAD*?
CHECK IT OUT! THEIR OWN BEYBLADE ARENA!
zwirrr
KA TANG

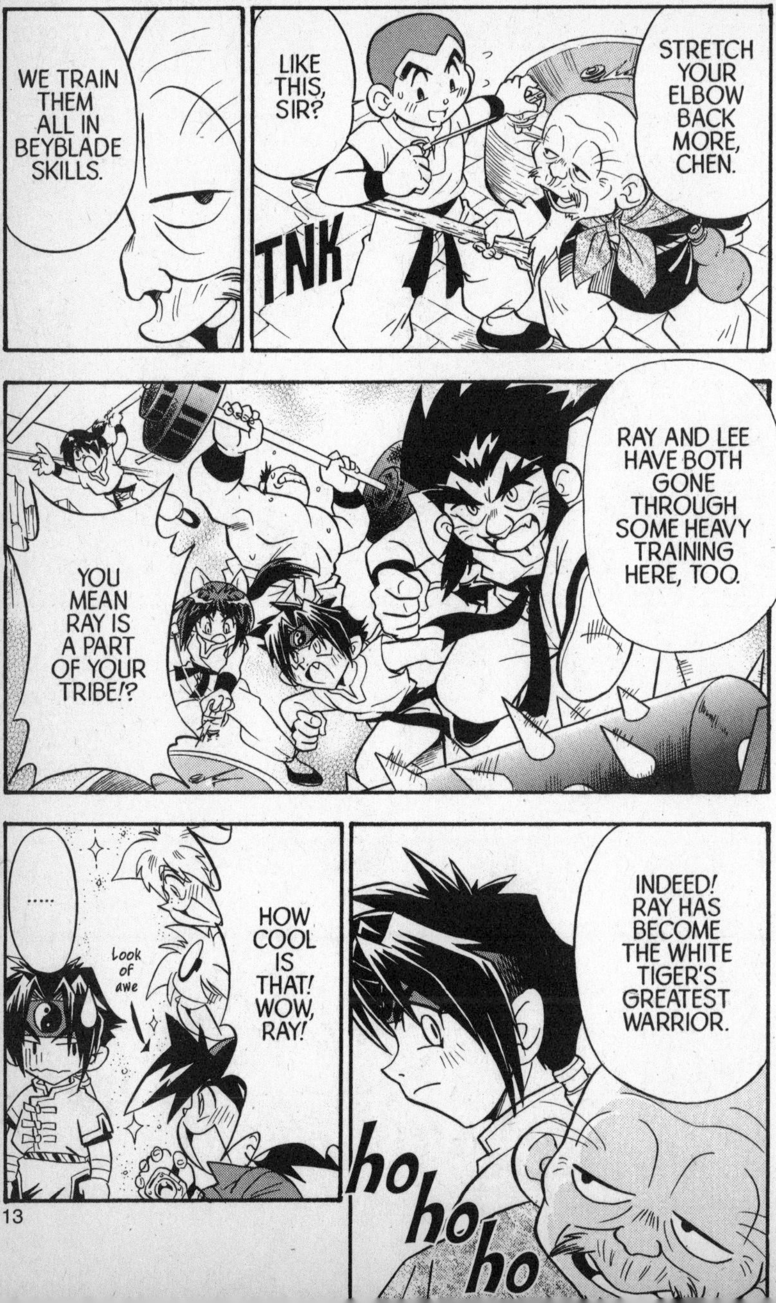
STRETCH YOUR ELBOW BACK MORE, CHEN.
LIKE THIS, SIR?
TNK
WE TRAIN THEM ALL IN BEYBLADE SKILLS.
RAY AND LEE HAVE BOTH GONE THROUGH SOME HEAVY TRAINING HERE, TOO.
YOU MEAN RAY IS A PART OF YOUR TRIBE!?
INDEED! RAY HAS BECOME THE WHITE TIGER'S GREATEST WARRIOR.
ho ho ho
HOW COOL IS THAT! WOW, RAY!
Look of awe
.....

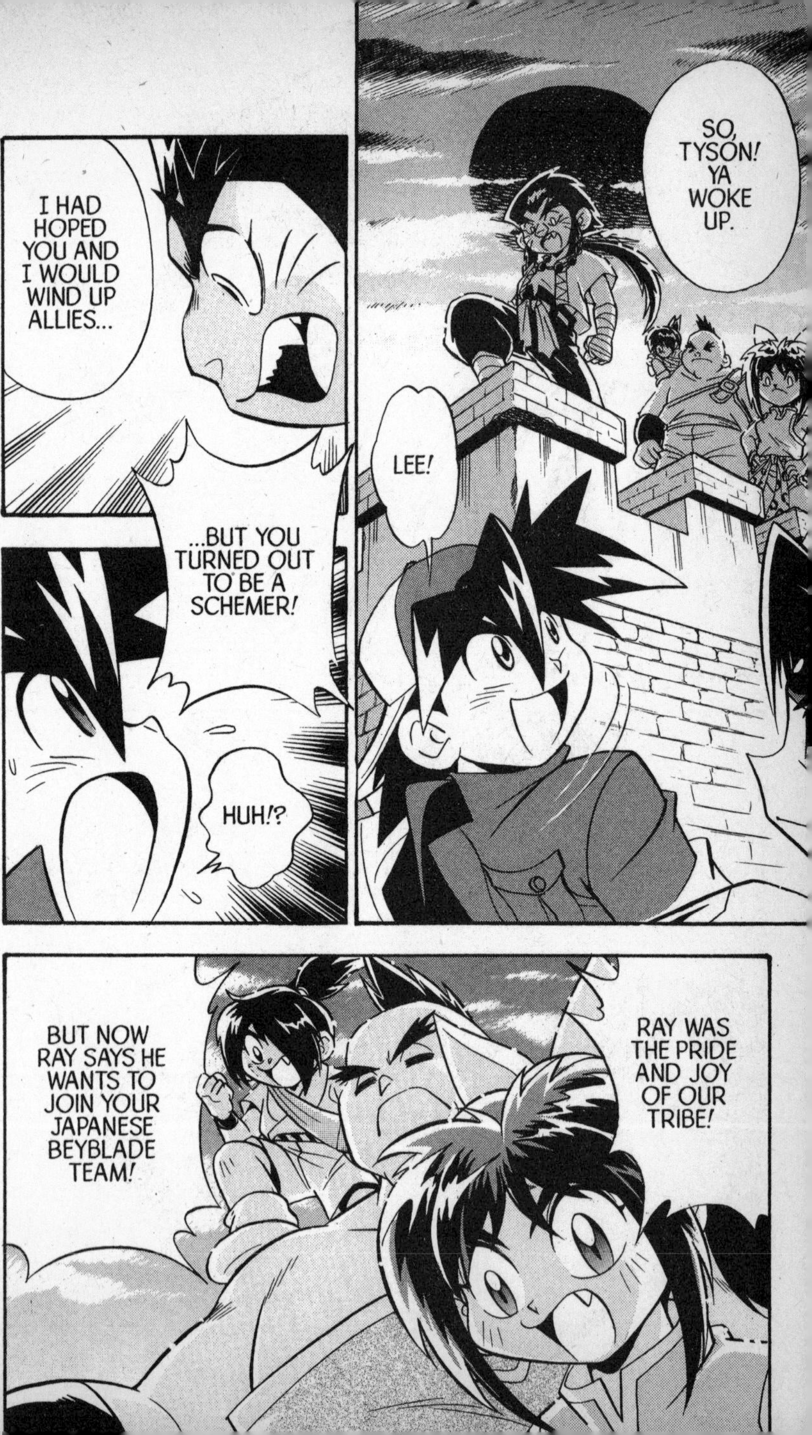
SO, TYSON! YA WOKE UP.
LEE!
I HAD HOPED YOU AND I WOULD WIND UP ALLIES...
...BUT YOU TURNED OUT TO BE A SCHEMER!
HUH!?
RAY WAS THE PRIDE AND JOY OF OUR TRIBE!
BUT NOW RAY SAYS HE WANTS TO JOIN YOUR JAPANESE BEYBLADE TEAM!

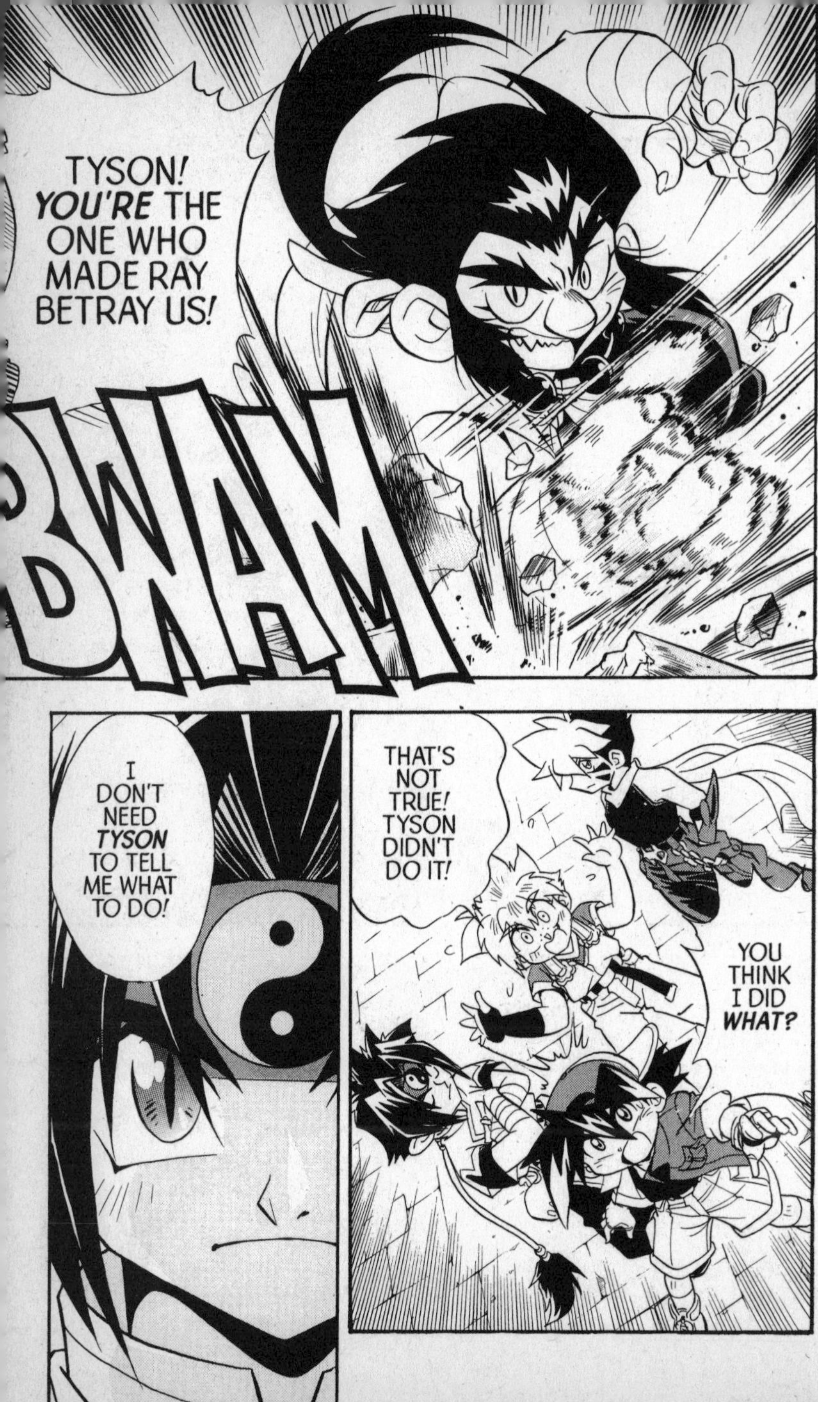
TYSON! YOU'RE THE ONE WHO MADE RAY BETRAY US!
BWAM
THAT'S NOT TRUE! TYSON DIDN'T DO IT!
YOU THINK I DID WHAT?
I DON'T NEED TYSON TO TELL ME WHAT TO DO!

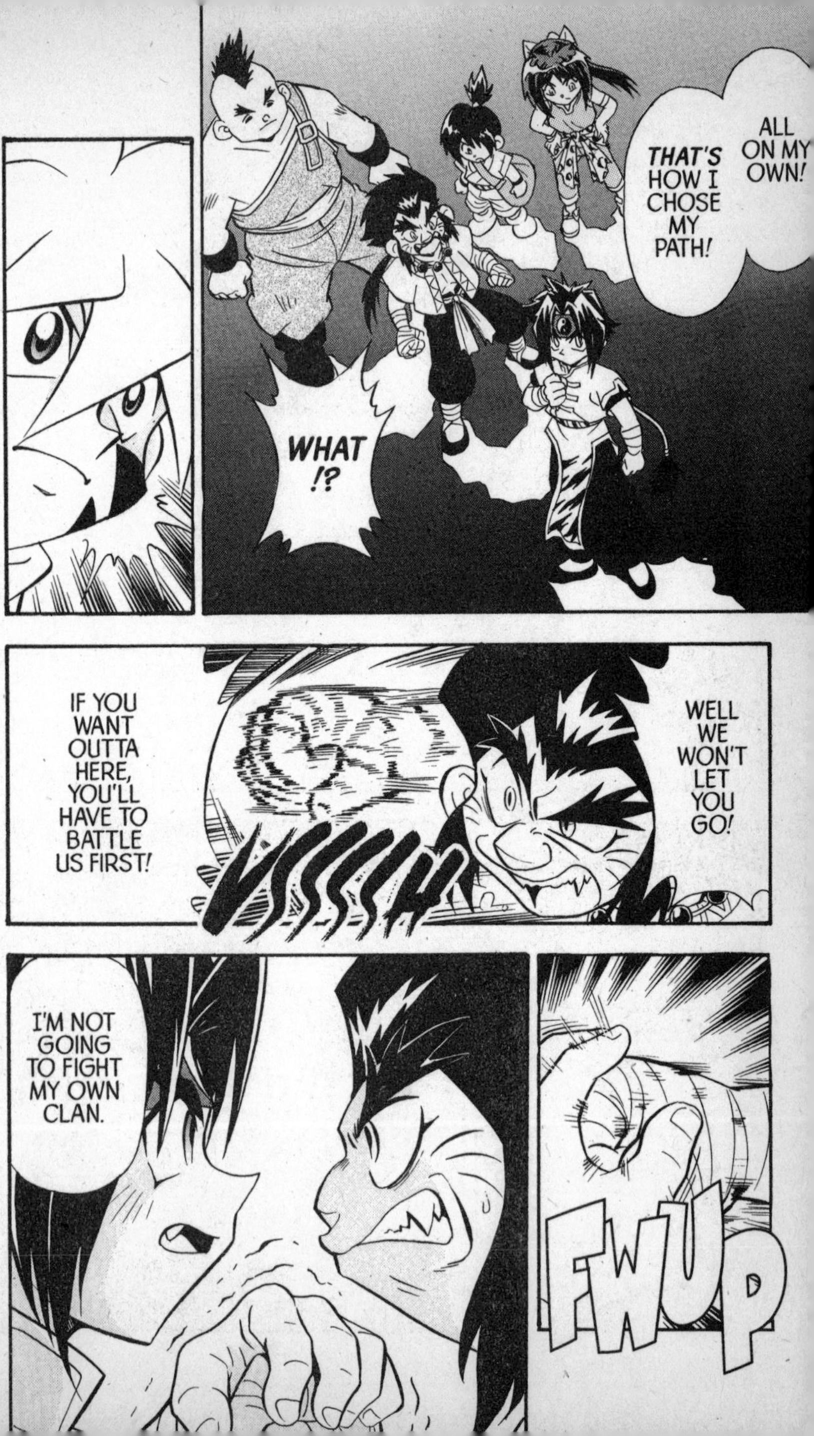
ALL ON MY OWN!
THAT'S HOW I CHOSE MY PATH!
WHAT !?
WELL WE WON'T LET YOU GO!
IF YOU WANT OUTTA HERE, YOU'LL HAVE TO BATTLE US FIRST!
VSSSSH
FWUP
I'M NOT GOING TO FIGHT MY OWN CLAN.

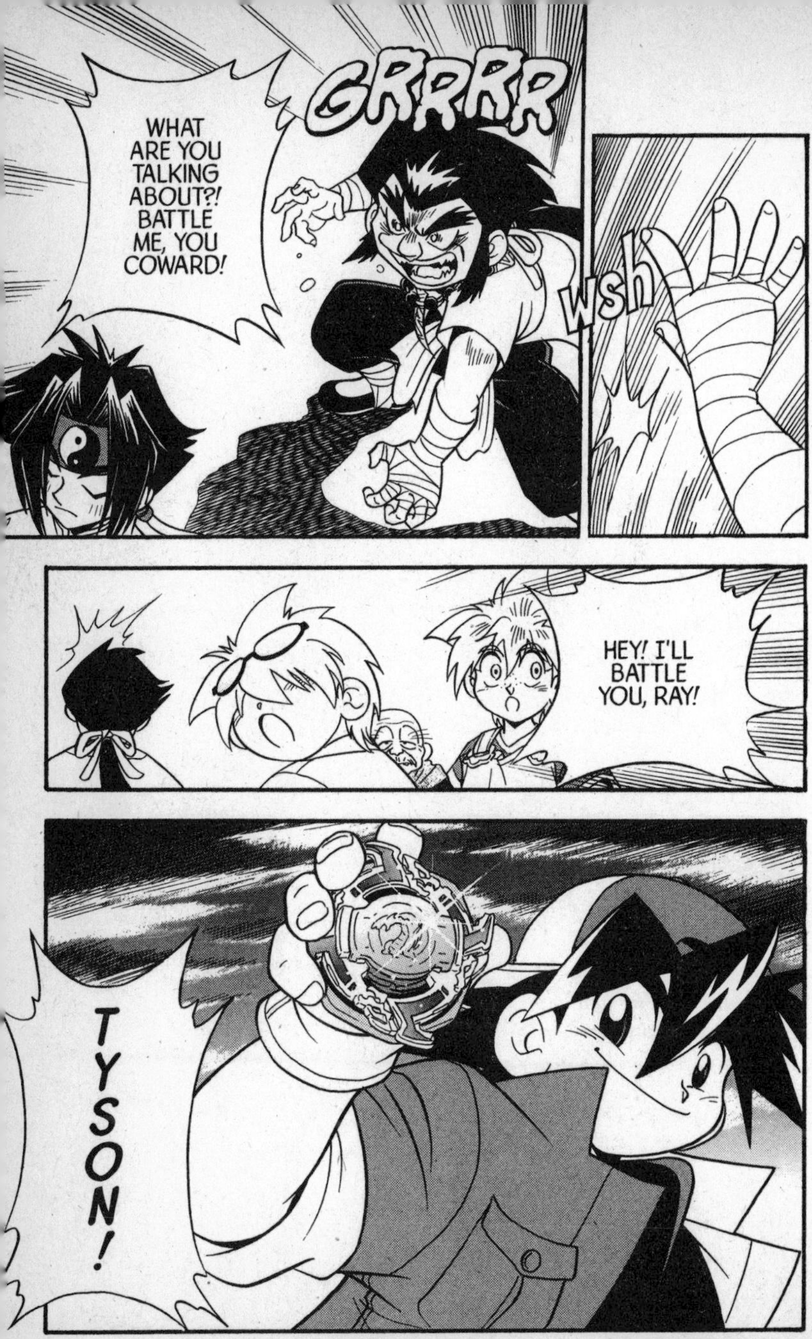
GRRRR
WHAT ARE YOU TALKING ABOUT?! BATTLE ME, YOU COWARD!
wsh
HEY! I'LL BATTLE YOU, RAY!
TYSON!

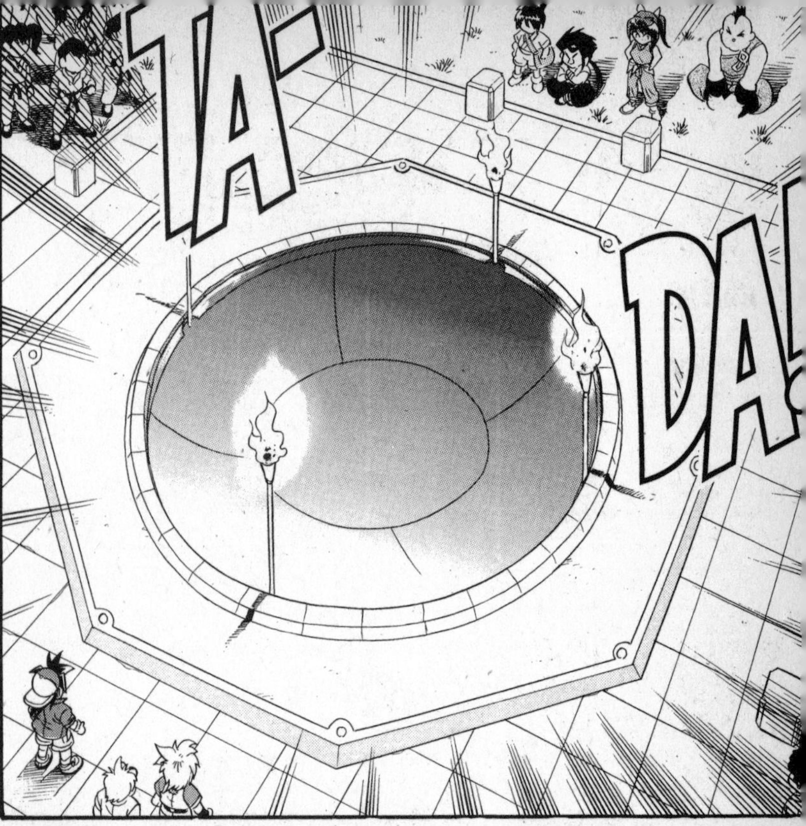
TA-
DA!
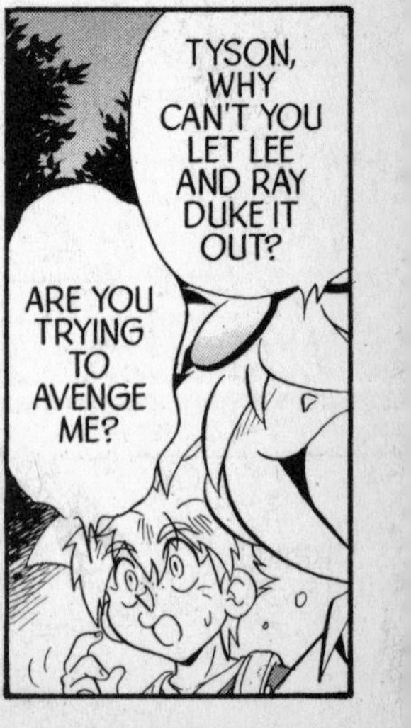
TYSON, WHY CAN'T YOU LET LEE AND RAY DUKE IT OUT?
ARE YOU TRYING TO AVENGE ME?
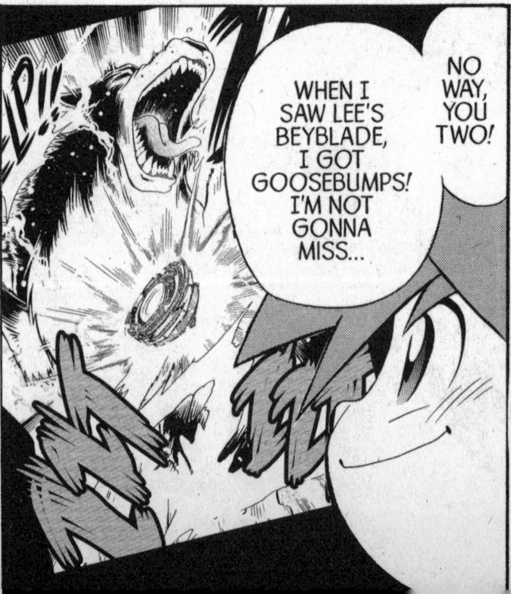
NO WAY, YOU TWO!
WHEN I SAW LEE'S BEYBLADE, I GOT GOOSEBUMPS! I'M NOT GONNA MISS...

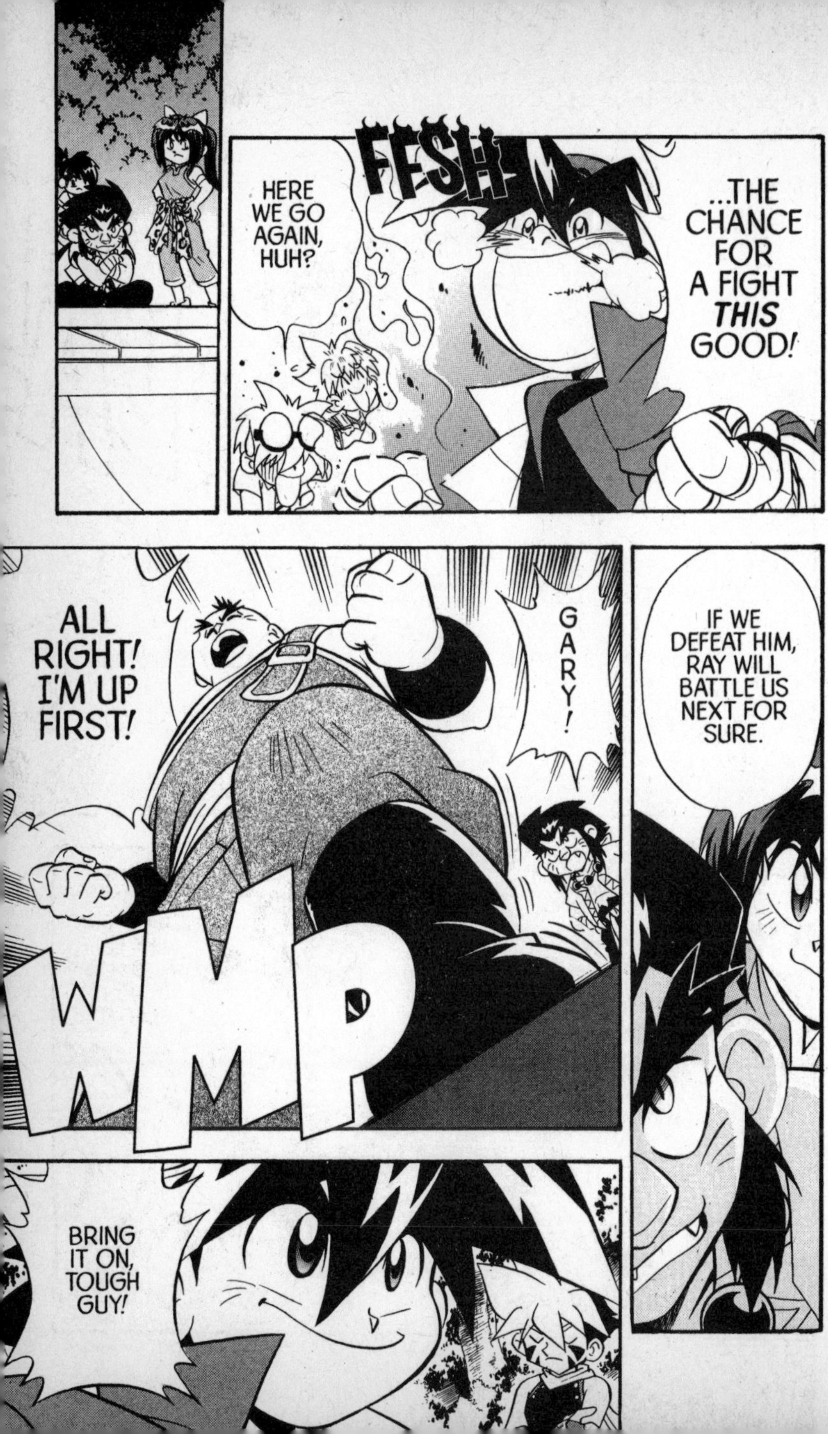
...THE CHANCE FOR A FIGHT THIS GOOD!
FFSH
HERE WE GO AGAIN, HUH?
IF WE DEFEAT HIM, RAY WILL BATTLE US NEXT FOR SURE.
GARY!
ALL RIGHT! I'M UP FIRST!
WMP
BRING IT ON, TOUGH GUY!

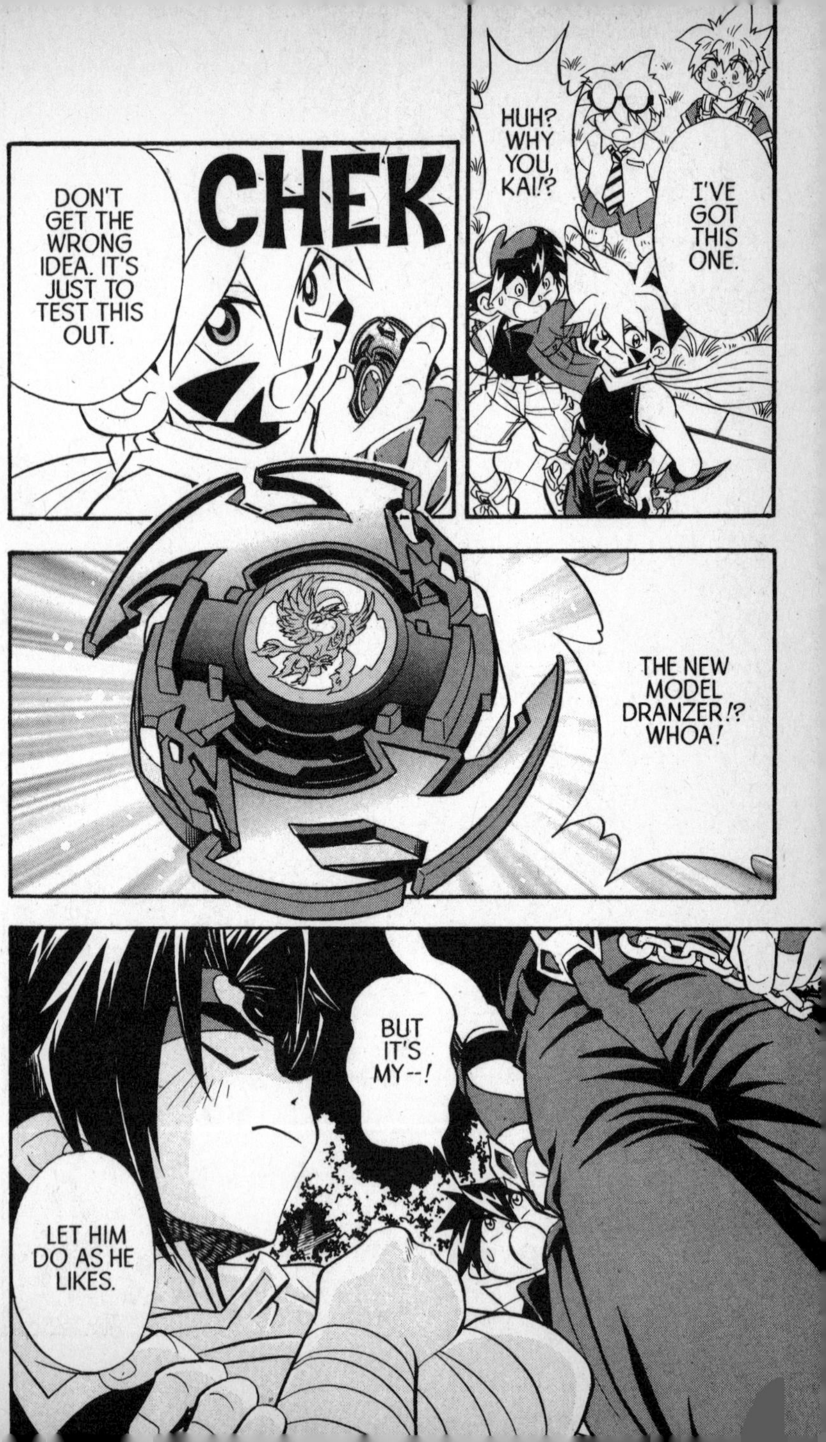
I'VE GOT THIS ONE.
HUH? WHY YOU, KAI!?
CHEK
DON'T GET THE WRONG IDEA. IT'S JUST TO TEST THIS OUT.
THE NEW MODEL DRANZER!? WHOA!
BUT IT'S MY--!
LET HIM DO AS HE LIKES.

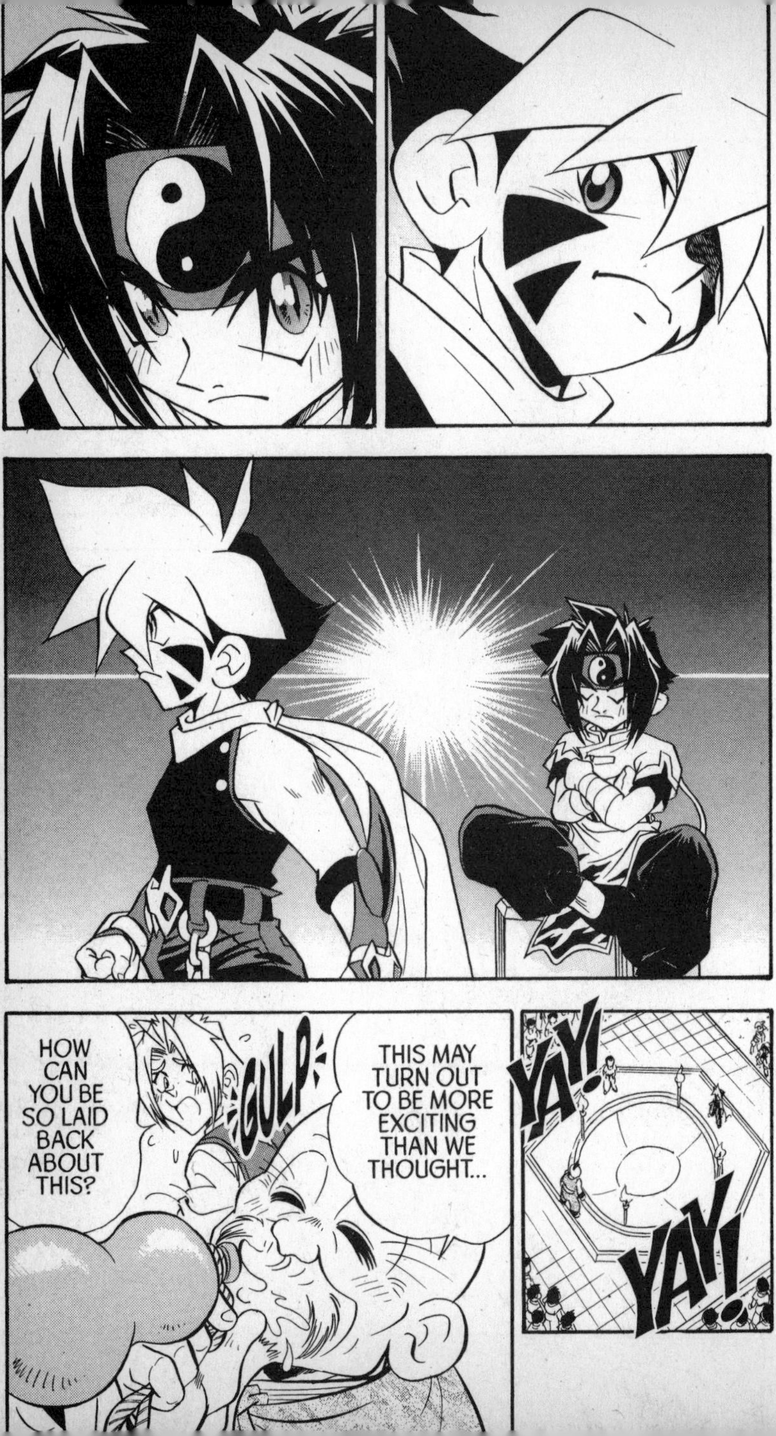
YAY!
YAY!
THIS MAY TURN OUT TO BE MORE EXCITING THAN WE THOUGHT...
GULP
HOW CAN YOU BE SO LAID BACK ABOUT THIS?

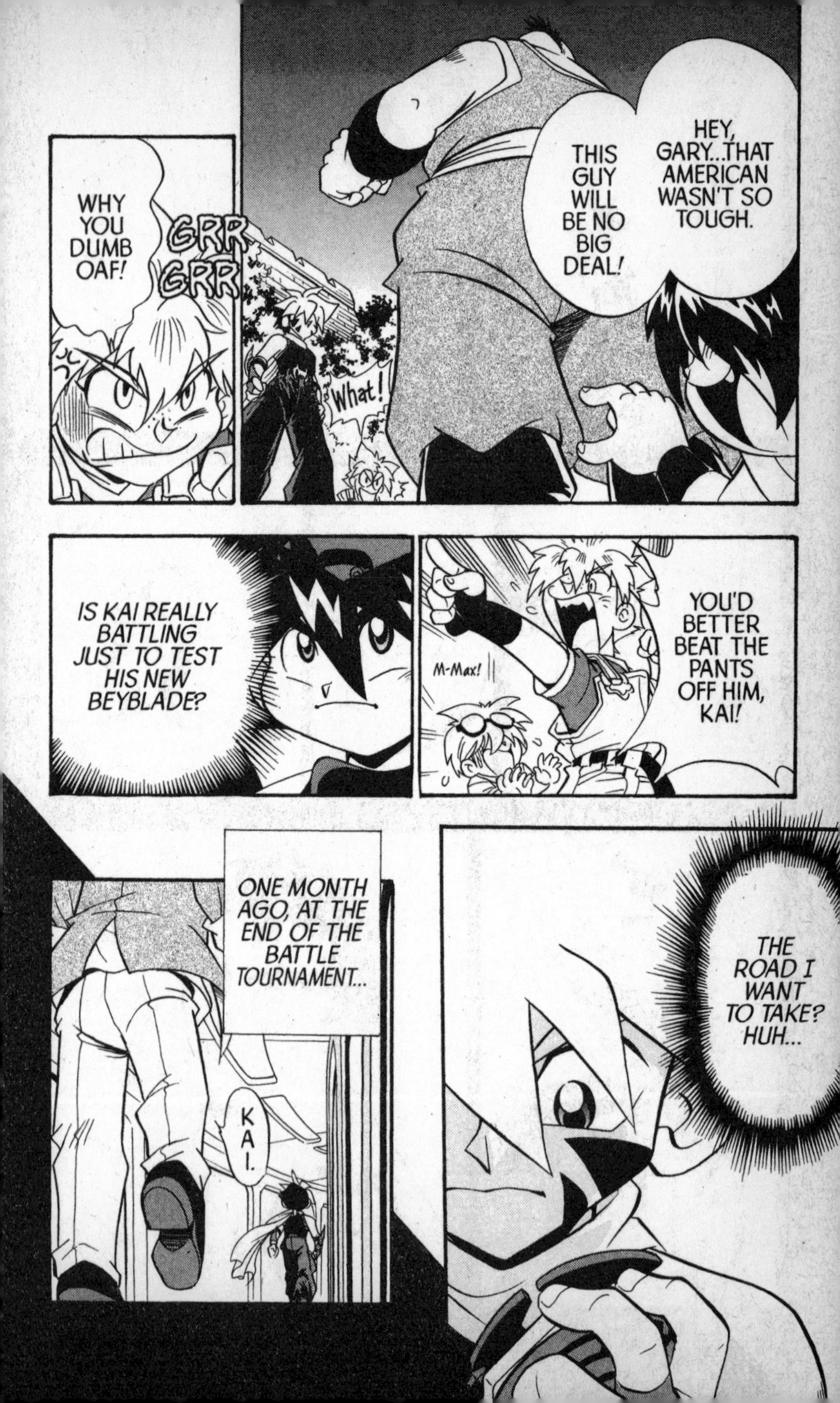
HEY, GARY...THAT AMERICAN WASN'T SO TOUGH.
THIS GUY WILL BE NO BIG DEAL!
What!
GRR GRR
WHY YOU DUMB OAF!
YOU'D BETTER BEAT THE PANTS OFF HIM, KAI!
M-Max!
IS KAI REALLY BATTLING JUST TO TEST HIS NEW BEYBLADE?
THE ROAD I WANT TO TAKE? HUH...
ONE MONTH AGO, AT THE END OF THE BATTLE TOURNAMENT...
KAI.

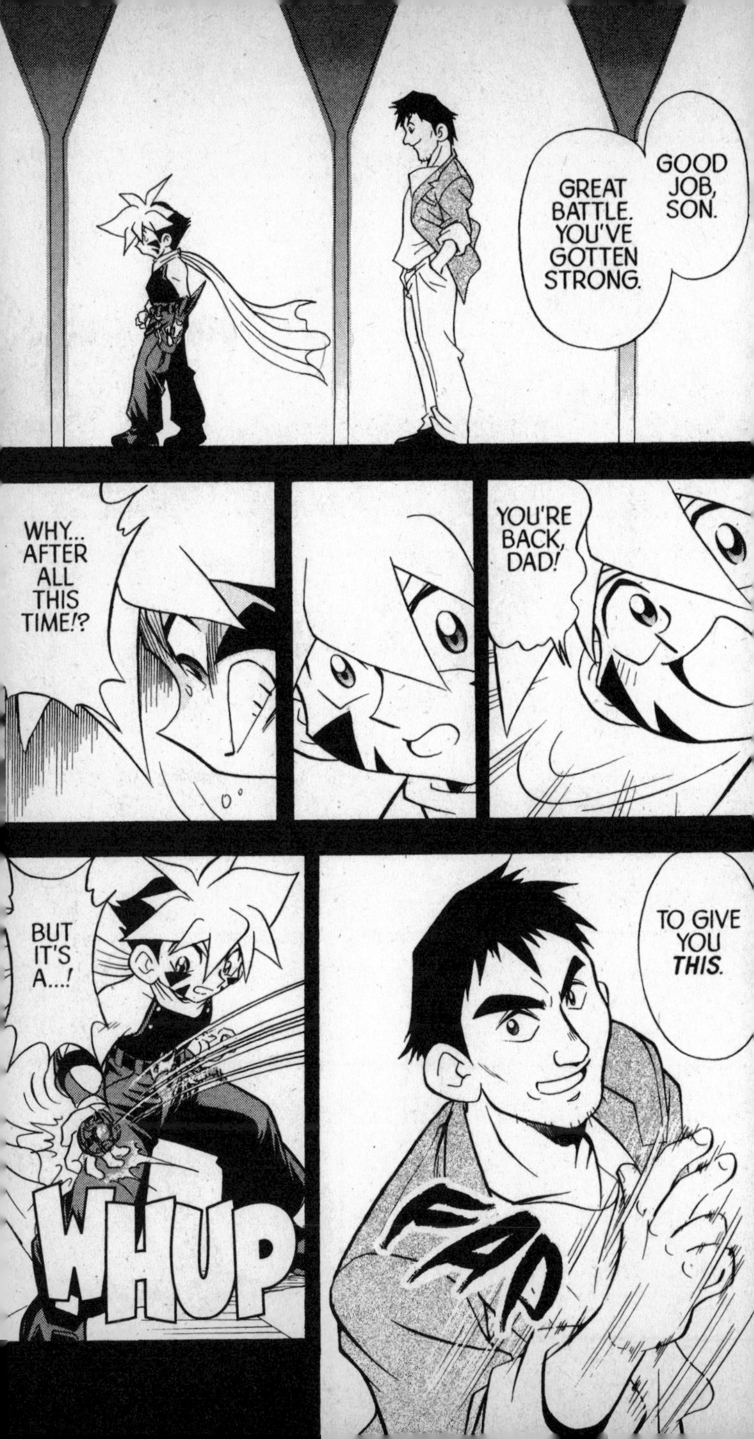
GOOD JOB, SON.
GREAT BATTLE. YOU'VE GOTTEN STRONG.
YOU'RE BACK, DAD!
WHY... AFTER ALL THIS TIME!?
TO GIVE YOU *THIS.*
BUT IT'S A...!
WHUP

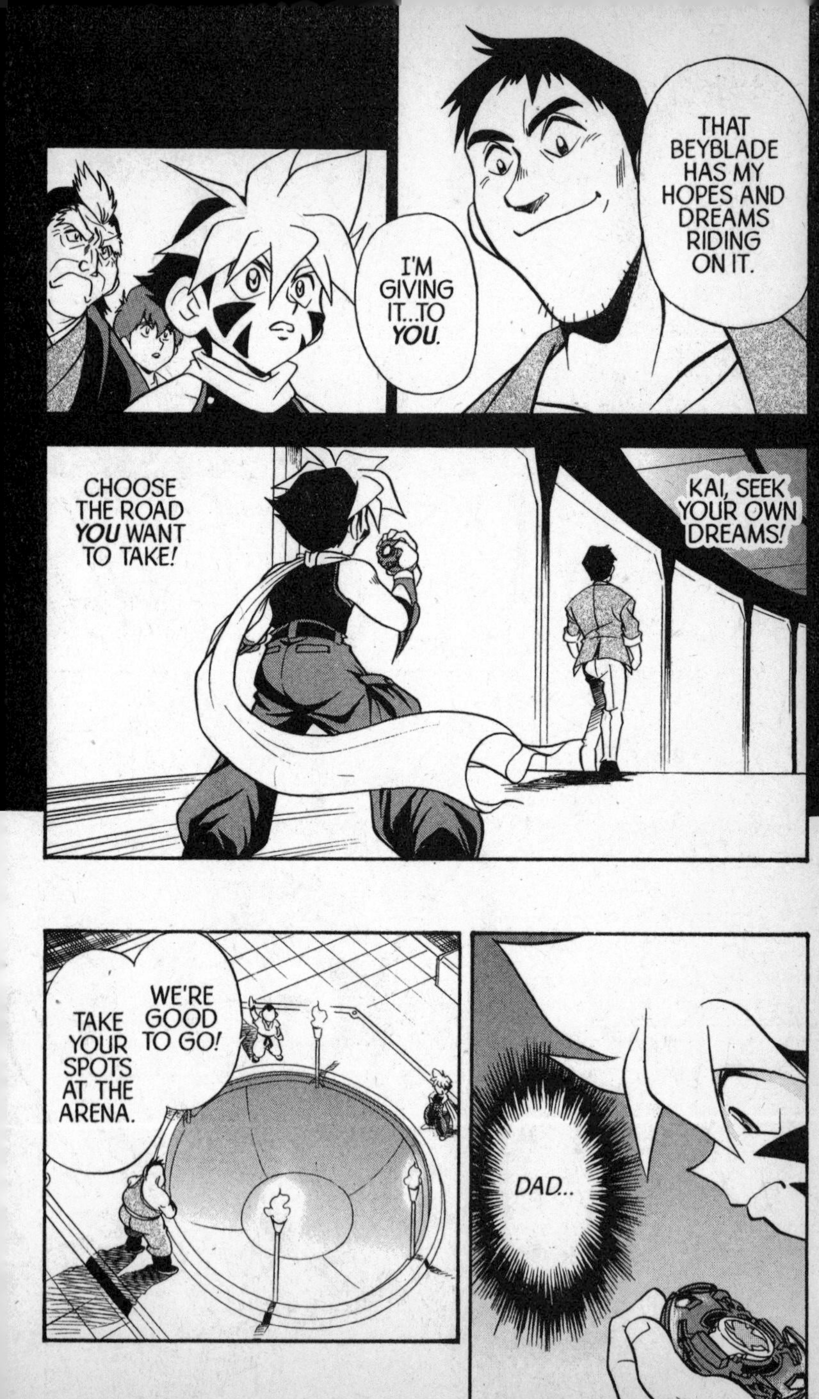
THAT BEYBLADE HAS MY HOPES AND DREAMS RIDING ON IT.
I'M GIVING IT...TO *YOU*.
KAI, SEEK YOUR OWN DREAMS!
CHOOSE THE ROAD *YOU* WANT TO TAKE!
DAD...
WE'RE GOOD TO GO!
TAKE YOUR SPOTS AT THE ARENA.

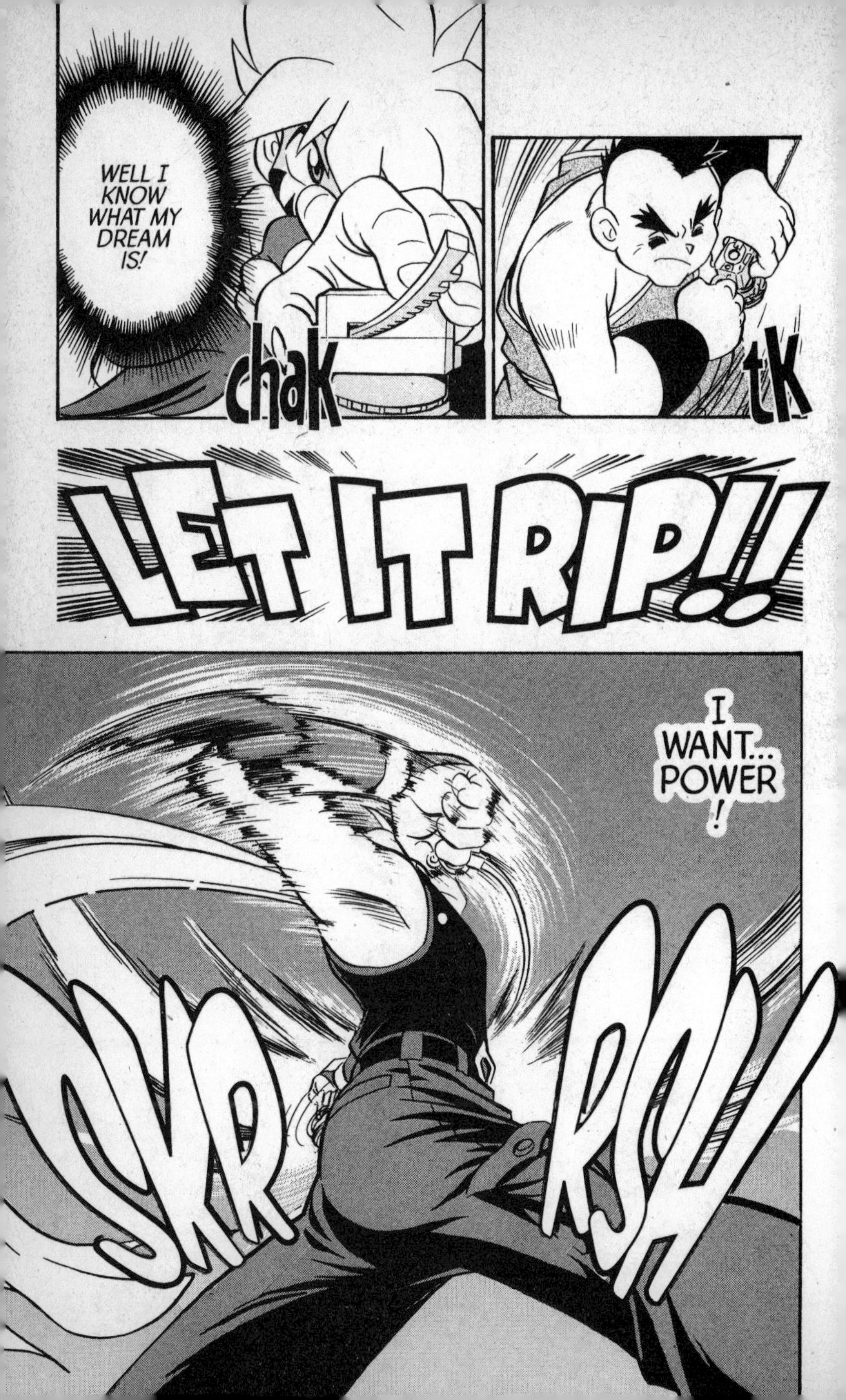
tK
WELL I KNOW WHAT MY DREAM IS!
chaK
LET IT RIP!!
I WANT... POWER!

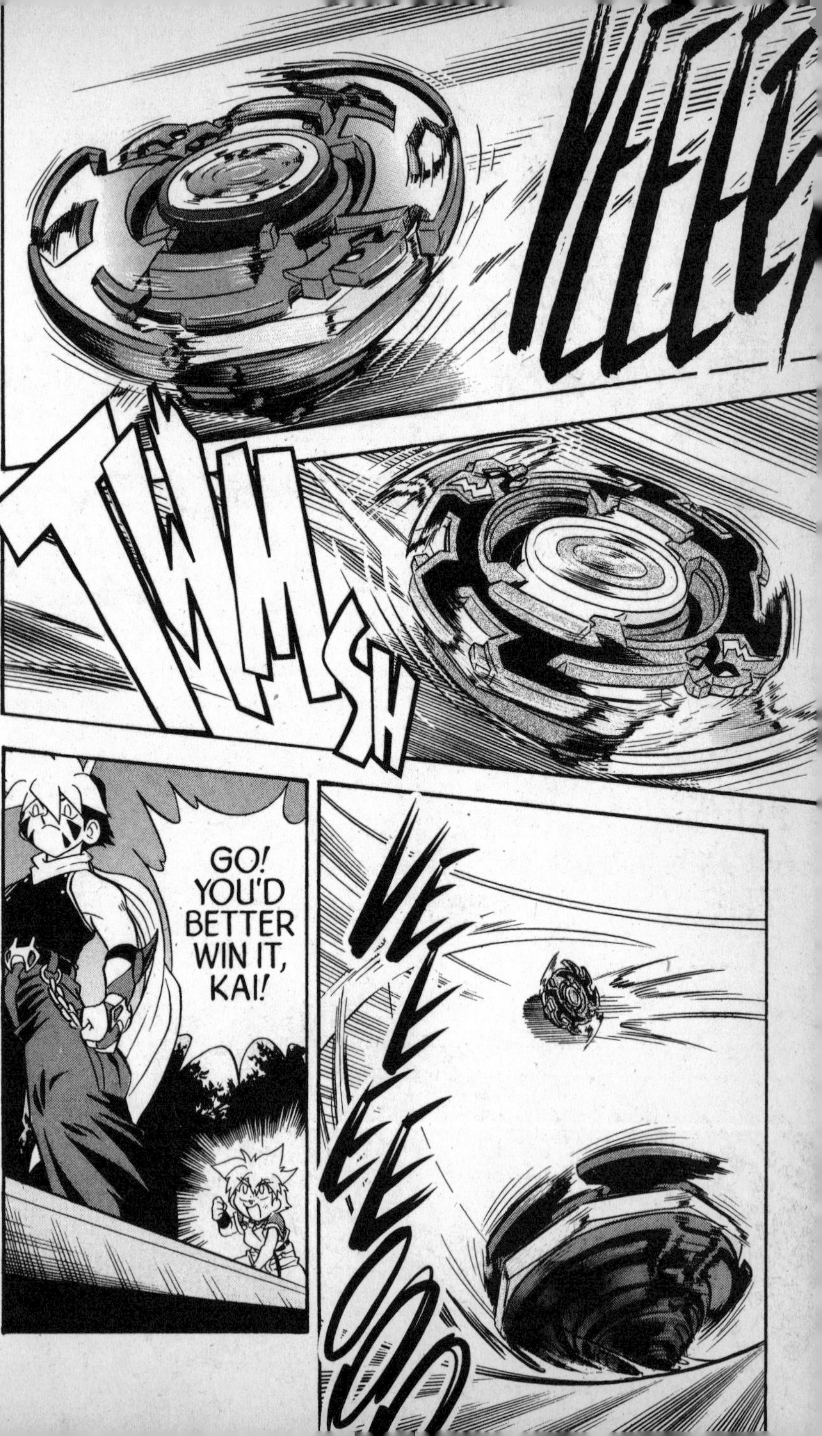
TWHASH
GO! YOU'D BETTER WIN IT, KAI!

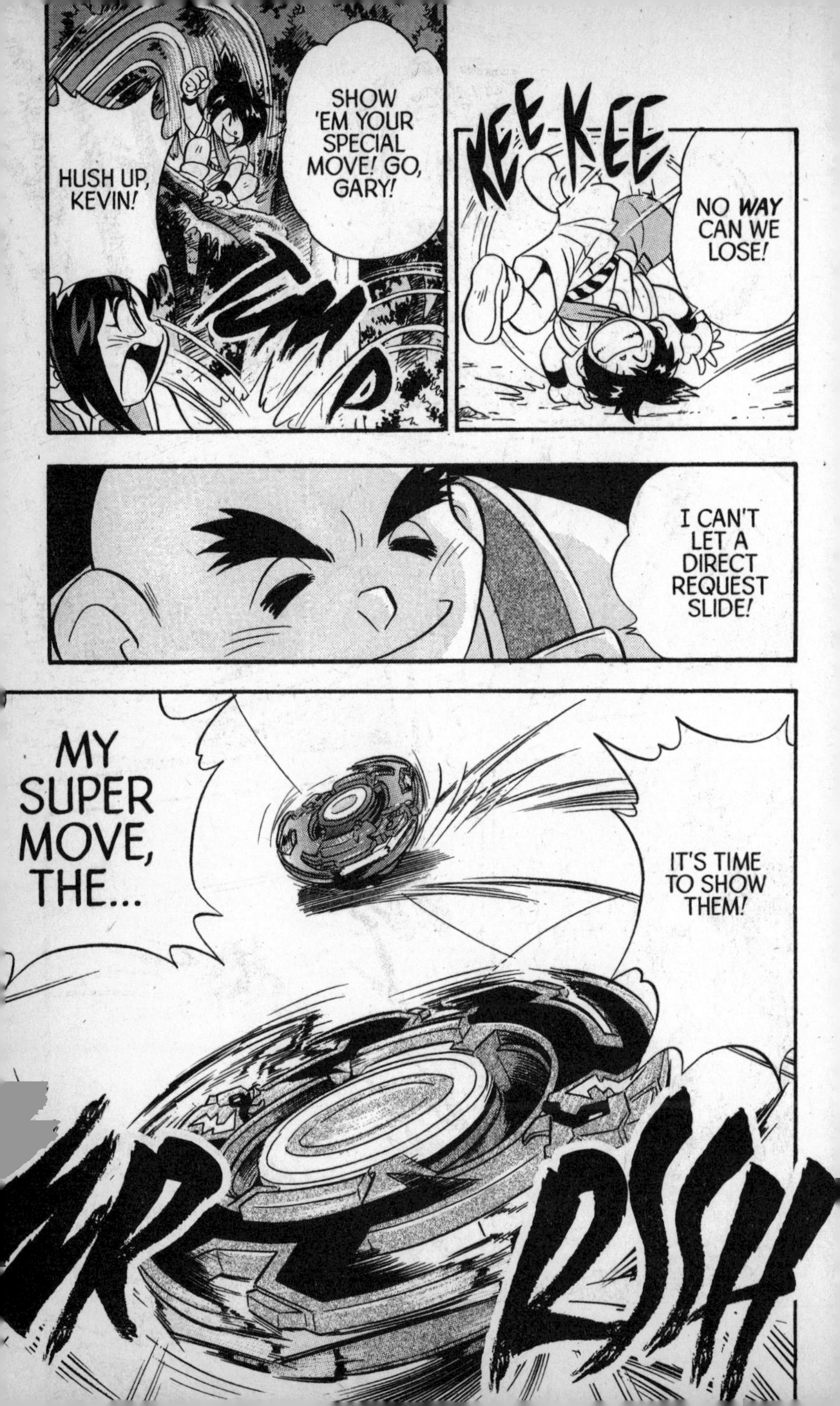
KEE-KEE
NO WAY CAN WE LOSE!
SHOW 'EM YOUR SPECIAL MOVE! GO, GARY!
HUSH UP, KEVIN!
THUMP
I CAN'T LET A DIRECT REQUEST SLIDE!
IT'S TIME TO SHOW THEM!
MY SUPER MOVE, THE...

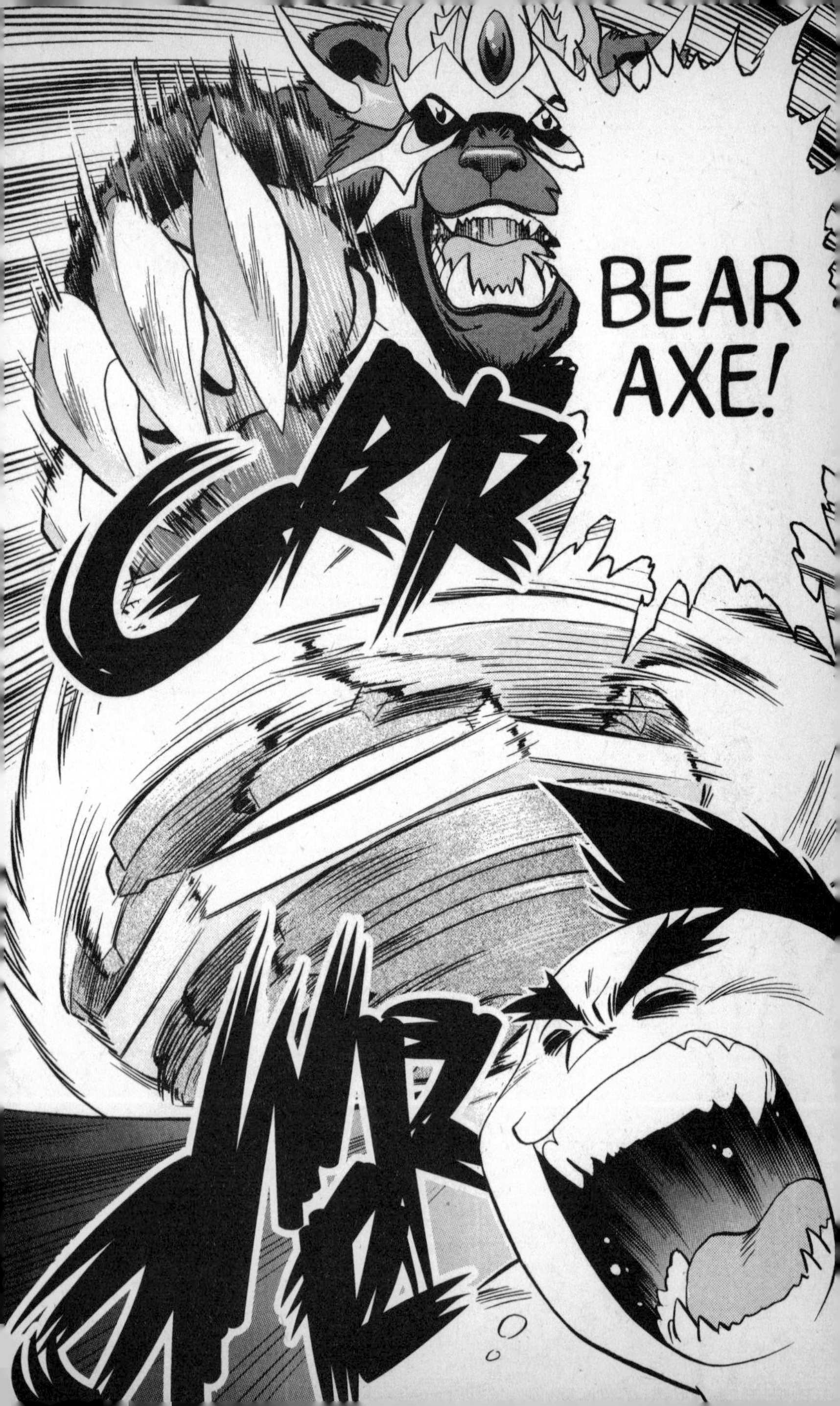
BEAR AXE!

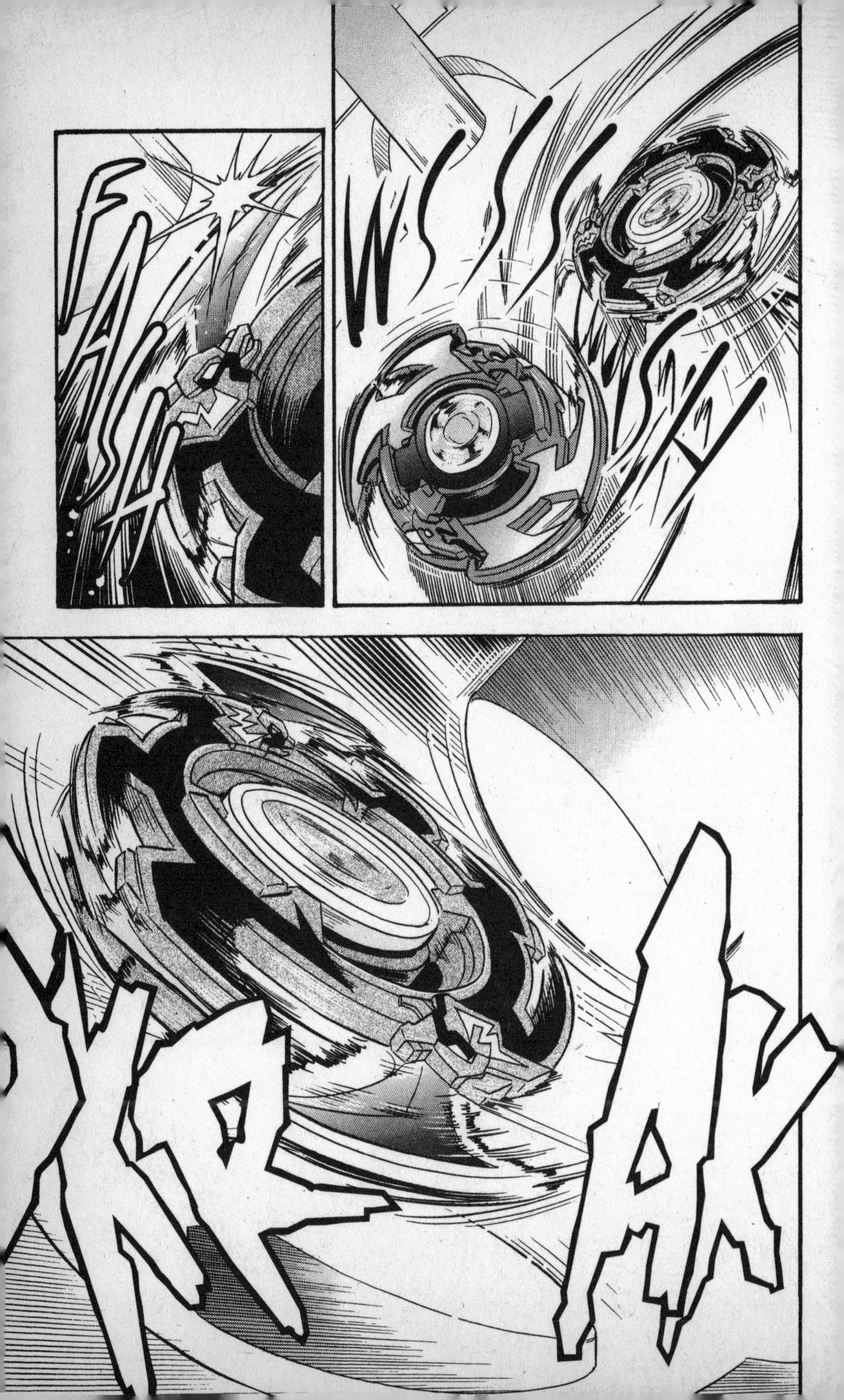

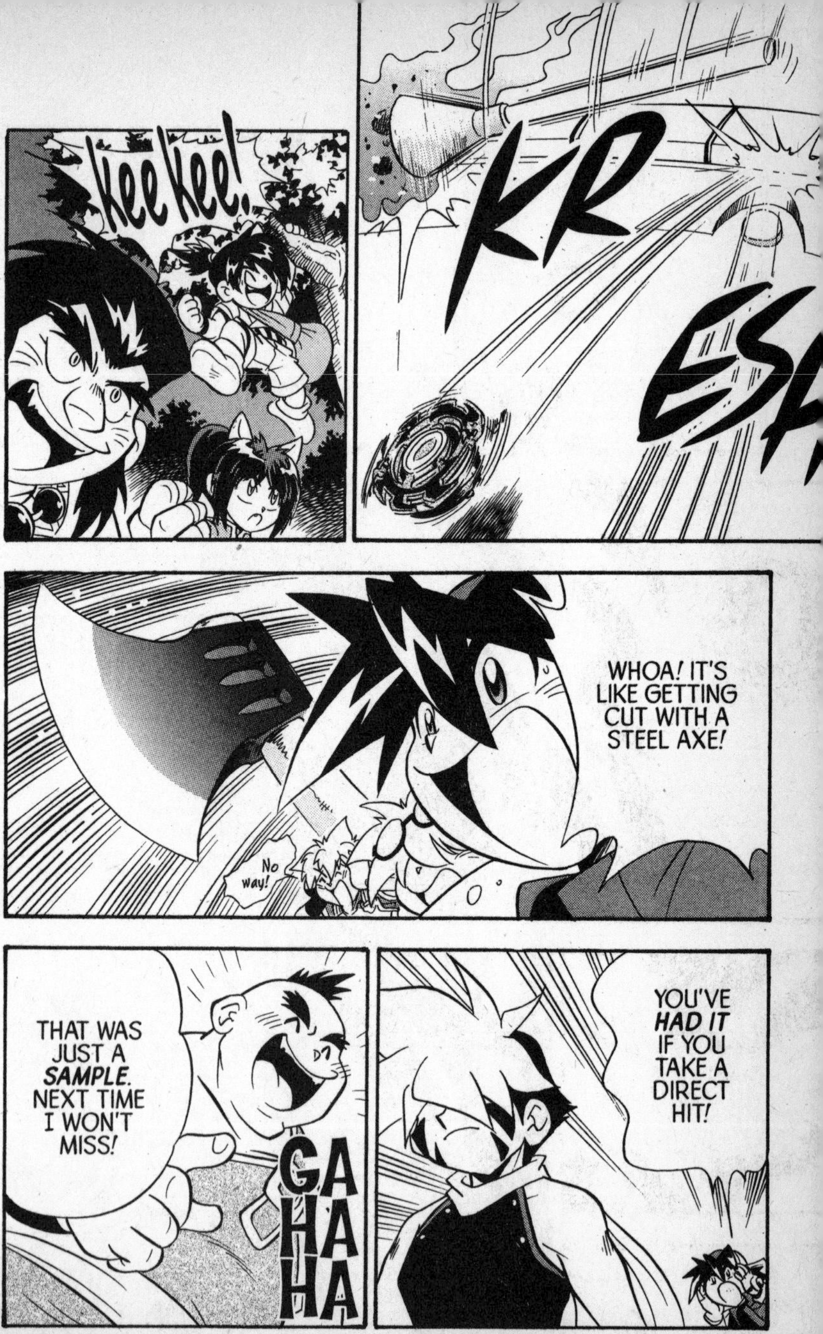
KR
ES
Kee Kee!
WHOA! IT'S LIKE GETTING CUT WITH A STEEL AXE!
No way!
YOU'VE *HAD IT* IF YOU TAKE A DIRECT HIT!
THAT WAS JUST A *SAMPLE*. NEXT TIME I WON'T MISS!
GAHAHAHA

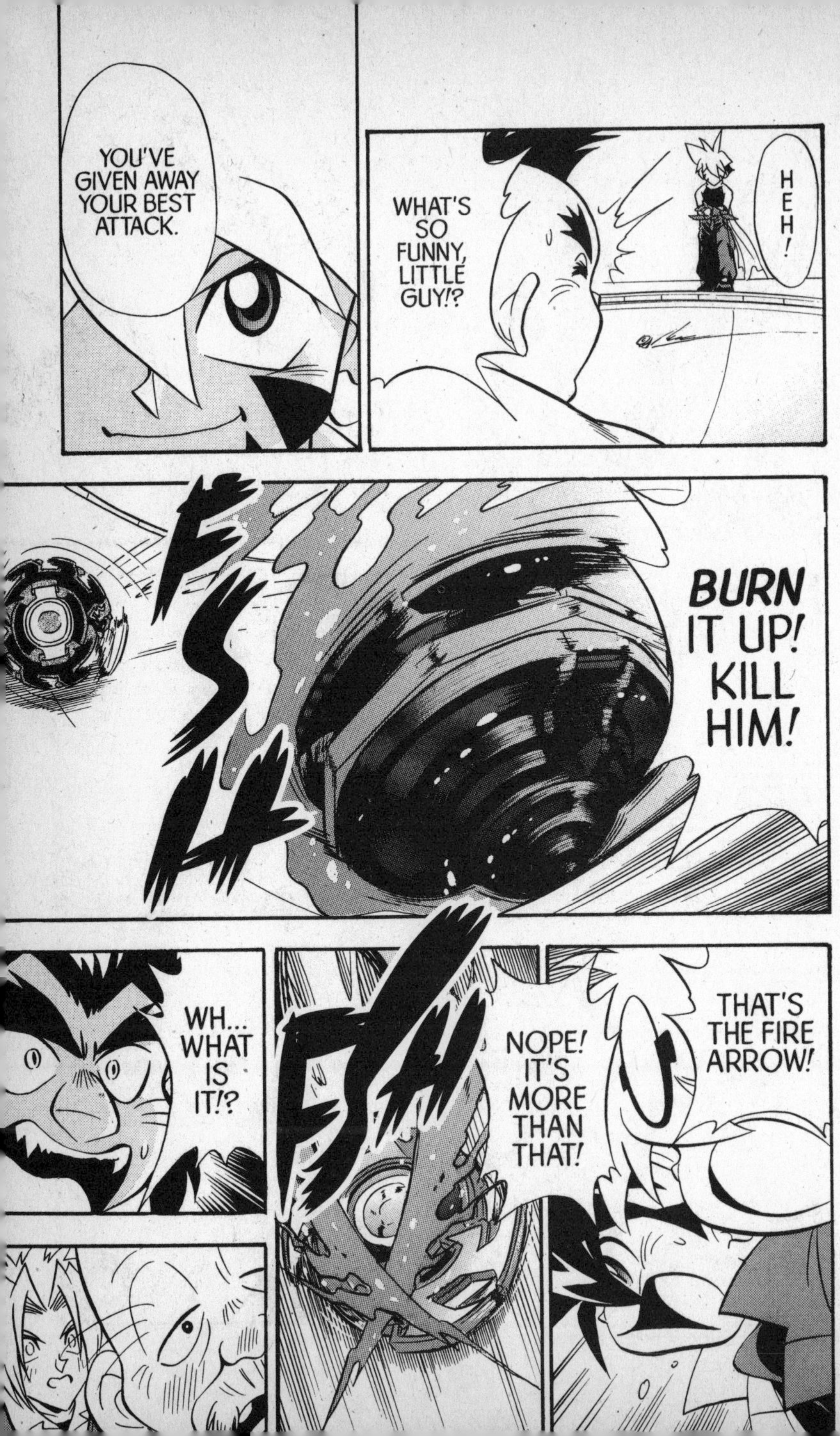
HEH!
WHAT'S SO FUNNY, LITTLE GUY!?
YOU'VE GIVEN AWAY YOUR BEST ATTACK.
BURN IT UP! KILL HIM!
THAT'S THE FIRE ARROW!
NOPE! IT'S MORE THAN THAT!
WH... WHAT IS IT!?

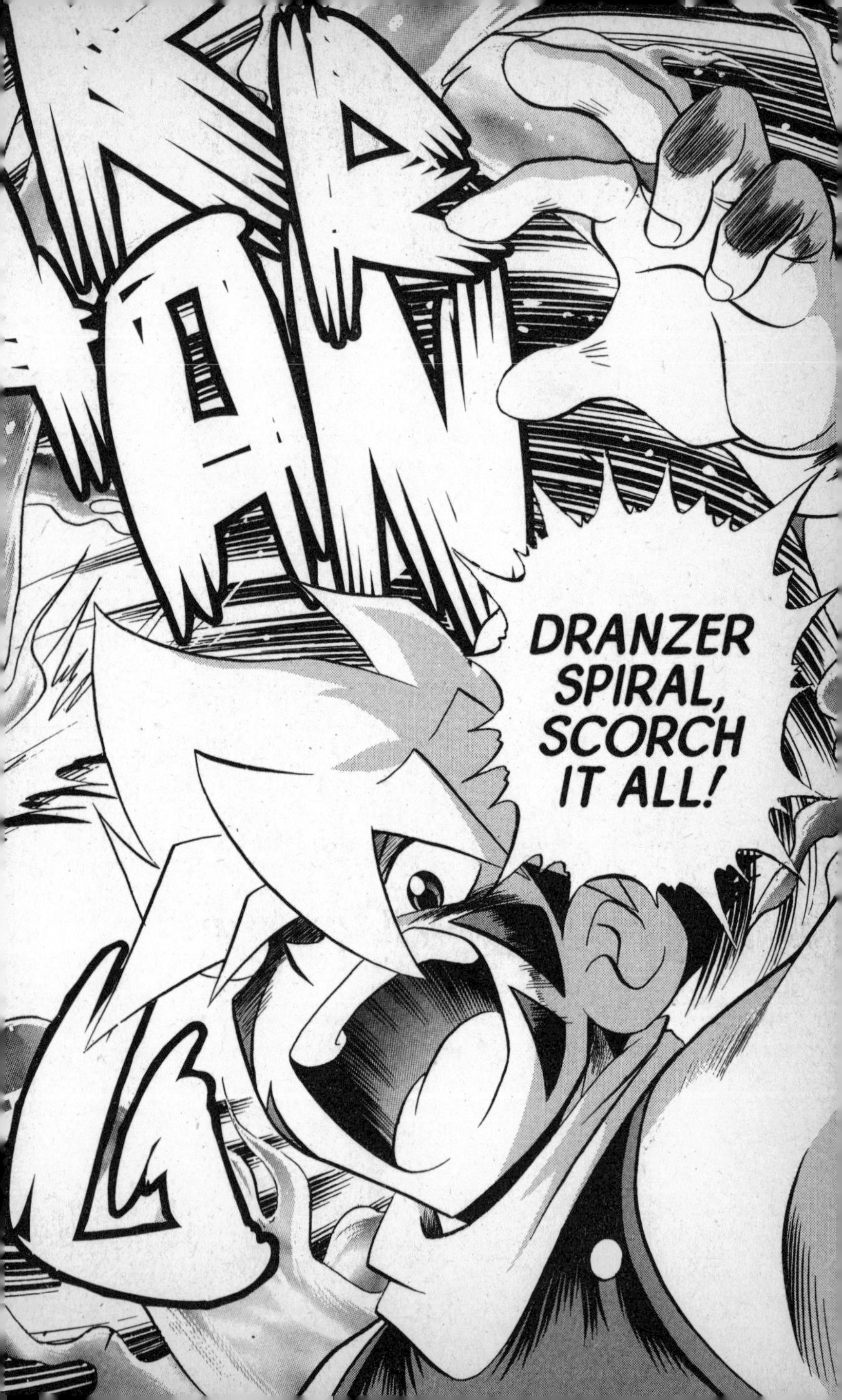
DRANZER SPIRAL, SCORCH IT ALL!

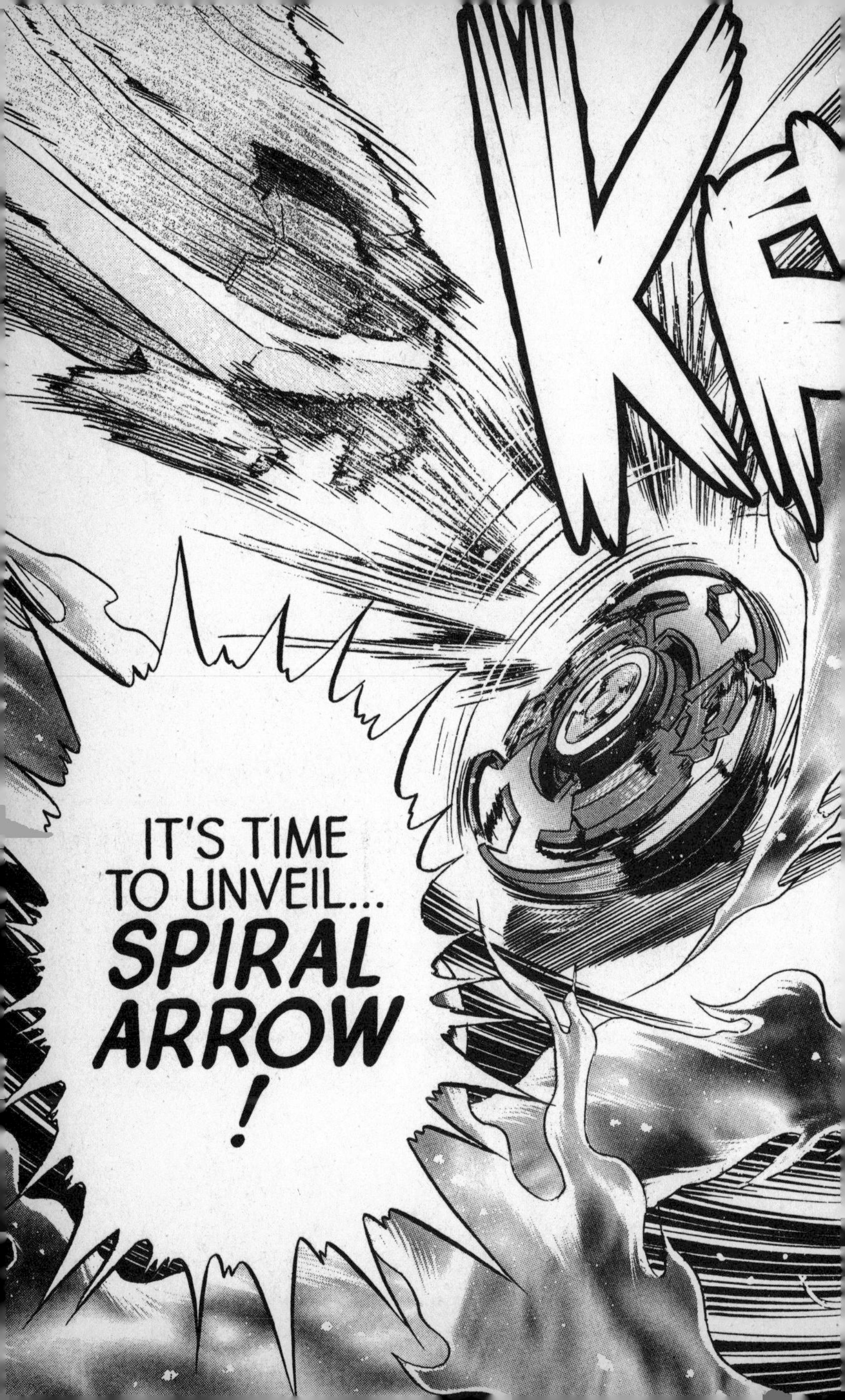
IT'S TIME TO UNVEIL... SPIRAL ARROW!

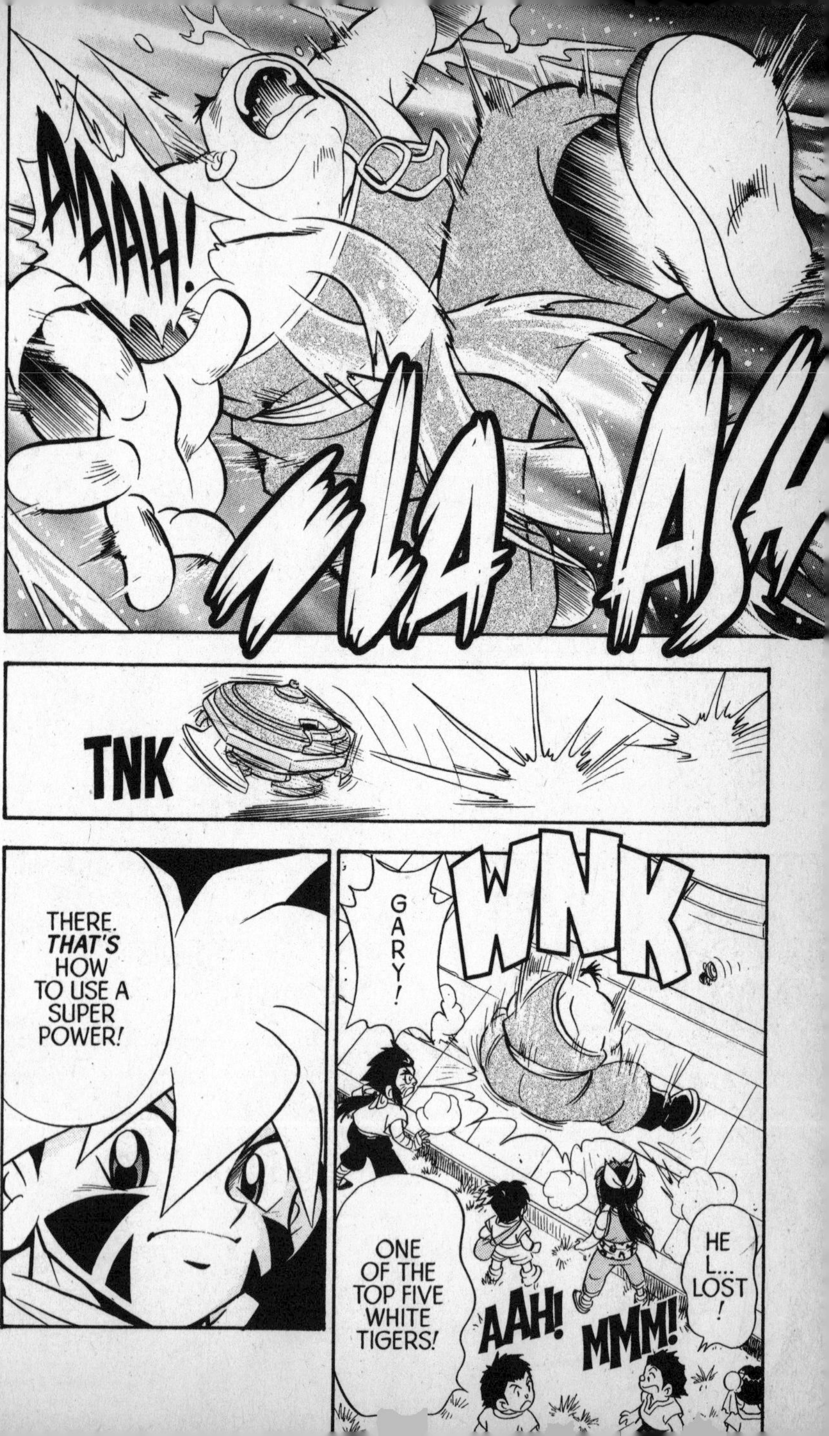
AAAH!
WAAAH
TNK
WNK
GARY!
HE L... LOST!
MMM!
AAH!
ONE OF THE TOP FIVE WHITE TIGERS!
THERE. *THAT'S* HOW TO USE A SUPER POWER!

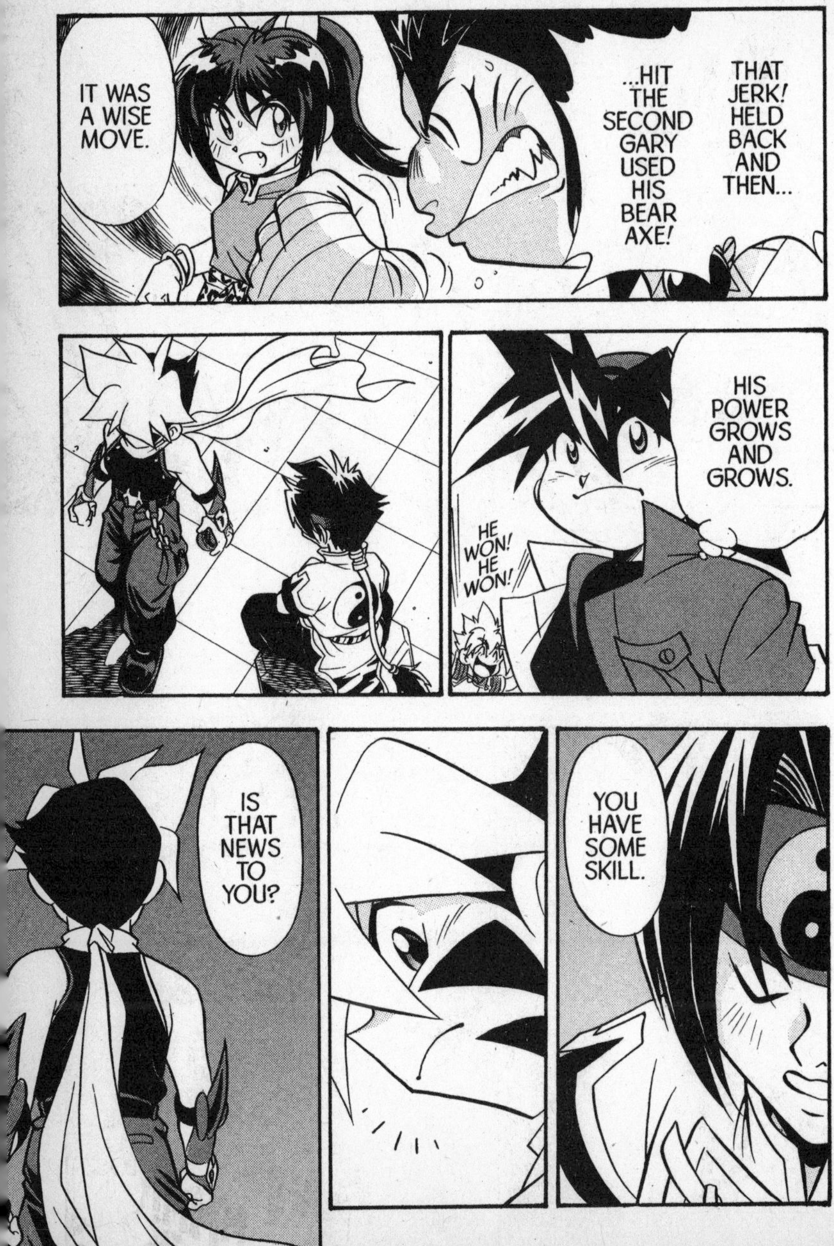
THAT JERK! HELD BACK AND THEN...
...HIT THE SECOND GARY USED HIS BEAR AXE!
IT WAS A WISE MOVE.
HIS POWER GROWS AND GROWS.
HE WON! HE WON!
YOU HAVE SOME SKILL.
IS THAT NEWS TO YOU?

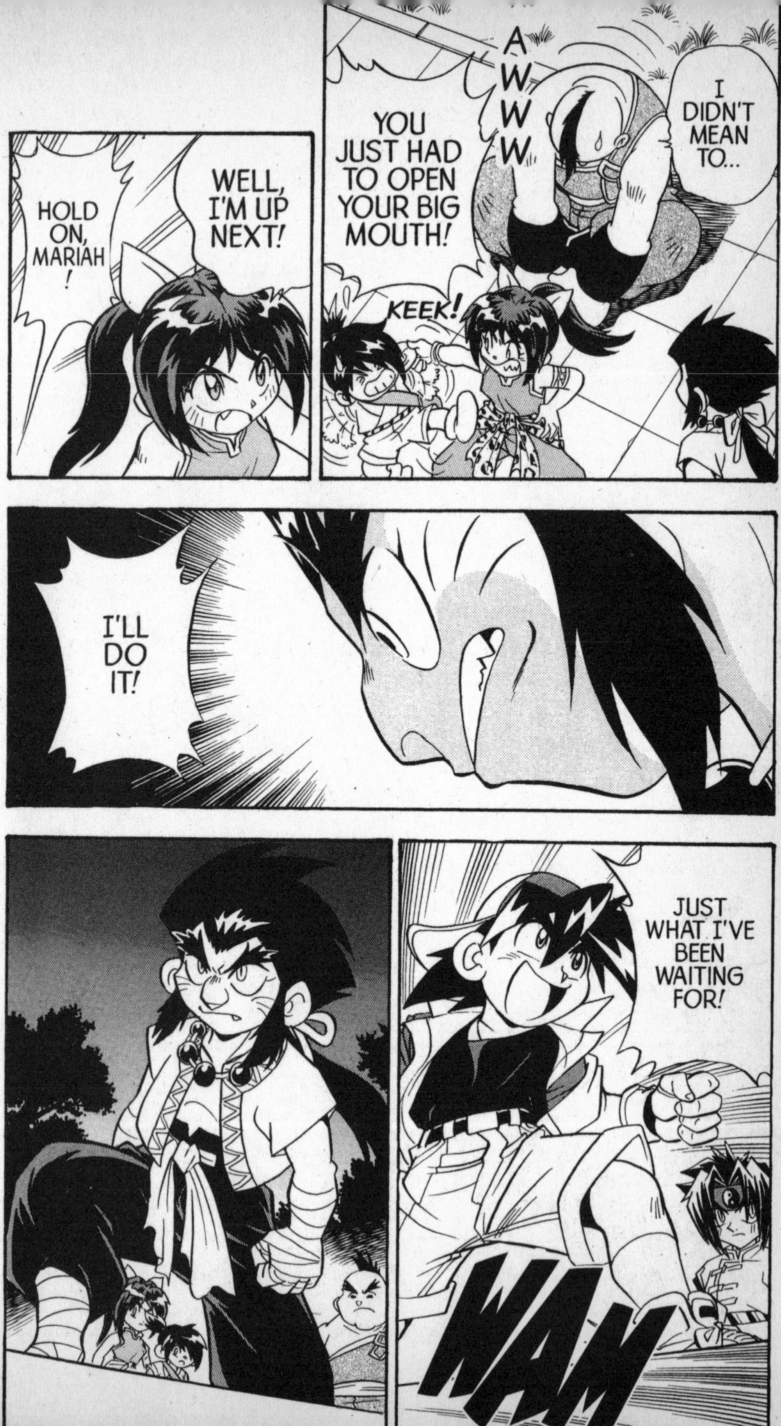
I DIDN'T MEAN TO...
AWWWW
YOU JUST HAD TO OPEN YOUR BIG MOUTH!
KEEK!
WELL, I'M UP NEXT!
HOLD ON, MARIAH!
I'LL DO IT!
JUST WHAT I'VE BEEN WAITING FOR!
WAM

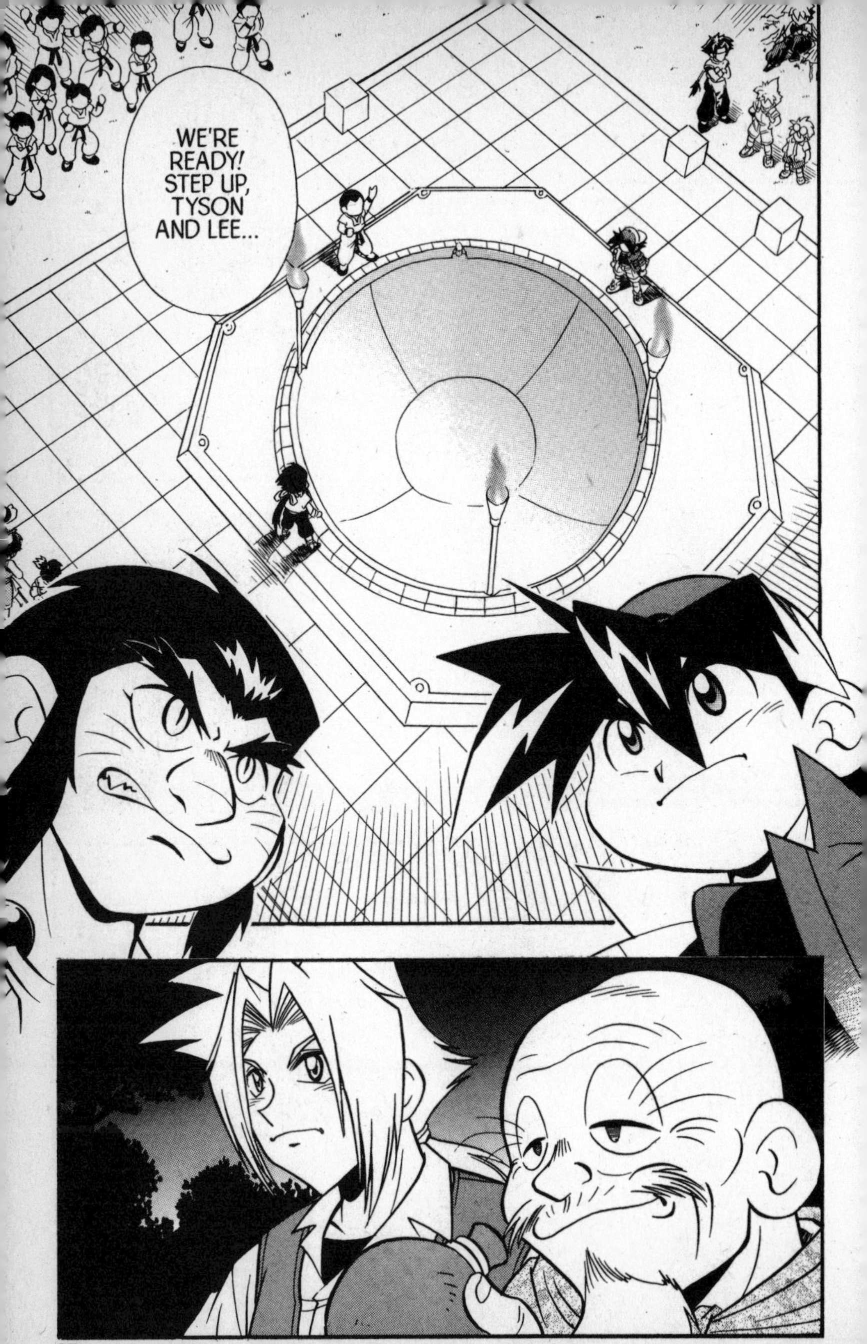
WE'RE READY! STEP UP, TYSON AND LEE...

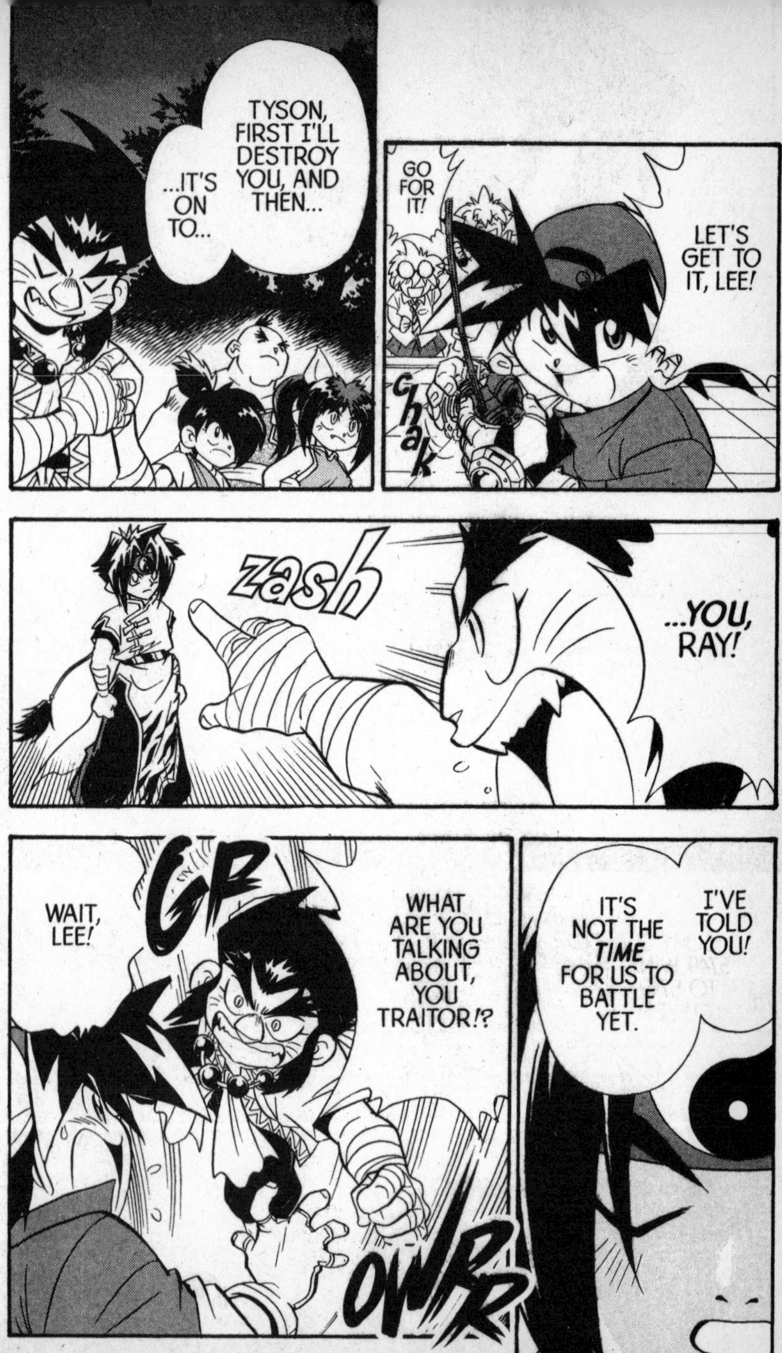
LET'S GET TO IT, LEE!
GO FOR IT!
chak
TYSON, FIRST I'LL DESTROY YOU, AND THEN...
...IT'S ON TO...
zash
...*YOU*, RAY!
I'VE TOLD YOU!
IT'S NOT THE *TIME* FOR US TO BATTLE YET.
GR
WHAT ARE YOU TALKING ABOUT, YOU TRAITOR!?
WAIT, LEE!
OWR

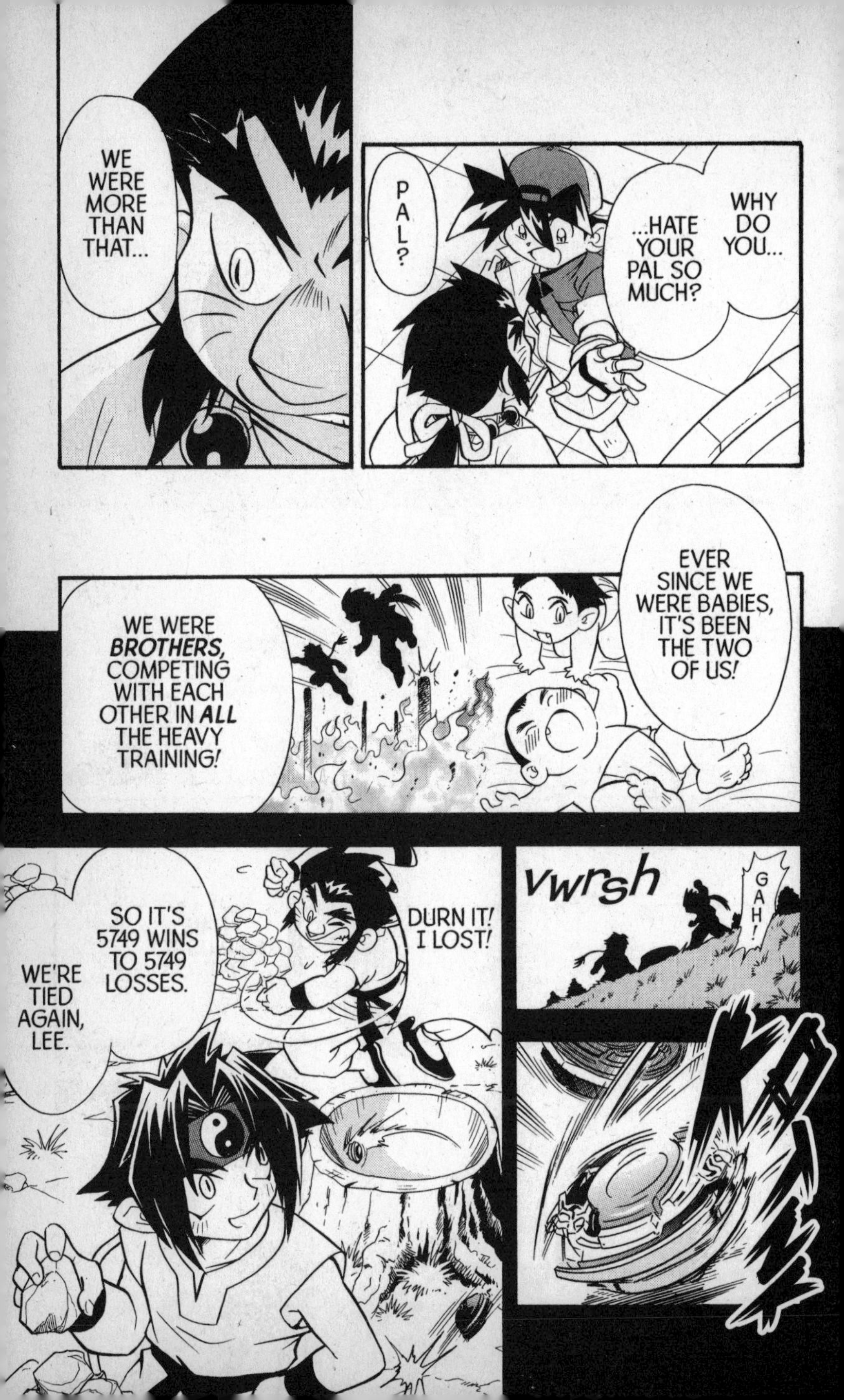
WHY DO YOU... ...HATE YOUR PAL SO MUCH?
PAL?
WE WERE MORE THAN THAT...
EVER SINCE WE WERE BABIES, IT'S BEEN THE TWO OF US!
WE WERE ***BROTHERS***, COMPETING WITH EACH OTHER IN ***ALL*** THE HEAVY TRAINING!
GAH!
vwrsh
DURN IT! I LOST!
SO IT'S 5749 WINS TO 5749 LOSSES.
WE'RE TIED AGAIN, LEE.

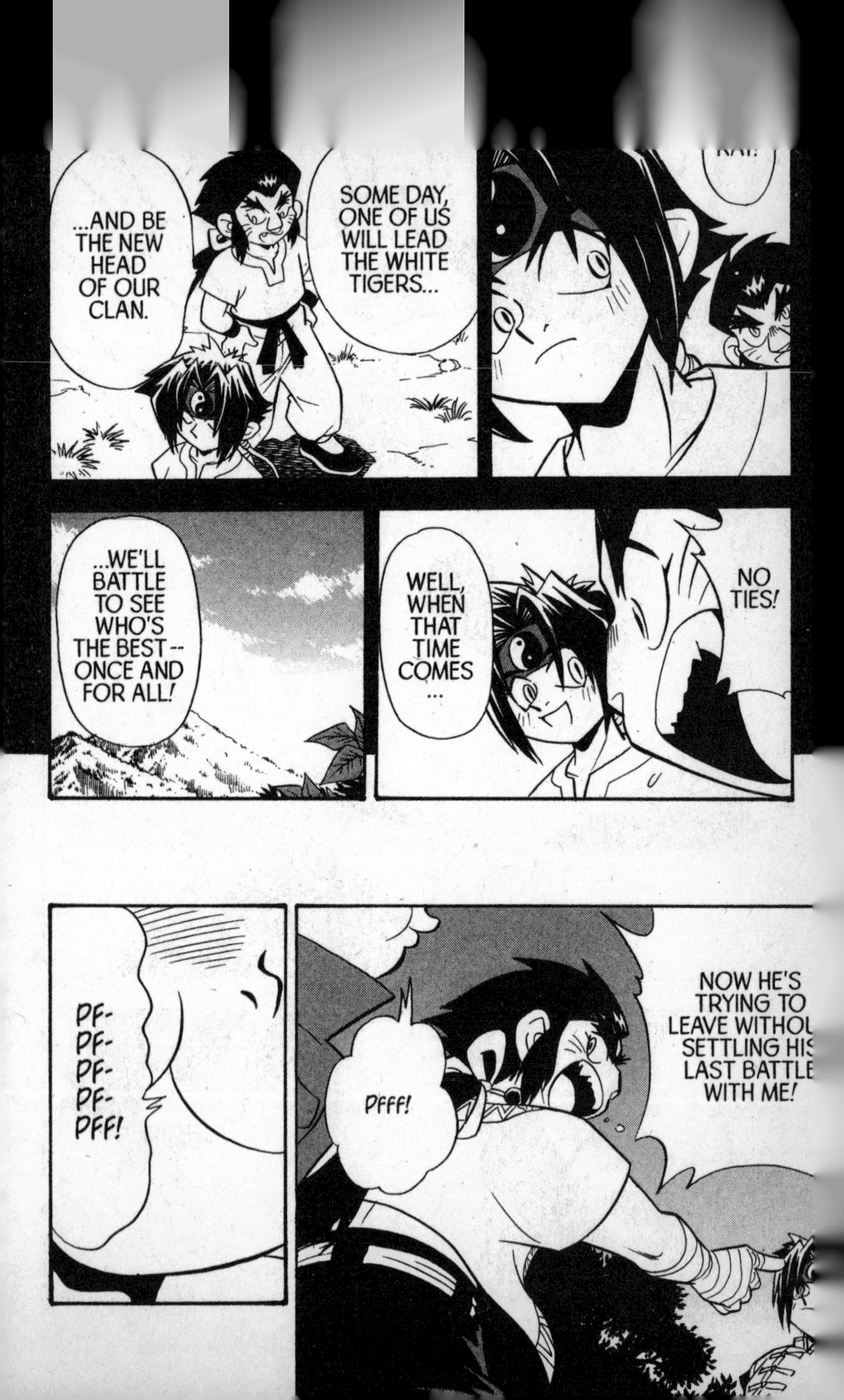
SOME DAY, ONE OF US WILL LEAD THE WHITE TIGERS...
...AND BE THE NEW HEAD OF OUR CLAN.
WELL, WHEN THAT TIME COMES...
...WE'LL BATTLE TO SEE WHO'S THE BEST -- ONCE AND FOR ALL!
NO TIES!
NOW HE'S TRYING TO LEAVE WITHOU SETTLING HIS LAST BATTLE WITH ME!
PFFF!
PF-PF-PF-PF-PFF!

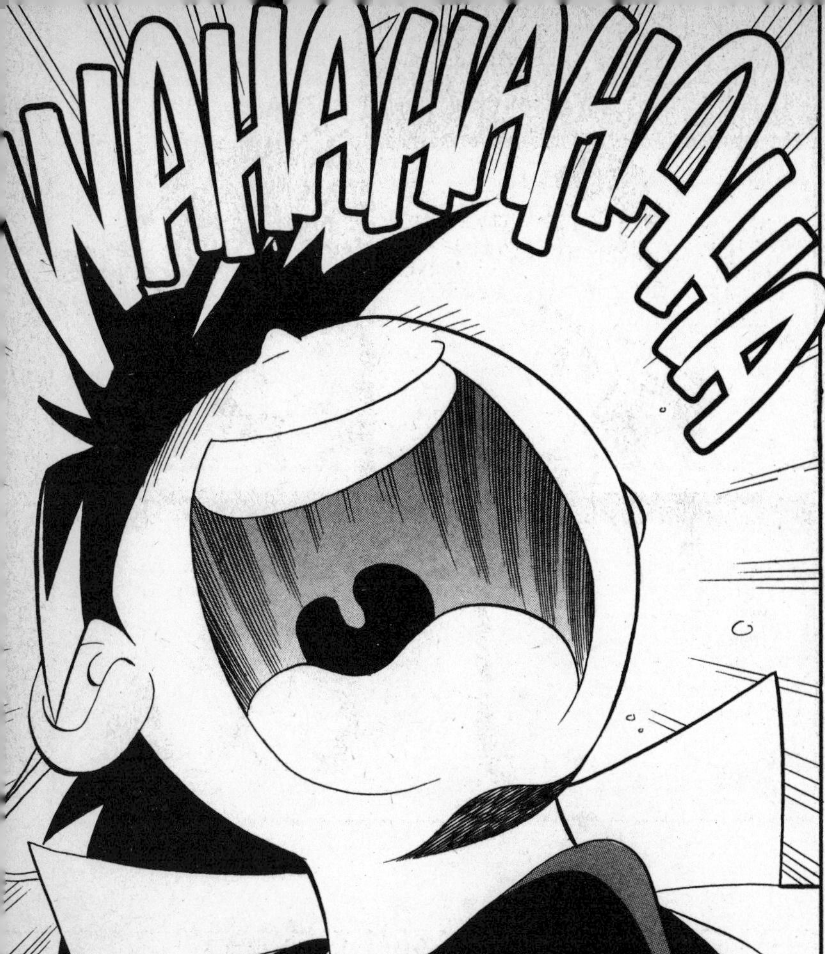
WAHAHAHAHA
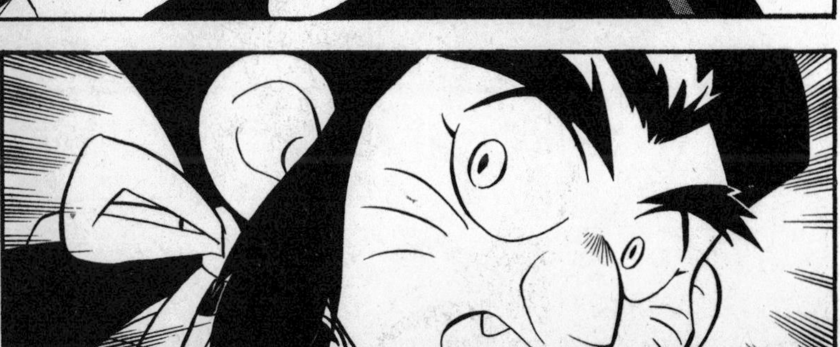

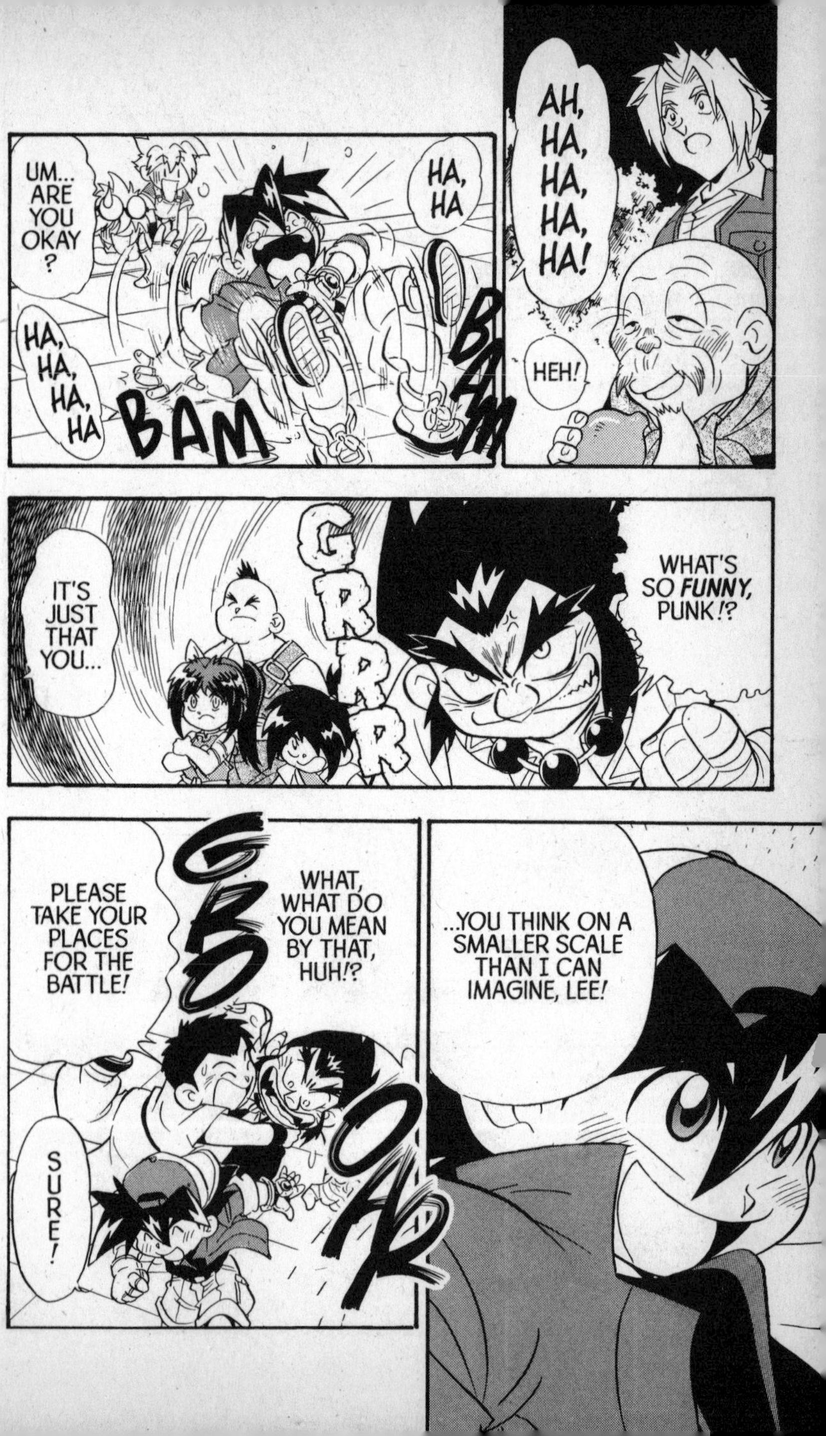
AH, HA, HA, HA, HA!
HEH!
HA, HA
UM... ARE YOU OKAY?
BAM
HA, HA, HA, HA
BAM
WHAT'S SO *FUNNY*, PUNK!?
GRRRR
IT'S JUST THAT YOU...
...YOU THINK ON A SMALLER SCALE THAN I CAN IMAGINE, LEE!
WHAT, WHAT DO YOU MEAN BY THAT, HUH!?
PLEASE TAKE YOUR PLACES FOR THE BATTLE!
SURE!

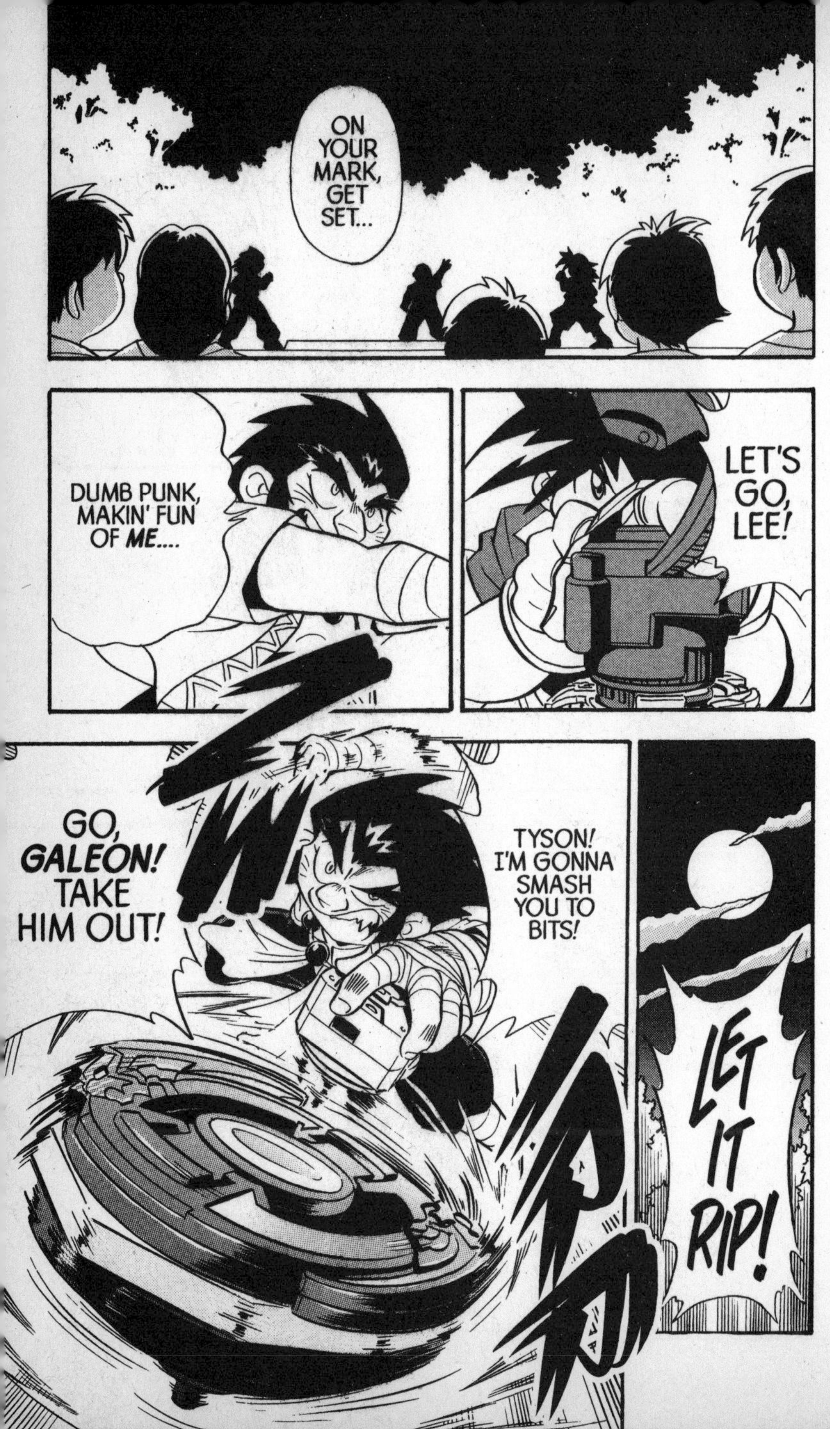
ON YOUR MARK, GET SET...
LET'S GO, LEE!
DUMB PUNK, MAKIN' FUN OF ***ME***....
LET IT RIP!
TYSON! I'M GONNA SMASH YOU TO BITS!
GO, ***GALEON!*** TAKE HIM OUT!

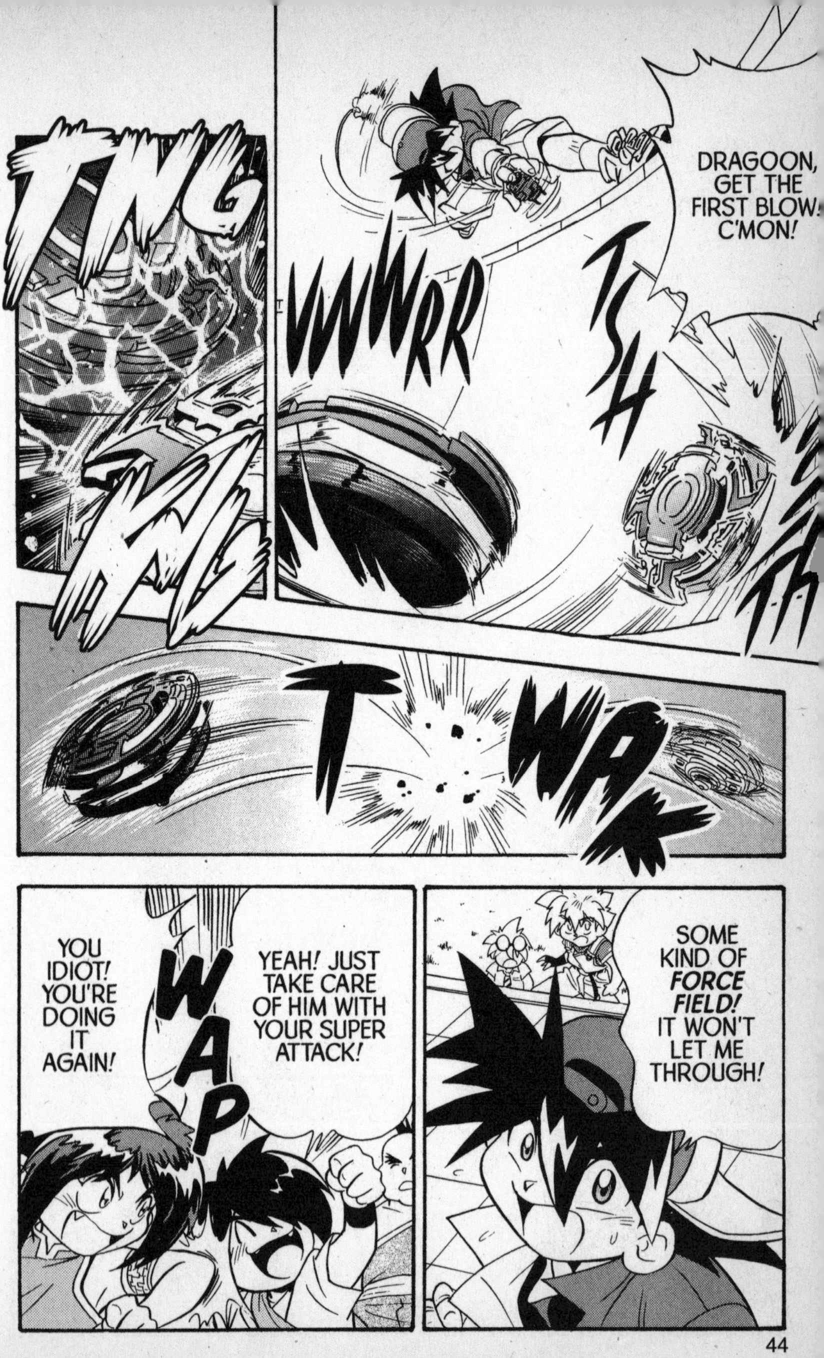
DRAGOON, GET THE FIRST BLOW! C'MON!
TSH
VVVWRR
TING
TWAK
SOME KIND OF *FORCE FIELD!* IT WON'T LET ME THROUGH!
YEAH! JUST TAKE CARE OF HIM WITH YOUR SUPER ATTACK!
WAP
YOU IDIOT! YOU'RE DOING IT AGAIN!

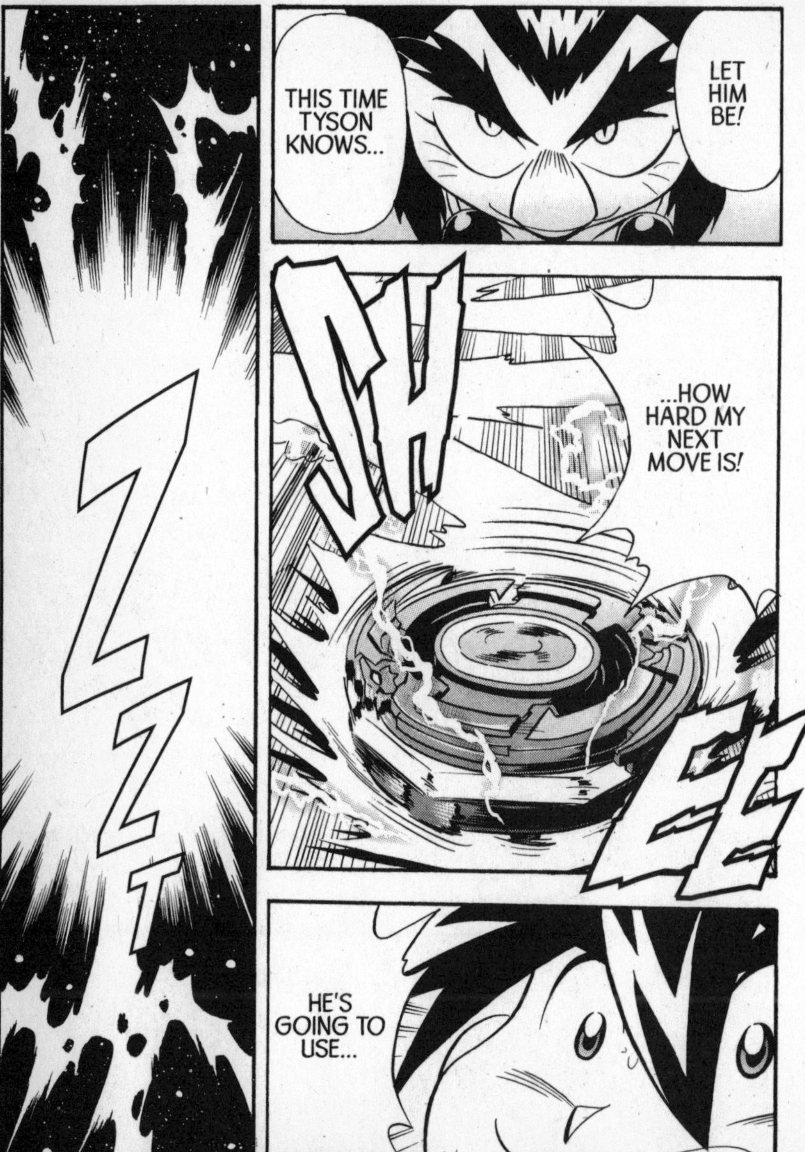
LET HIM BE!
THIS TIME TYSON KNOWS...
SH
...HOW HARD MY NEXT MOVE IS!
EE
HE'S GOING TO USE...
ZZZT

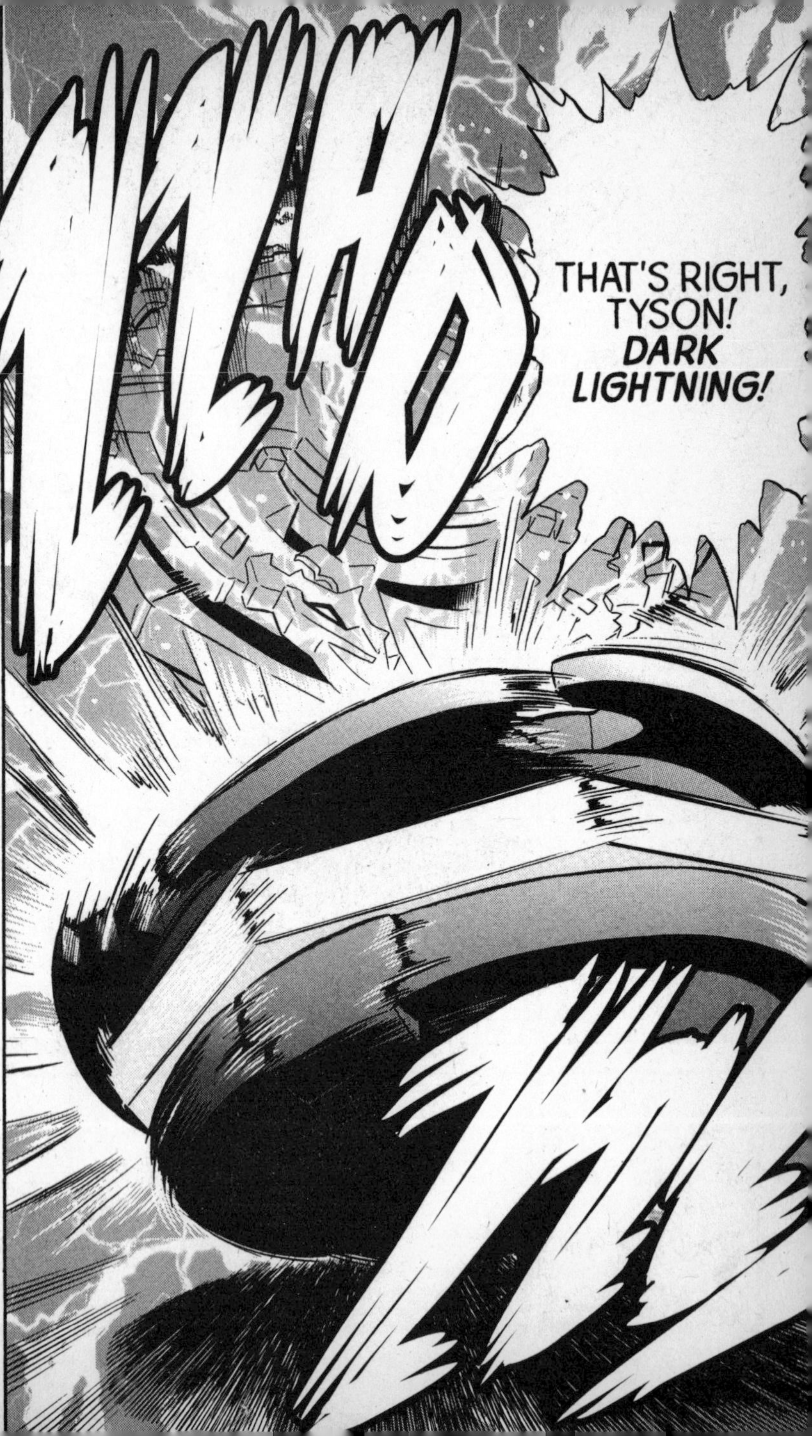
THAT'S RIGHT, TYSON! *DARK LIGHTNING!*

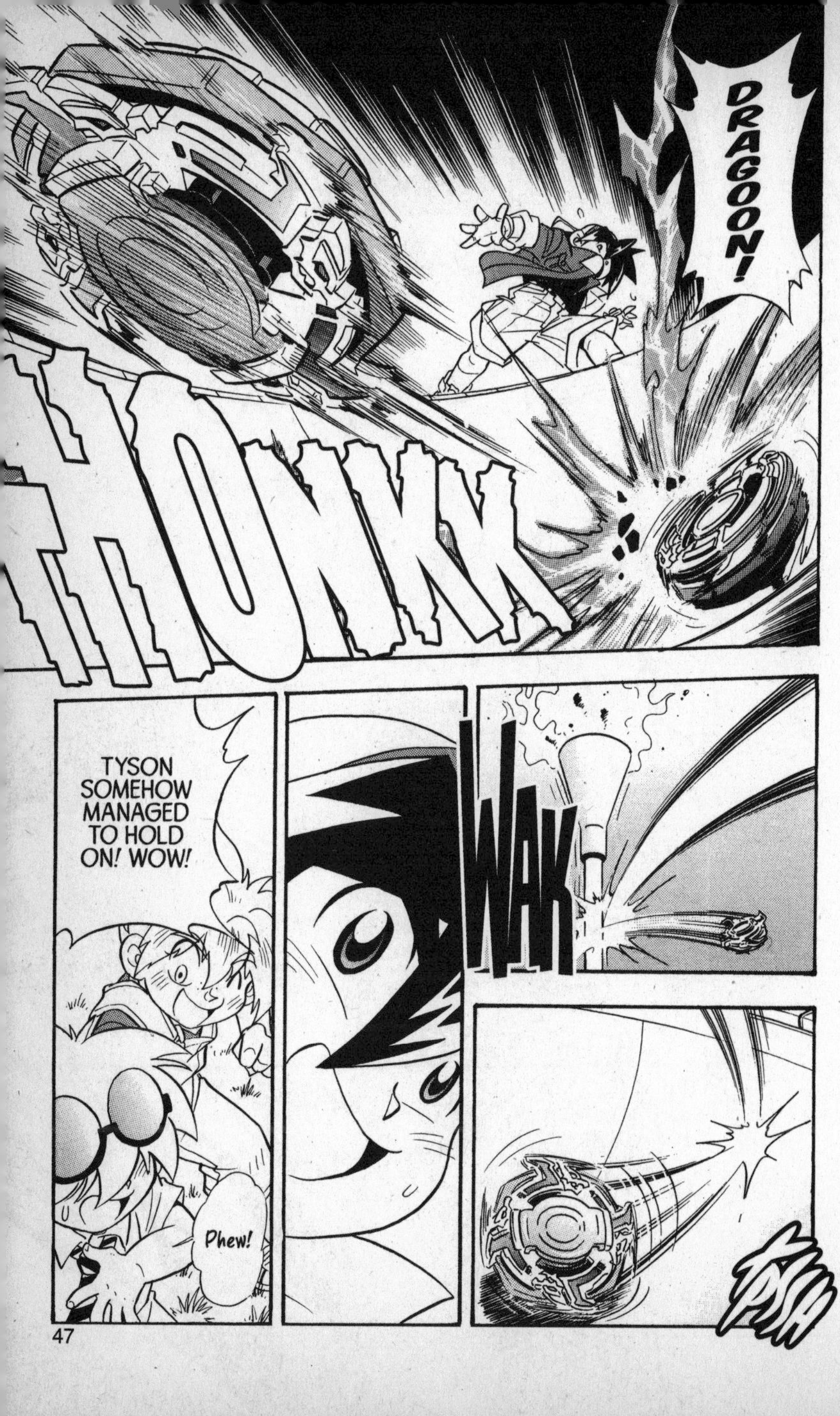
DRAGOOON!
THONKK
WAK
PSSH
TYSON SOMEHOW MANAGED TO HOLD ON! WOW!
Phew!

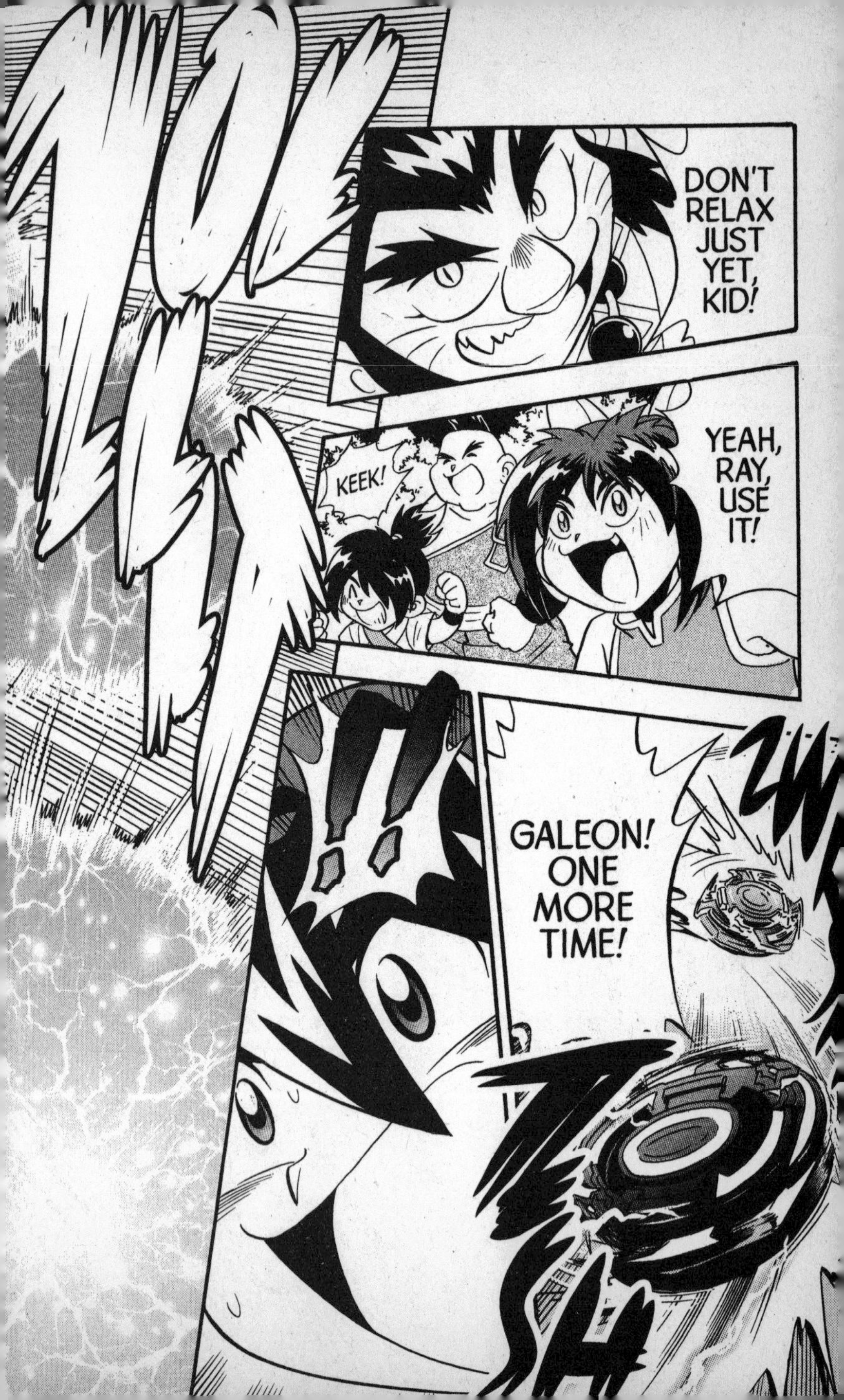
DON'T RELAX JUST YET, KID!
YEAH, RAY, USE IT!
KEEK!
GALEON! ONE MORE TIME!

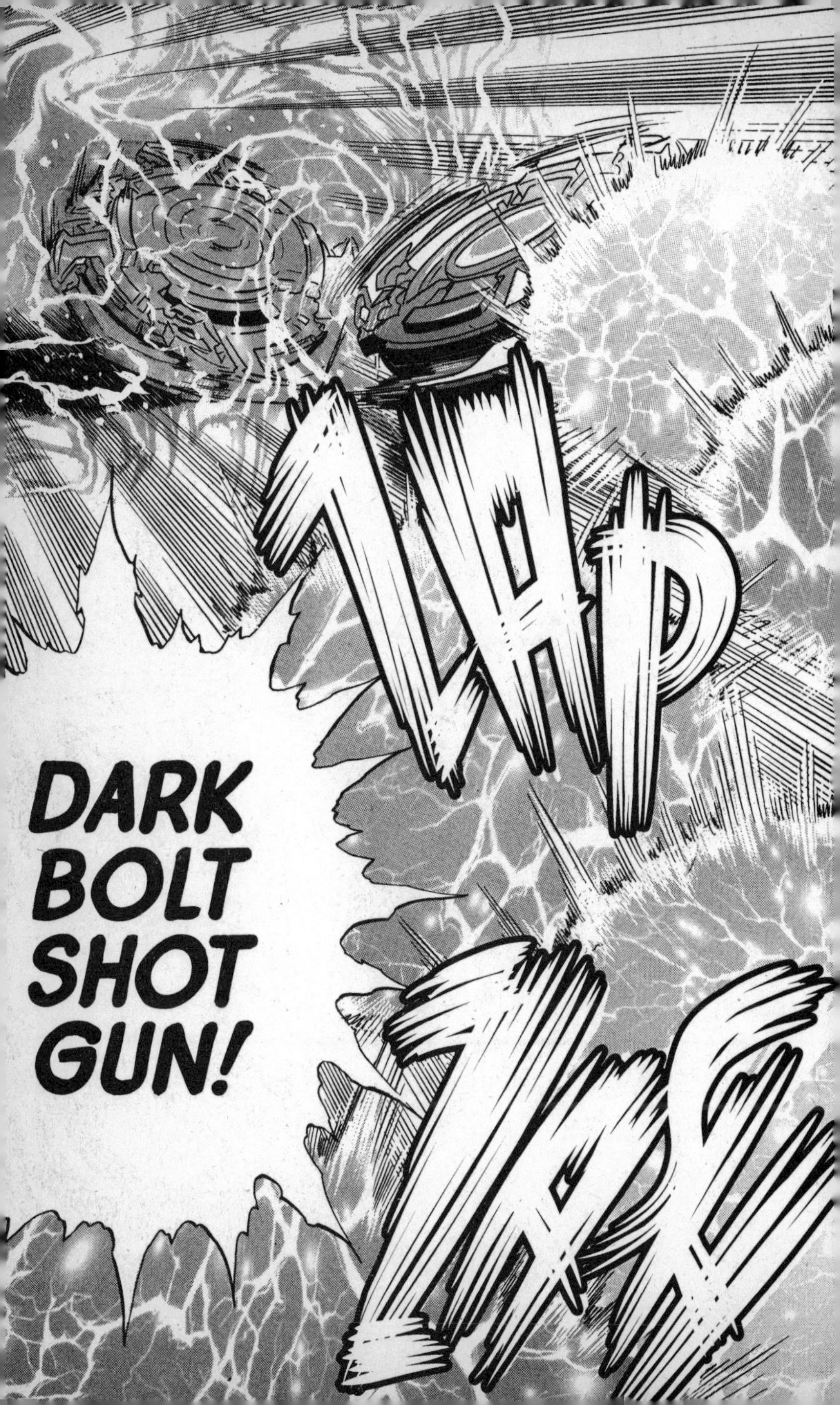
ZZAP
DARK BOLT SHOT GUN!
ZZAP

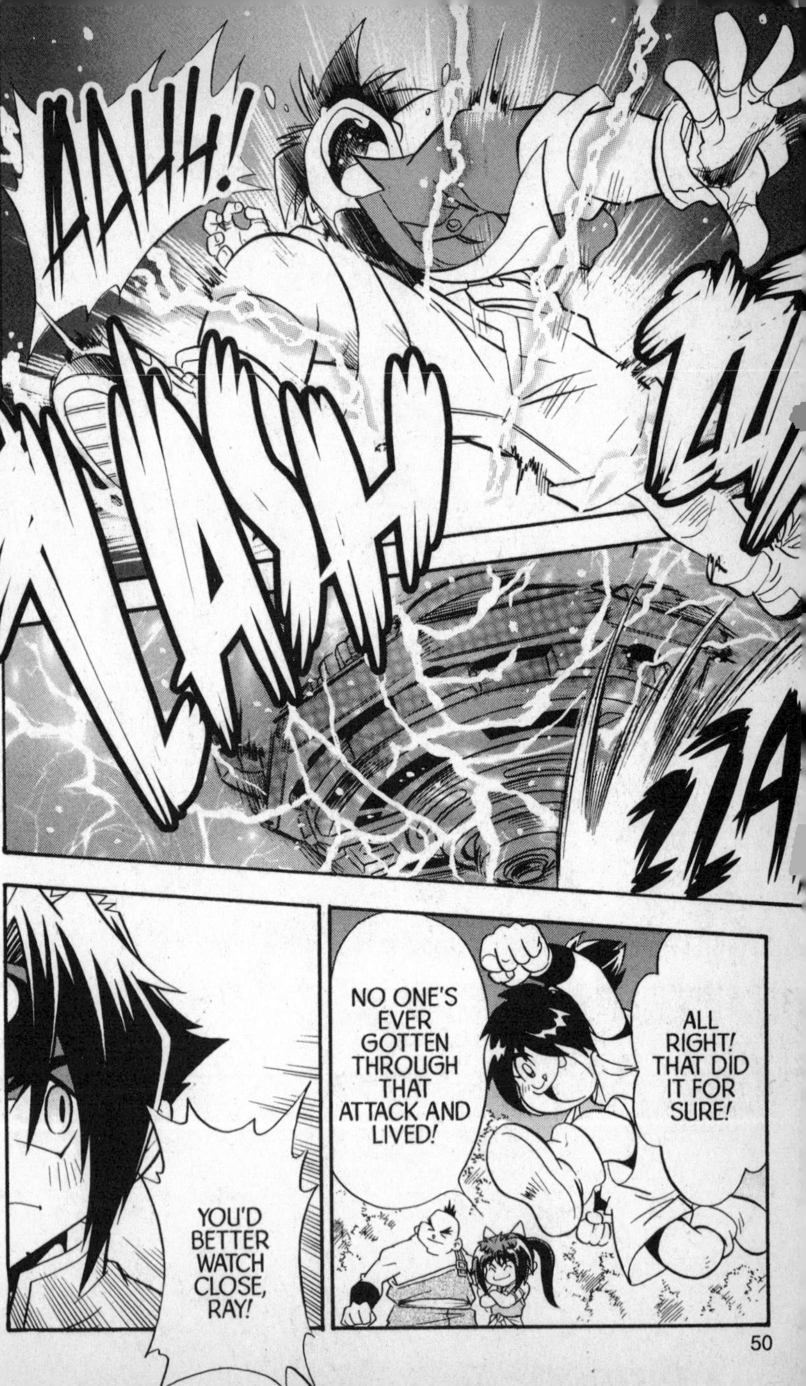
AAHH!
FLASH
ALL RIGHT! THAT DID IT FOR SURE!
NO ONE'S EVER GOTTEN THROUGH THAT ATTACK AND LIVED!
YOU'D BETTER WATCH CLOSE, RAY!

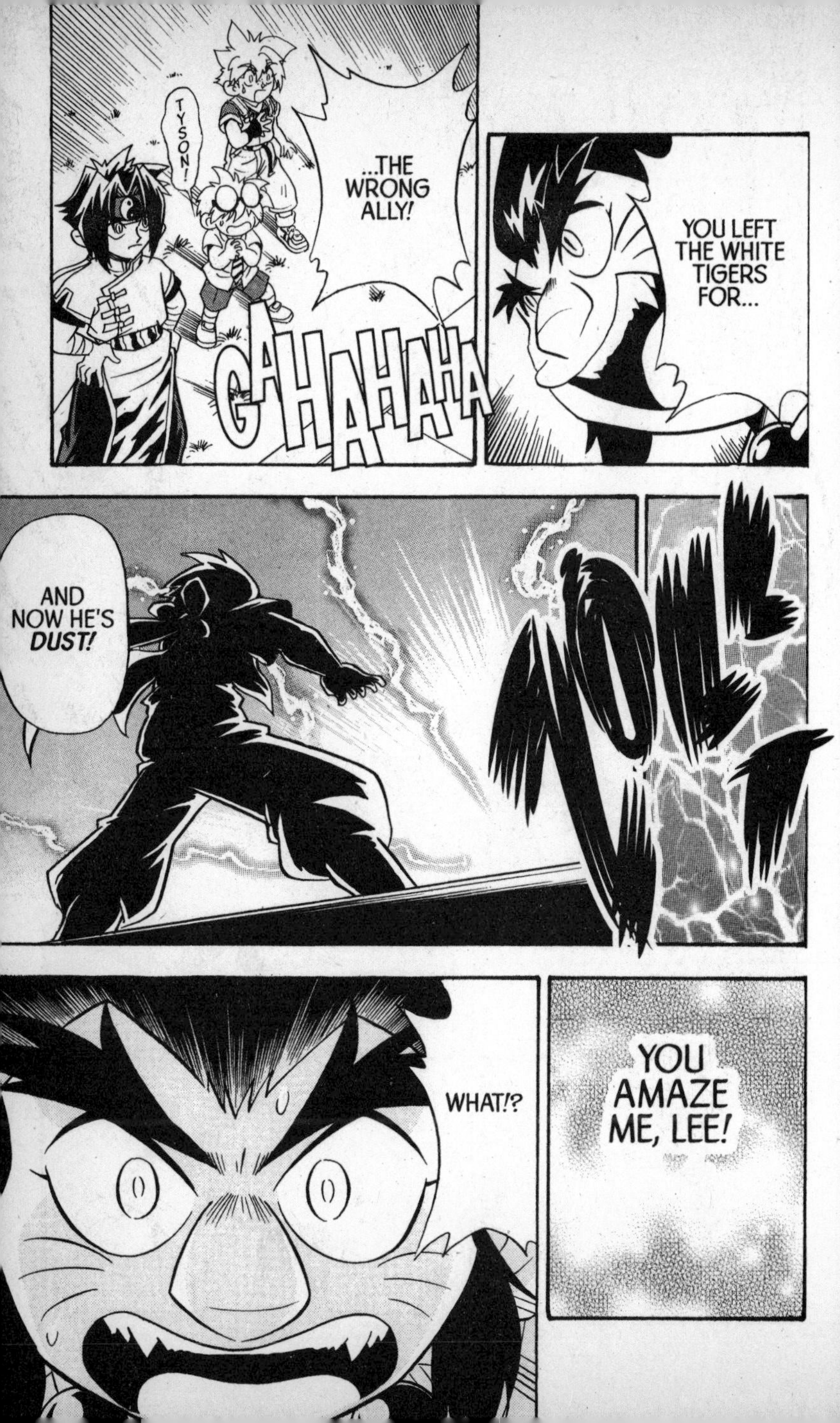
YOU LEFT THE WHITE TIGERS FOR...
...THE WRONG ALLY!
TYSON!
GAHAHAHA
AND NOW HE'S *DUST!*
YOU AMAZE ME, LEE!
WHAT!?

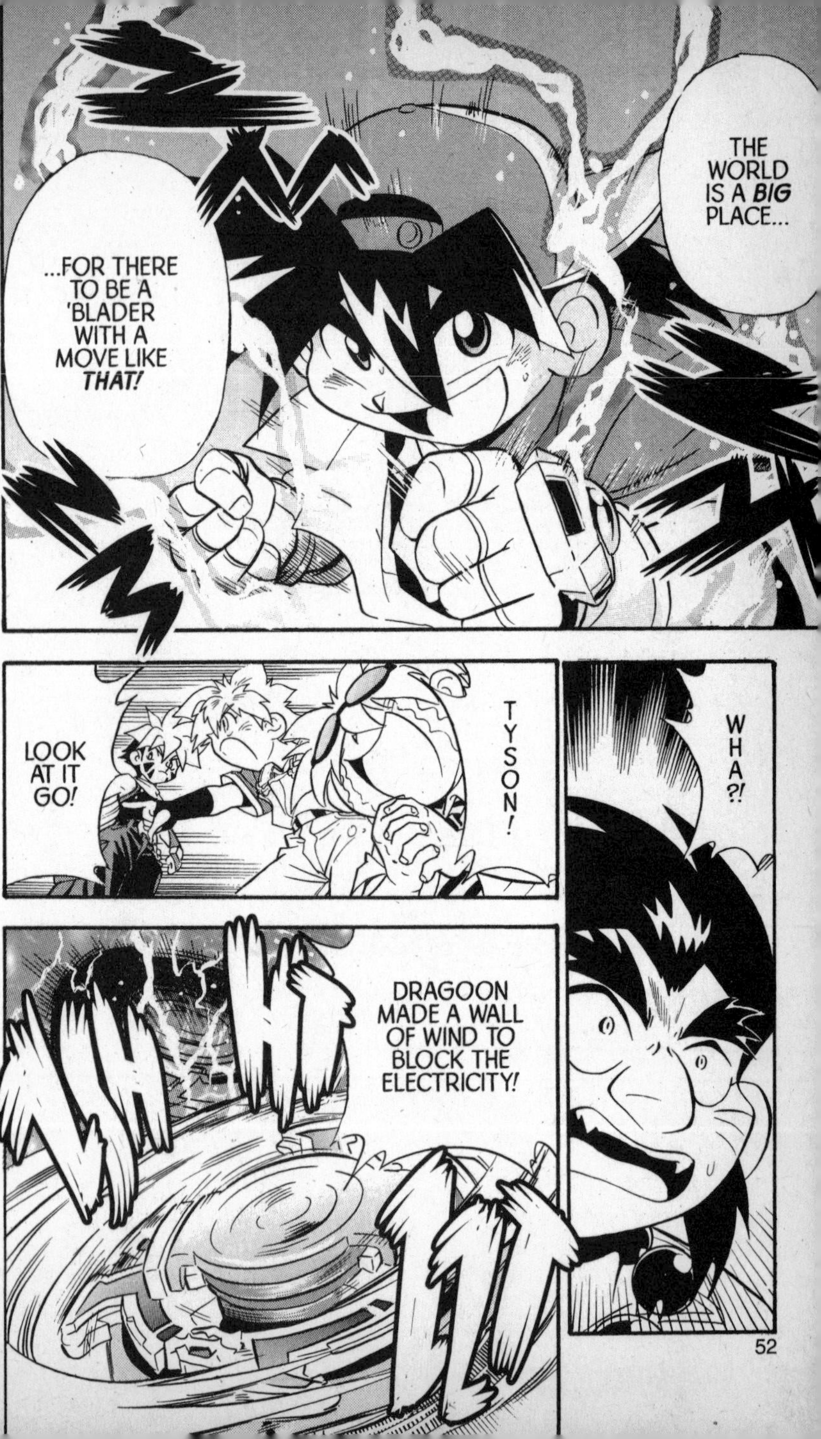
THE WORLD IS A *BIG* PLACE...
...FOR THERE TO BE A 'BLADER WITH A MOVE LIKE *THAT!*
WHA?!
TYSON!
LOOK AT IT GO!
DRAGOON MADE A WALL OF WIND TO BLOCK THE ELECTRICITY!

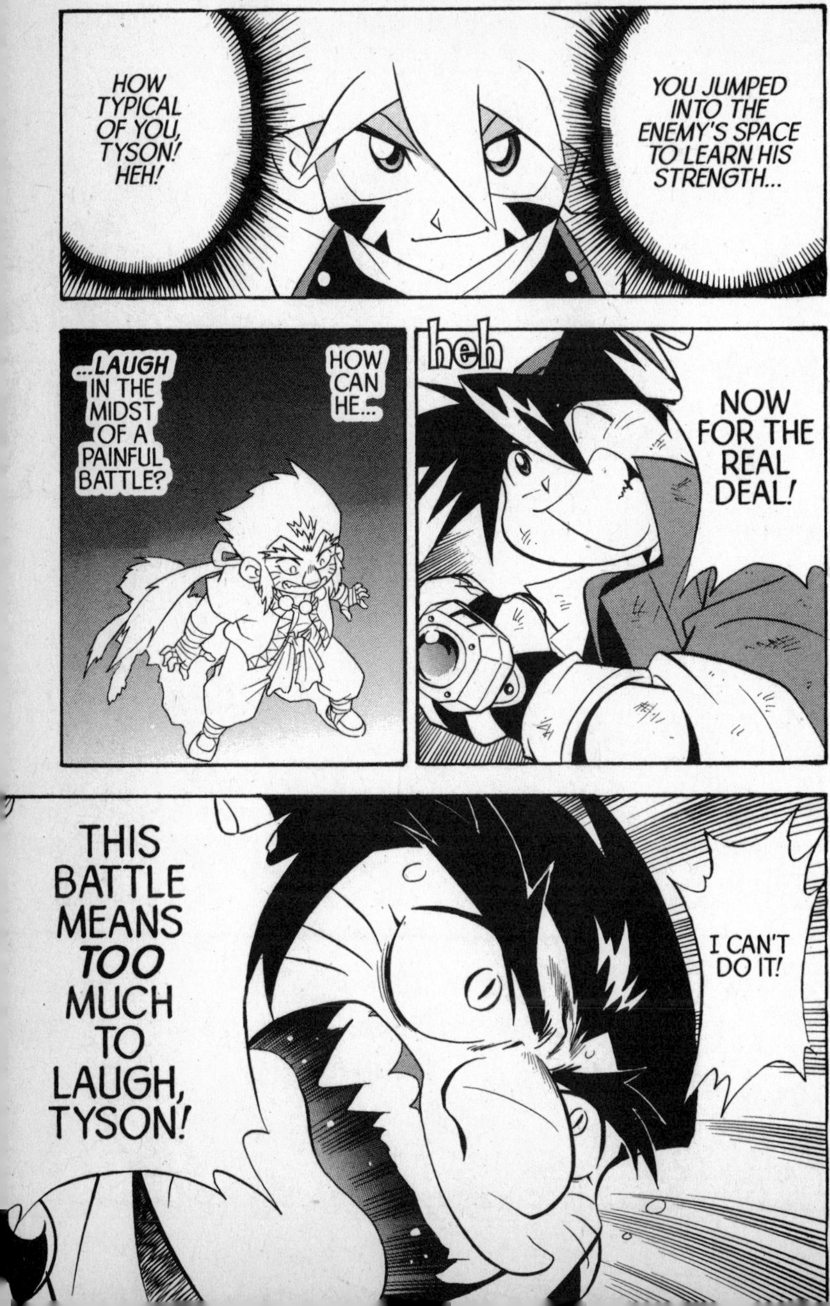
YOU JUMPED INTO THE ENEMY'S SPACE TO LEARN HIS STRENGTH...
HOW TYPICAL OF YOU, TYSON! HEH!
heh
NOW FOR THE REAL DEAL!
HOW CAN HE...
...LAUGH IN THE MIDST OF A PAINFUL BATTLE?
I CAN'T DO IT!
THIS BATTLE MEANS TOO MUCH TO LAUGH, TYSON!

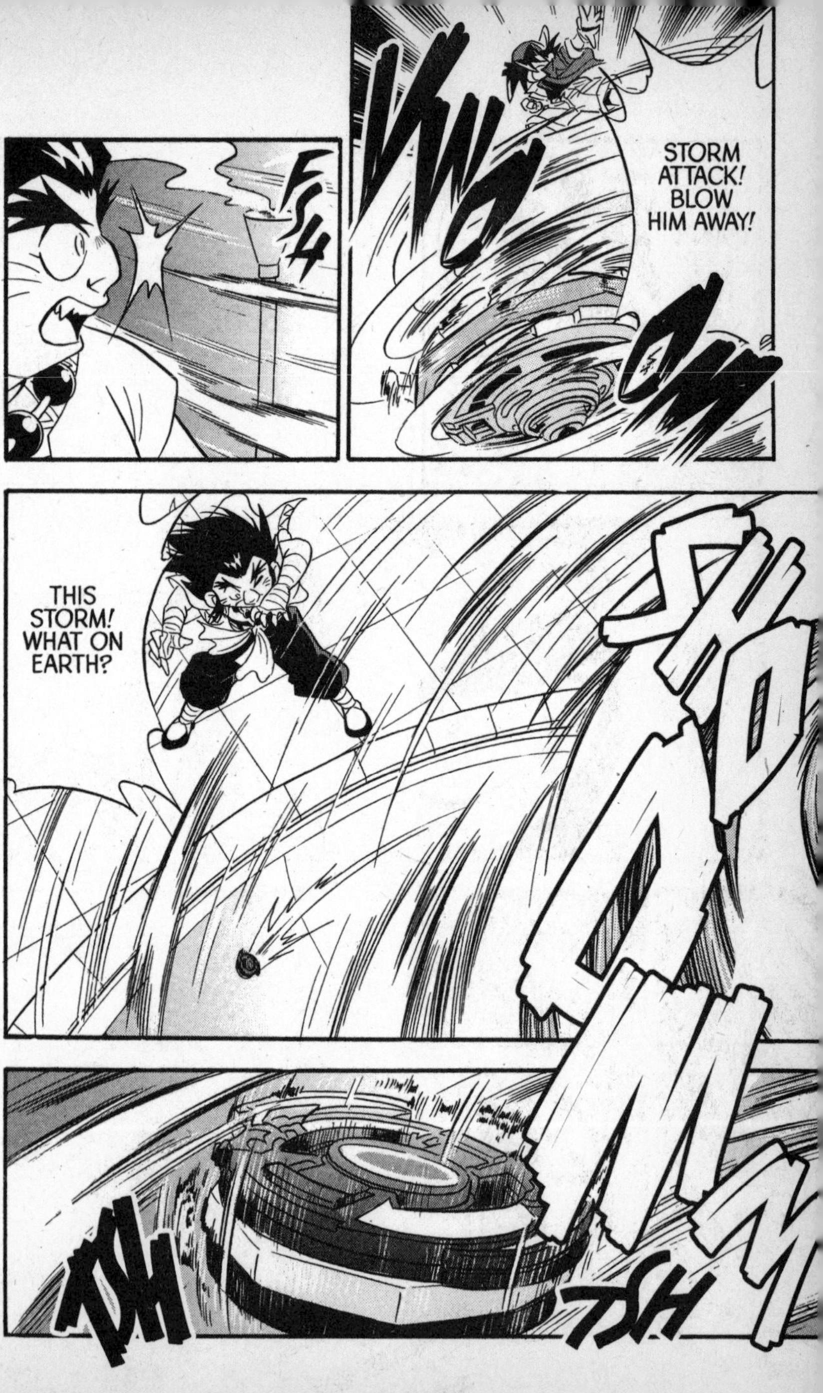
STORM ATTACK! BLOW HIM AWAY!
THIS STORM! WHAT ON EARTH?
TSH
TSH

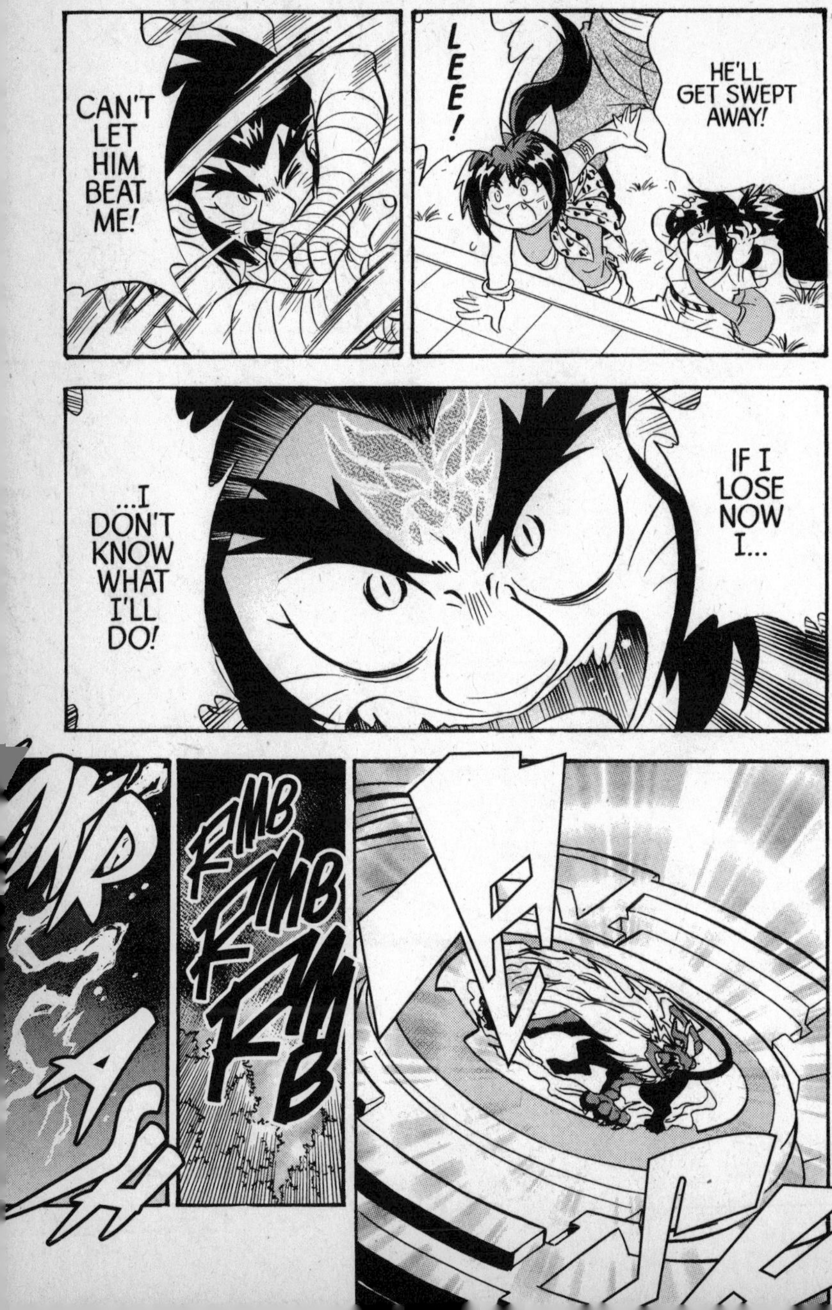
HE'LL GET SWEPT AWAY!
LEE!
CAN'T LET HIM BEAT ME!
IF I LOSE NOW I...
...I DON'T KNOW WHAT I'LL DO!

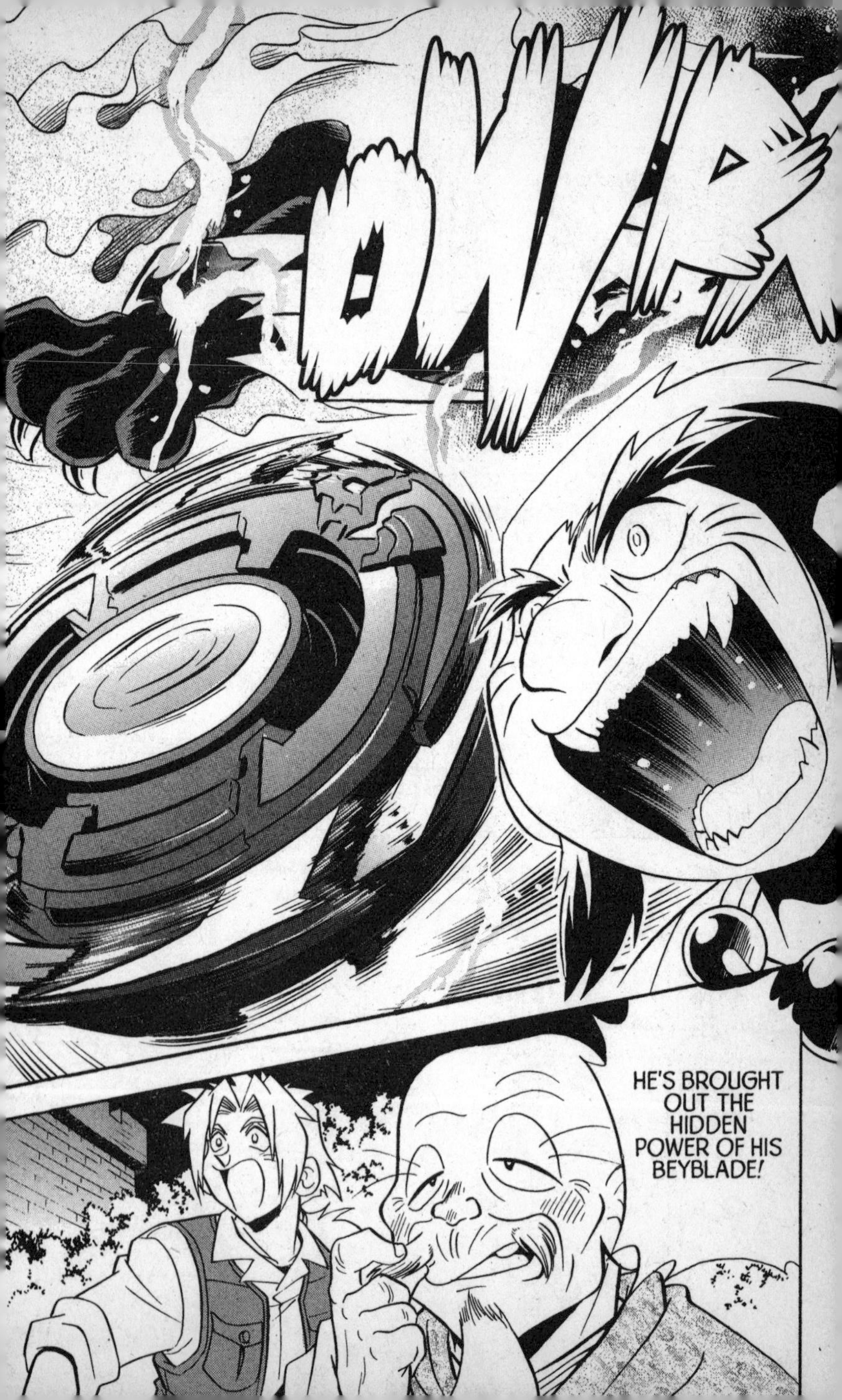

HE'S BROUGHT OUT THE HIDDEN POWER OF HIS BEYBLADE!

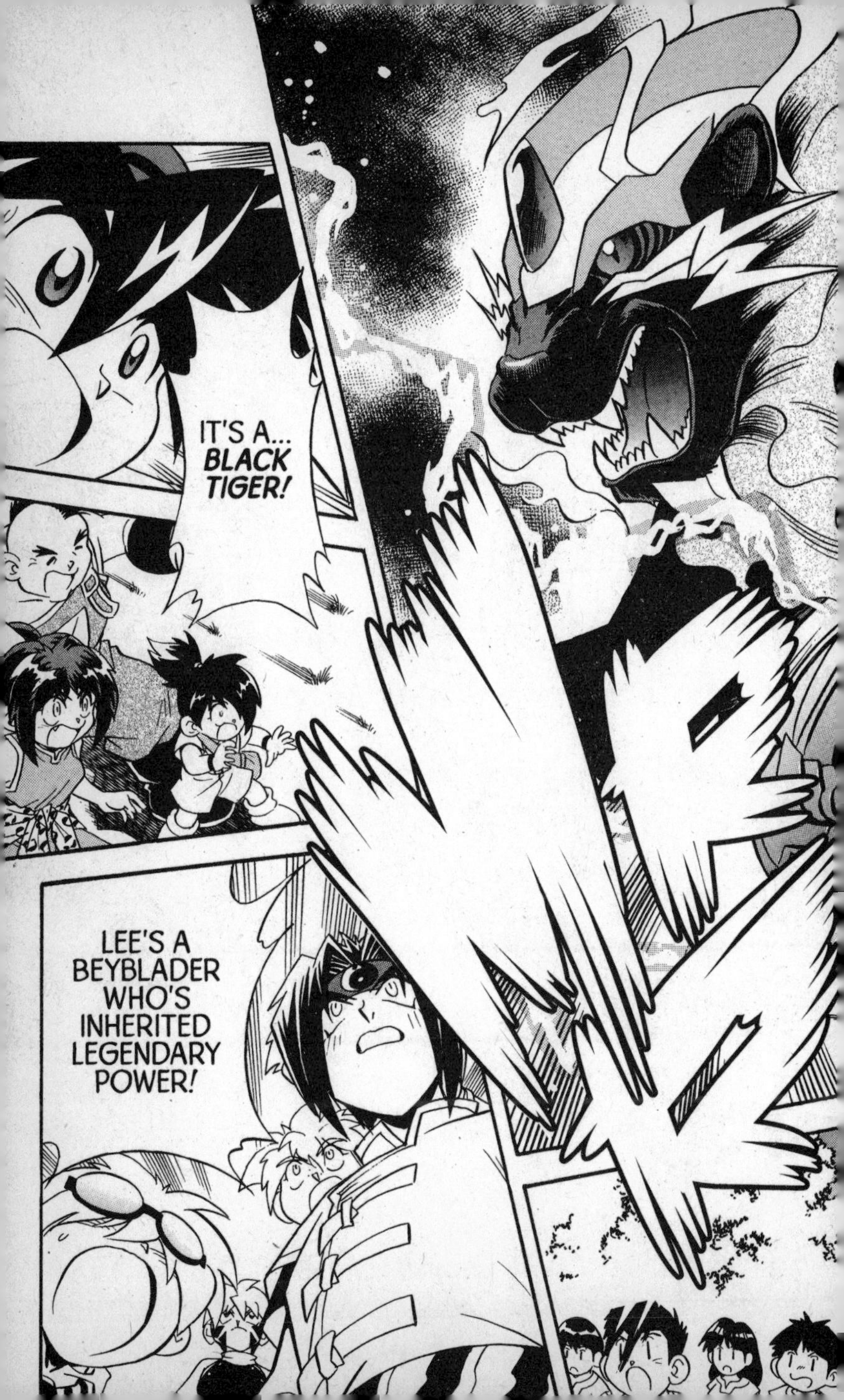
IT'S A... BLACK TIGER!
LEE'S A BEYBLADER WHO'S INHERITED LEGENDARY POWER!

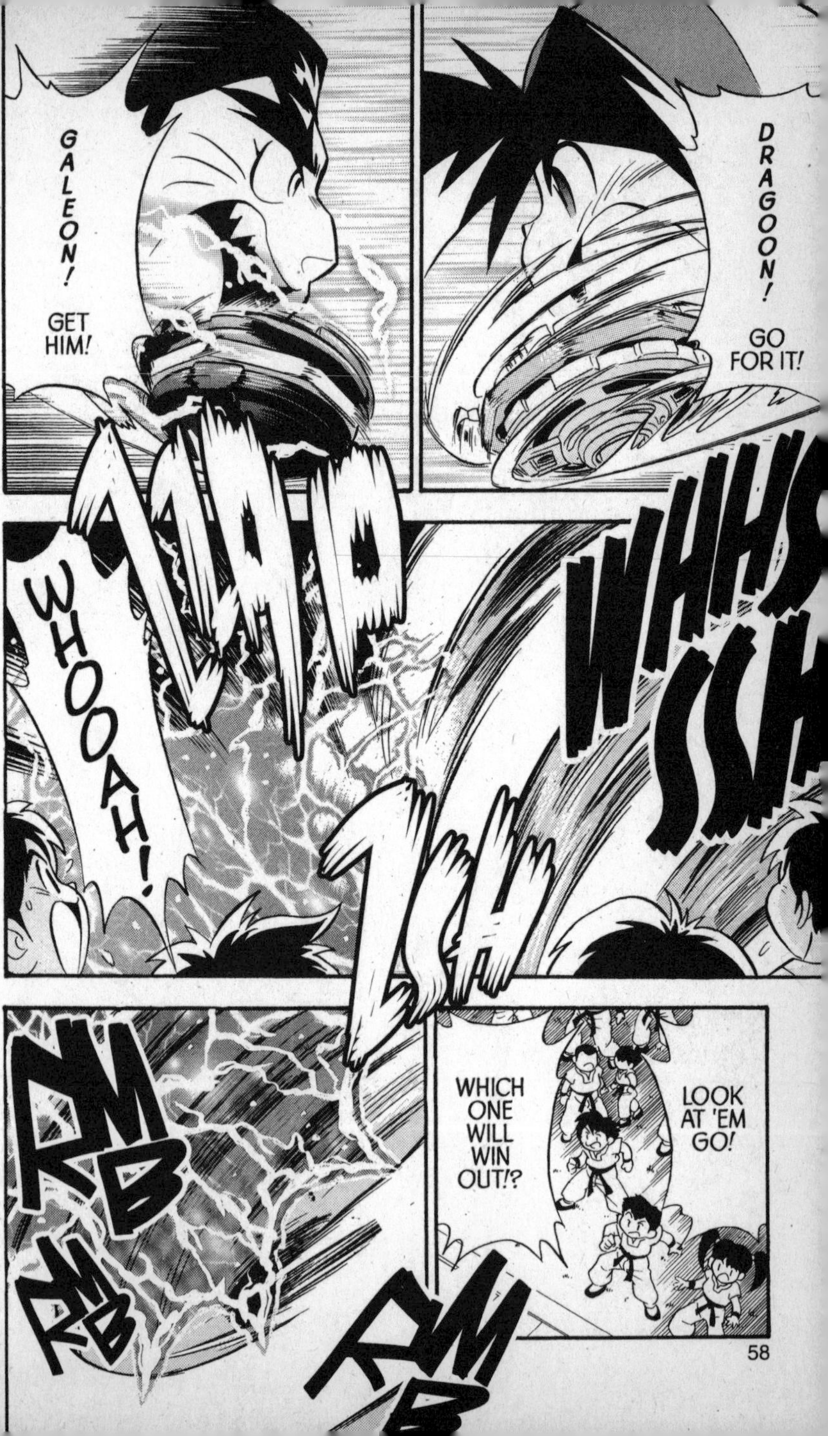
DRAGOOON!
GO FOR IT!
GALEEON!
GET HIM!
WHOOAH!
LOOK AT 'EM GO!
WHICH ONE WILL WIN OUT!?

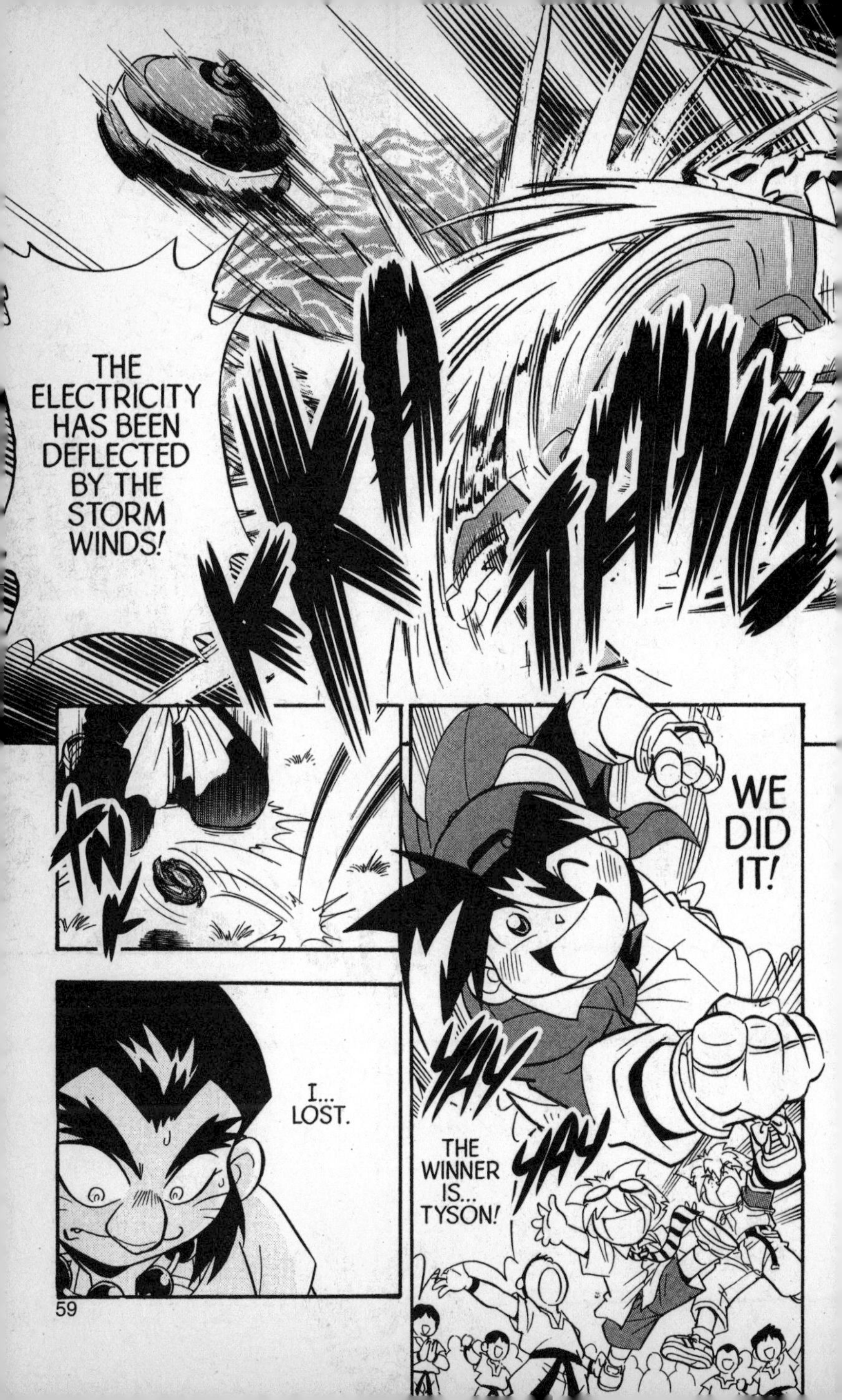
THE ELECTRICITY HAS BEEN DEFLECTED BY THE STORM WINDS!
WE DID IT!
YAY
YAY
THE WINNER IS... TYSON!
I... LOST.

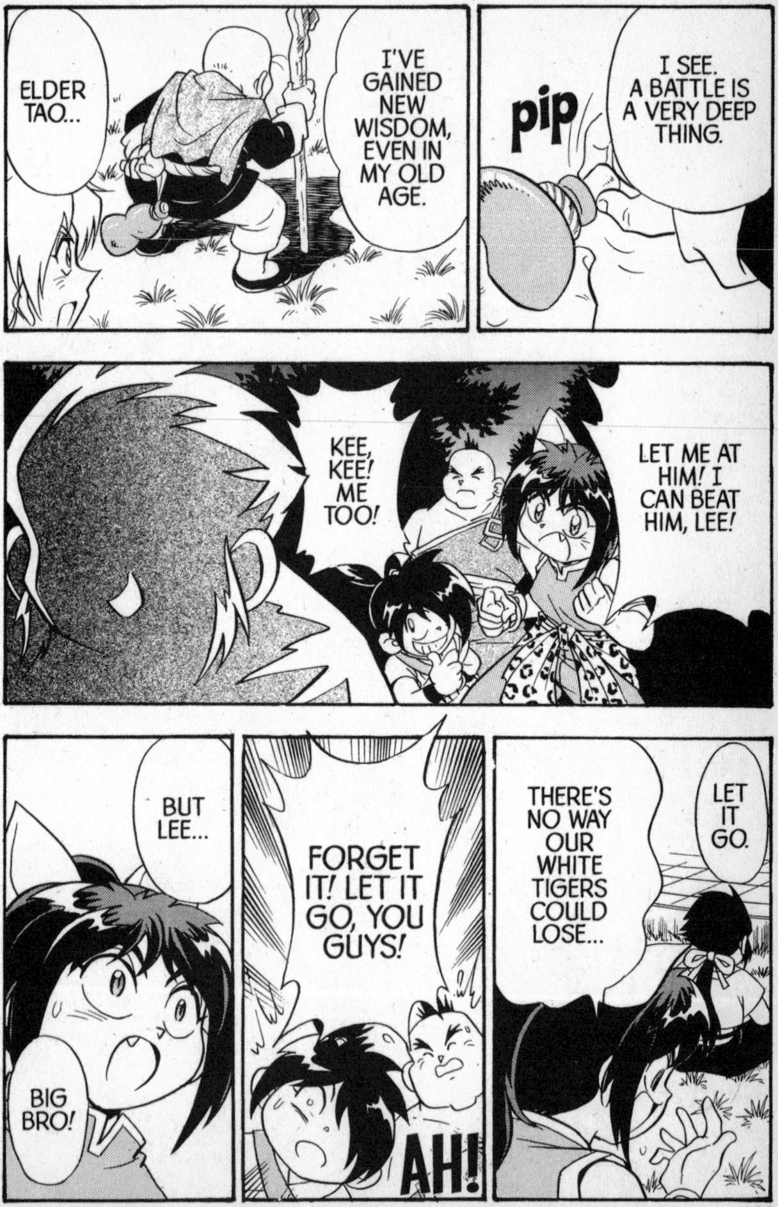
pip
I SEE. A BATTLE IS A VERY DEEP THING.
I'VE GAINED NEW WISDOM, EVEN IN MY OLD AGE.
ELDER TAO...
LET ME AT HIM! I CAN BEAT HIM, LEE!
KEE, KEE! ME TOO!
LET IT GO.
THERE'S NO WAY OUR WHITE TIGERS COULD LOSE...
FORGET IT! LET IT GO, YOU GUYS!
AH!
BUT LEE...
BIG BRO!

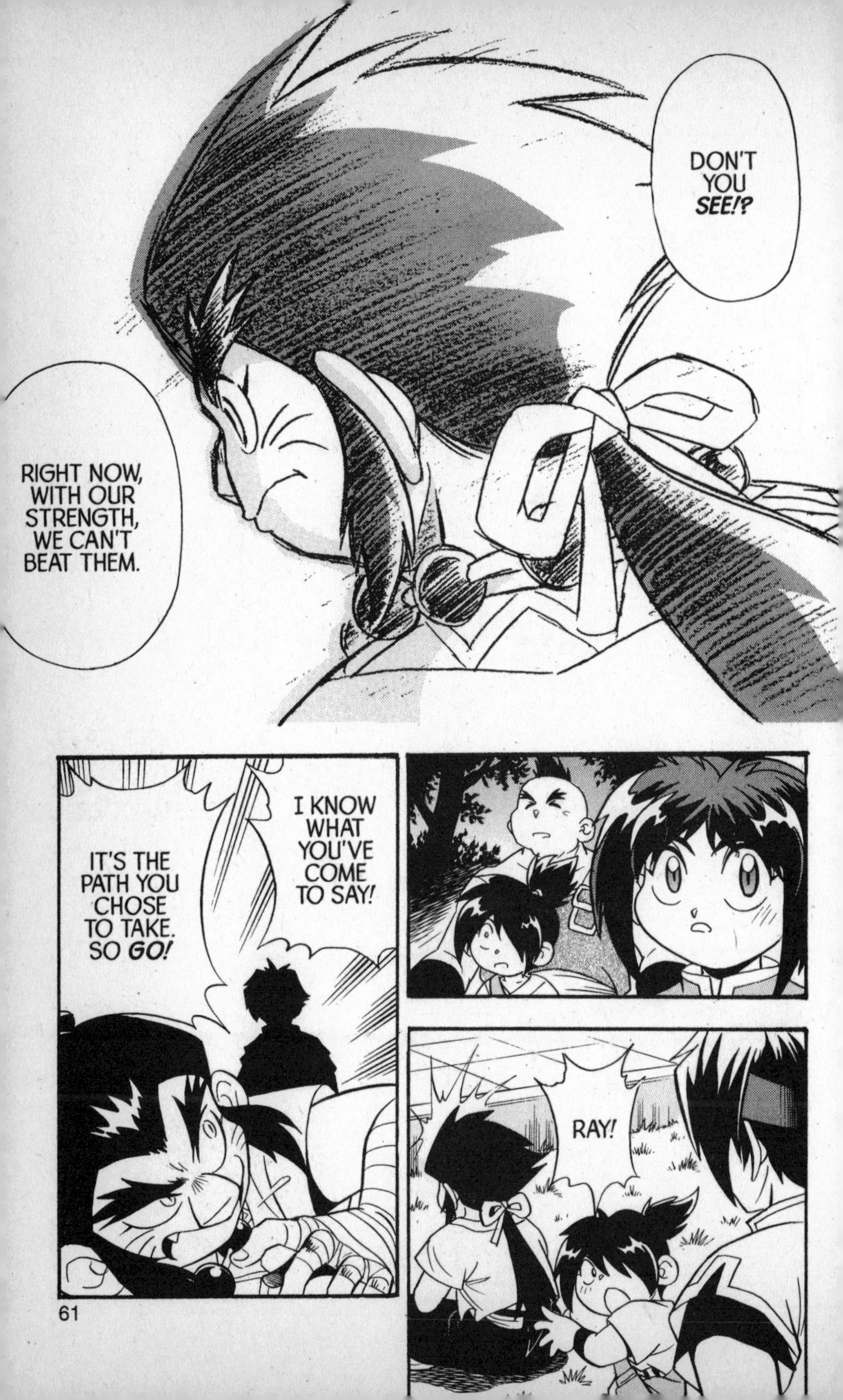
DON'T YOU *SEE!?*
RIGHT NOW, WITH OUR STRENGTH, WE CAN'T BEAT THEM.
RAY!
I KNOW WHAT YOU'VE COME TO SAY!
IT'S THE PATH YOU CHOSE TO TAKE. SO *GO!*

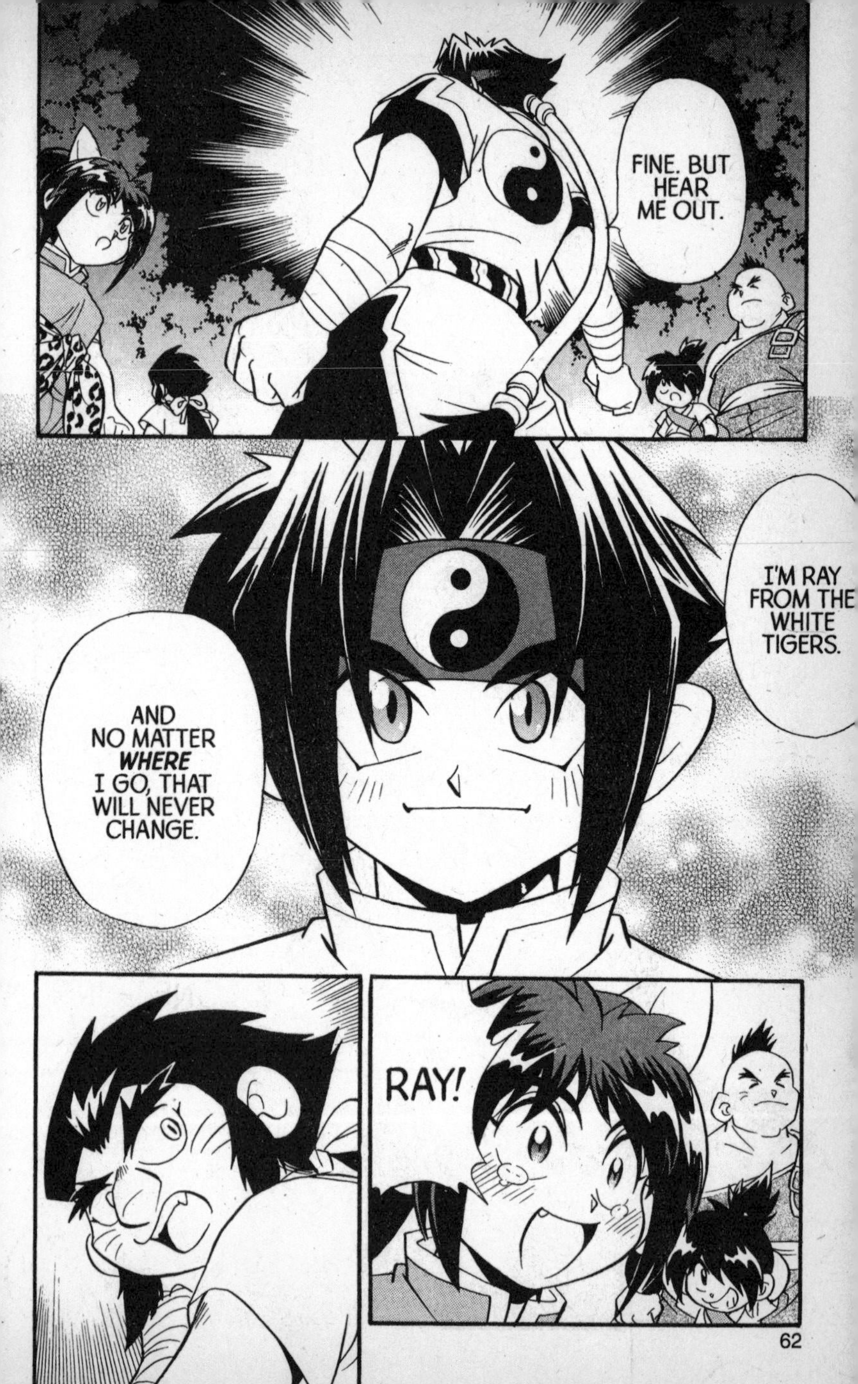
FINE. BUT HEAR ME OUT.
I'M RAY FROM THE WHITE TIGERS.
AND NO MATTER *WHERE* I GO, THAT WILL NEVER CHANGE.
RAY!

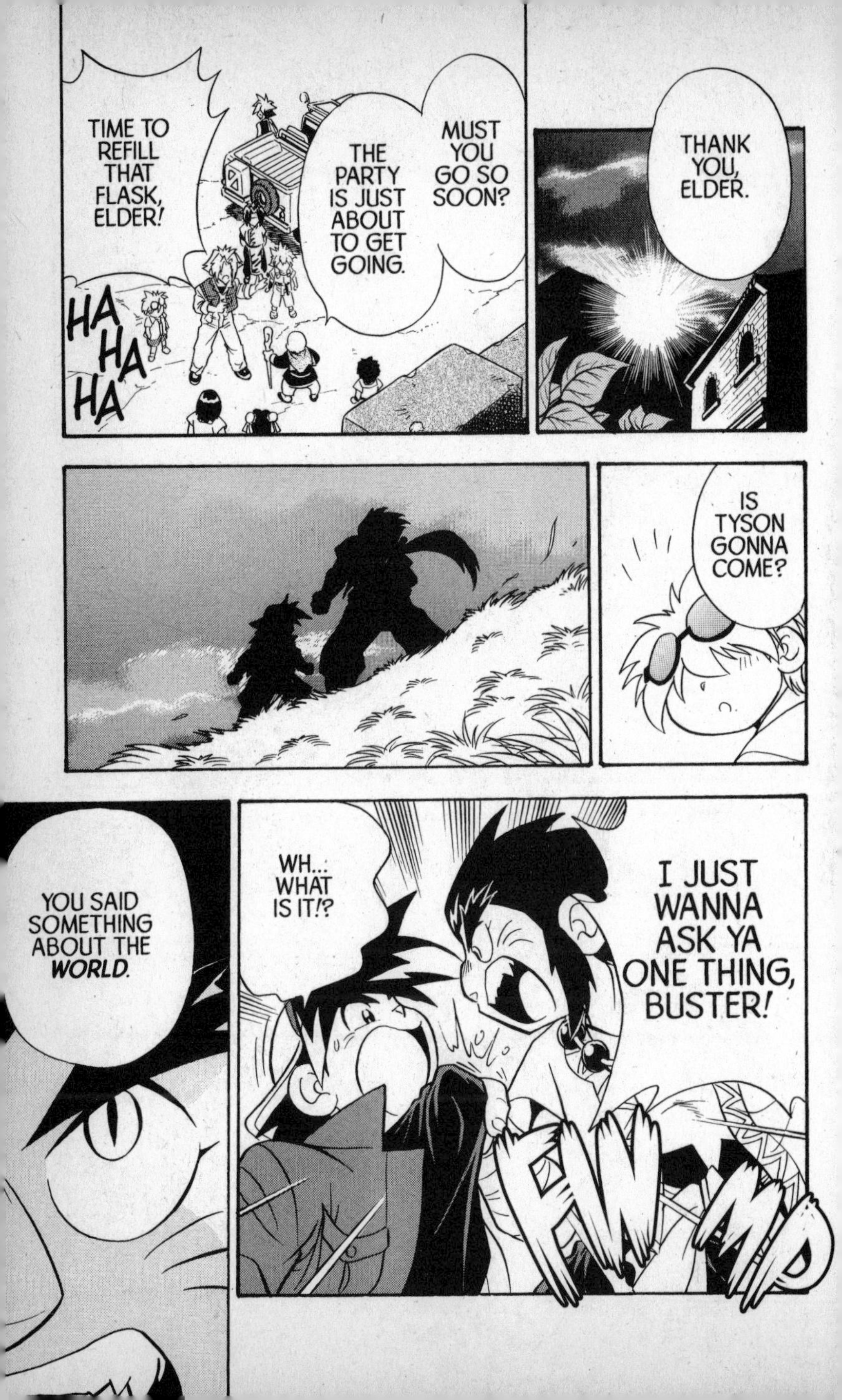
THANK YOU, ELDER.
MUST YOU GO SO SOON?
THE PARTY IS JUST ABOUT TO GET GOING.
TIME TO REFILL THAT FLASK, ELDER!
HA HA HA
IS TYSON GONNA COME?
I JUST WANNA ASK YA ONE THING, BUSTER!
WH... WHAT IS IT!?
YOU SAID SOMETHING ABOUT THE *WORLD*.

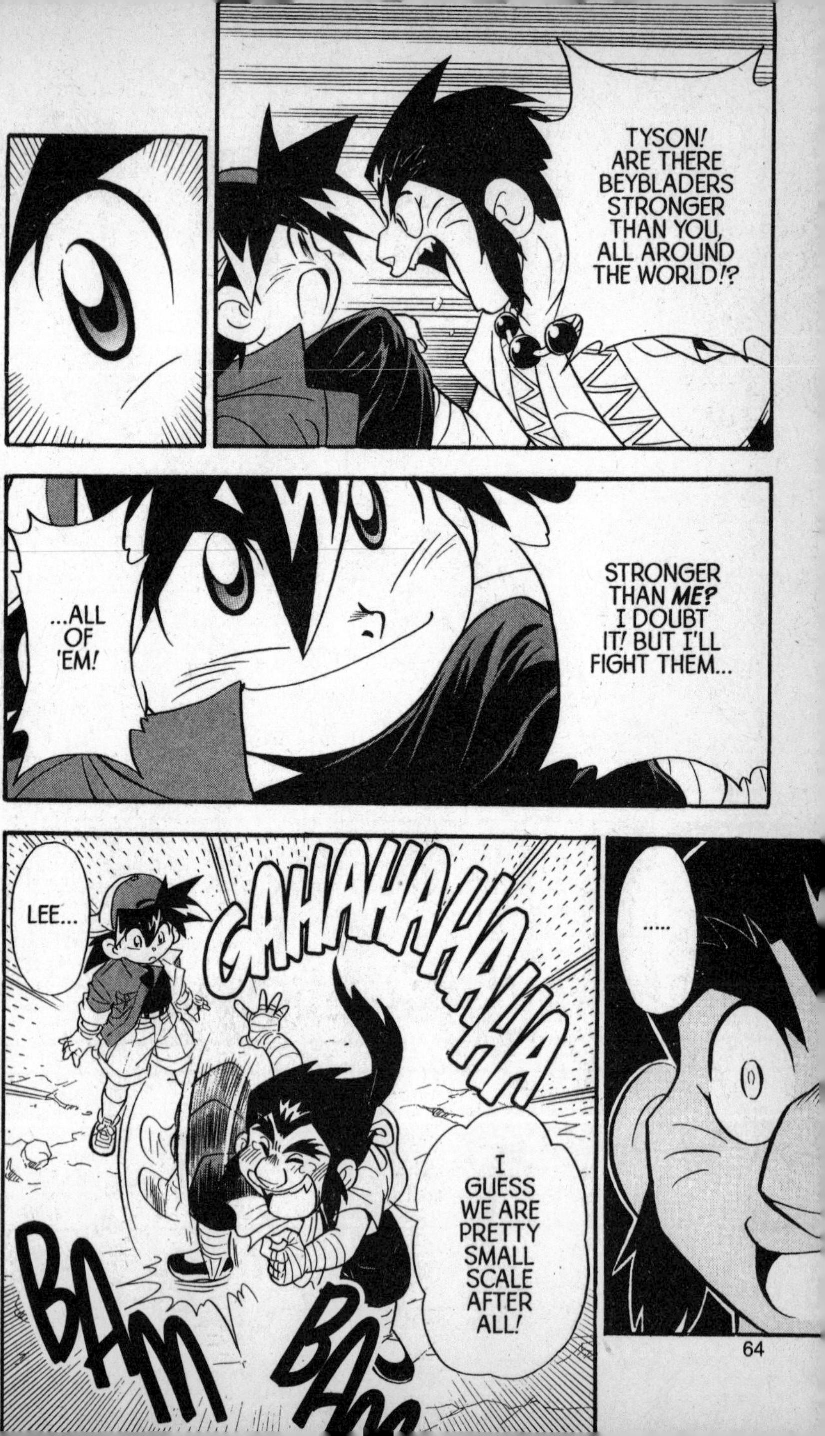
TYSON! ARE THERE BEYBLADERS STRONGER THAN YOU, ALL AROUND THE WORLD!?
STRONGER THAN *ME?* I DOUBT IT! BUT I'LL FIGHT THEM...
...ALL OF 'EM!
.....
GAHAHAHAHAHA
LEE...
I GUESS WE ARE PRETTY SMALL SCALE AFTER ALL!
BAM
BAM

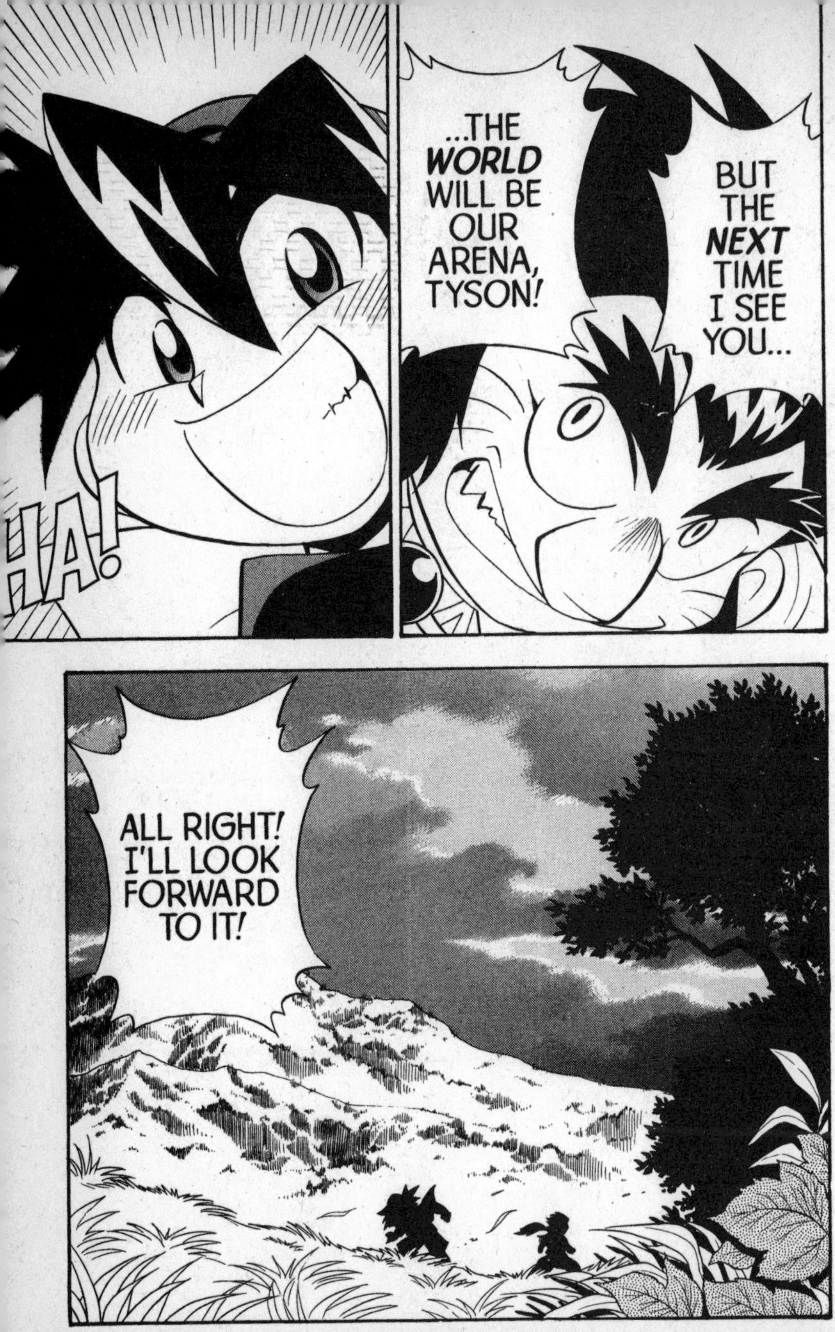
BUT THE NEXT TIME I SEE YOU...
...THE WORLD WILL BE OUR ARENA, TYSON!
HA!
ALL RIGHT! I'LL LOOK FORWARD TO IT!

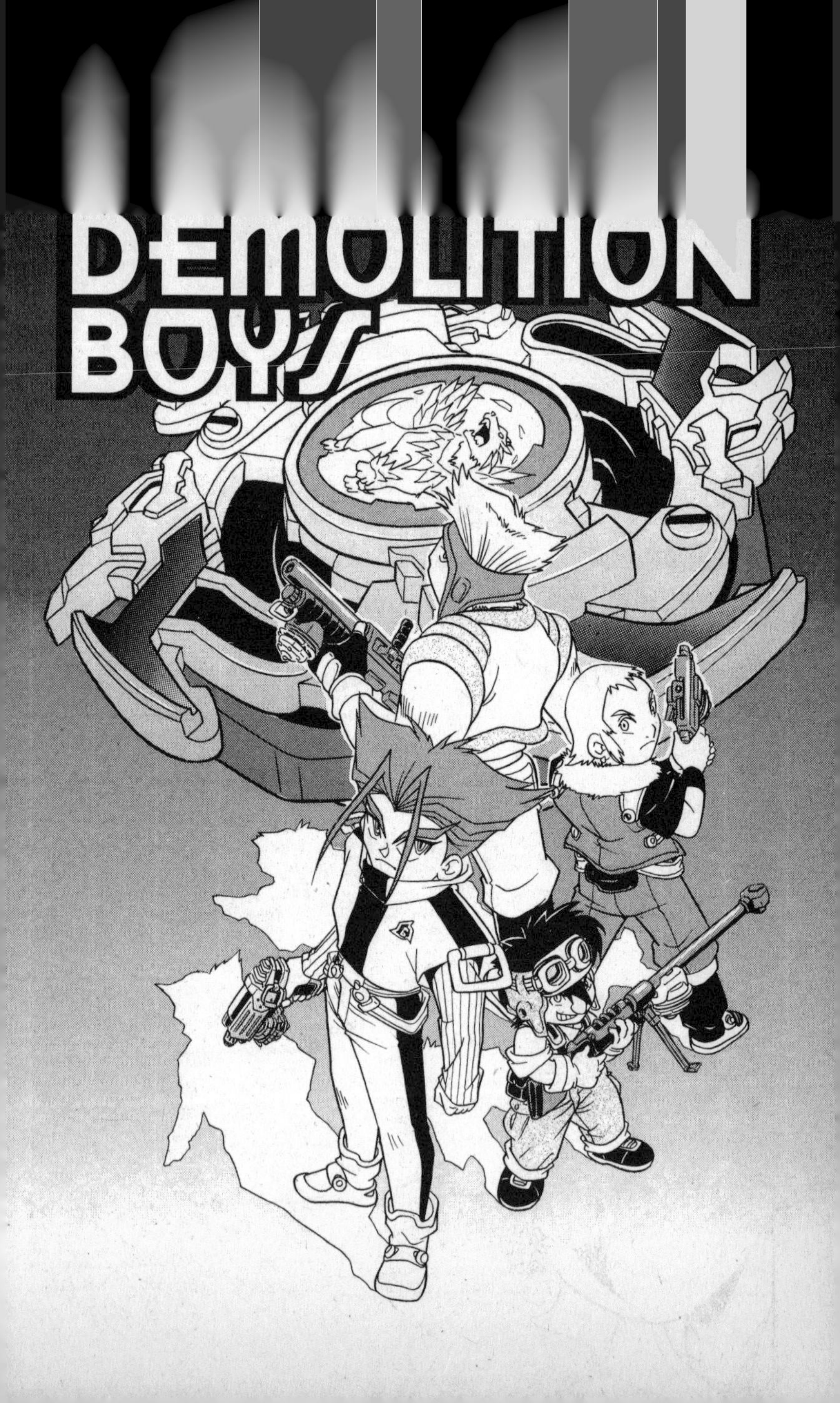
DEMOLITION
BOYS

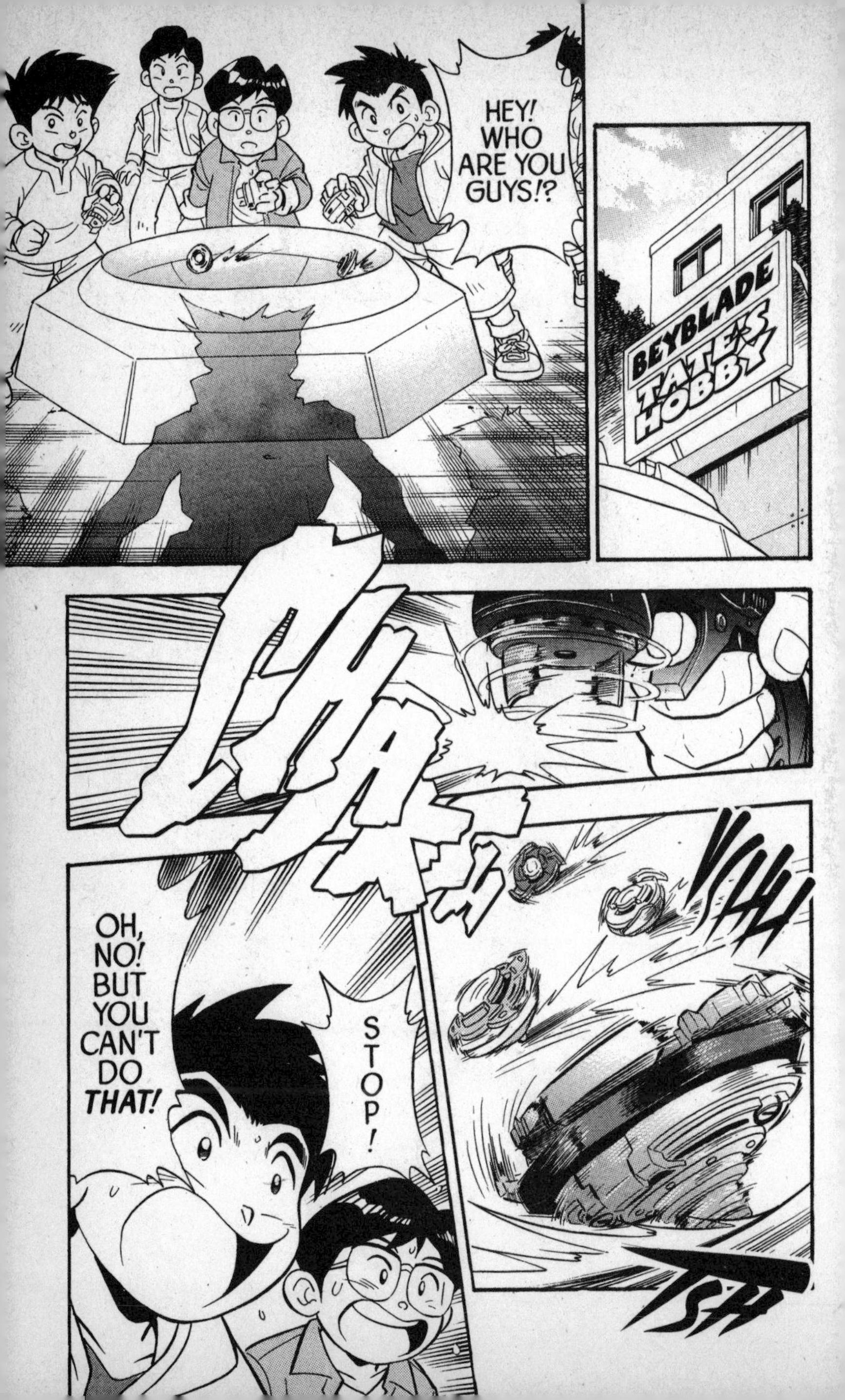
BEYBLADE
TATE'S HOBBY
HEY! WHO ARE YOU GUYS!?
TSH
STOP!
OH, NO! BUT YOU CAN'T DO *THAT!*

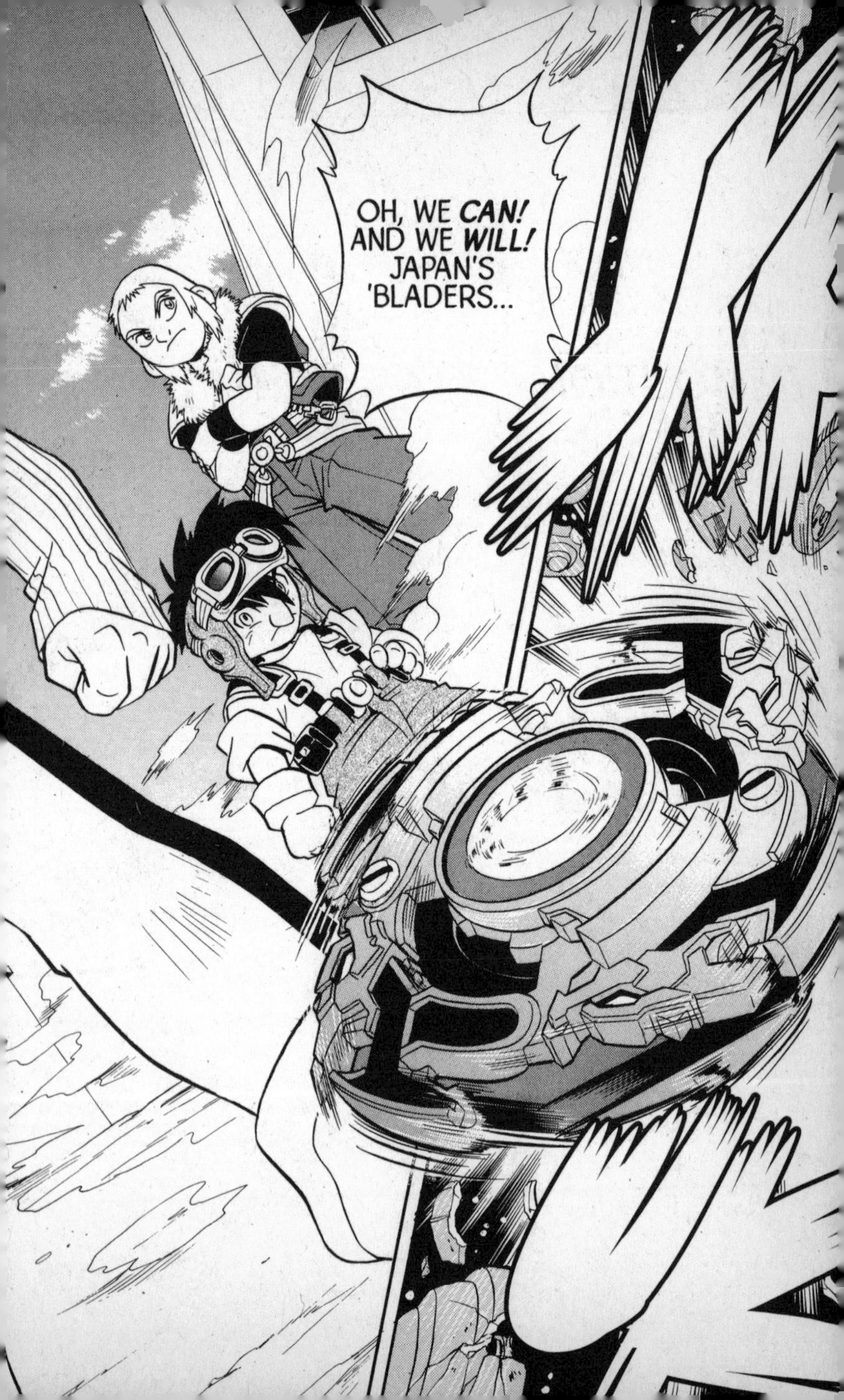
OH, WE CAN! AND WE WILL! JAPAN'S 'BLADERS...

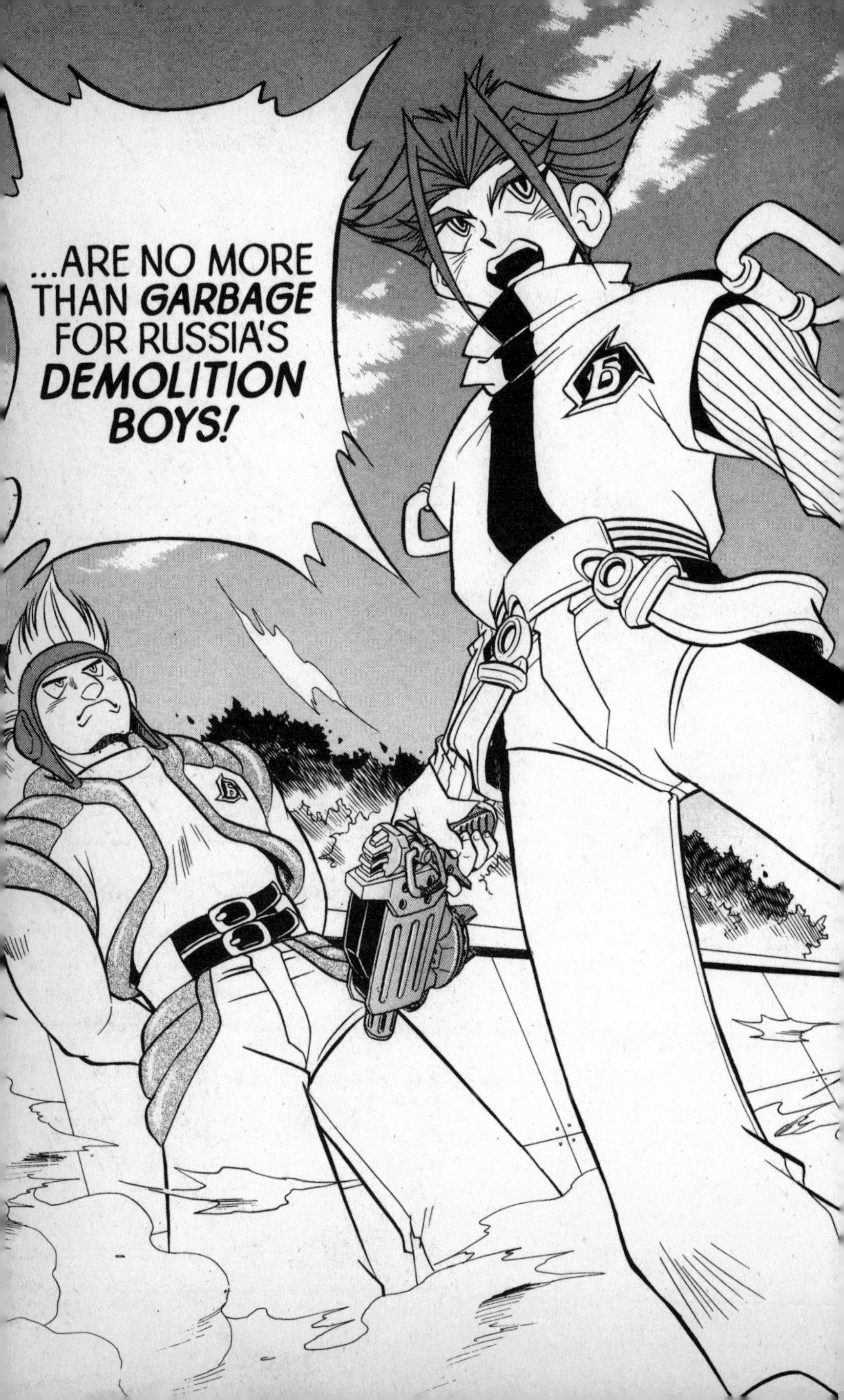
...ARE NO MORE THAN *GARBAGE* FOR RUSSIA'S *DEMOLITION BOYS!*

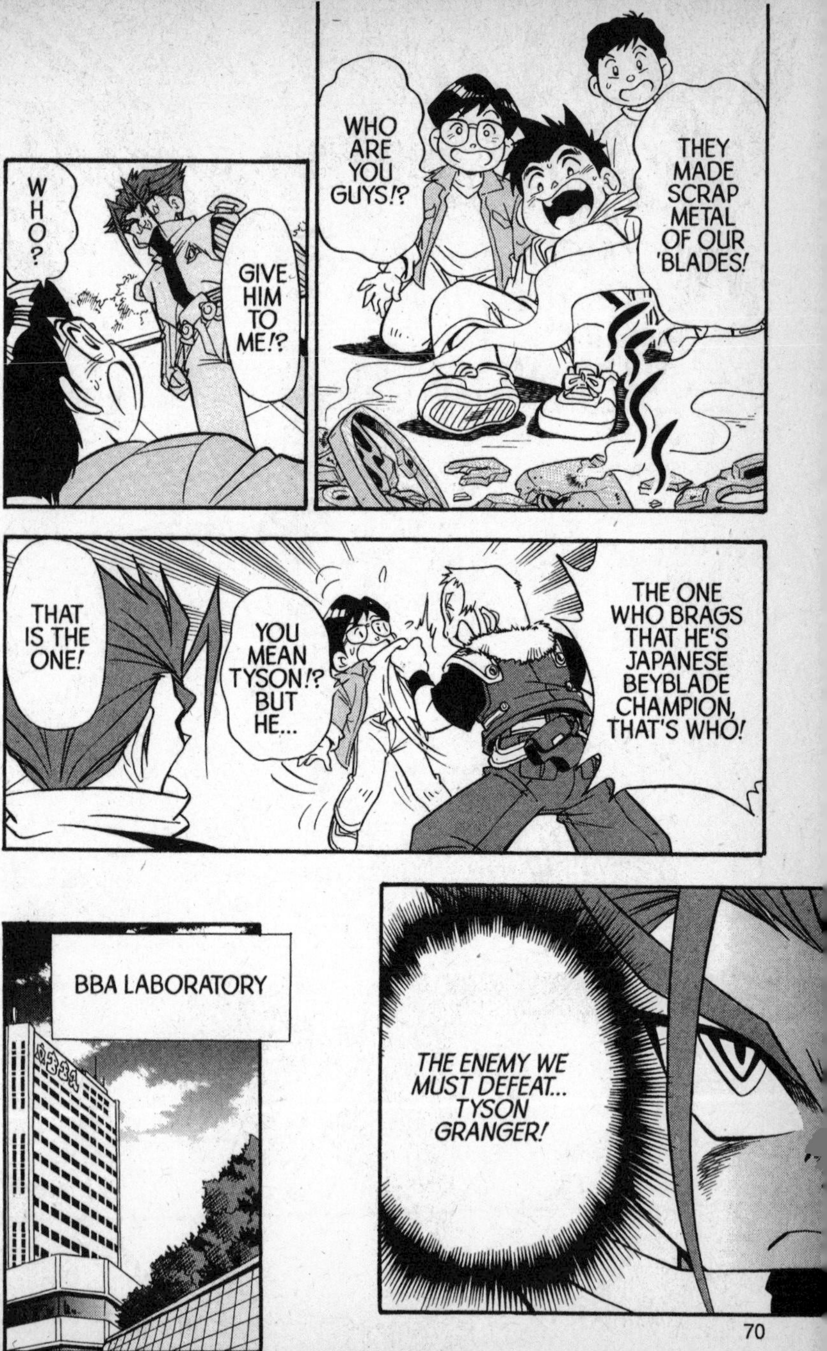
THEY MADE SCRAP METAL OF OUR 'BLADES!
WHO ARE YOU GUYS!?
GIVE HIM TO ME!?
WHO?
THE ONE WHO BRAGS THAT HE'S JAPANESE BEYBLADE CHAMPION, THAT'S WHO!
YOU MEAN TYSON!? BUT HE...
THAT IS THE ONE!
THE ENEMY WE MUST DEFEAT... TYSON GRANGER!
BBA LABORATORY

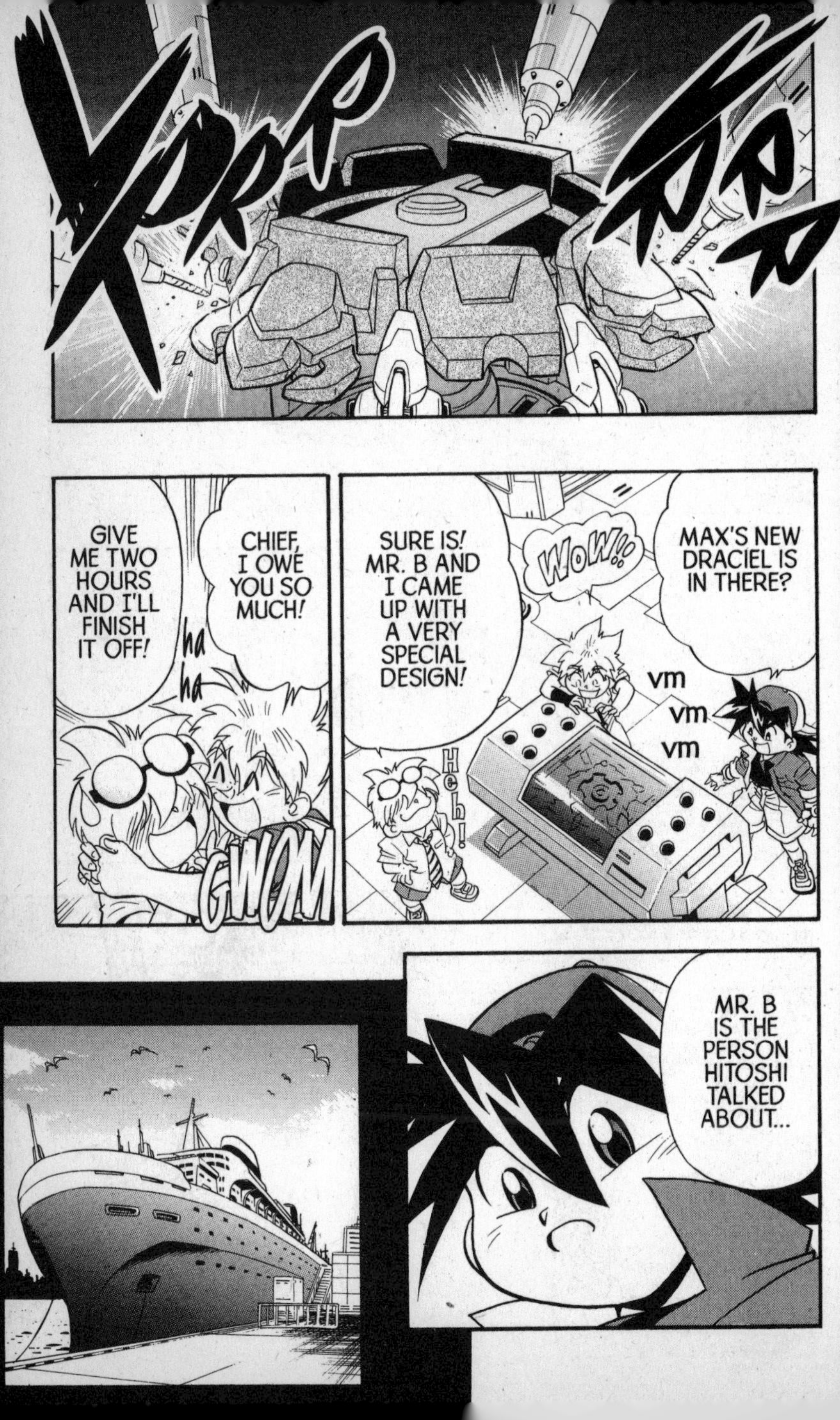
MAX'S NEW DRACIEL IS IN THERE?
WOW!!
vm vm vm
SURE IS! MR. B AND I CAME UP WITH A VERY SPECIAL DESIGN!
Heh!
CHIEF, I OWE YOU SO MUCH!
GIVE ME TWO HOURS AND I'LL FINISH IT OFF!
ha ha
GWOM
MR. B IS THE PERSON HITOSHI TALKED ABOUT...

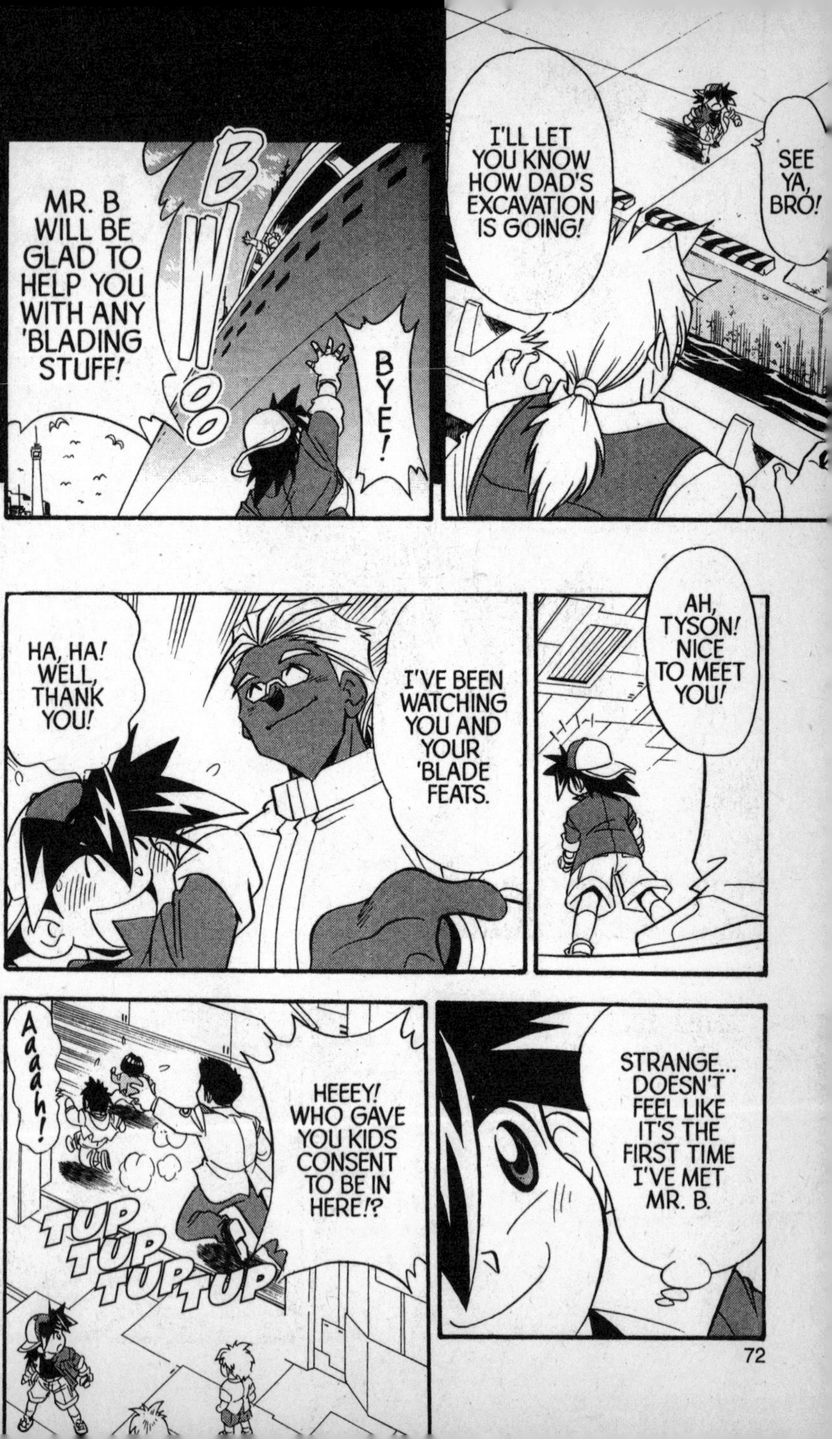
I'LL LET YOU KNOW HOW DAD'S EXCAVATION IS GOING!
SEE YA, BRO!
BWOO
BYE!
MR. B WILL BE GLAD TO HELP YOU WITH ANY 'BLADING STUFF!
AH, TYSON! NICE TO MEET YOU!
I'VE BEEN WATCHING YOU AND YOUR 'BLADE FEATS.
HA, HA! WELL, THANK YOU!
STRANGE... DOESN'T FEEL LIKE IT'S THE FIRST TIME I'VE MET MR. B.
HEEEY! WHO GAVE YOU KIDS CONSENT TO BE IN HERE!?
Aaaah!
TUP TUP TUP TUP

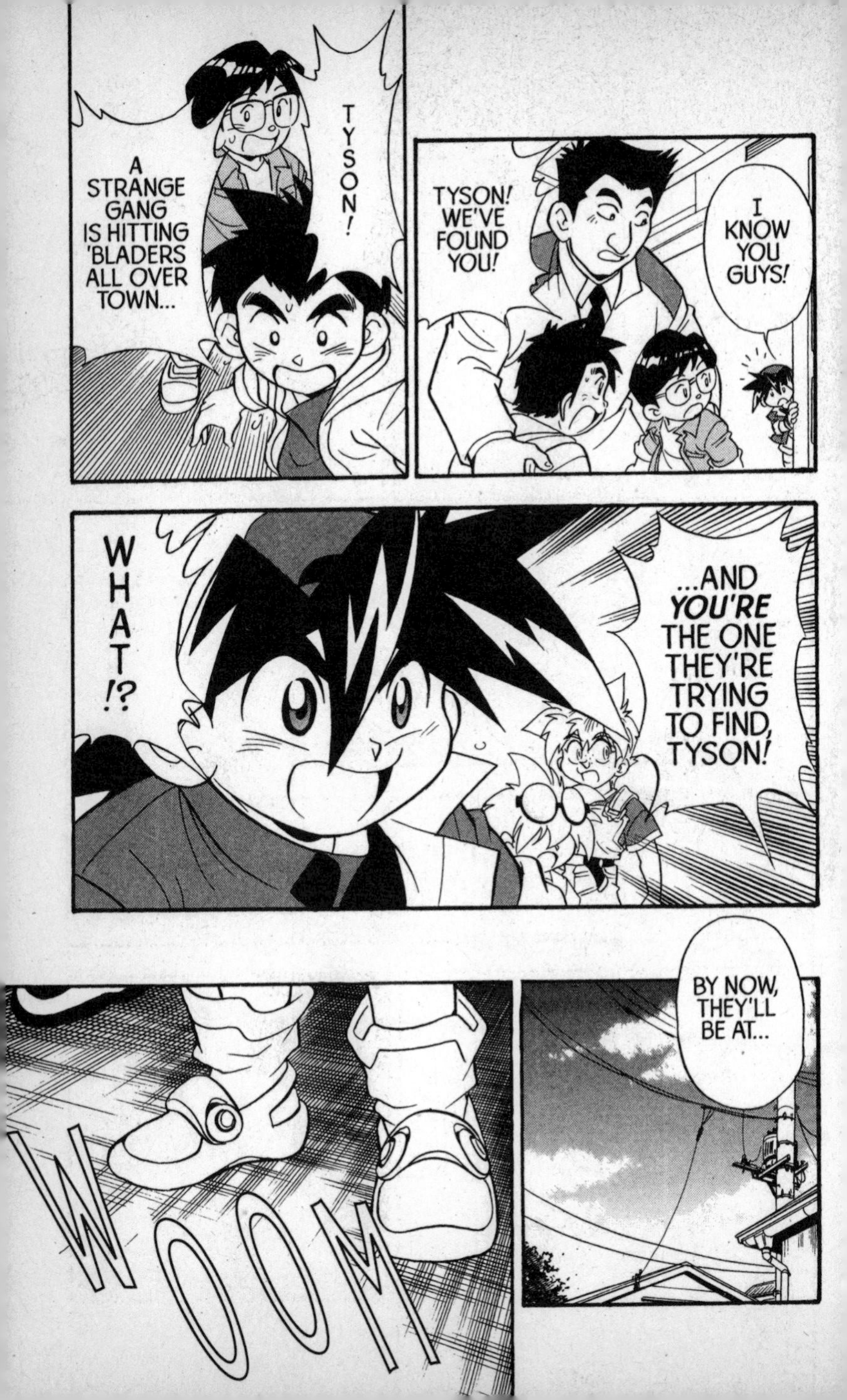
TYSON! WE'VE FOUND YOU!
I KNOW YOU GUYS!
TYSON!
A STRANGE GANG IS HITTING 'BLADERS ALL OVER TOWN...
...AND *YOU'RE* THE ONE THEY'RE TRYING TO FIND, TYSON!
WHAT!?
BY NOW, THEY'LL BE AT...
WOOM

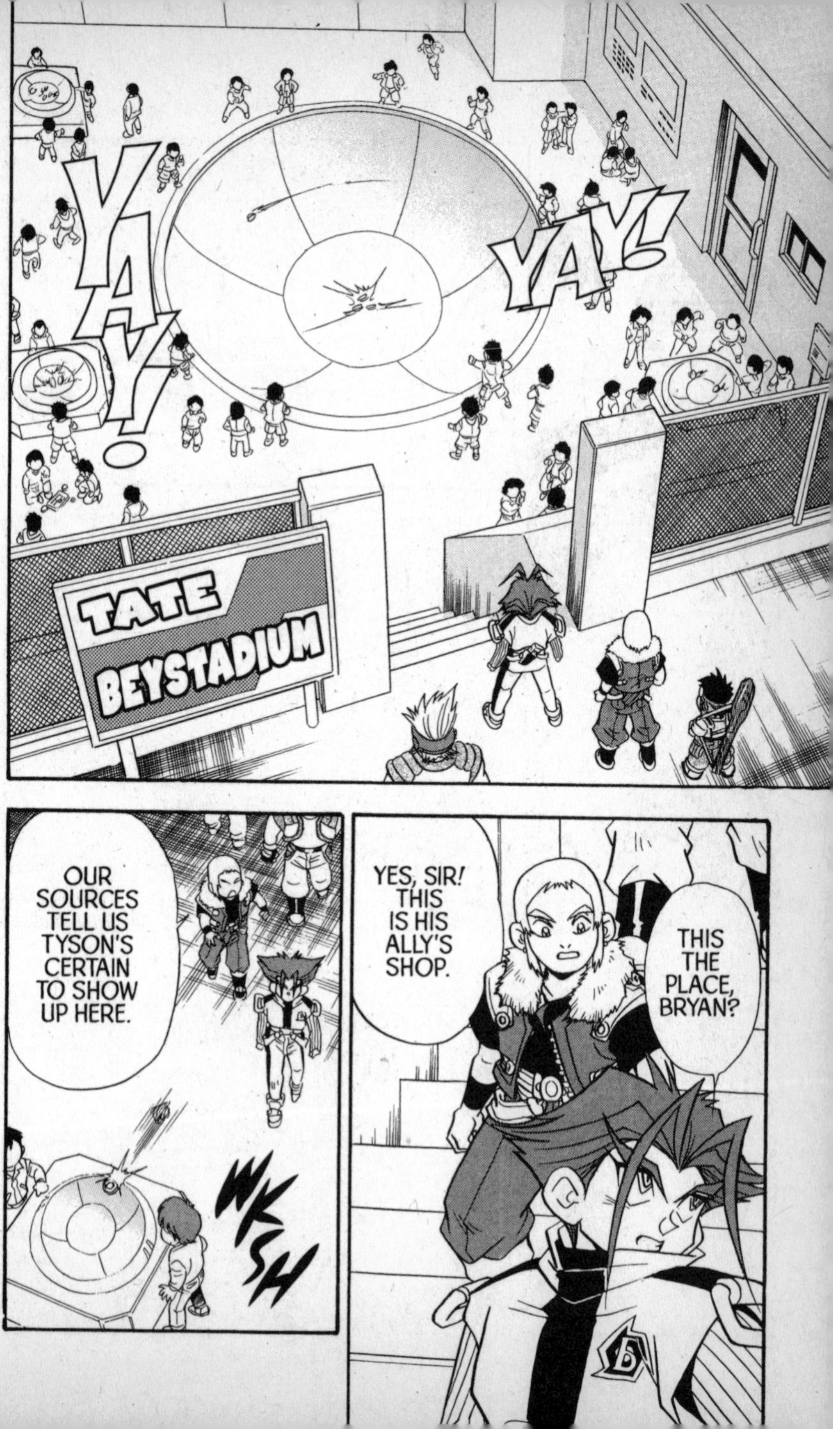
YAY!
YAY!
TATE BEYSTADIUM
THIS THE PLACE, BRYAN?
YES, SIR! THIS IS HIS ALLY'S SHOP.
OUR SOURCES TELL US TYSON'S CERTAIN TO SHOW UP HERE.
WKSH

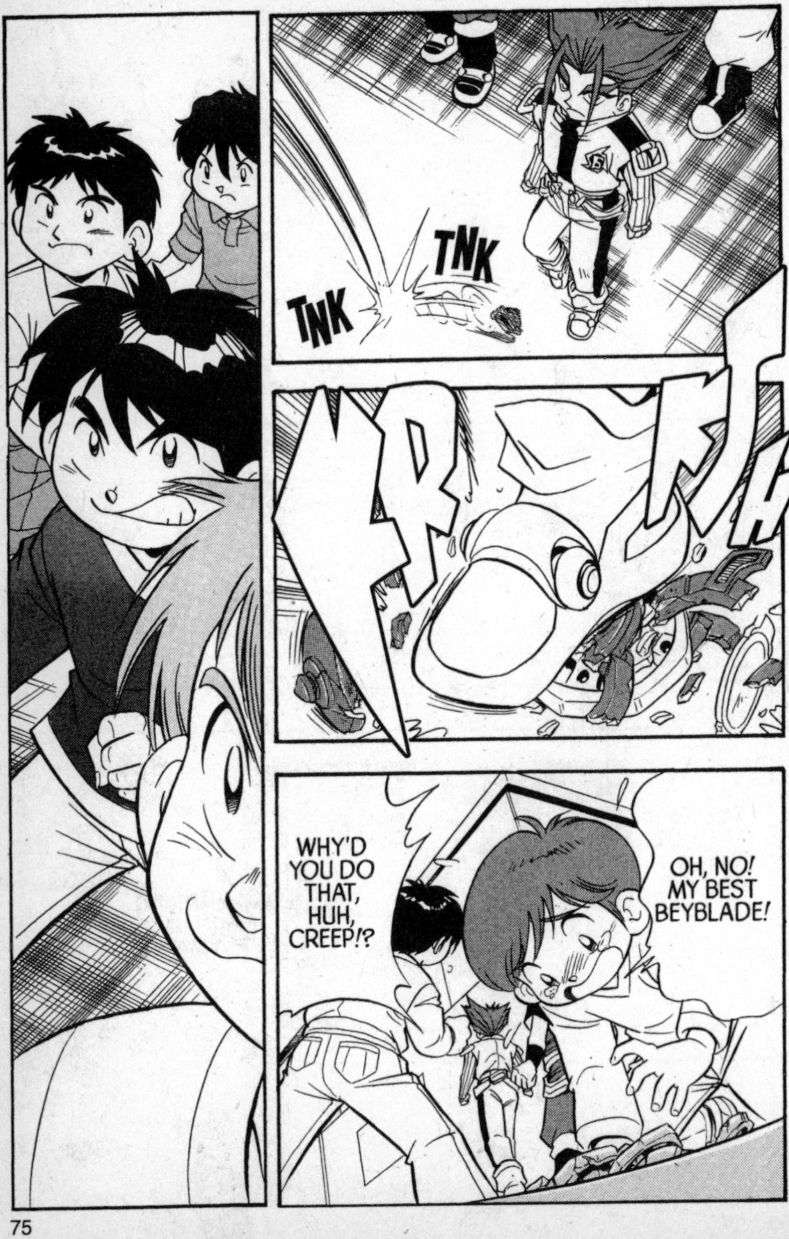
TNK
TNK
OH, NO! MY BEST BEYBLADE!
WHY'D YOU DO THAT, HUH, CREEP!?

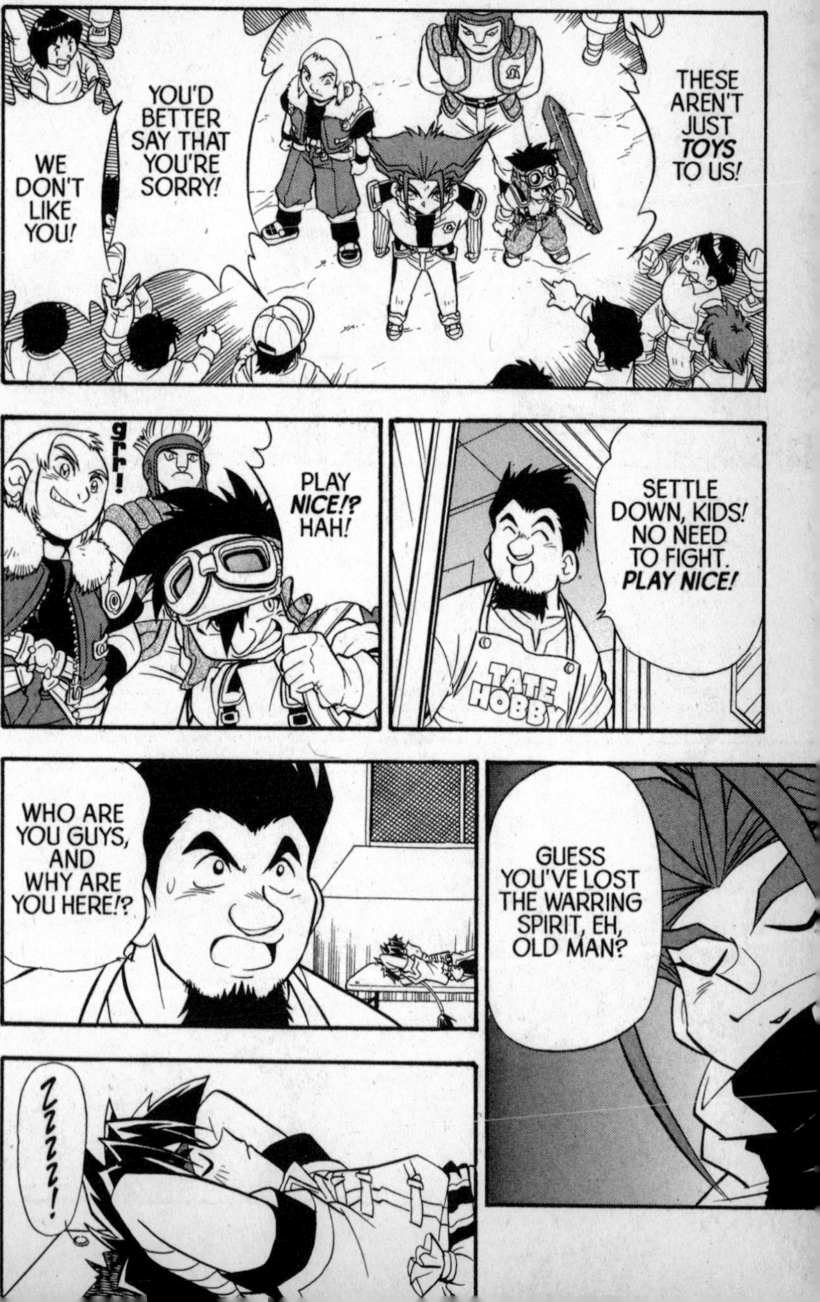
THESE AREN'T JUST *TOYS* TO US!
YOU'D BETTER SAY THAT YOU'RE SORRY!
WE DON'T LIKE YOU!
SETTLE DOWN, KIDS! NO NEED TO FIGHT. *PLAY NICE!*
TATE HOBBY
PLAY *NICE!?* HAH!
grr!
GUESS YOU'VE LOST THE WARRING SPIRIT, EH, OLD MAN?
WHO ARE YOU GUYS, AND WHY ARE YOU HERE!?
ZZZZ!

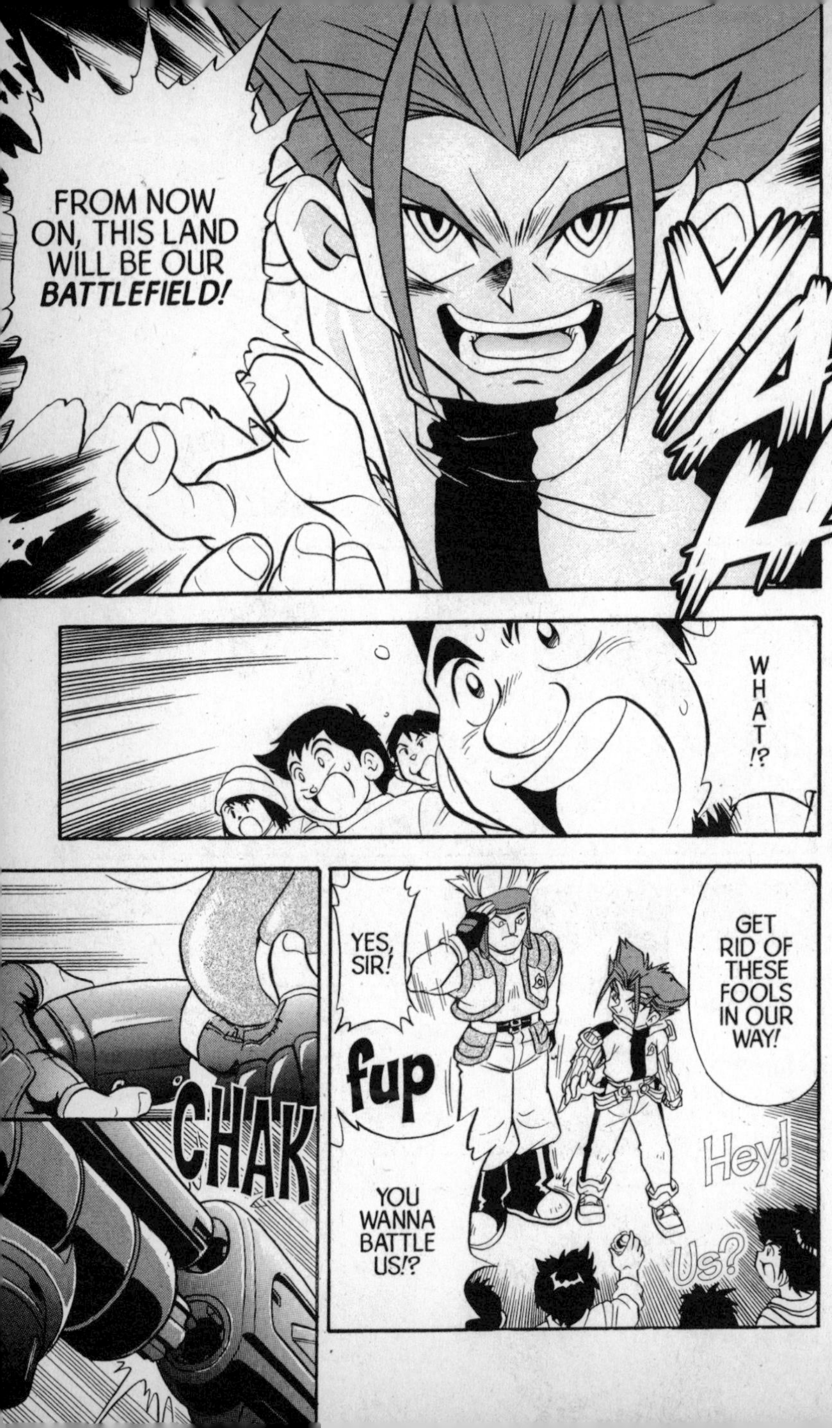
FROM NOW ON, THIS LAND WILL BE OUR *BATTLEFIELD!*
WHAT!?
GET RID OF THESE FOOLS IN OUR WAY!
YES, SIR!
fup
Hey!
Us?
YOU WANNA BATTLE US!?
CHAK

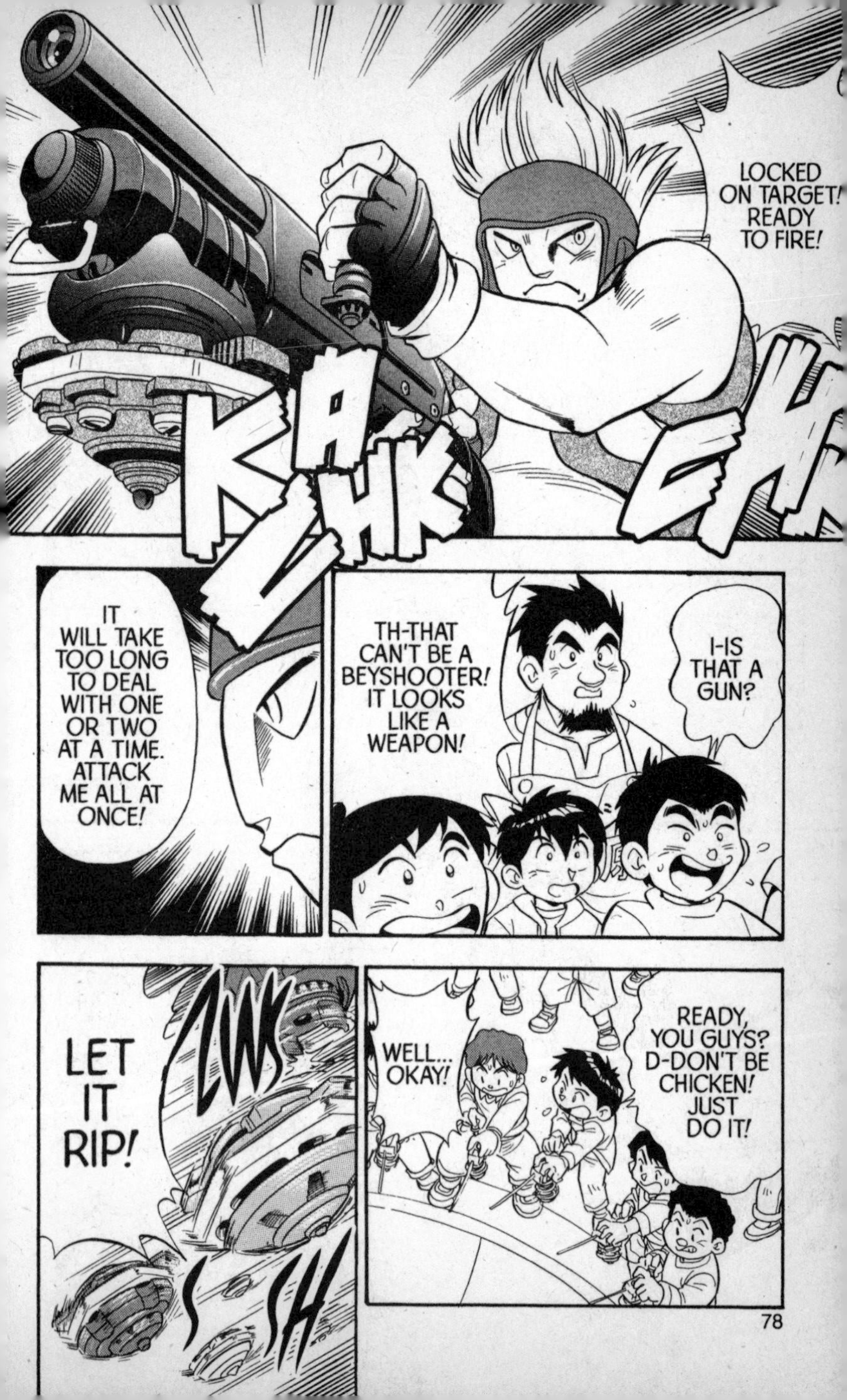
LOCKED ON TARGET! READY TO FIRE!
I-IS THAT A GUN?
TH-THAT CAN'T BE A BEYSHOOTER! IT LOOKS LIKE A WEAPON!
IT WILL TAKE TOO LONG TO DEAL WITH ONE OR TWO AT A TIME. ATTACK ME ALL AT ONCE!
READY, YOU GUYS? D-DON'T BE CHICKEN! JUST DO IT!
WELL... OKAY!
LET IT RIP!

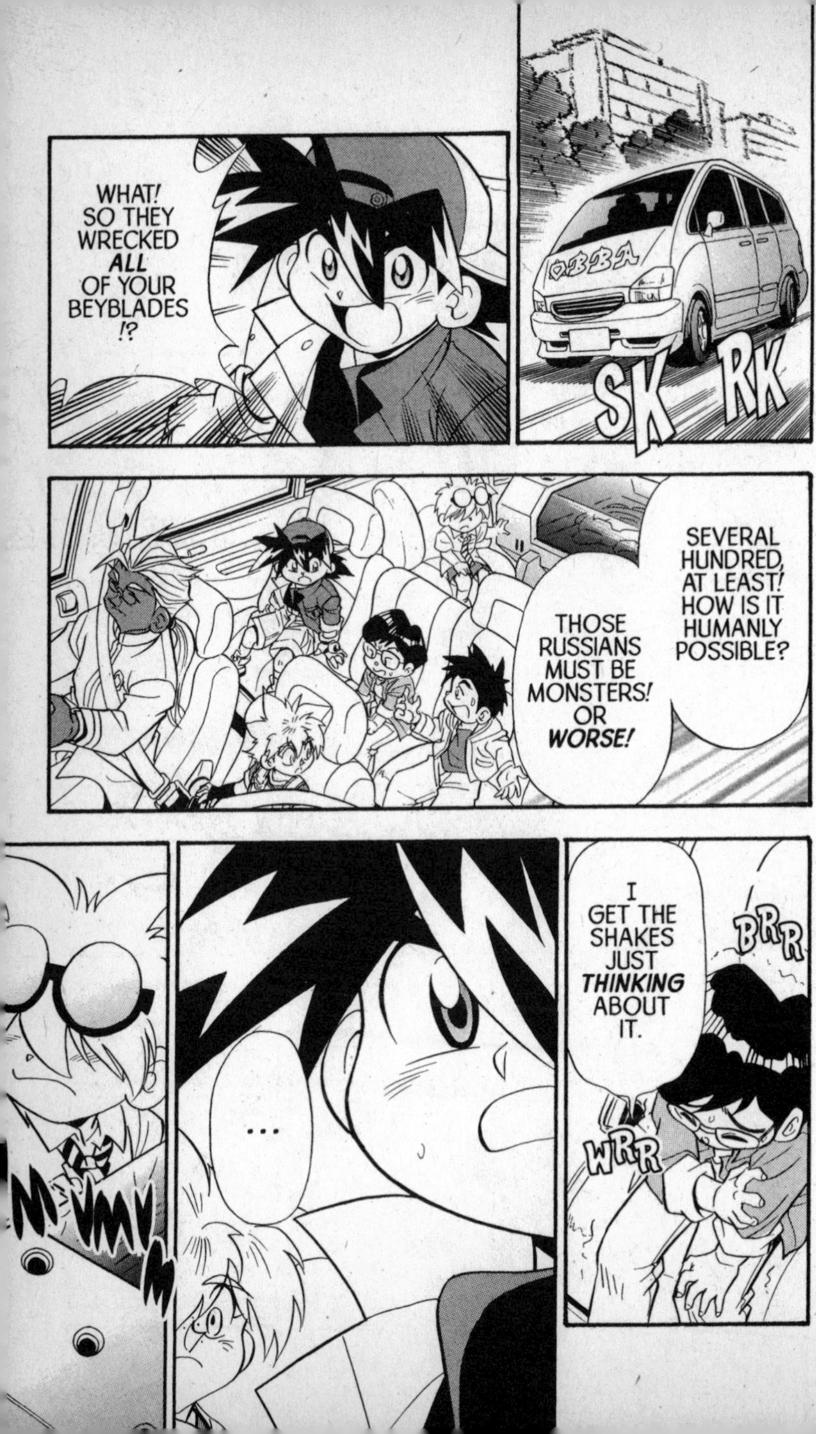
SK RK
WHAT! SO THEY WRECKED *ALL* OF YOUR BEYBLADES !?
SEVERAL HUNDRED, AT LEAST! HOW IS IT HUMANLY POSSIBLE?
THOSE RUSSIANS MUST BE MONSTERS! OR *WORSE!*
I GET THE SHAKES JUST *THINKING* ABOUT IT.
BRR
WRR
...

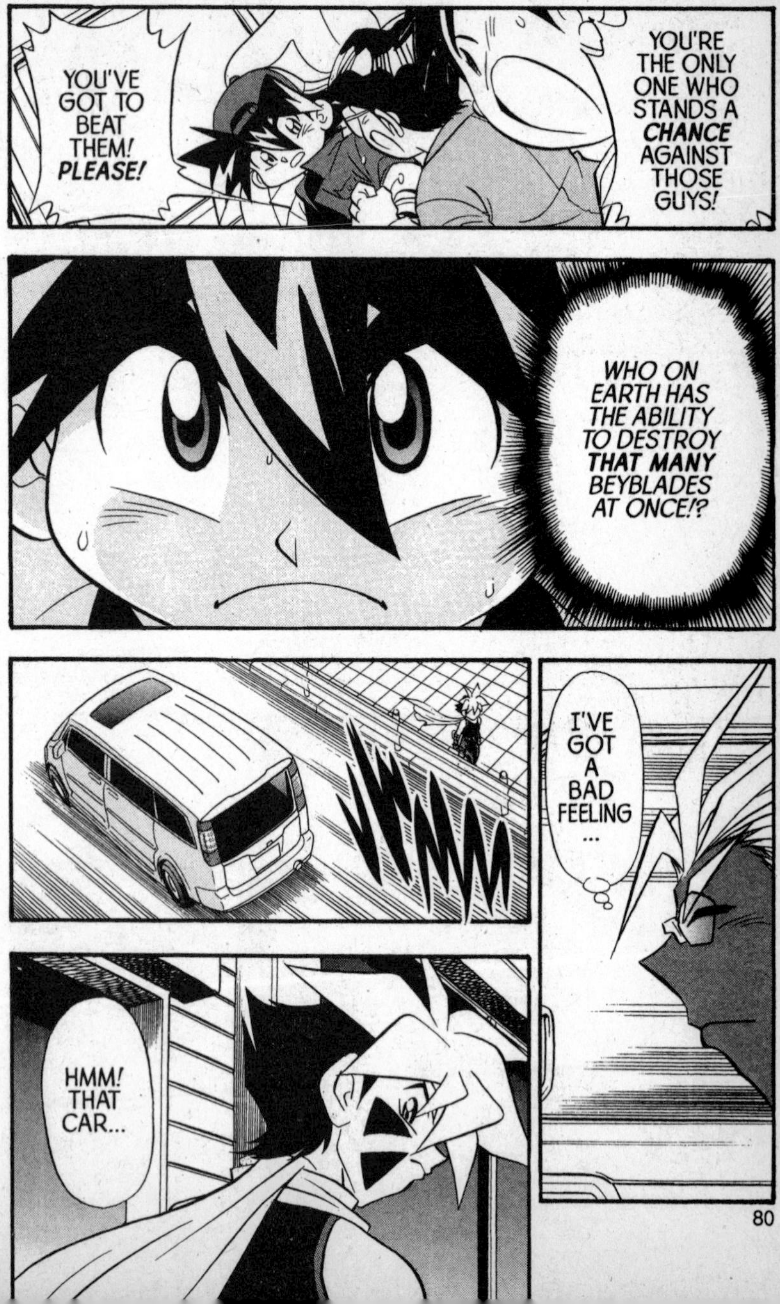
YOU'RE THE ONLY ONE WHO STANDS A ***CHANCE*** AGAINST THOSE GUYS!
YOU'VE GOT TO BEAT THEM! ***PLEASE!***
WHO ON EARTH HAS THE ABILITY TO DESTROY ***THAT MANY*** *BEYBLADES AT ONCE!?*
I'VE GOT A BAD FEELING ...
HMM! THAT CAR...

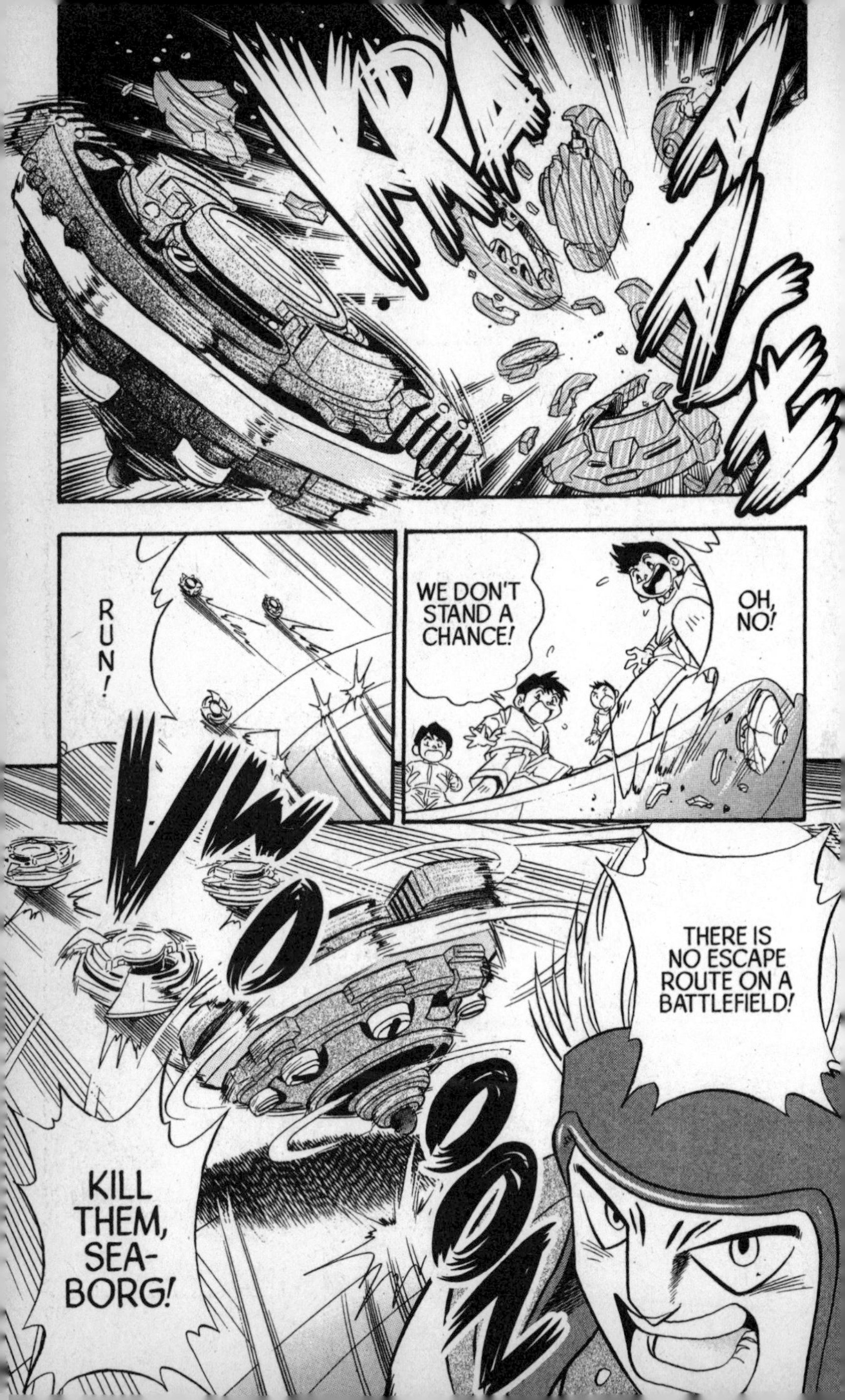
OH, NO!
WE DON'T STAND A CHANCE!
RUN!
THERE IS NO ESCAPE ROUTE ON A BATTLEFIELD!
KILL THEM, SEA-BORG!

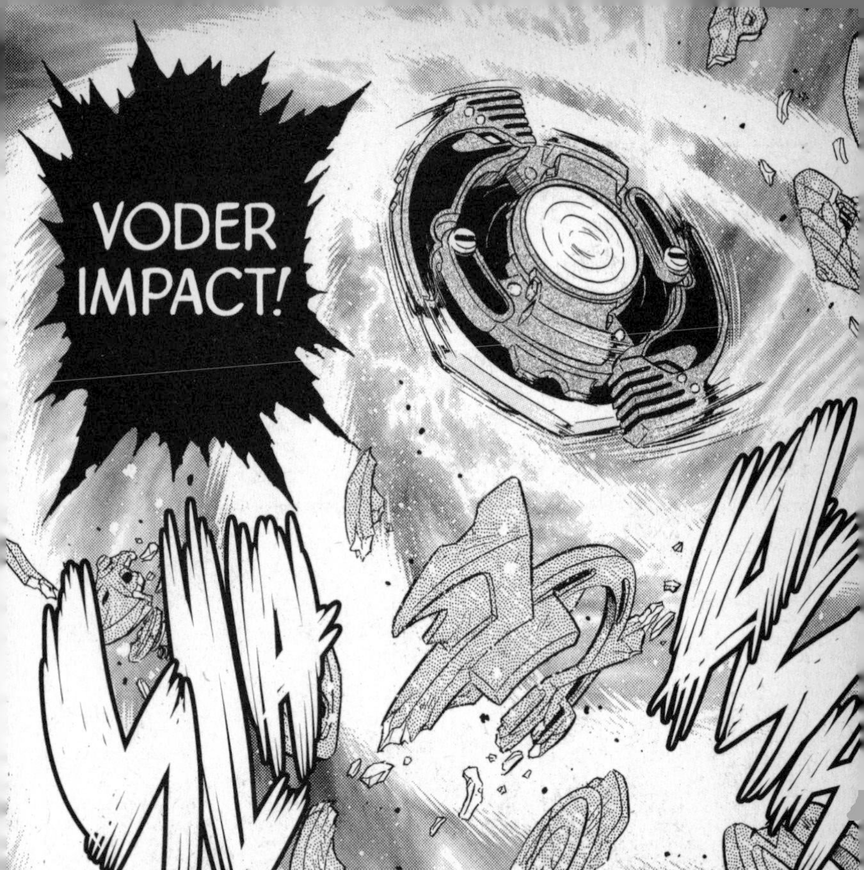
VODER IMPACT!

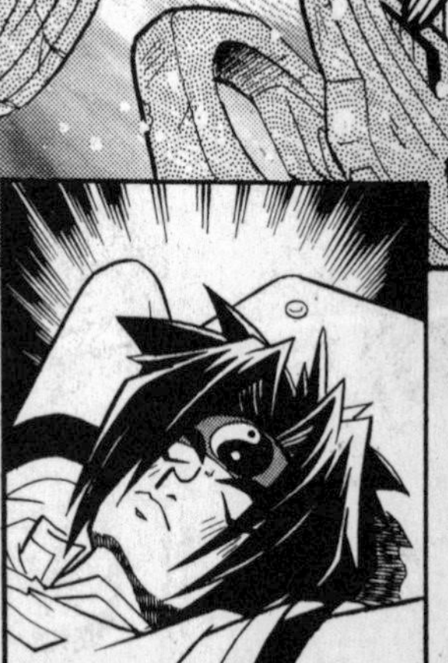

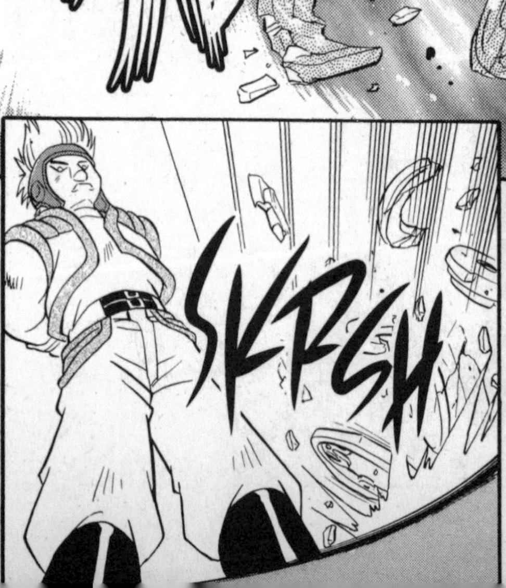
SKRSH

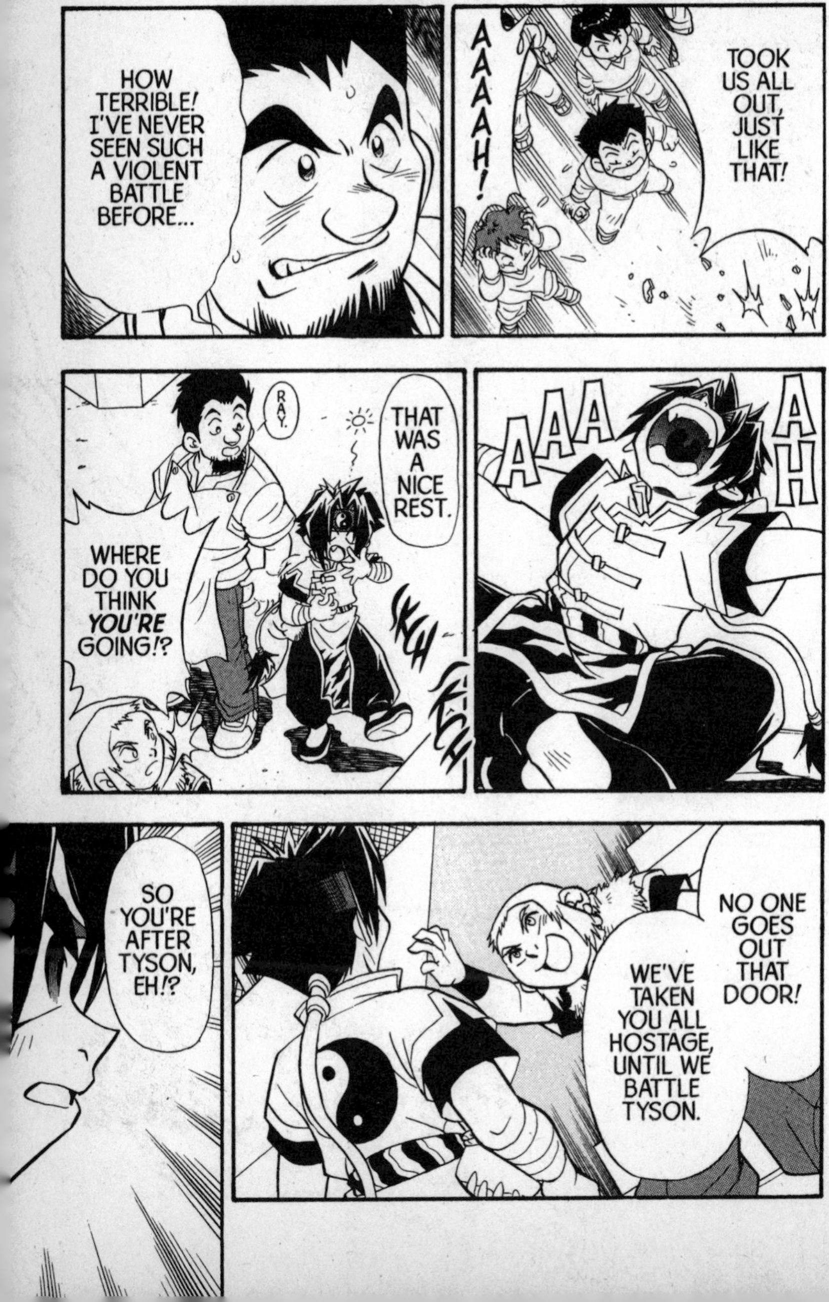
TOOK US ALL OUT, JUST LIKE THAT!
AAAAAH!
HOW TERRIBLE! I'VE NEVER SEEN SUCH A VIOLENT BATTLE BEFORE...
AAAAH
THAT WAS A NICE REST.
RAY.
WHERE DO YOU THINK *YOU'RE* GOING!?
NO ONE GOES OUT THAT DOOR!
WE'VE TAKEN YOU ALL HOSTAGE, UNTIL WE BATTLE TYSON.
SO YOU'RE AFTER TYSON, EH!?

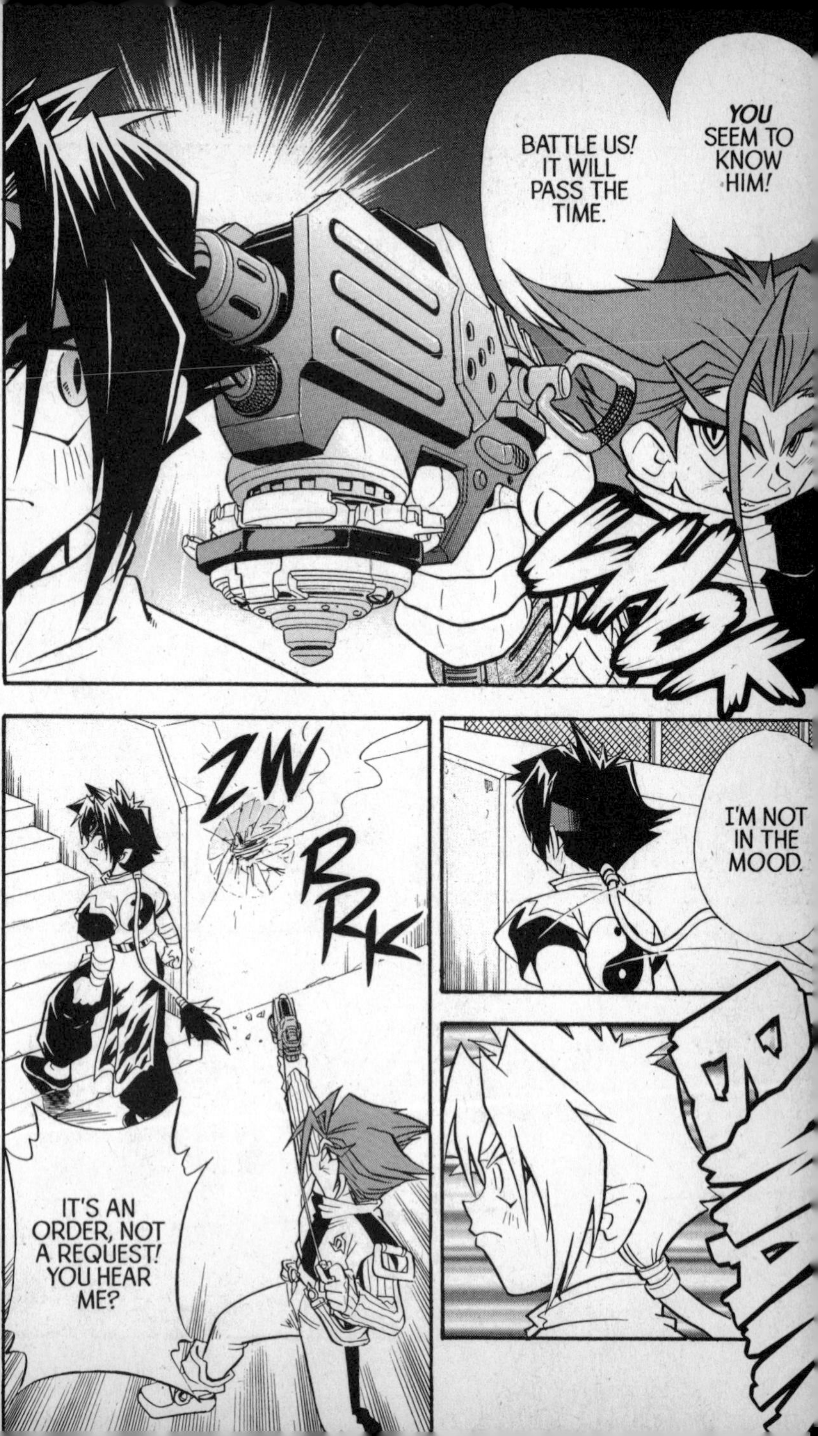
YOU SEEM TO KNOW HIM!
BATTLE US! IT WILL PASS THE TIME.
I'M NOT IN THE MOOD.
ZWRRK
IT'S AN ORDER, NOT A REQUEST! YOU HEAR ME?

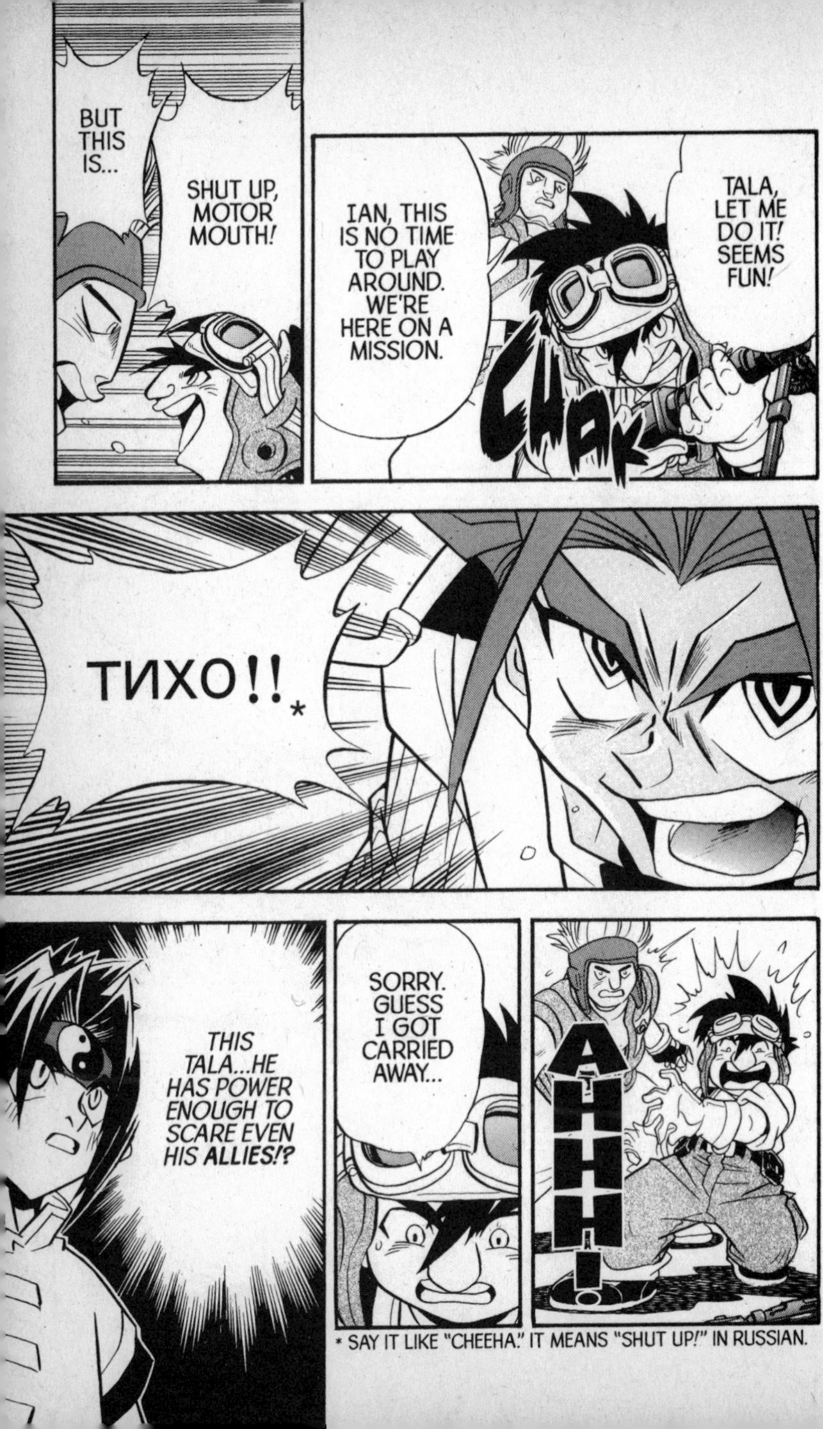
TALA, LET ME DO IT! SEEMS FUN!
IAN, THIS IS NO TIME TO PLAY AROUND. WE'RE HERE ON A MISSION.
CHAK
BUT THIS IS...
SHUT UP, MOTOR MOUTH!
ТИХО!!*
AHHHH!
SORRY. GUESS I GOT CARRIED AWAY...
THIS TALA...HE HAS POWER ENOUGH TO SCARE EVEN HIS **ALLIES!?**

* SAY IT LIKE "CHEEHA." IT MEANS "SHUT UP!" IN RUSSIAN.

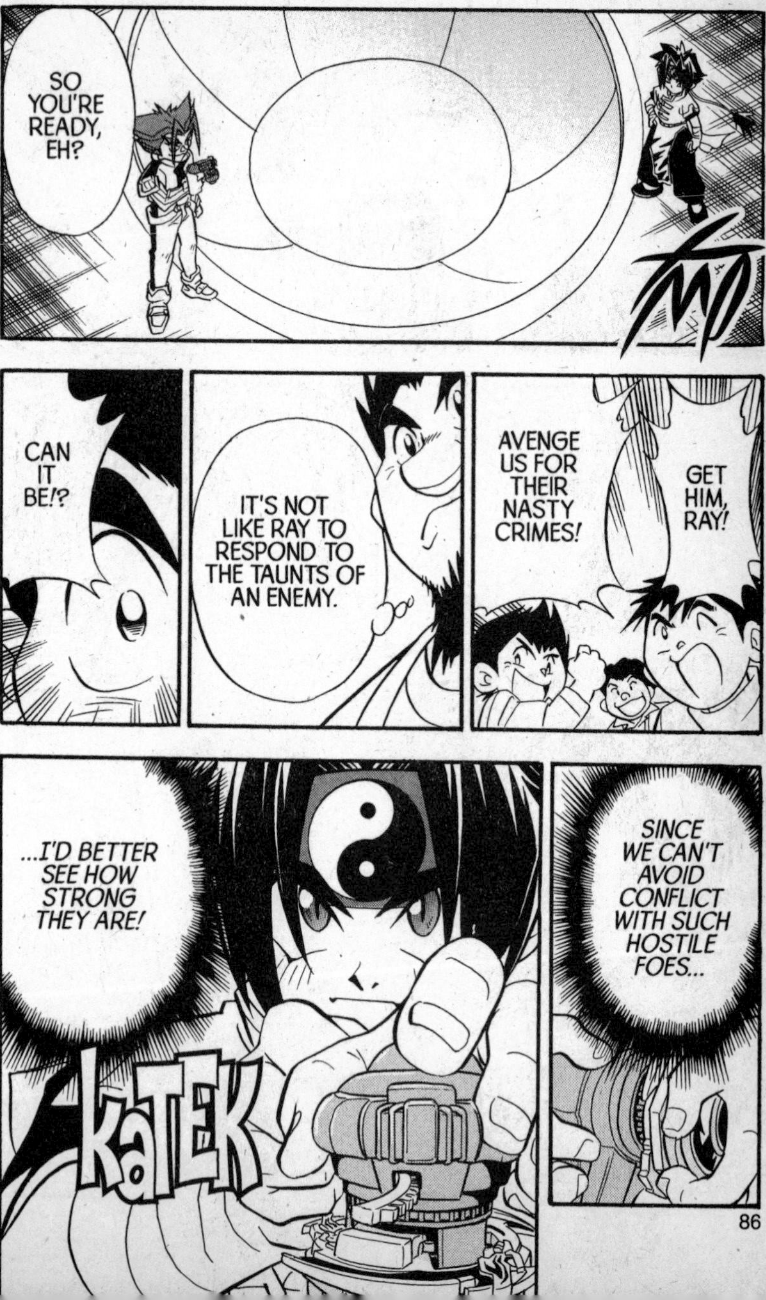
SO YOU'RE READY, EH?
GET HIM, RAY!
AVENGE US FOR THEIR NASTY CRIMES!
IT'S NOT LIKE RAY TO RESPOND TO THE TAUNTS OF AN ENEMY.
CAN IT BE!?
SINCE WE CAN'T AVOID CONFLICT WITH SUCH HOSTILE FOES...
...I'D BETTER SEE HOW STRONG THEY ARE!
KaTEK

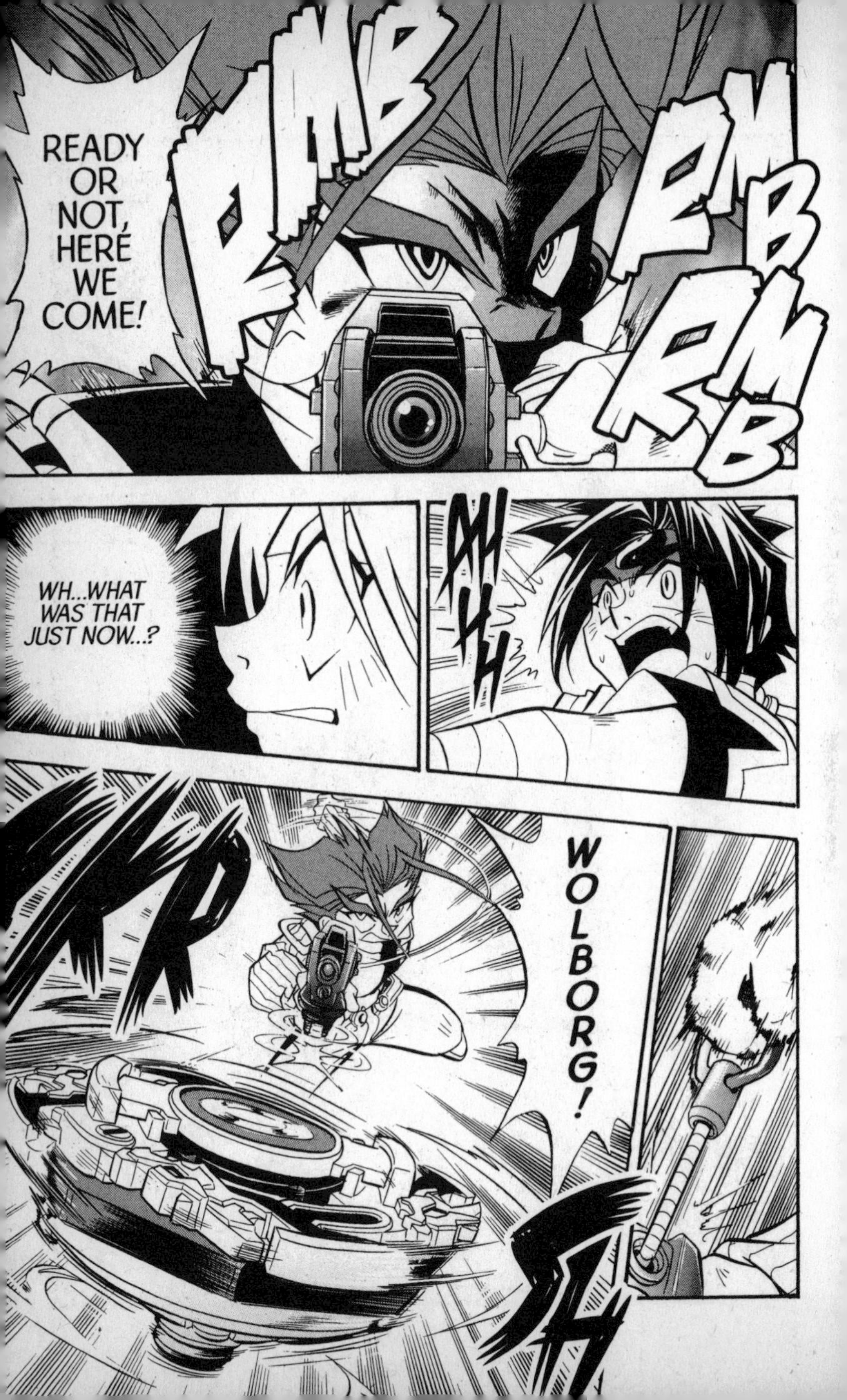
READY OR NOT, HERE WE COME!
WH...WHAT WAS THAT JUST NOW...?
WOLBORG!

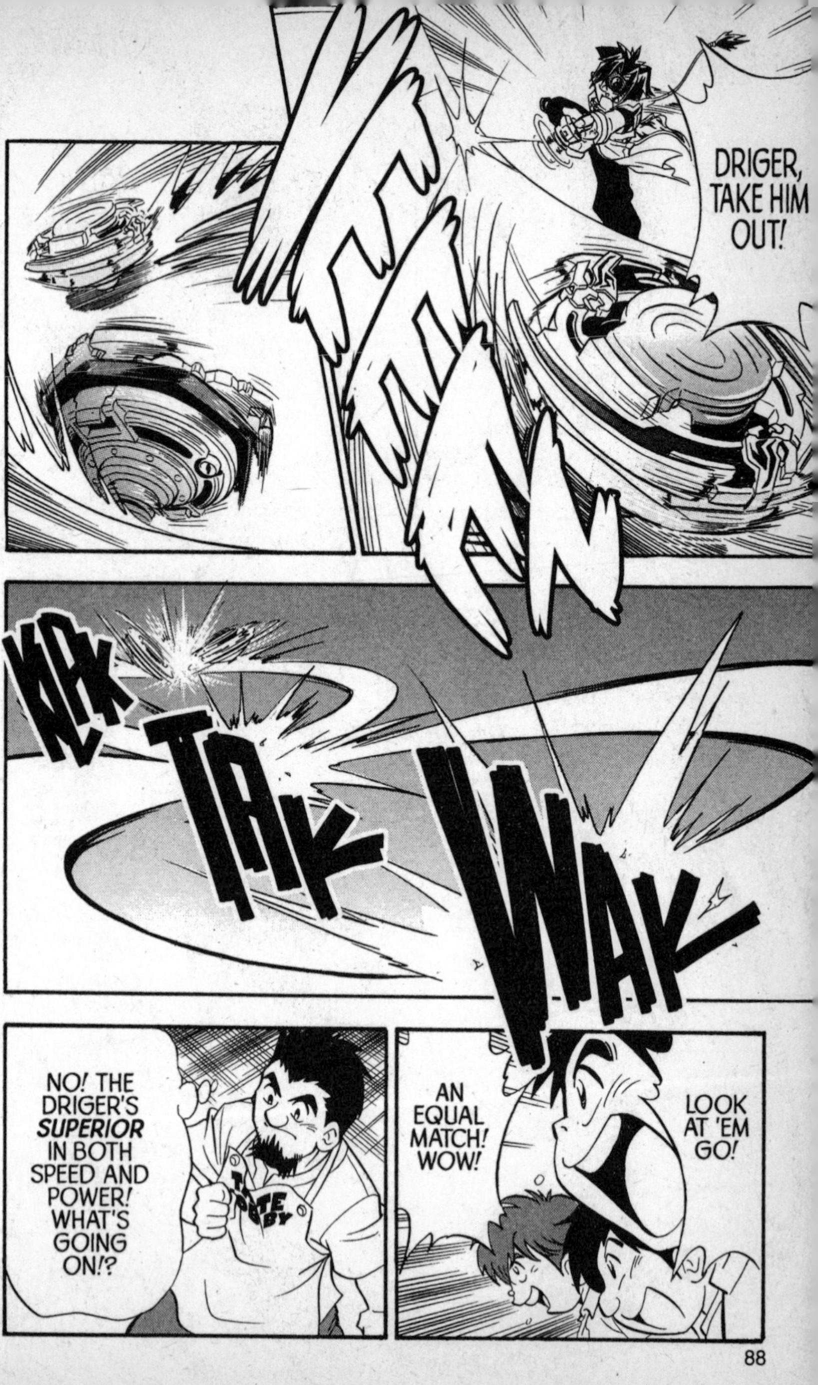
DRIGER, TAKE HIM OUT!
KRAK
TAK
WAK
LOOK AT 'EM GO!
AN EQUAL MATCH! WOW!
NO! THE DRIGER'S *SUPERIOR* IN BOTH SPEED AND POWER! WHAT'S GOING ON!?

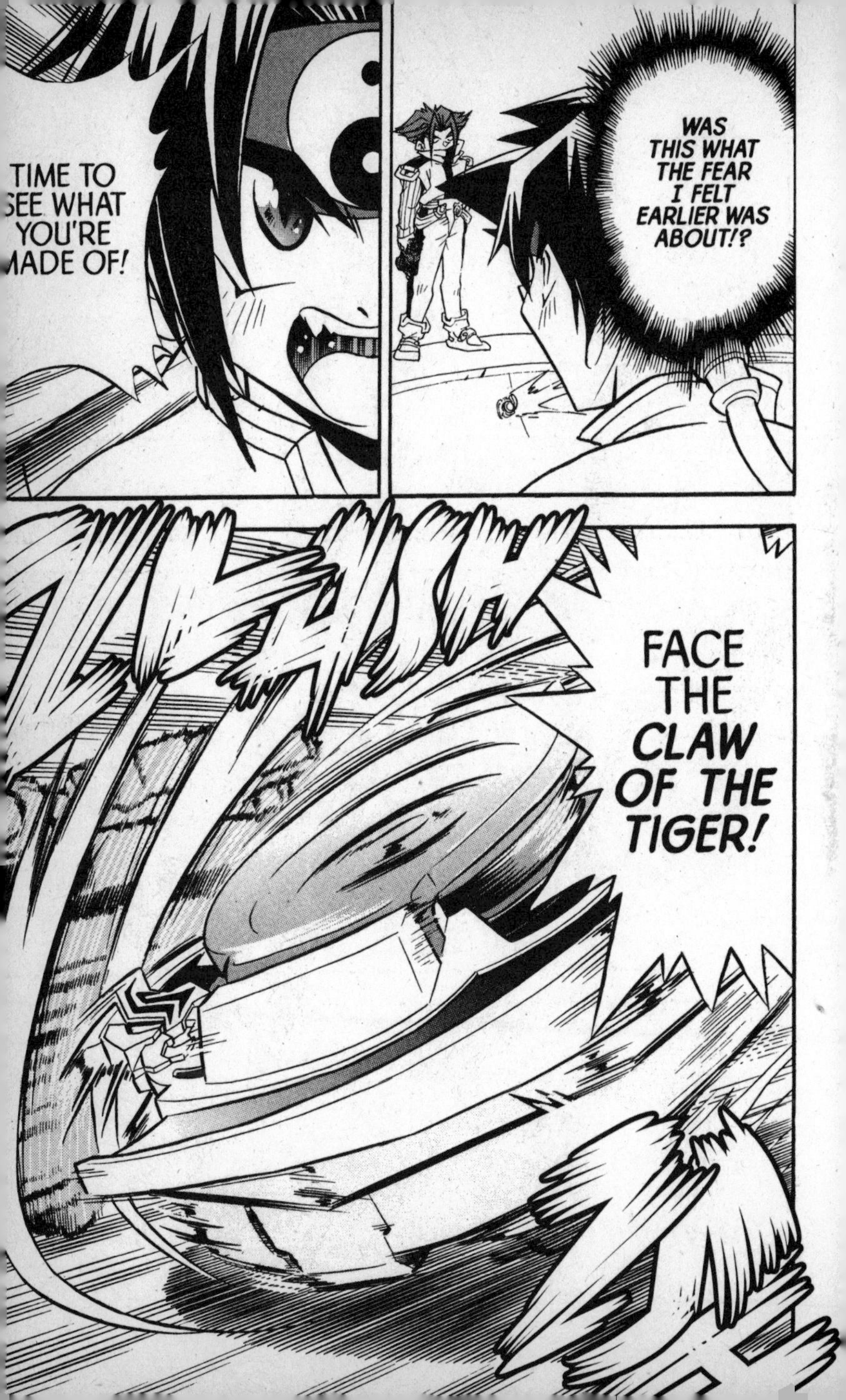
WAS THIS WHAT THE FEAR I FELT EARLIER WAS ABOUT!?
TIME TO SEE WHAT YOU'RE MADE OF!
FACE THE CLAW OF THE TIGER!

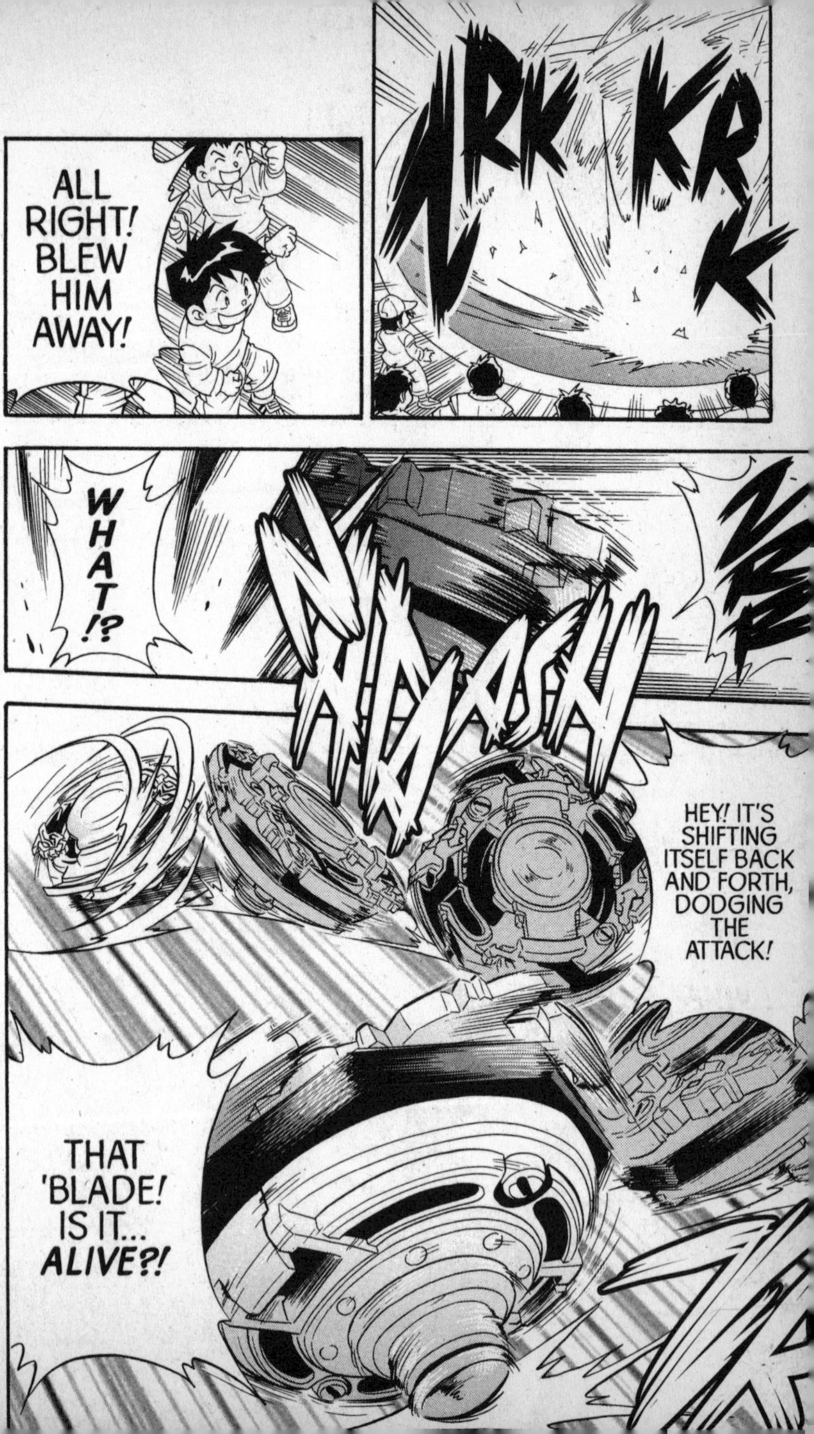
ALL RIGHT! BLEW HIM AWAY!
WHAT!?
HEY! IT'S SHIFTING ITSELF BACK AND FORTH, DODGING THE ATTACK!
THAT 'BLADE! IS IT... ALIVE?!

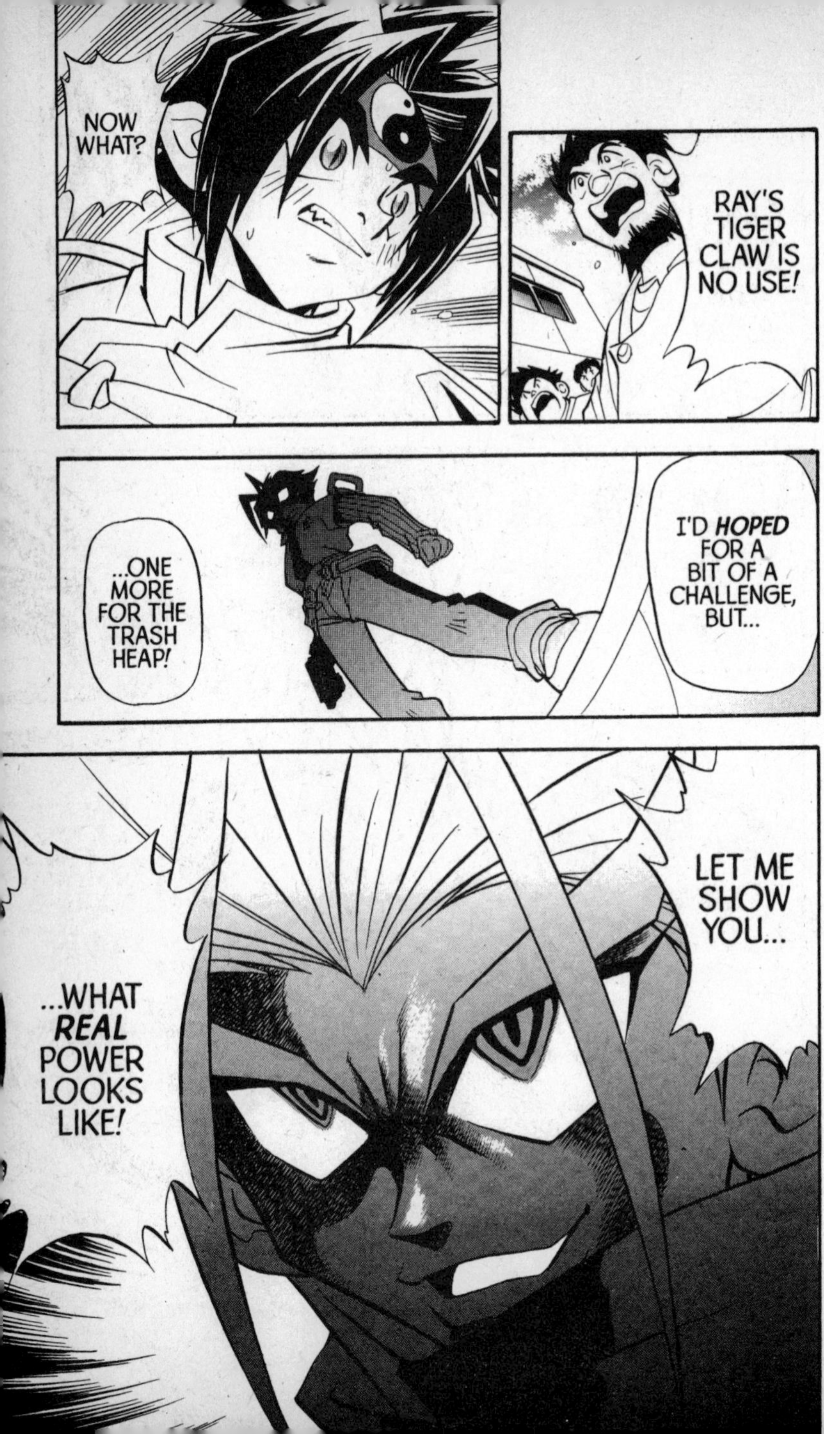
RAY'S TIGER CLAW IS NO USE!
NOW WHAT?
I'D *HOPED* FOR A BIT OF A CHALLENGE, BUT...
...ONE MORE FOR THE TRASH HEAP!
LET ME SHOW YOU...
...WHAT *REAL* POWER LOOKS LIKE!

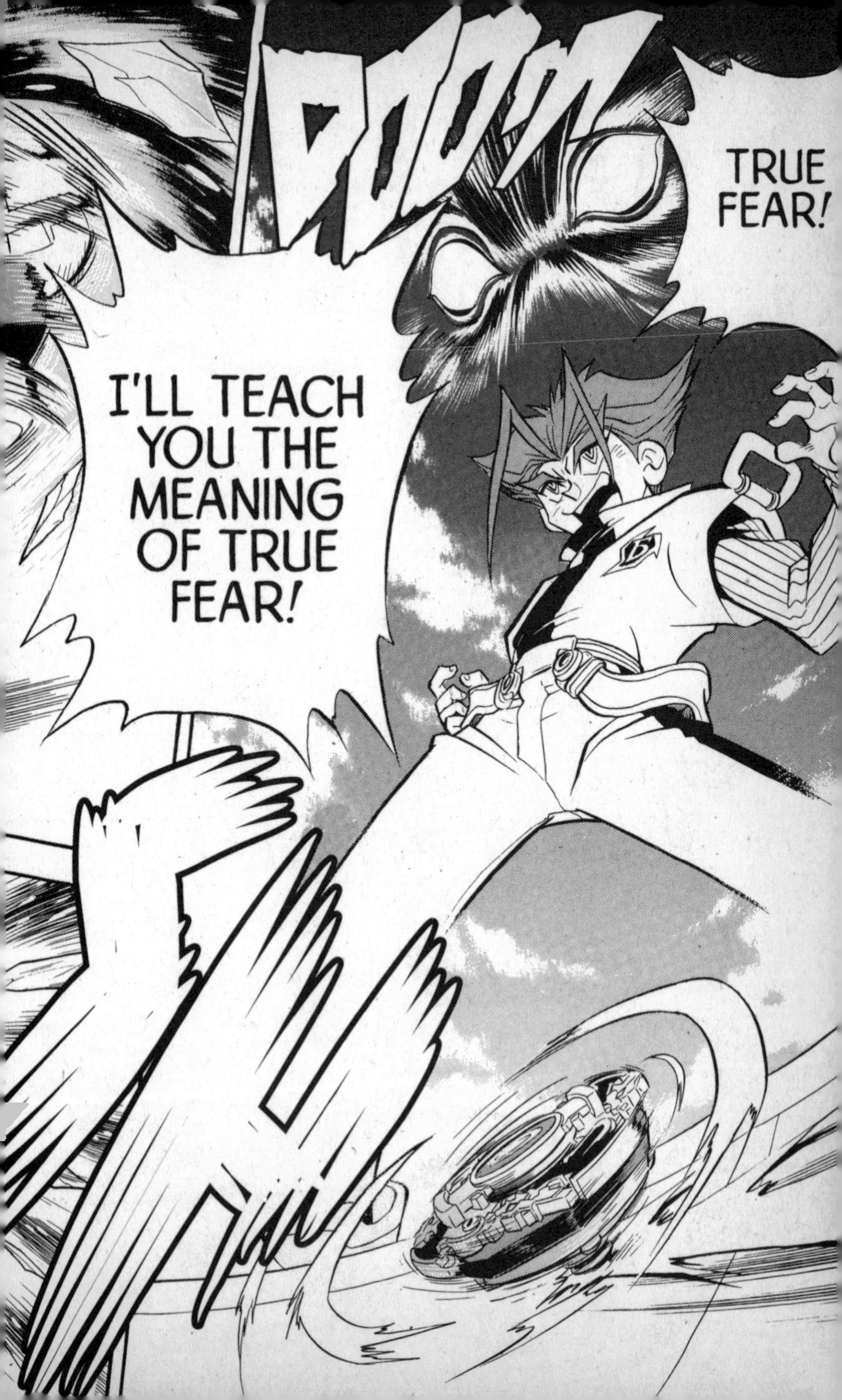
BOOM
TRUE FEAR!
I'LL TEACH YOU THE MEANING OF TRUE FEAR!

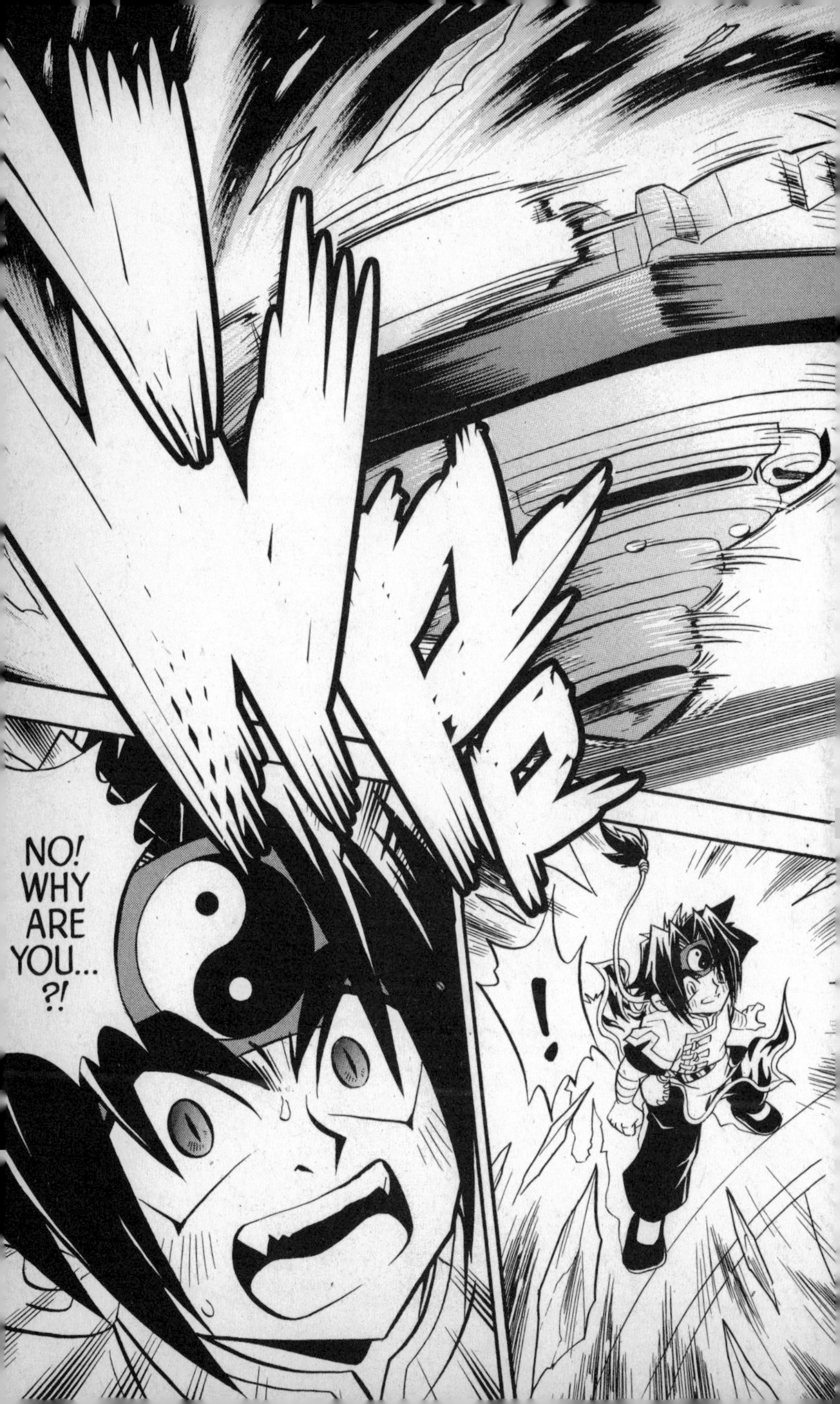
!
NO! WHY ARE YOU...?!

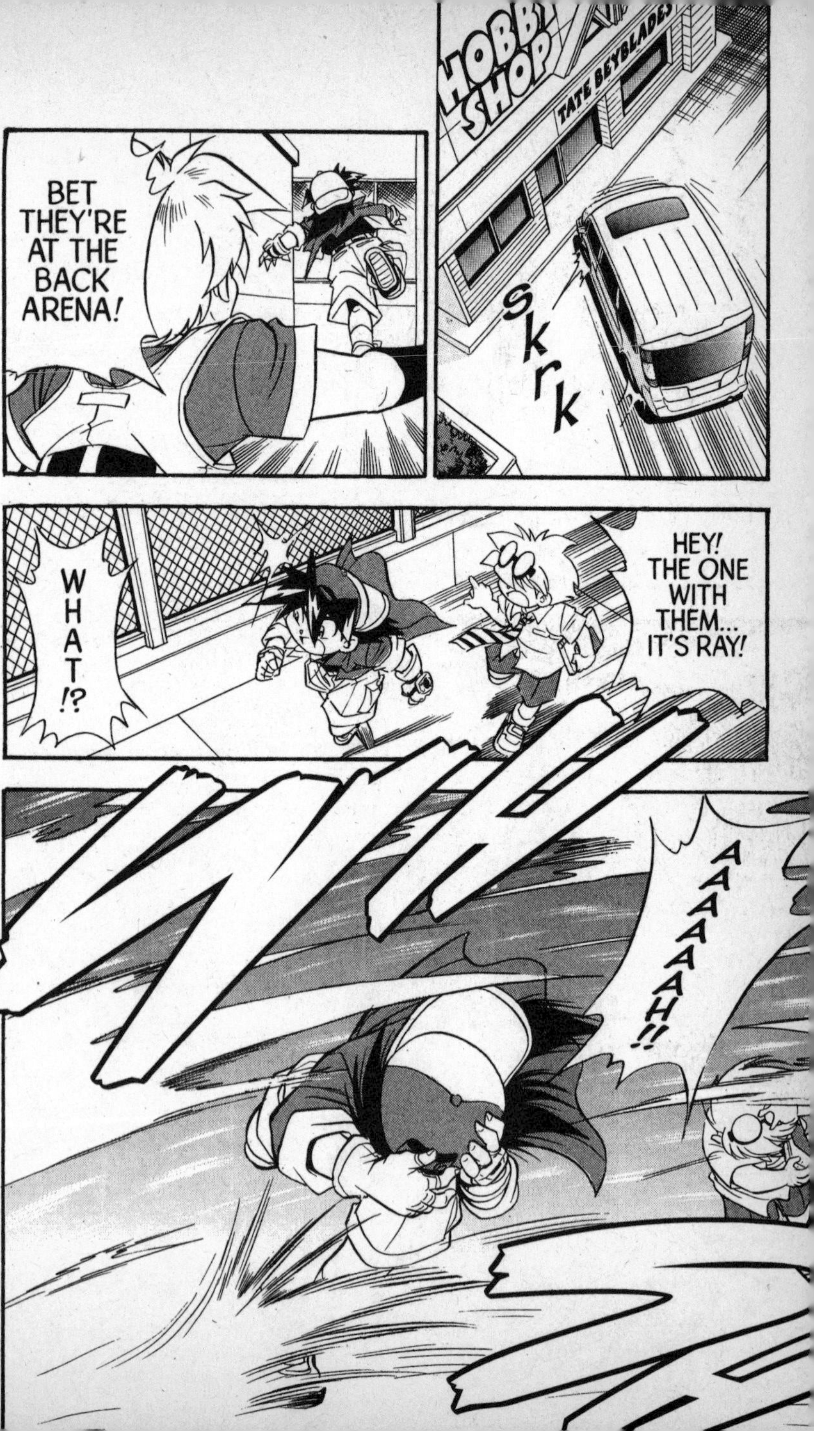
HOBBY SHOP
TATE BEYBLADES
Skrk
BET THEY'RE AT THE BACK ARENA!
HEY! THE ONE WITH THEM... IT'S RAY!
WHAT!?
AAAAAAH!!

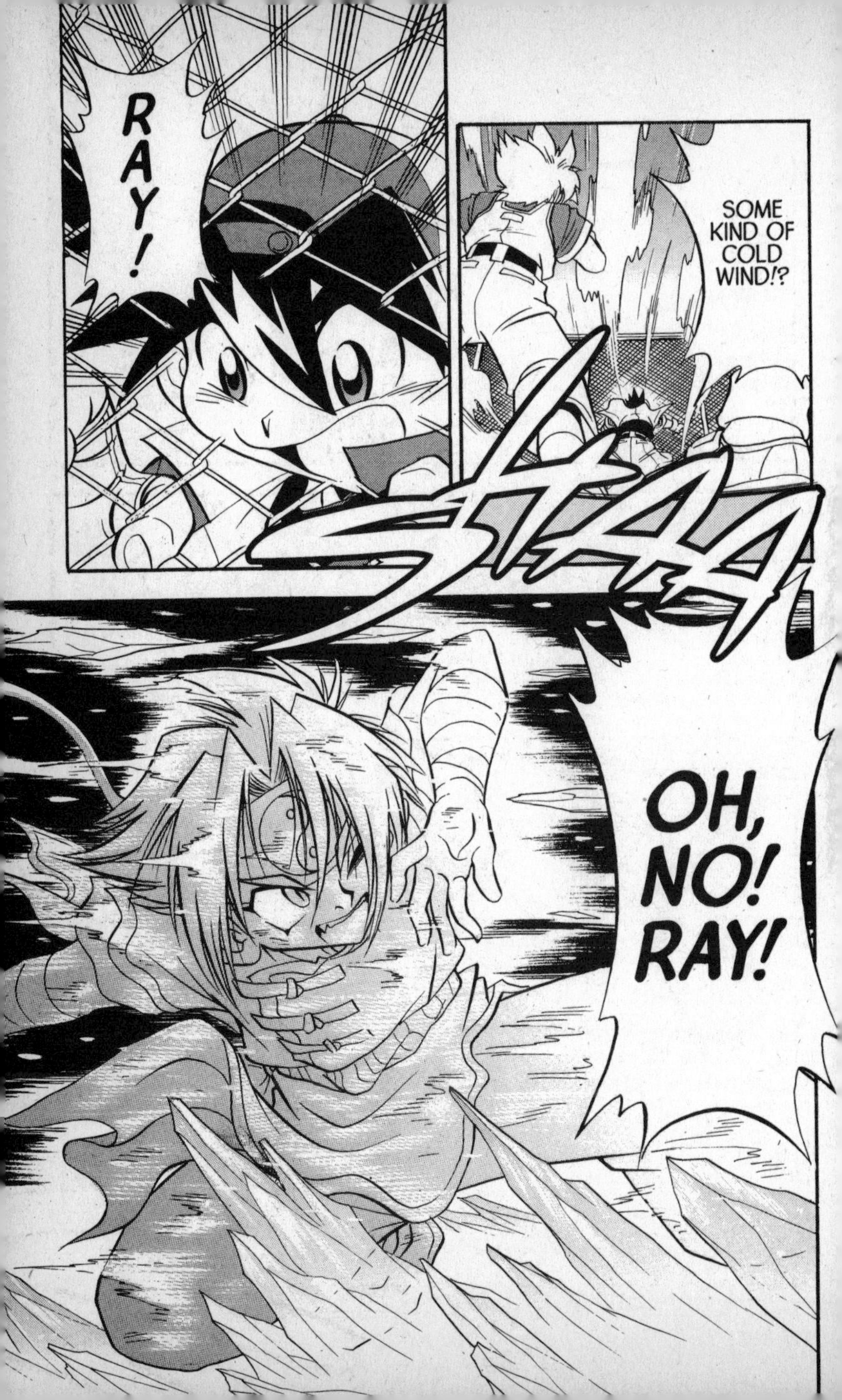
SOME KIND OF COLD WIND!?
RAY!
SHAA
OH, NO! RAY!

KRRA

WSD

RAY!

THEY GOT HIM!

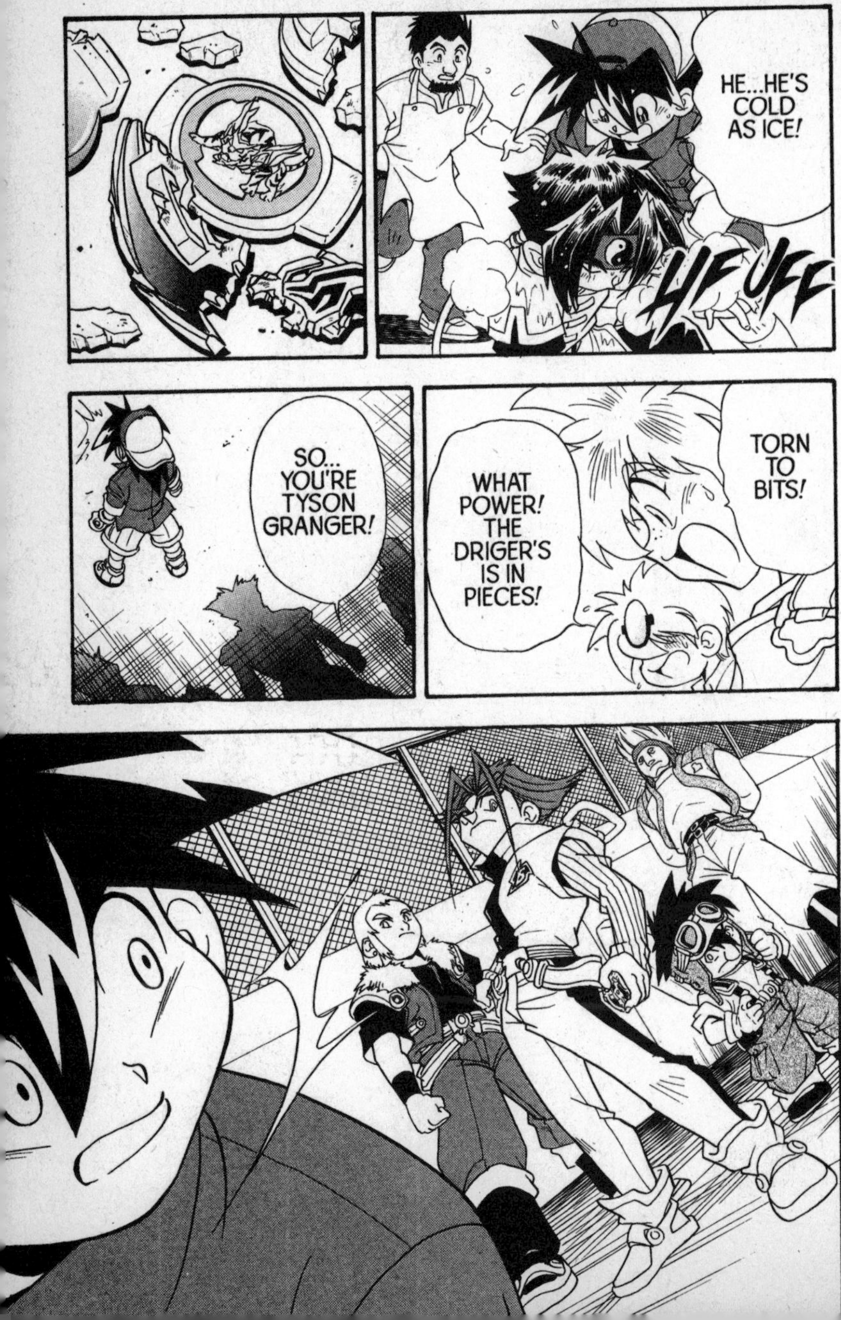
HE...HE'S COLD AS ICE!
TORN TO BITS!
WHAT POWER! THE DRIGER'S IS IN PIECES!
SO... YOU'RE TYSON GRANGER!

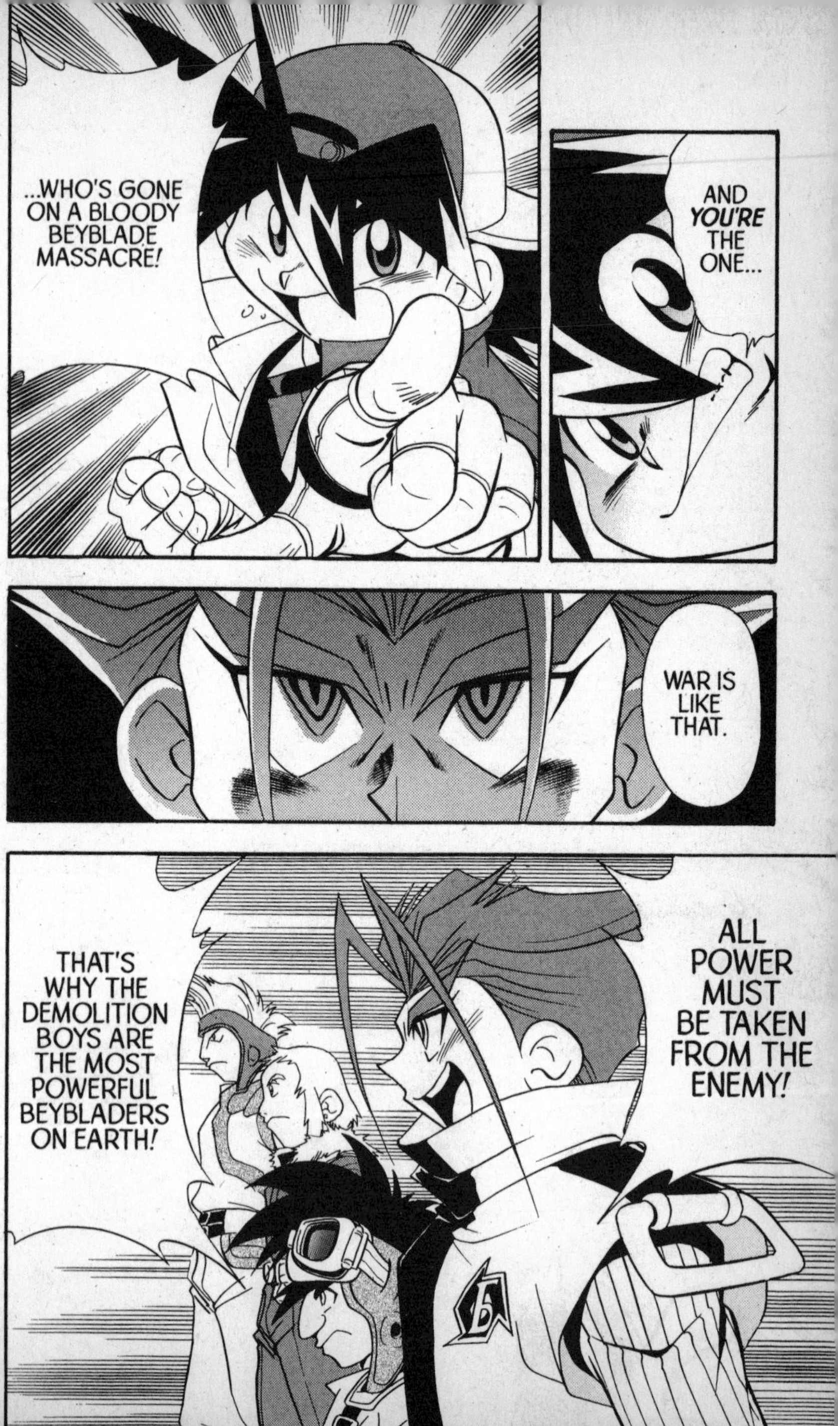
AND YOU'RE THE ONE...
...WHO'S GONE ON A BLOODY BEYBLADE MASSACRE!
WAR IS LIKE THAT.
ALL POWER MUST BE TAKEN FROM THE ENEMY!
THAT'S WHY THE DEMOLITION BOYS ARE THE MOST POWERFUL BEYBLADERS ON EARTH!

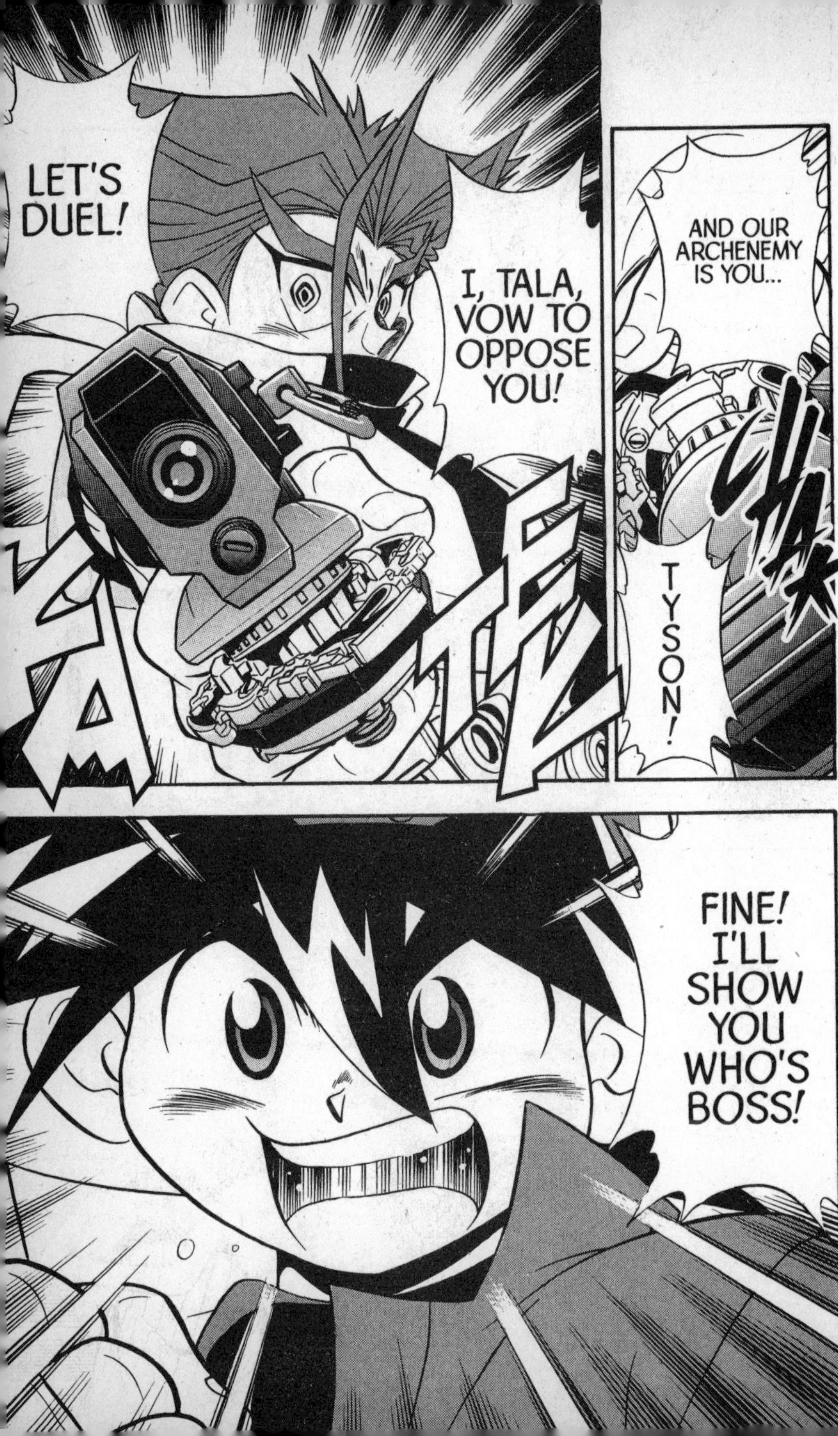
AND OUR ARCHENEMY IS YOU...
TYSON!
I, TALA, VOW TO OPPOSE YOU!
LET'S DUEL!
FINE! I'LL SHOW YOU WHO'S BOSS!

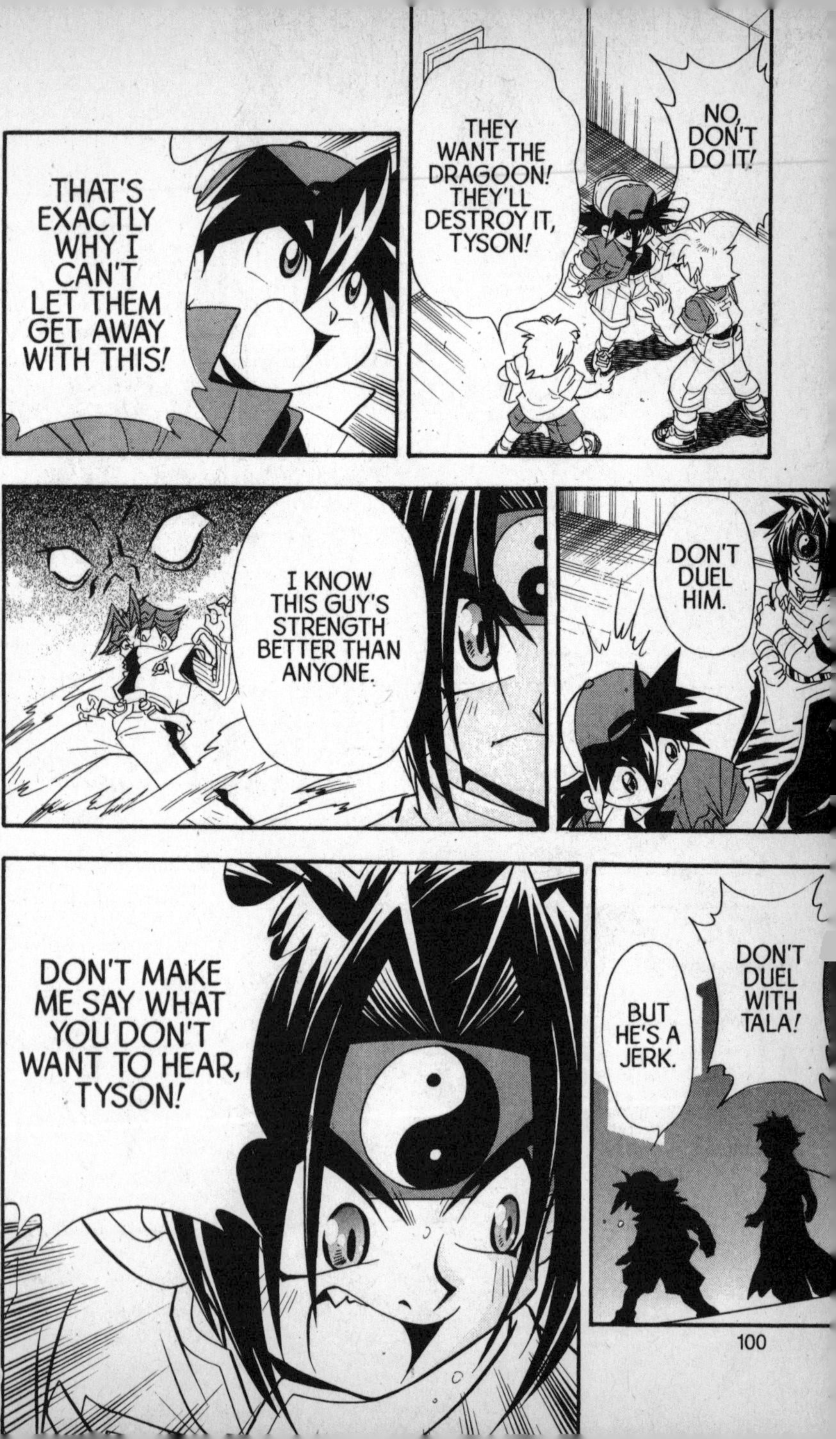
NO, DON'T DO IT!
THEY WANT THE DRAGOON! THEY'LL DESTROY IT, TYSON!
THAT'S EXACTLY WHY I CAN'T LET THEM GET AWAY WITH THIS!
DON'T DUEL HIM.
I KNOW THIS GUY'S STRENGTH BETTER THAN ANYONE.
DON'T DUEL WITH TALA!
BUT HE'S A JERK.
DON'T MAKE ME SAY WHAT YOU DON'T WANT TO HEAR, TYSON!

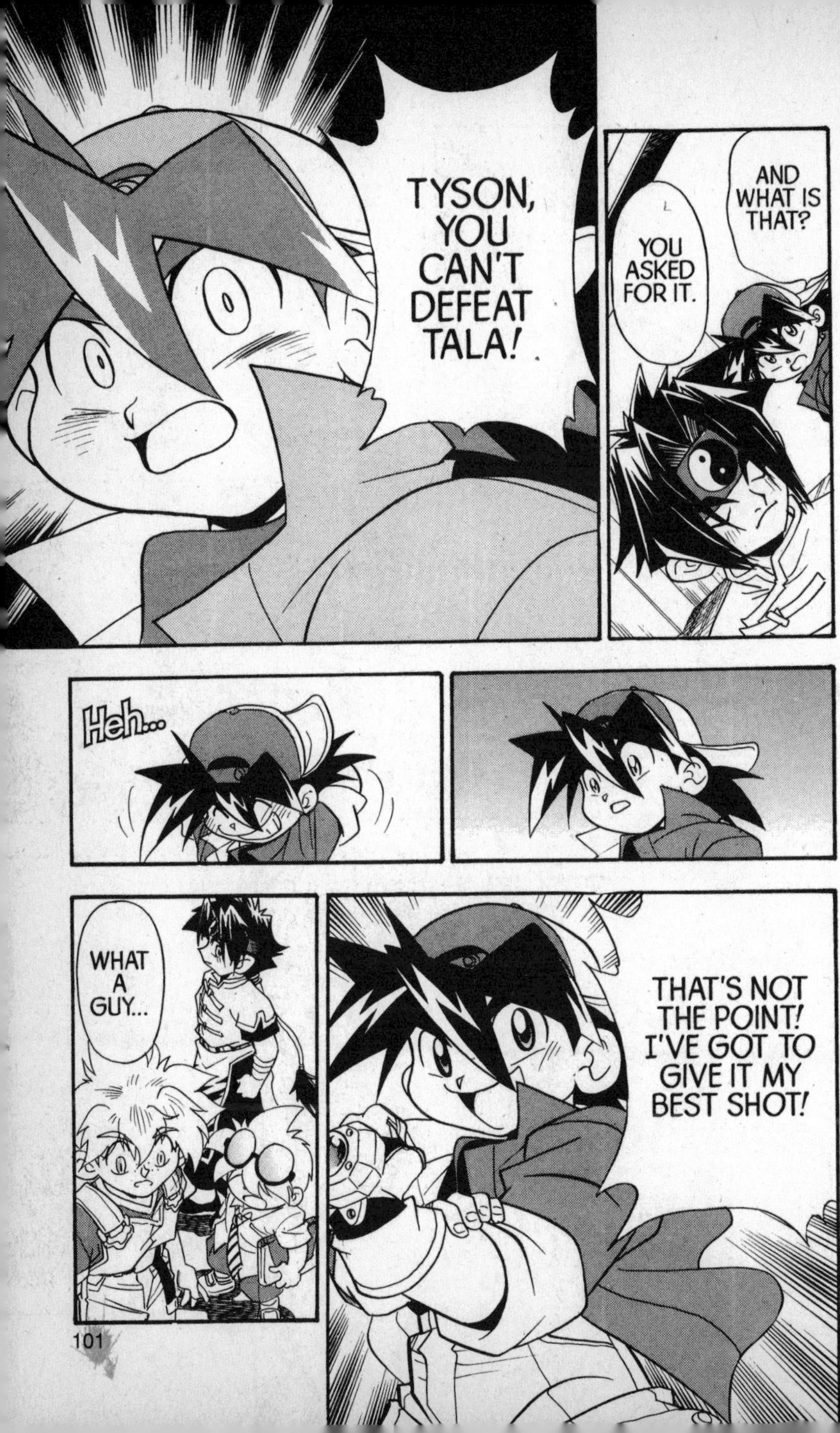
TYSON, YOU CAN'T DEFEAT TALA!
YOU ASKED FOR IT.
AND WHAT IS THAT?
Heh...
WHAT A GUY...
THAT'S NOT THE POINT! I'VE GOT TO GIVE IT MY BEST SHOT!

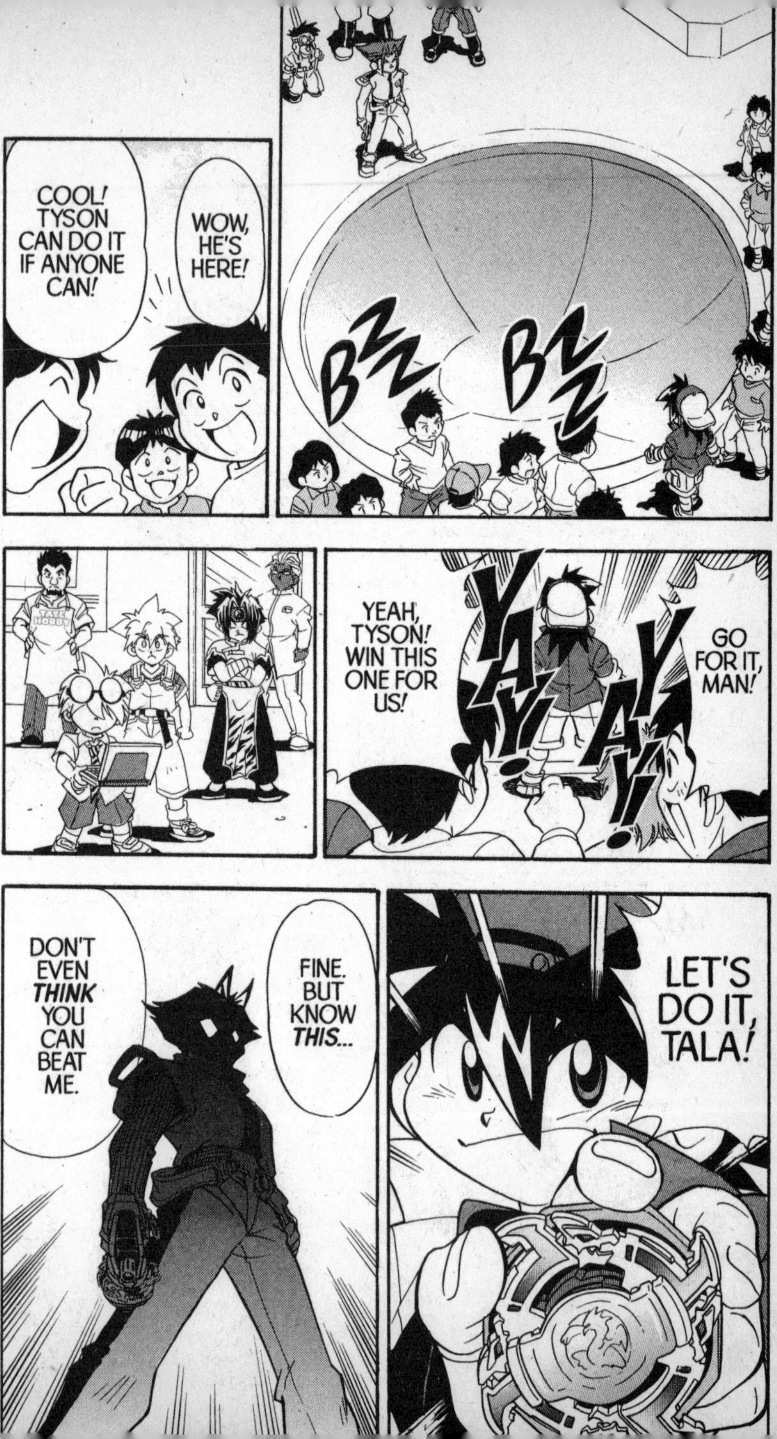
BZZ
BZZ
WOW, HE'S HERE!
COOL! TYSON CAN DO IT IF ANYONE CAN!
GO FOR IT, MAN!
YAY!
YAY!
YEAH, TYSON! WIN THIS ONE FOR US!
LET'S DO IT, TALA!
FINE. BUT KNOW *THIS*...
DON'T EVEN *THINK* YOU CAN BEAT ME.

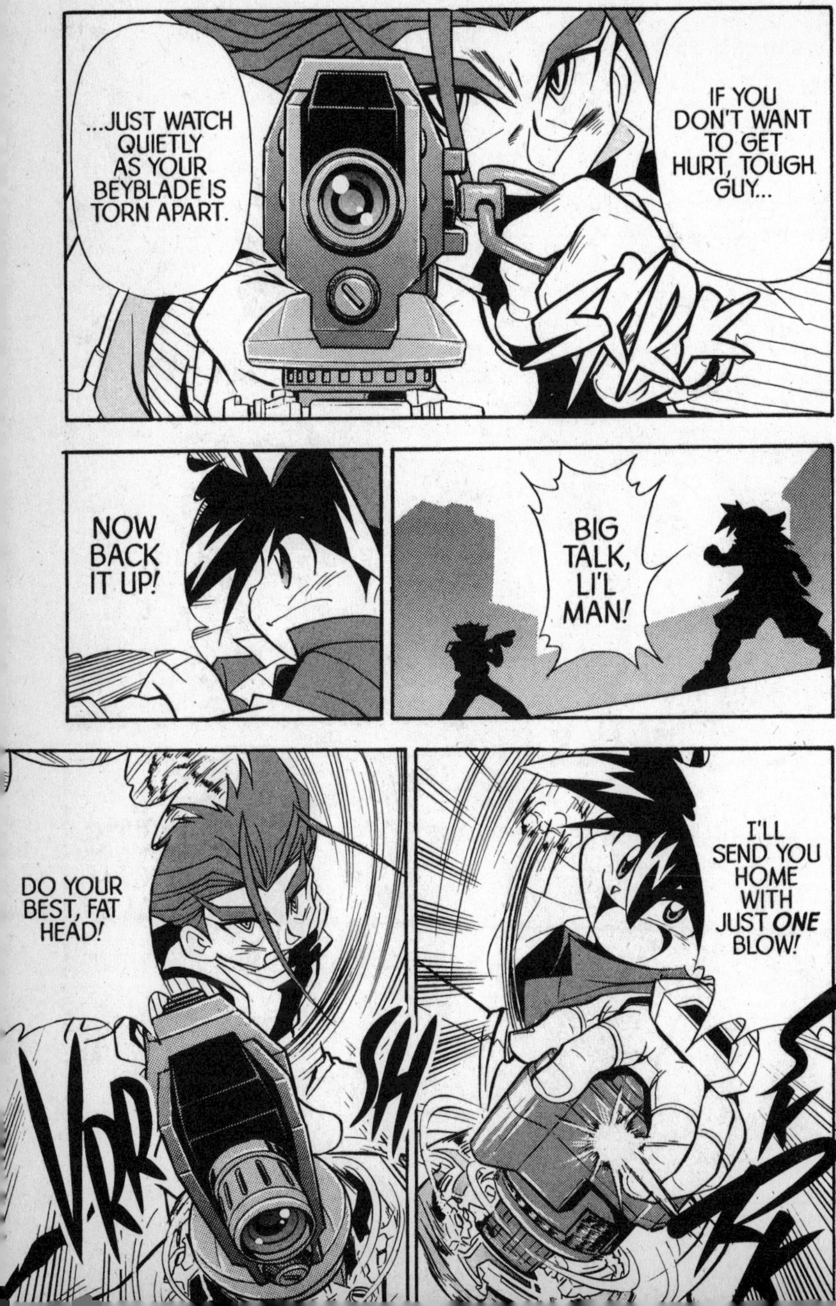
IF YOU DON'T WANT TO GET HURT, TOUGH GUY...
...JUST WATCH QUIETLY AS YOUR BEYBLADE IS TORN APART.
BIG TALK, LI'L MAN!
NOW BACK IT UP!
I'LL SEND YOU HOME WITH JUST *ONE* BLOW!
DO YOUR BEST, FAT HEAD!

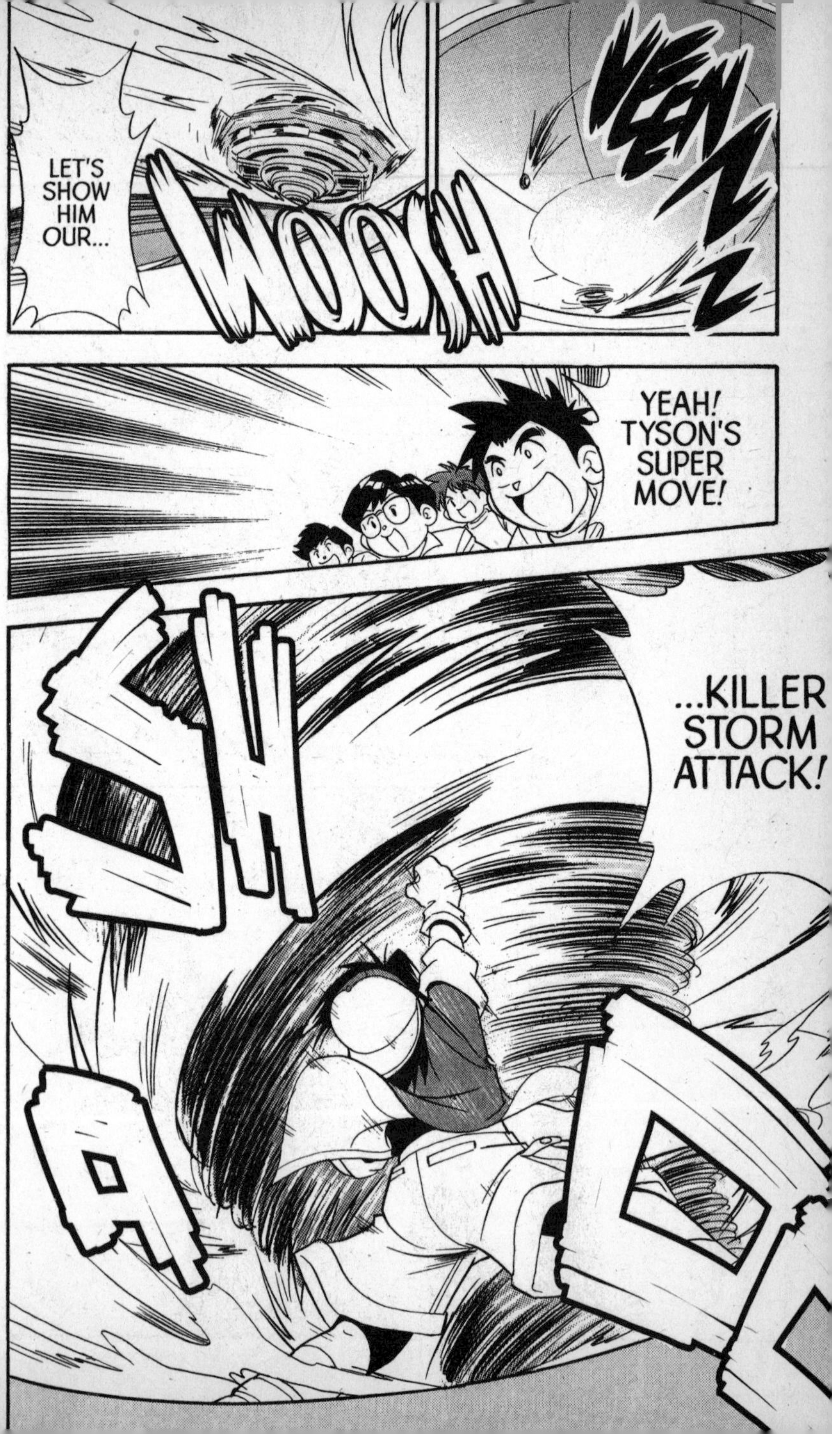
LET'S SHOW HIM OUR...
WOOSH
YEAH! TYSON'S SUPER MOVE!
...KILLER STORM ATTACK!

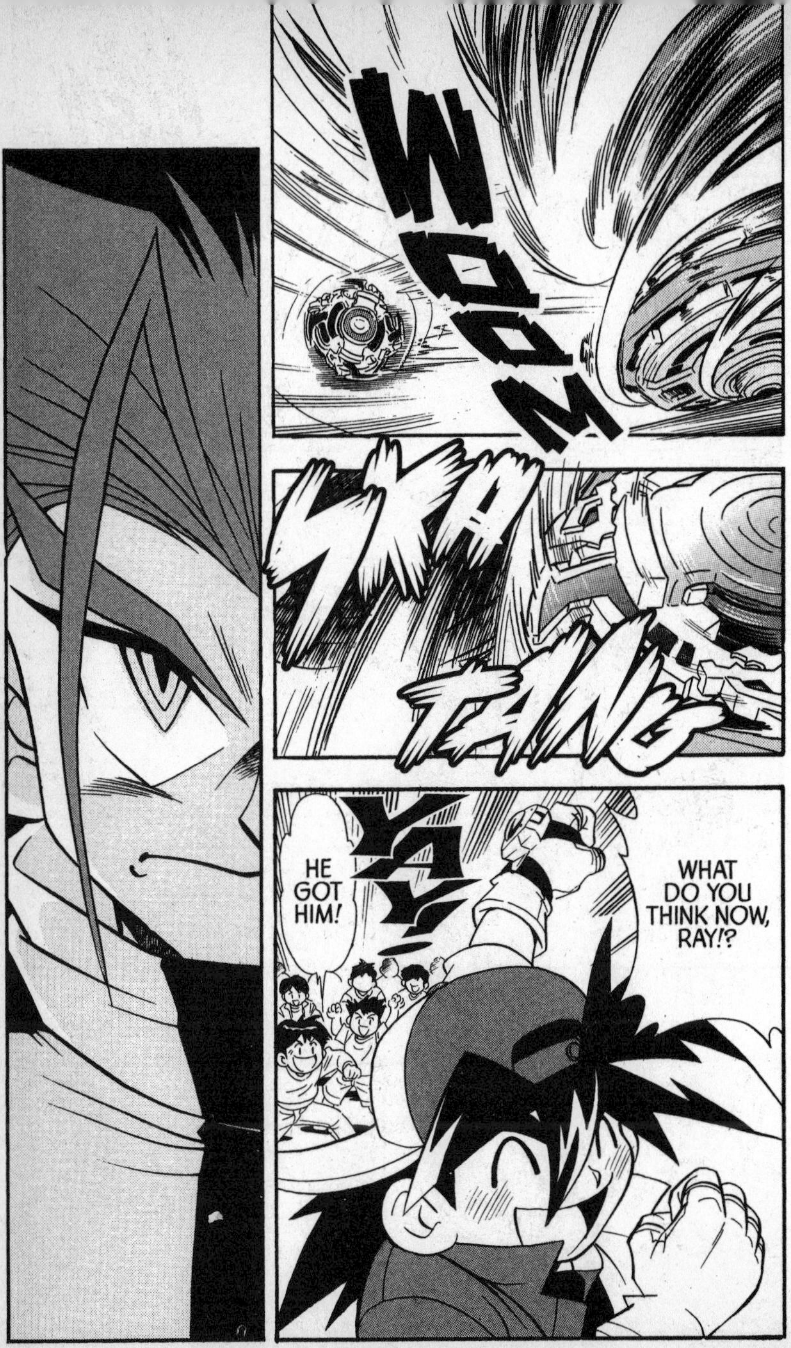
TANG
WHAT DO YOU THINK NOW, RAY!?
YAY
HE GOT HIM!

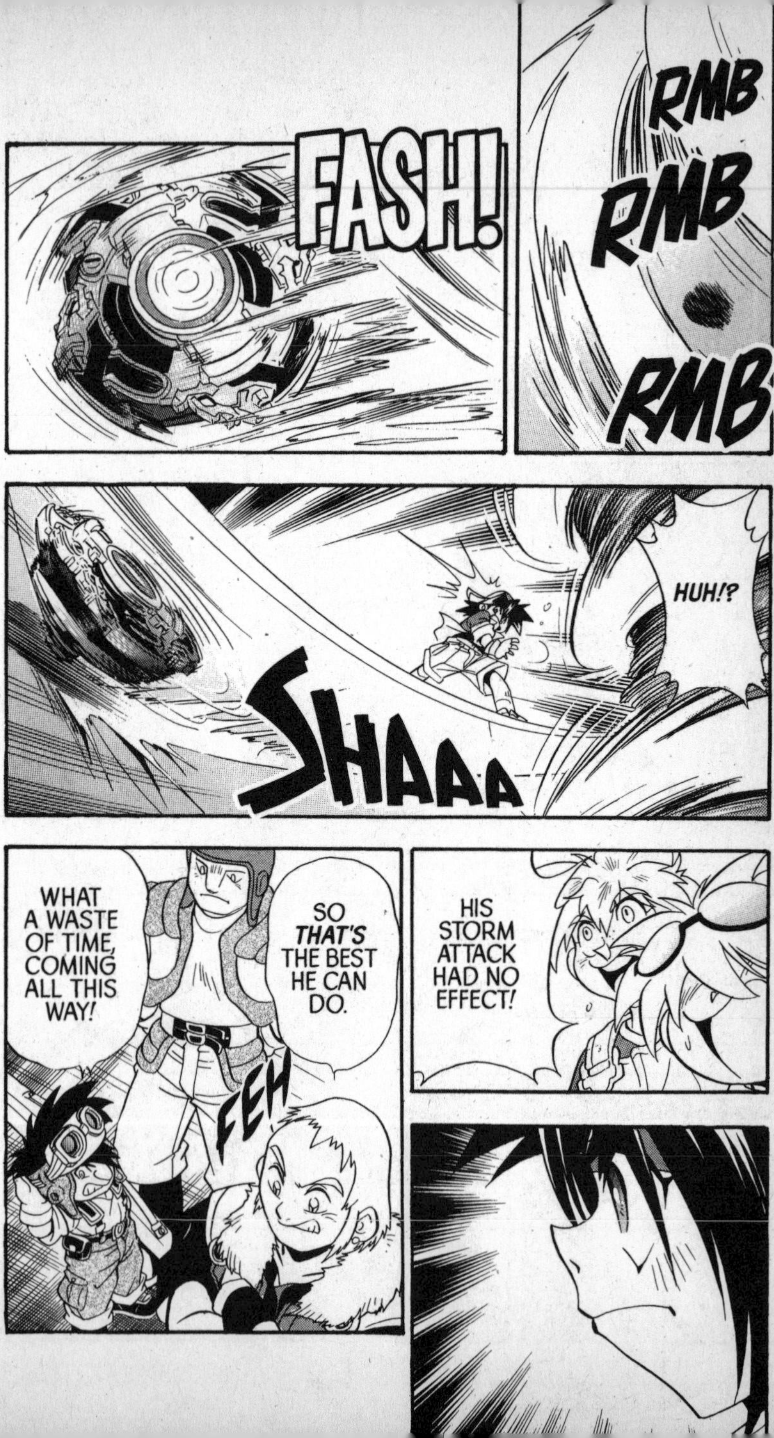
RMB
RMB
RMB
FASH!
HUH!?
SHAAA
HIS STORM ATTACK HAD NO EFFECT!
SO *THAT'S* THE BEST HE CAN DO.
WHAT A WASTE OF TIME, COMING ALL THIS WAY!
FEH

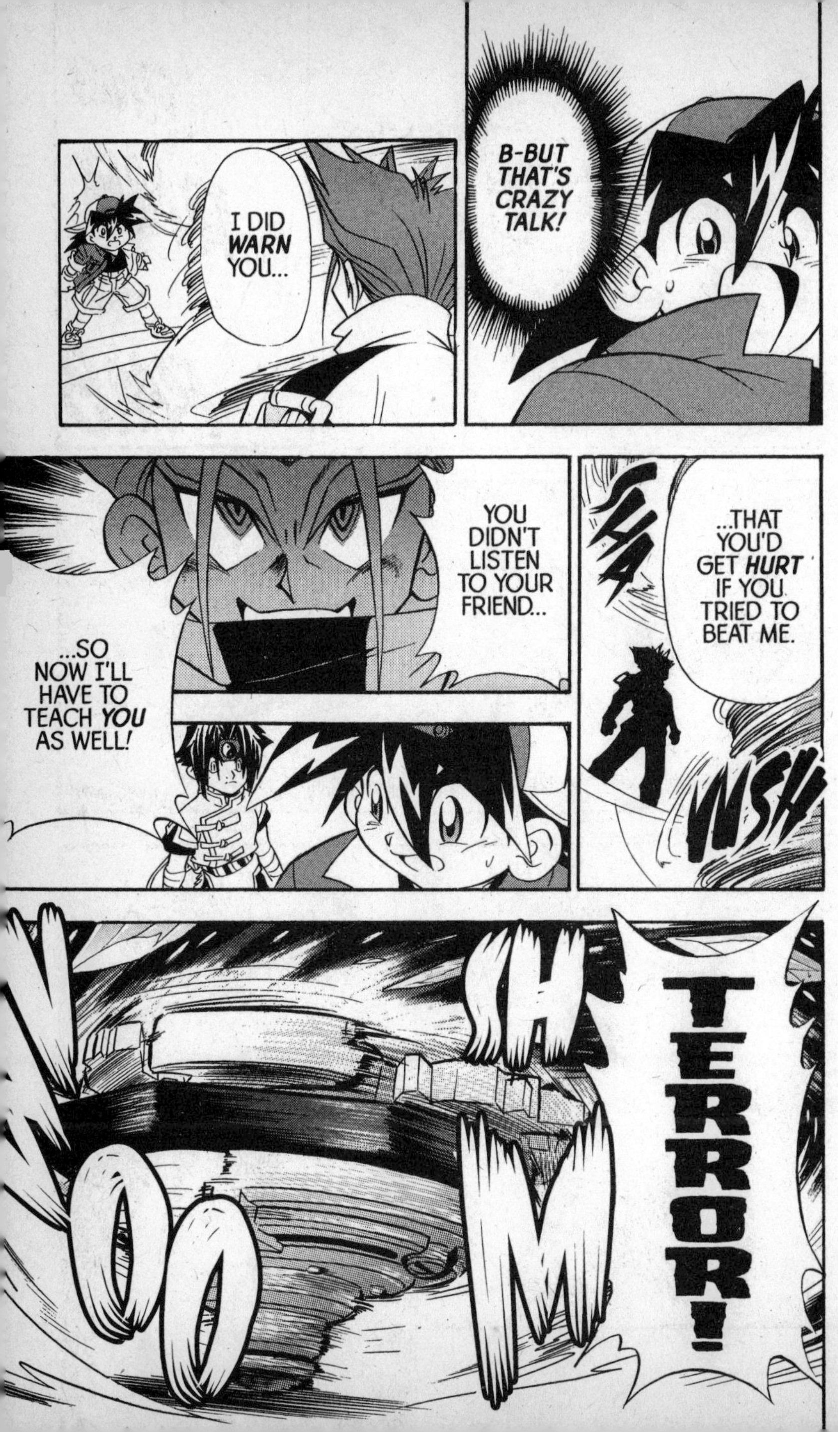
B-BUT THAT'S CRAZY TALK!
I DID WARN YOU...
...THAT YOU'D GET HURT IF YOU TRIED TO BEAT ME.
YOU DIDN'T LISTEN TO YOUR FRIEND...
...SO NOW I'LL HAVE TO TEACH YOU AS WELL!
TERROR!

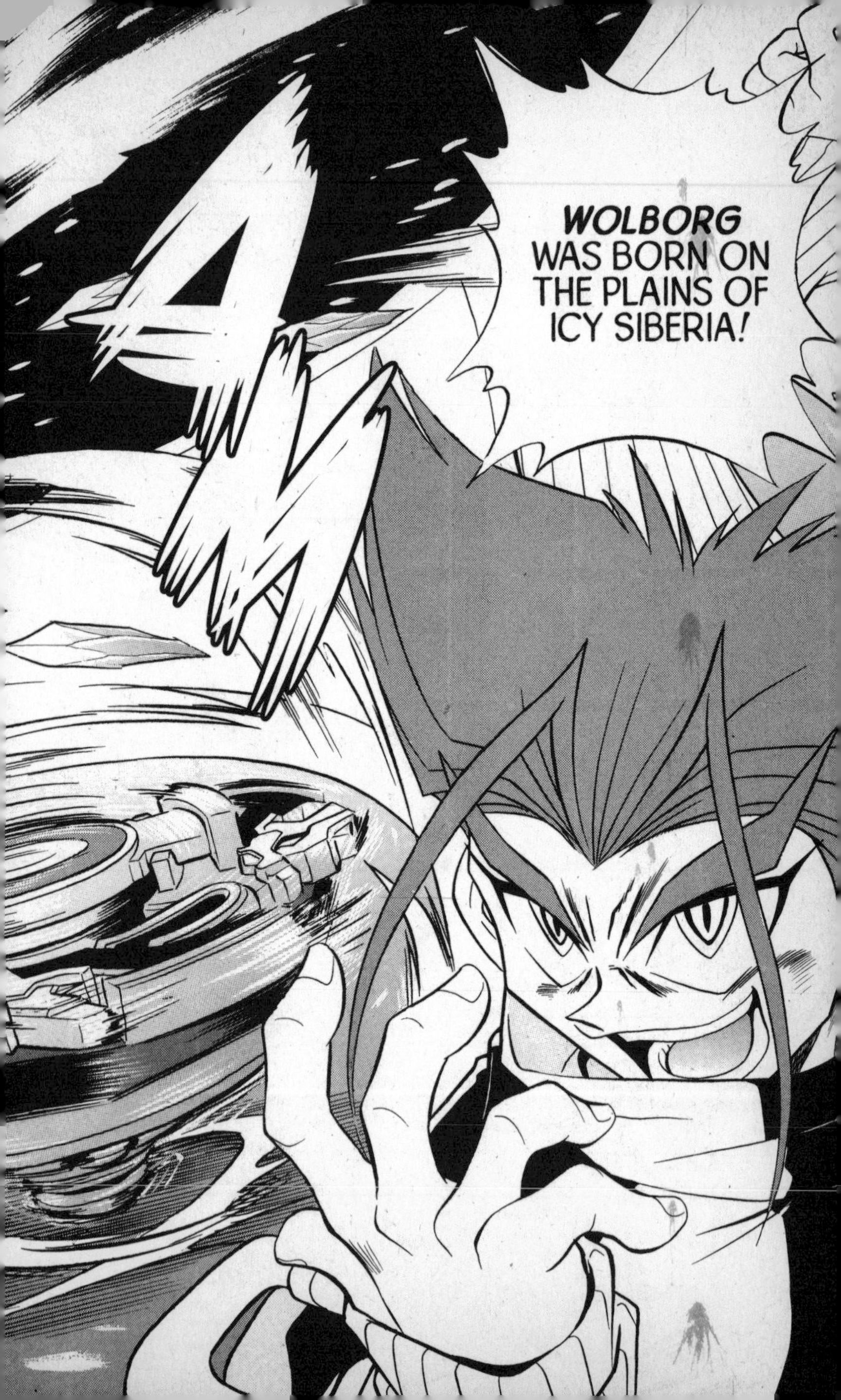
WOLBORG WAS BORN ON THE PLAINS OF ICY SIBERIA!

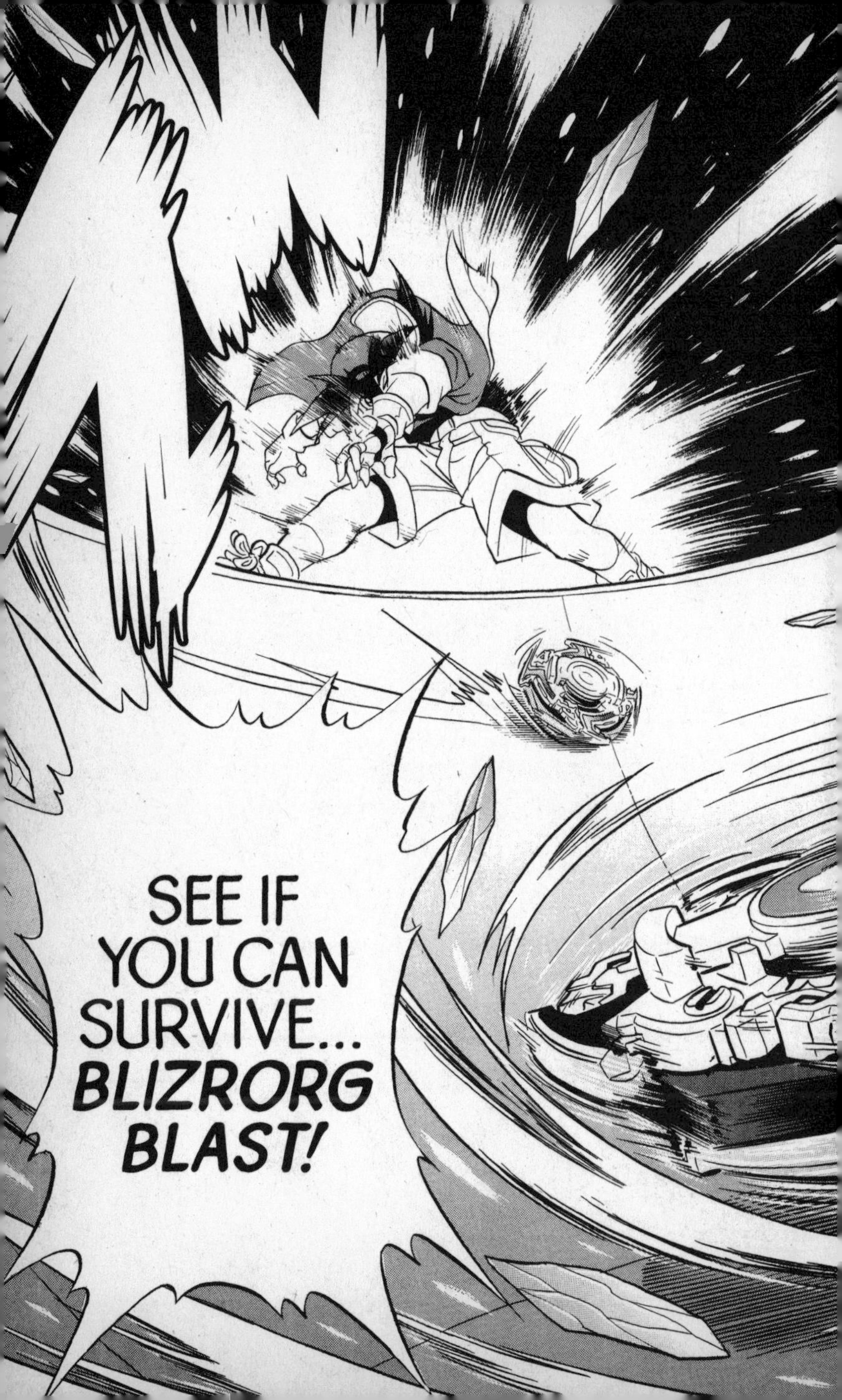
SEE IF YOU CAN SURVIVE... BLIZRORG BLAST!

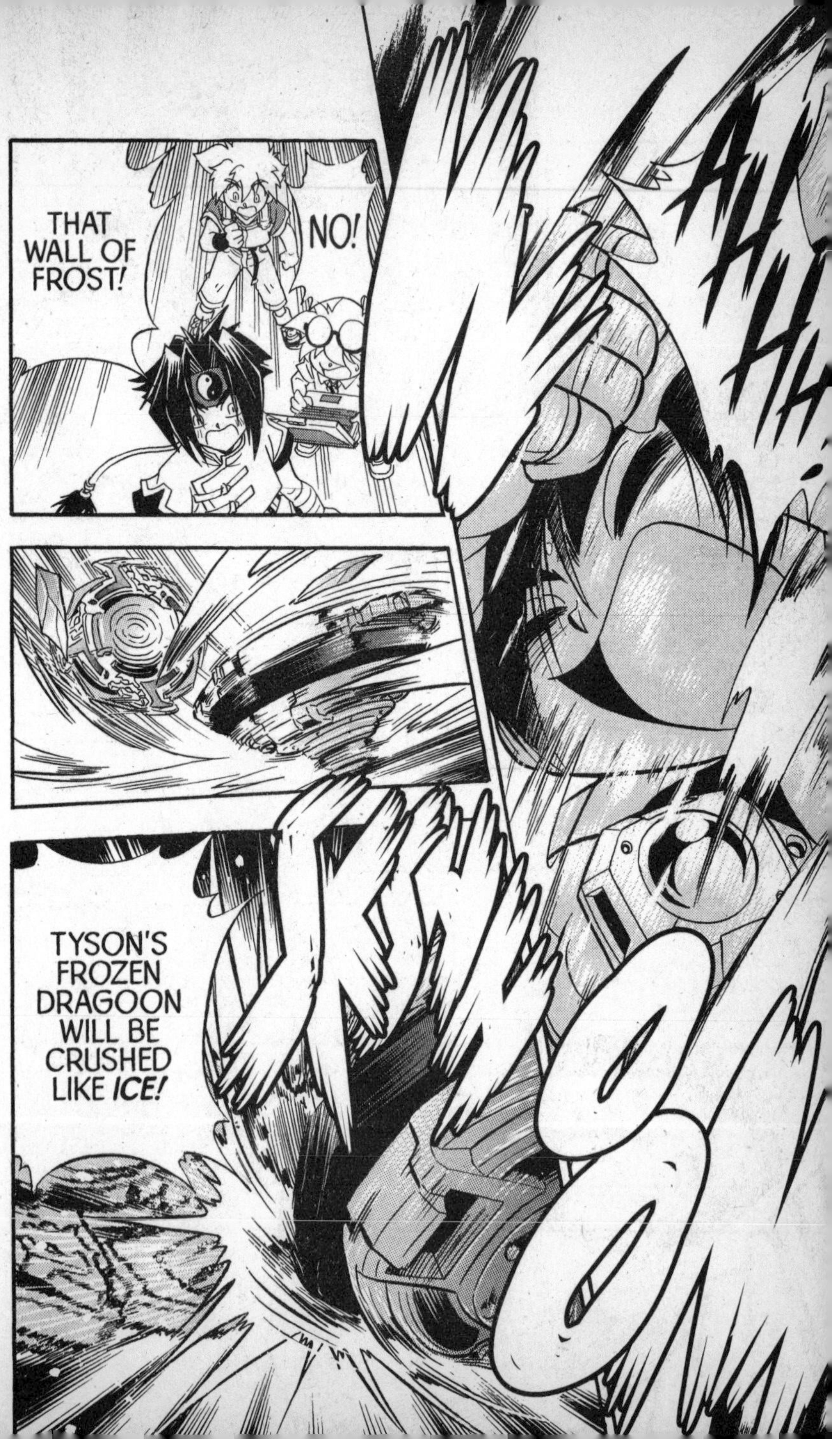
NO!
THAT WALL OF FROST!
TYSON'S FROZEN DRAGOON WILL BE CRUSHED LIKE *ICE!*

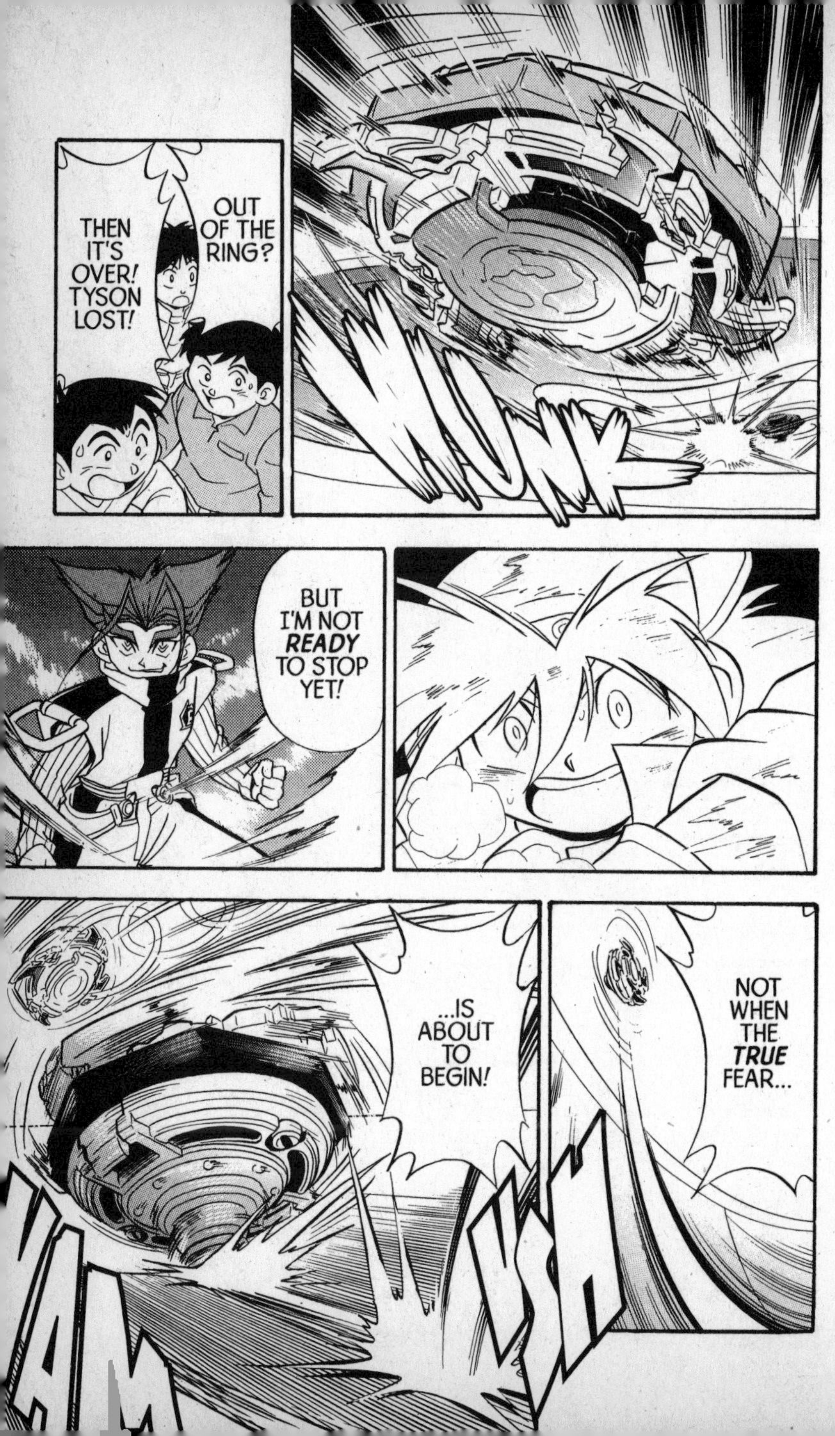
WHUNK
OUT OF THE RING?
THEN IT'S OVER! TYSON LOST!
BUT I'M NOT ***READY*** TO STOP YET!
NOT WHEN THE ***TRUE*** FEAR...
...IS ABOUT TO BEGIN!

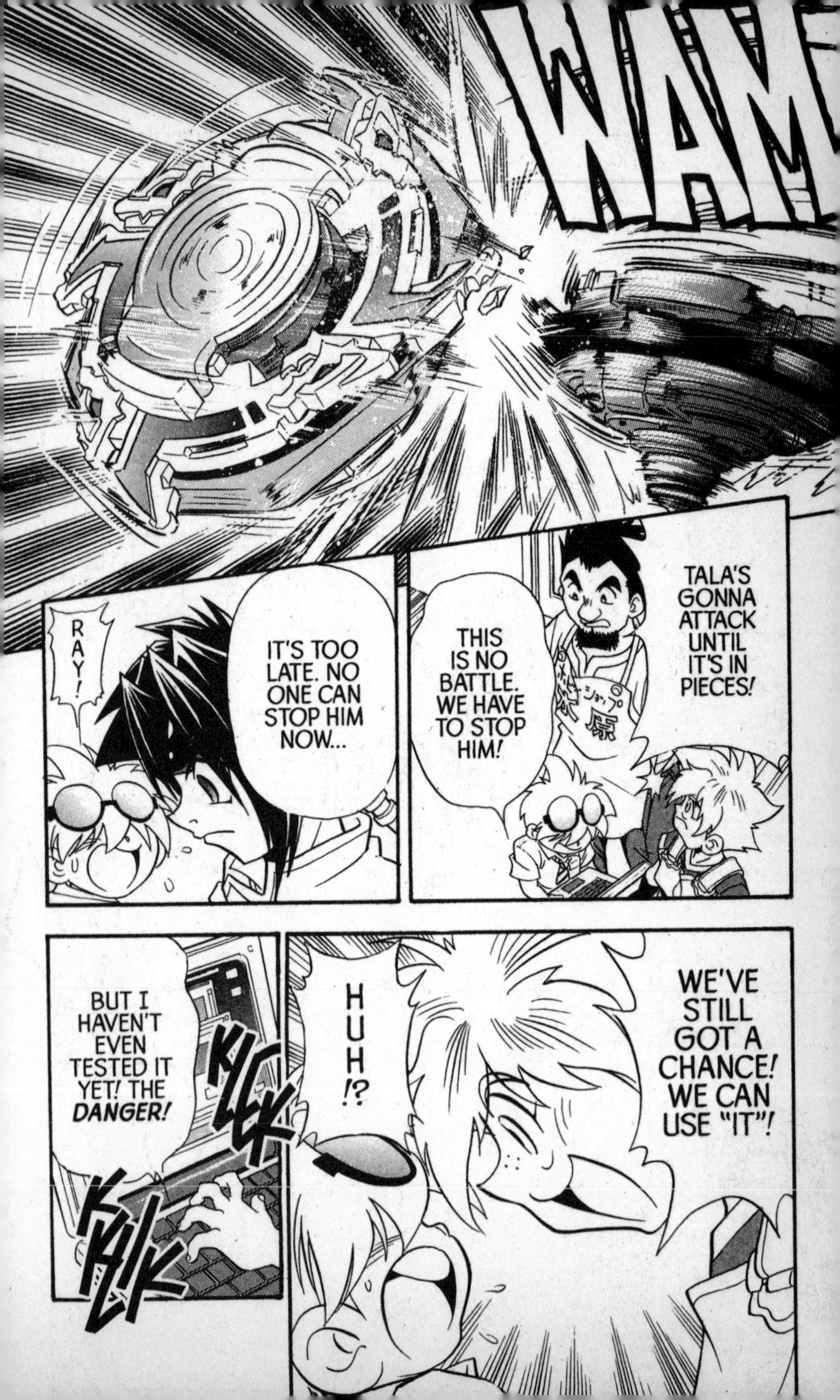
WAM
TALA'S GONNA ATTACK UNTIL IT'S IN PIECES!
THIS IS NO BATTLE. WE HAVE TO STOP HIM!
IT'S TOO LATE. NO ONE CAN STOP HIM NOW...
RAY!
WE'VE STILL GOT A CHANCE! WE CAN USE "IT"!
HUH!?
BUT I HAVEN'T EVEN TESTED IT YET! THE *DANGER!*

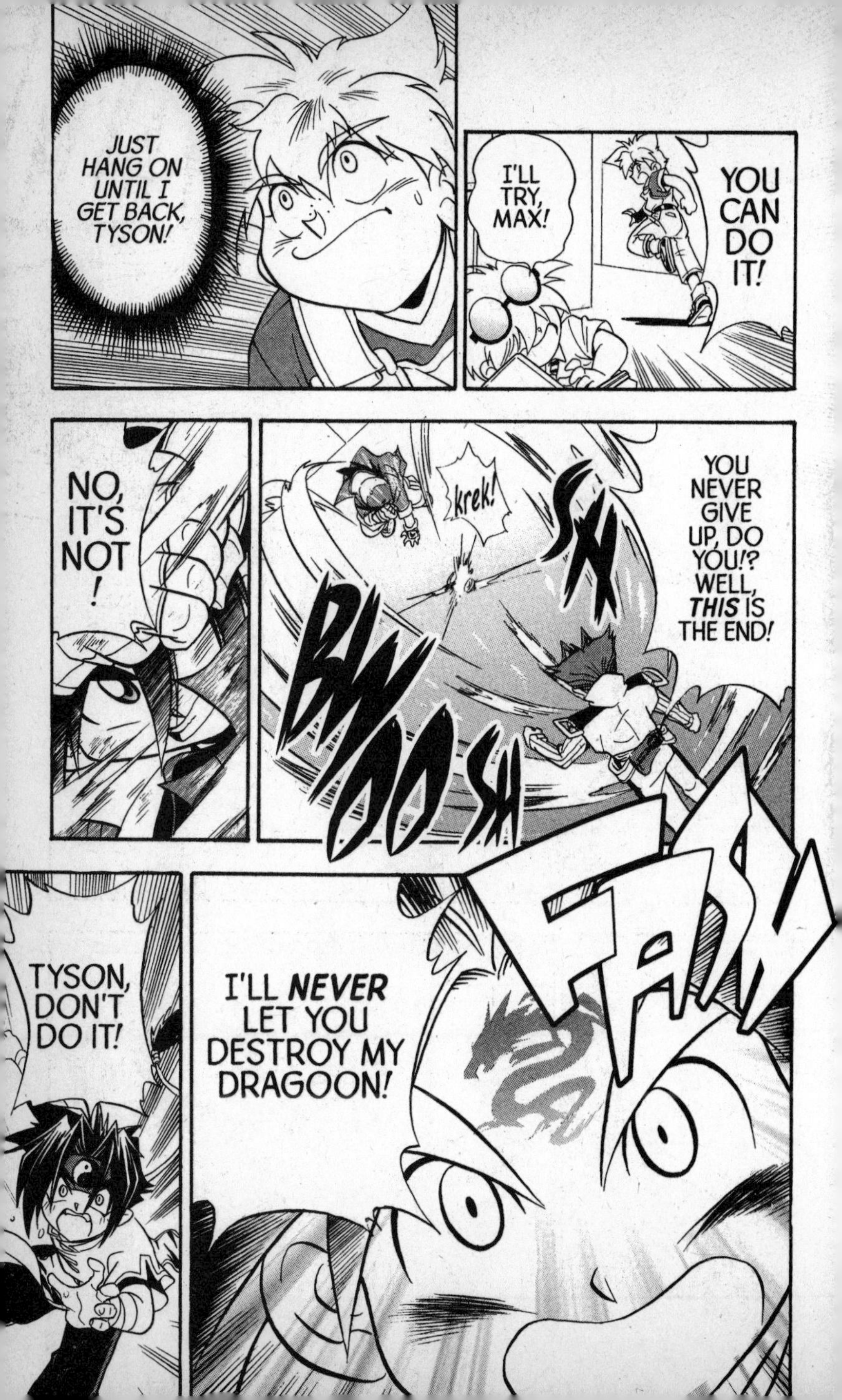
JUST HANG ON UNTIL I GET BACK, TYSON!
I'LL TRY, MAX!
YOU CAN DO IT!
NO, IT'S NOT!
krek!
YOU NEVER GIVE UP, DO YOU!? WELL, THIS IS THE END!
TYSON, DON'T DO IT!
I'LL NEVER LET YOU DESTROY MY DRAGOON!

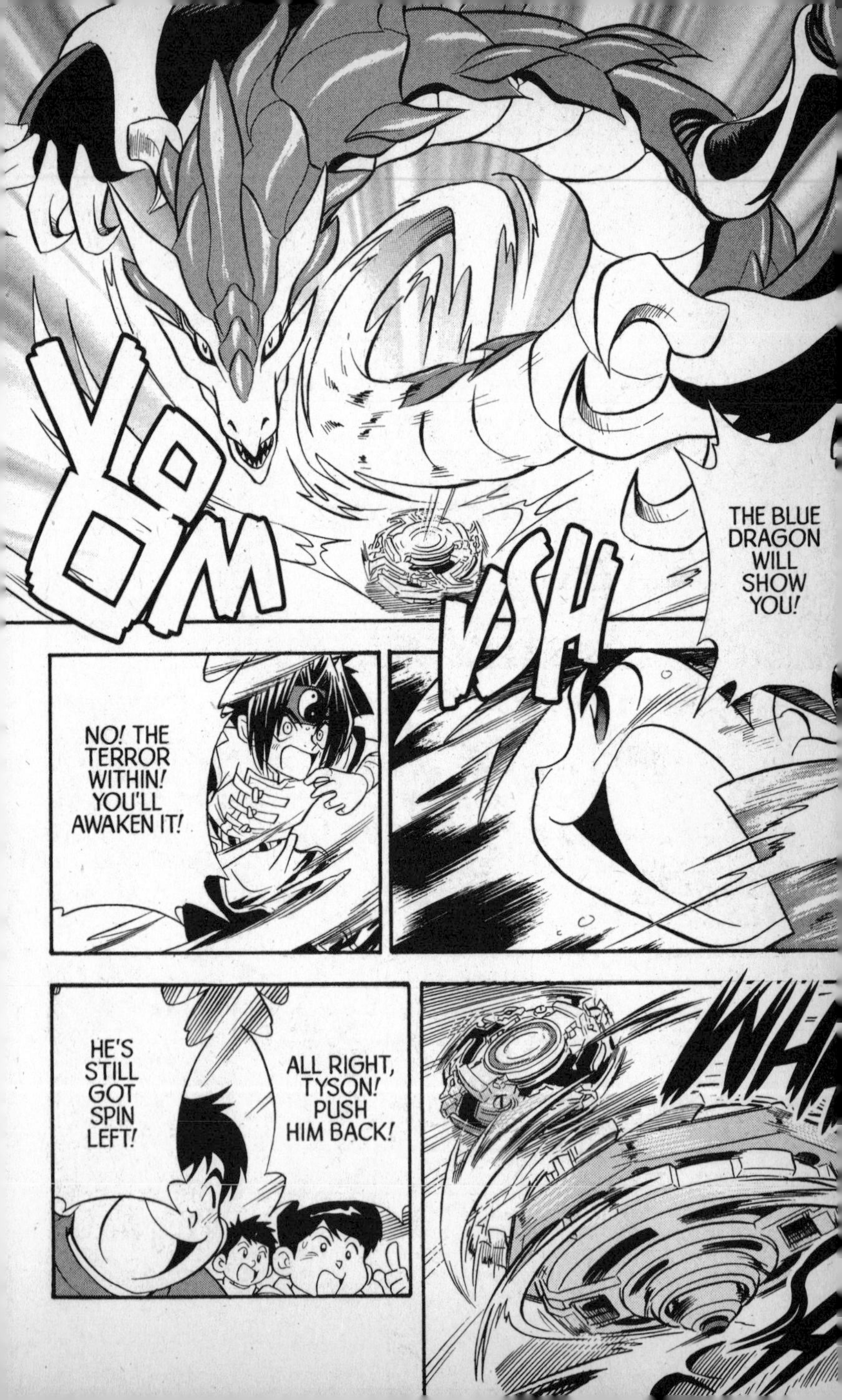
THE BLUE DRAGON WILL SHOW YOU!
VOOM
VSH
NO! THE TERROR WITHIN! YOU'LL AWAKEN IT!
ALL RIGHT, TYSON! PUSH HIM BACK!
HE'S STILL GOT SPIN LEFT!

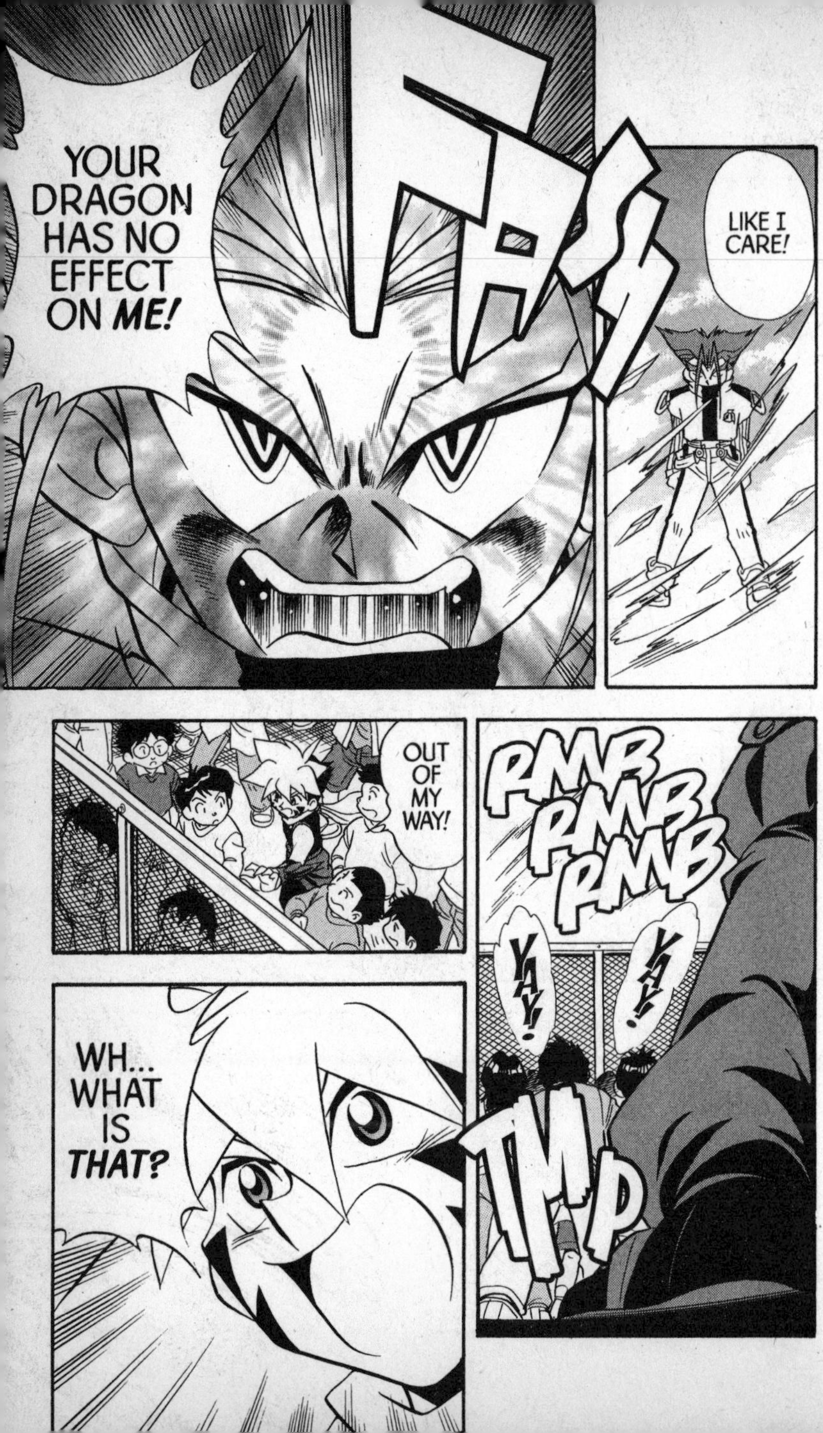
YOUR DRAGON HAS NO EFFECT ON *ME!*
LIKE I CARE!
OUT OF MY WAY!
WH... WHAT IS *THAT?*
RMB RMB RMB
YAY!
YAY!
TMP

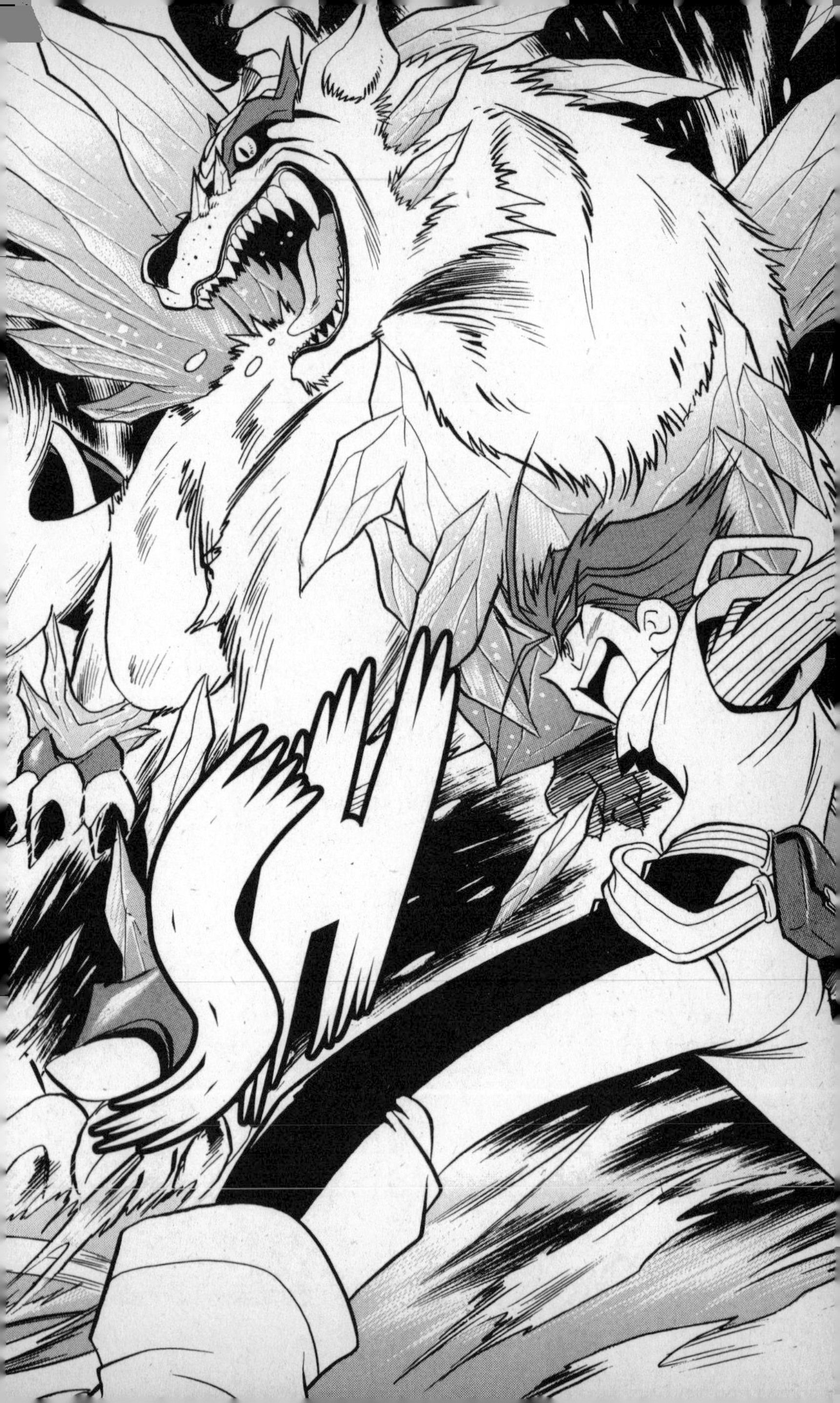

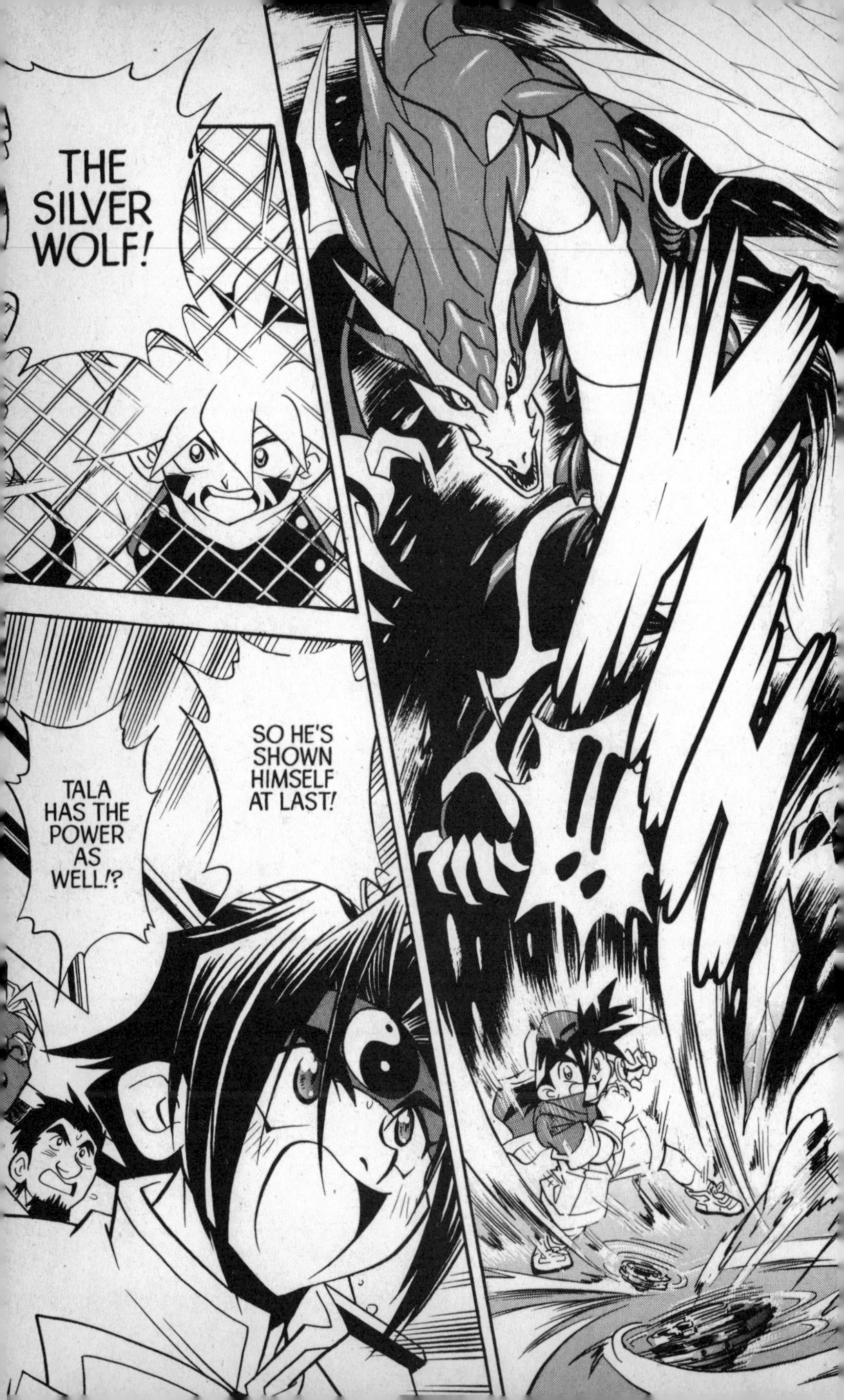
!!
THE SILVER WOLF!
SO HE'S SHOWN HIMSELF AT LAST!
TALA HAS THE POWER AS WELL!?

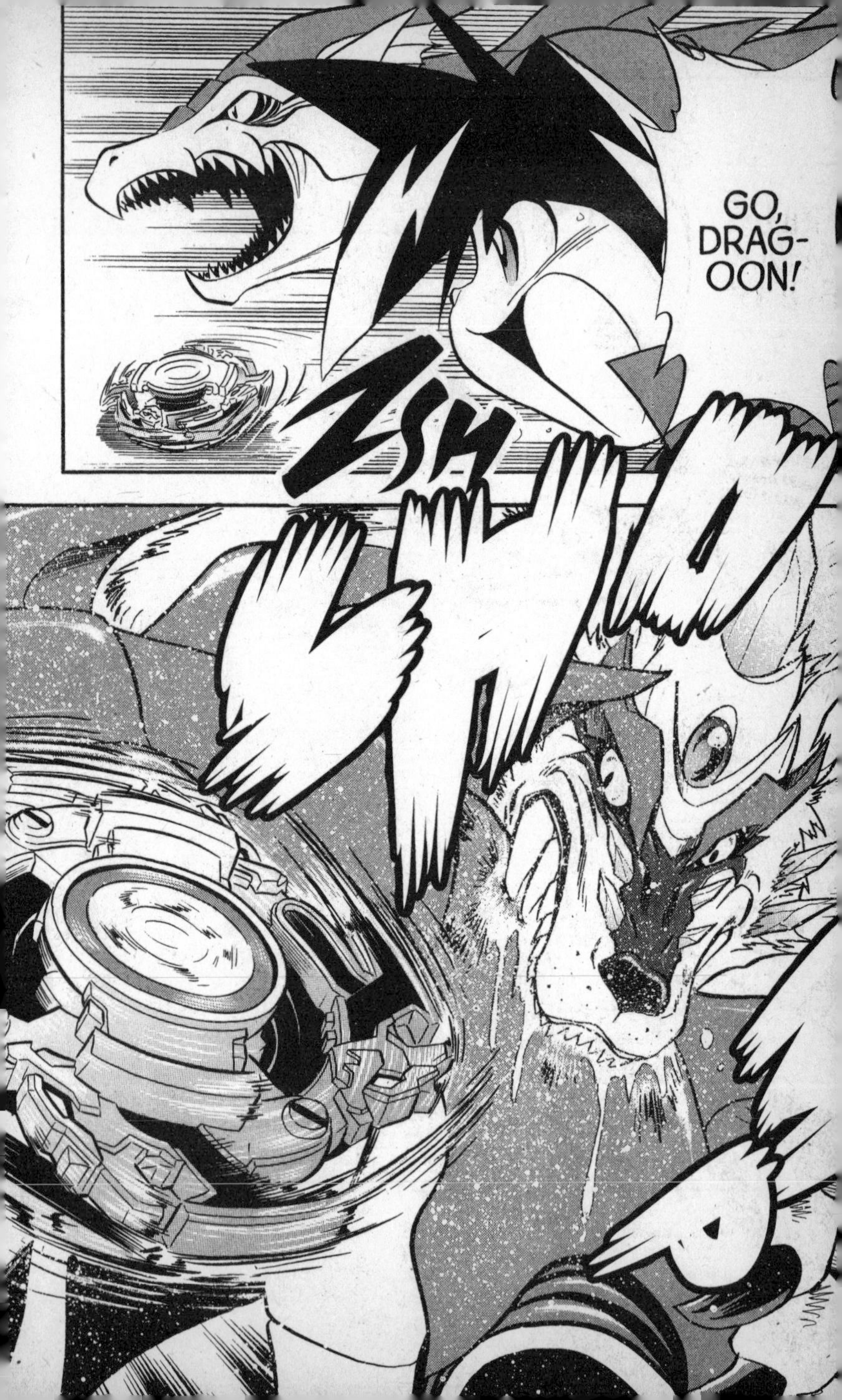
GO, DRAG-OON!

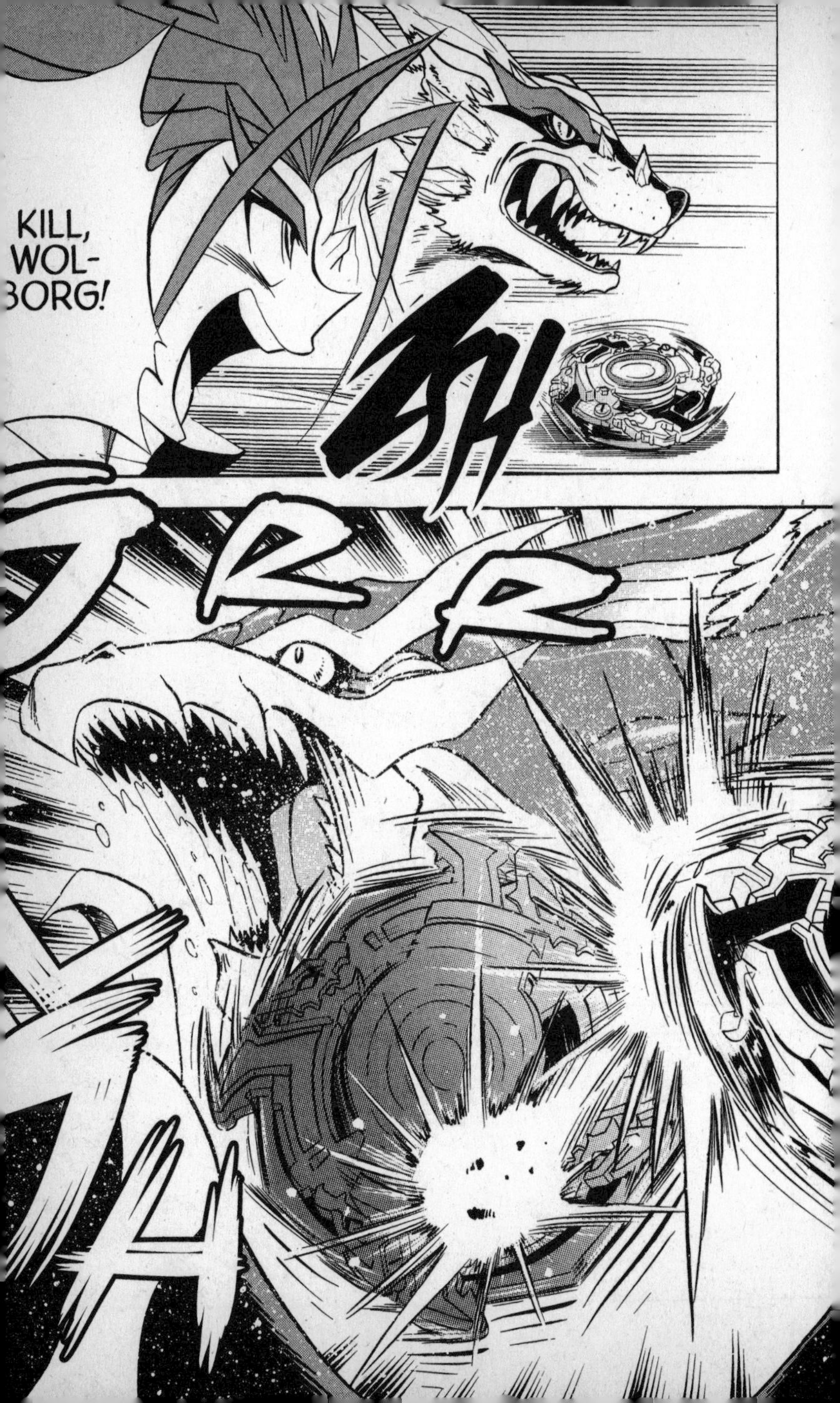
KILL, WOL-BORG!
SH
ZRR
GA

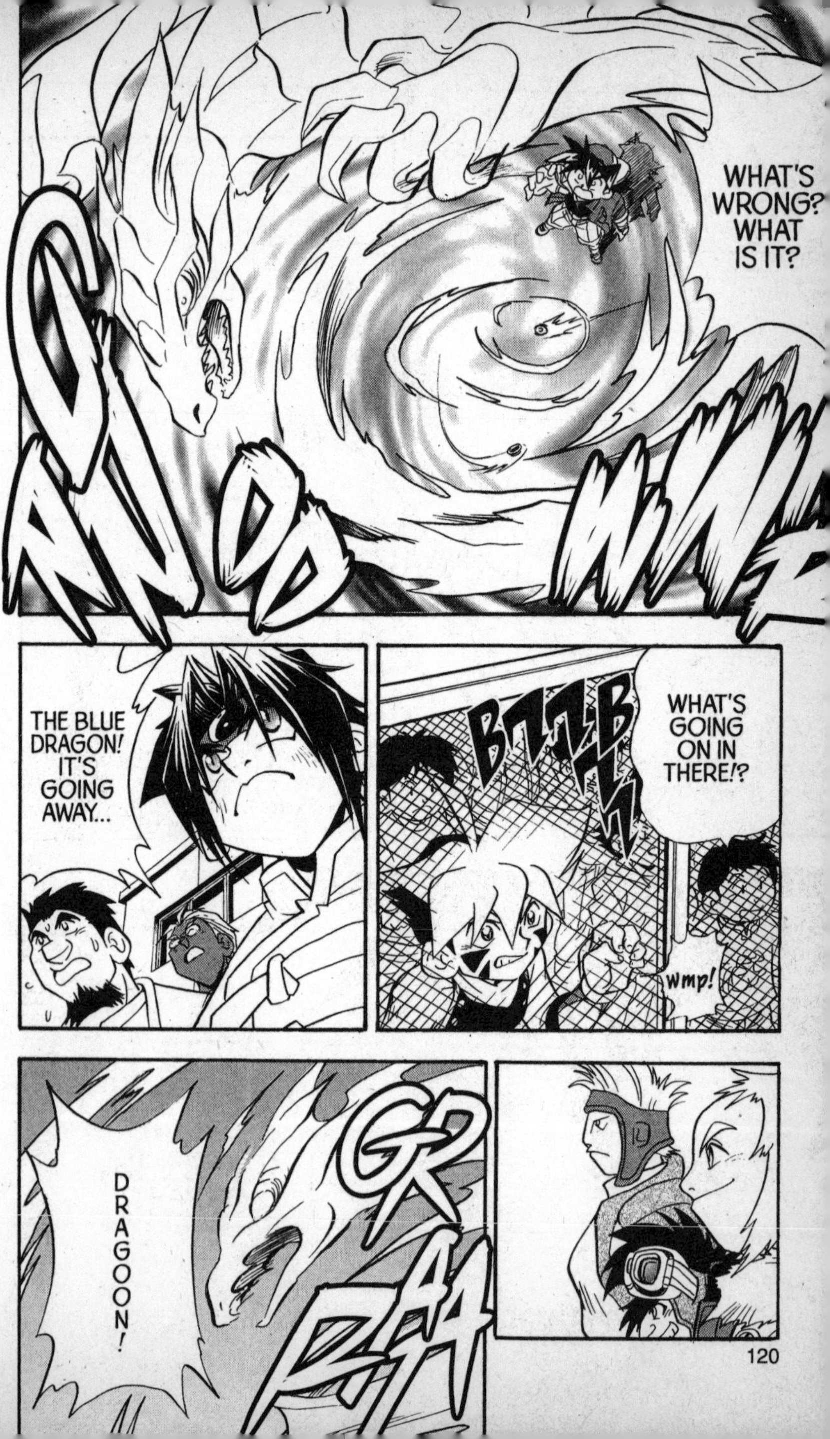
WHAT'S WRONG? WHAT IS IT?
WHAT'S GOING ON IN THERE!?
wmp!
THE BLUE DRAGON! IT'S GOING AWAY...
DRAGOON!

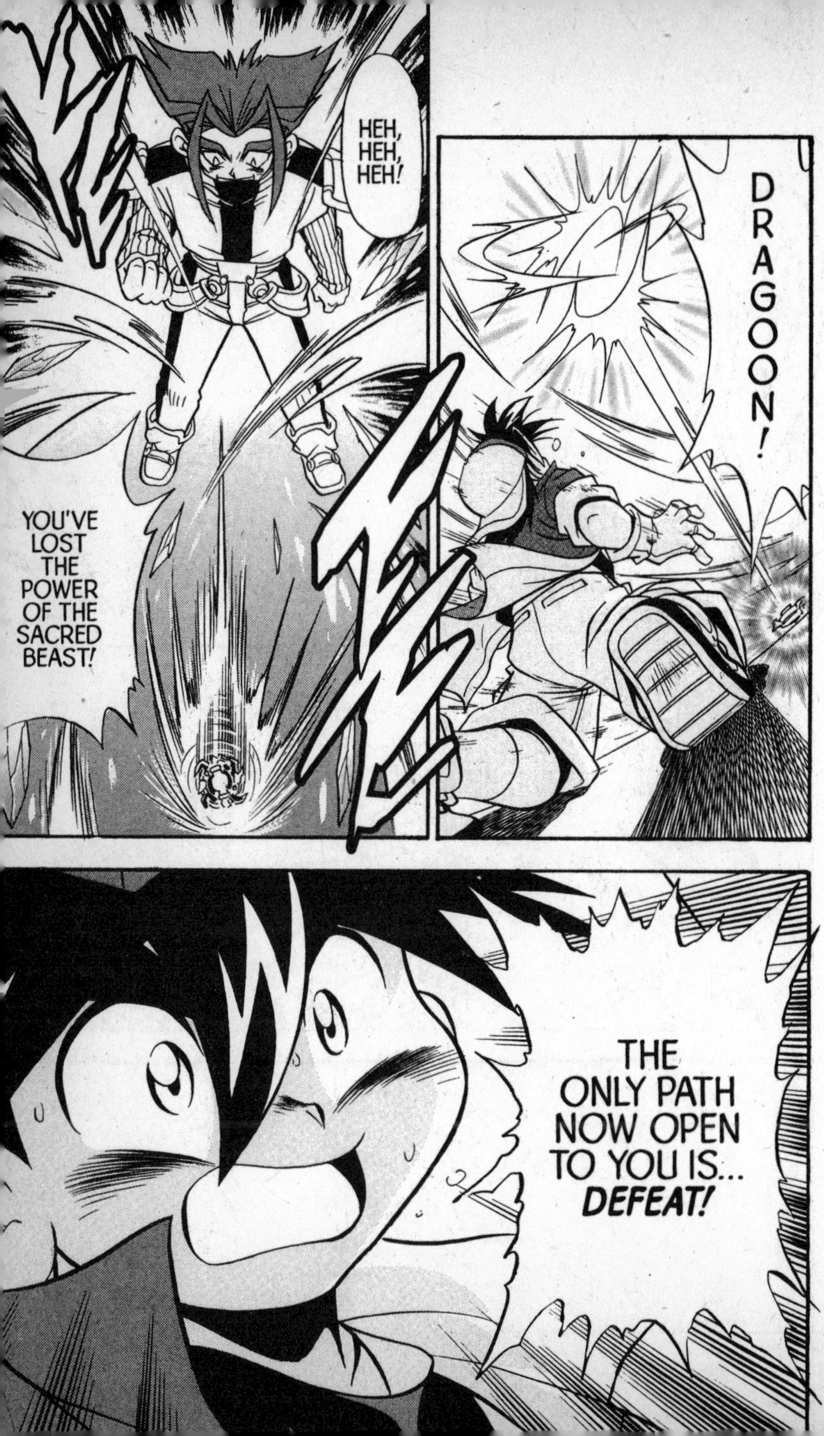
DRAGOOON!
HEH, HEH, HEH!
YOU'VE LOST THE POWER OF THE SACRED BEAST!
THE ONLY PATH NOW OPEN TO YOU IS... *DEFEAT!*

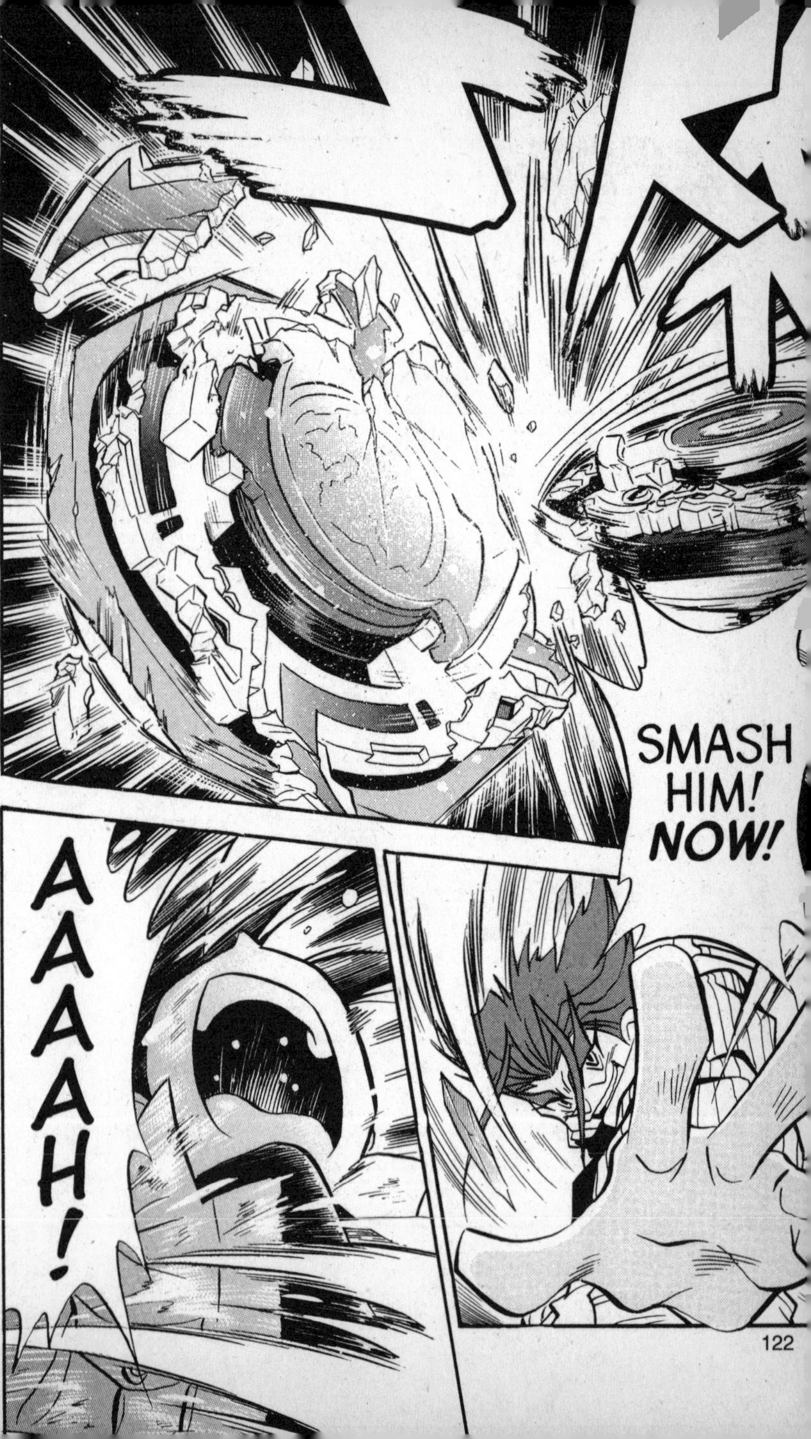
SMASH HIM! NOW!
AAAAAH!

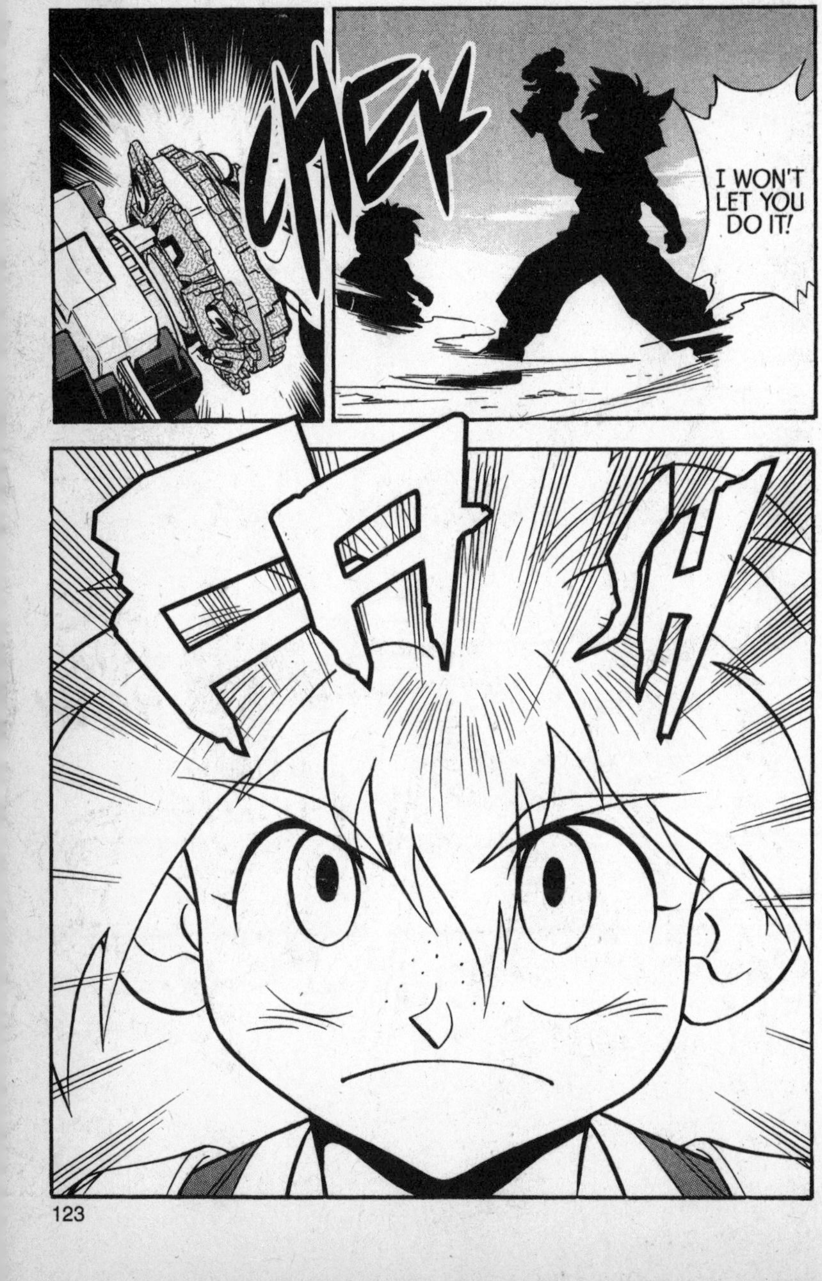
I WON'T LET YOU DO IT!

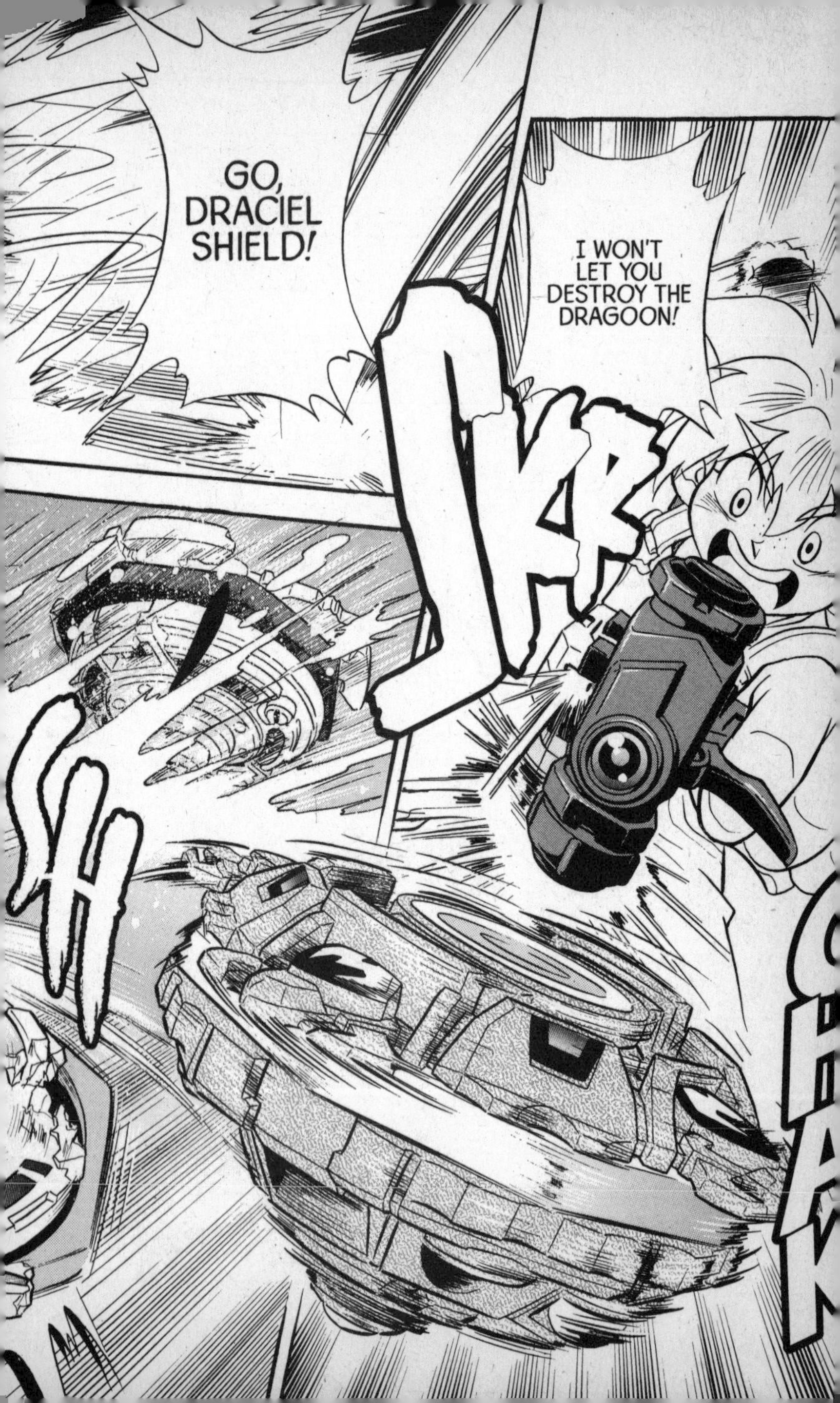
I WON'T LET YOU DESTROY THE DRAGOON!
GO, DRACIEL SHIELD!

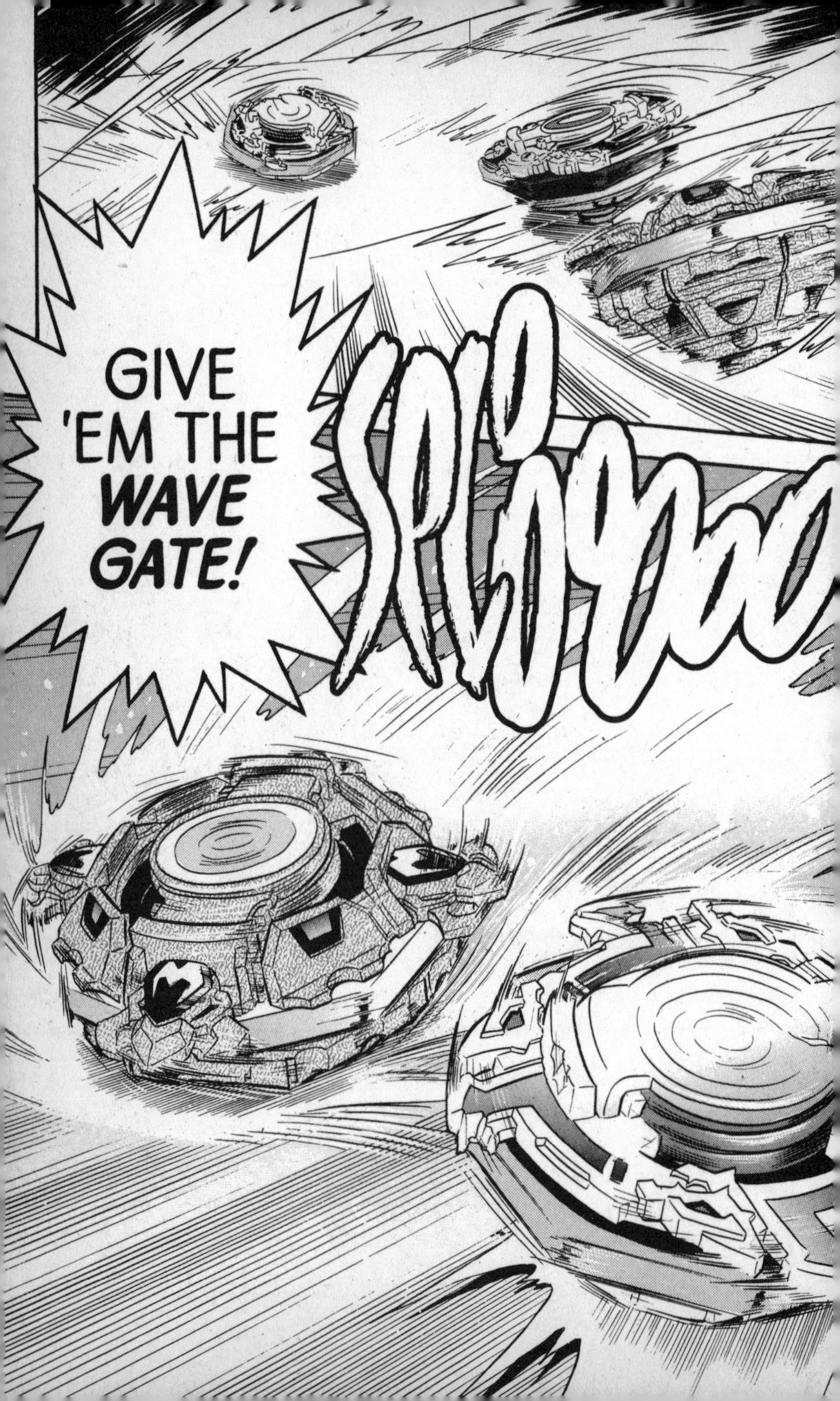
GIVE 'EM THE ***WAVE GATE!***

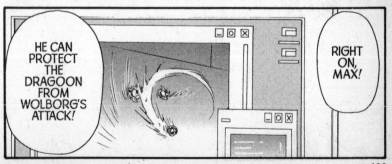

HE CAN PROTECT THE DRAGOON FROM WOLBORG'S ATTACK!

RIGHT ON, MAX!

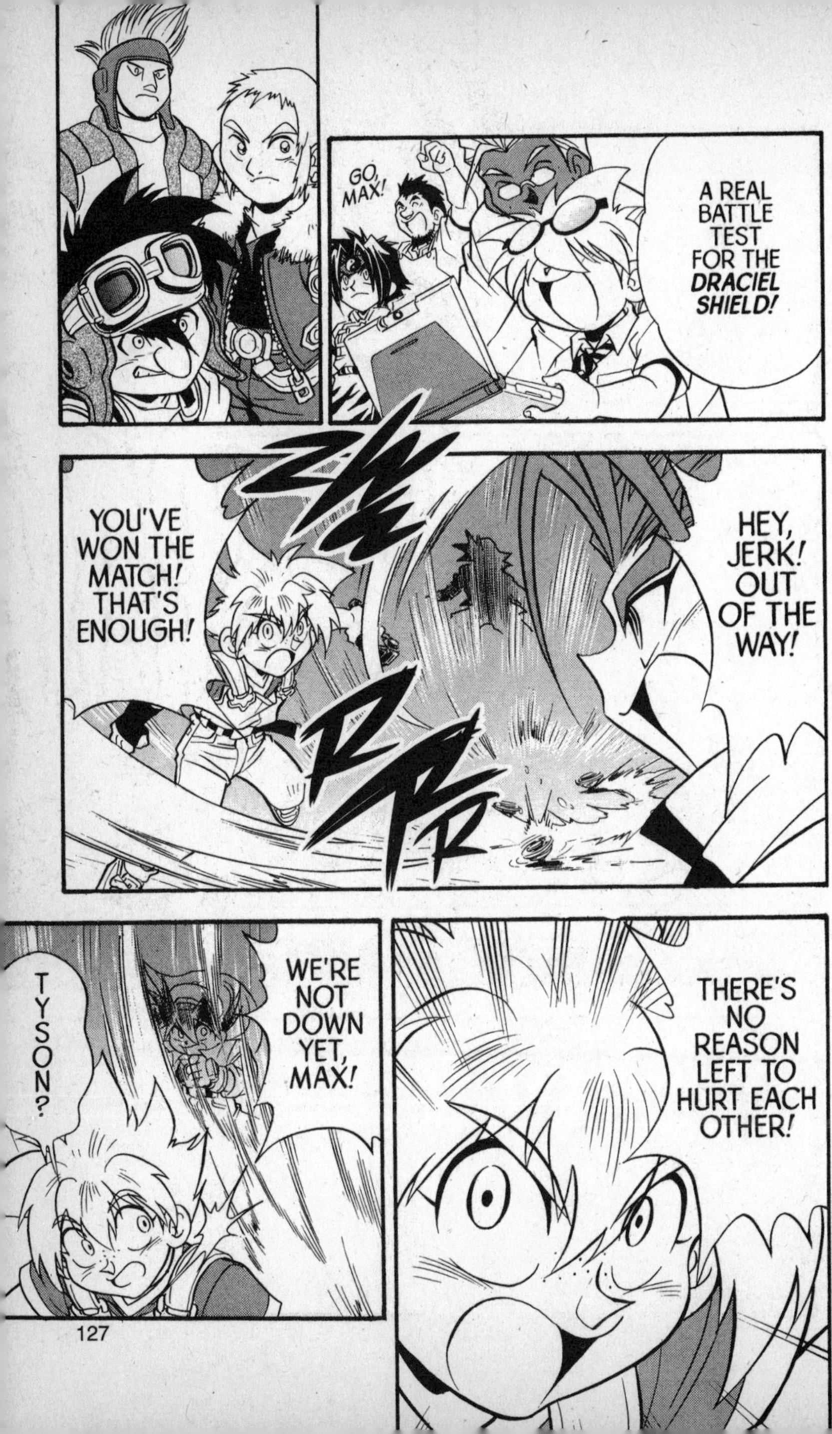
A REAL BATTLE TEST FOR THE DRACIEL SHIELD!
GO, MAX!
HEY, JERK! OUT OF THE WAY!
YOU'VE WON THE MATCH! THAT'S ENOUGH!
THERE'S NO REASON LEFT TO HURT EACH OTHER!
WE'RE NOT DOWN YET, MAX!
TYSON?

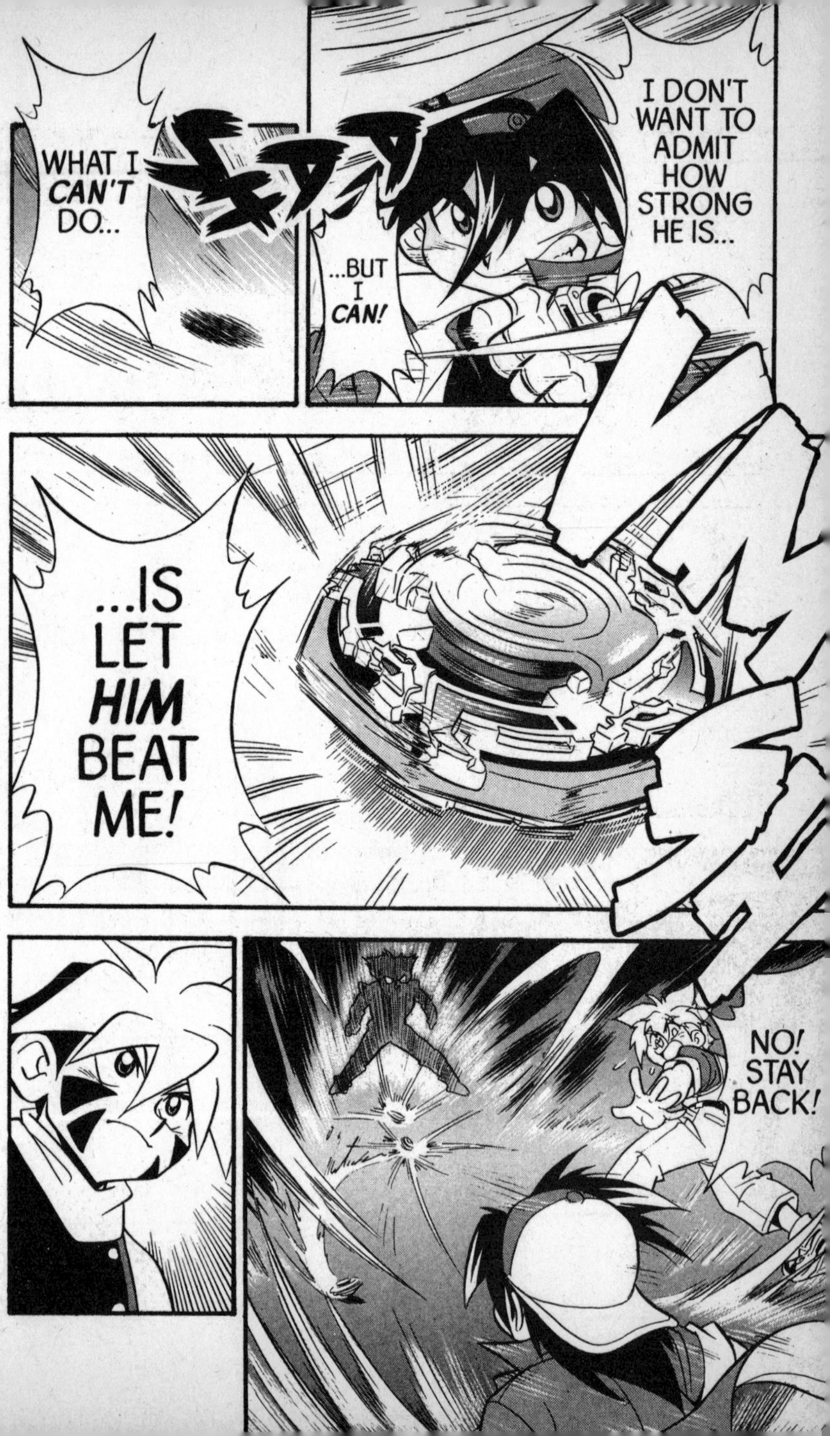
I DON'T WANT TO ADMIT HOW STRONG HE IS...
...BUT I *CAN!*
WHAT I *CAN'T* DO...
...IS LET ***HIM*** BEAT ME!
NO! STAY BACK!

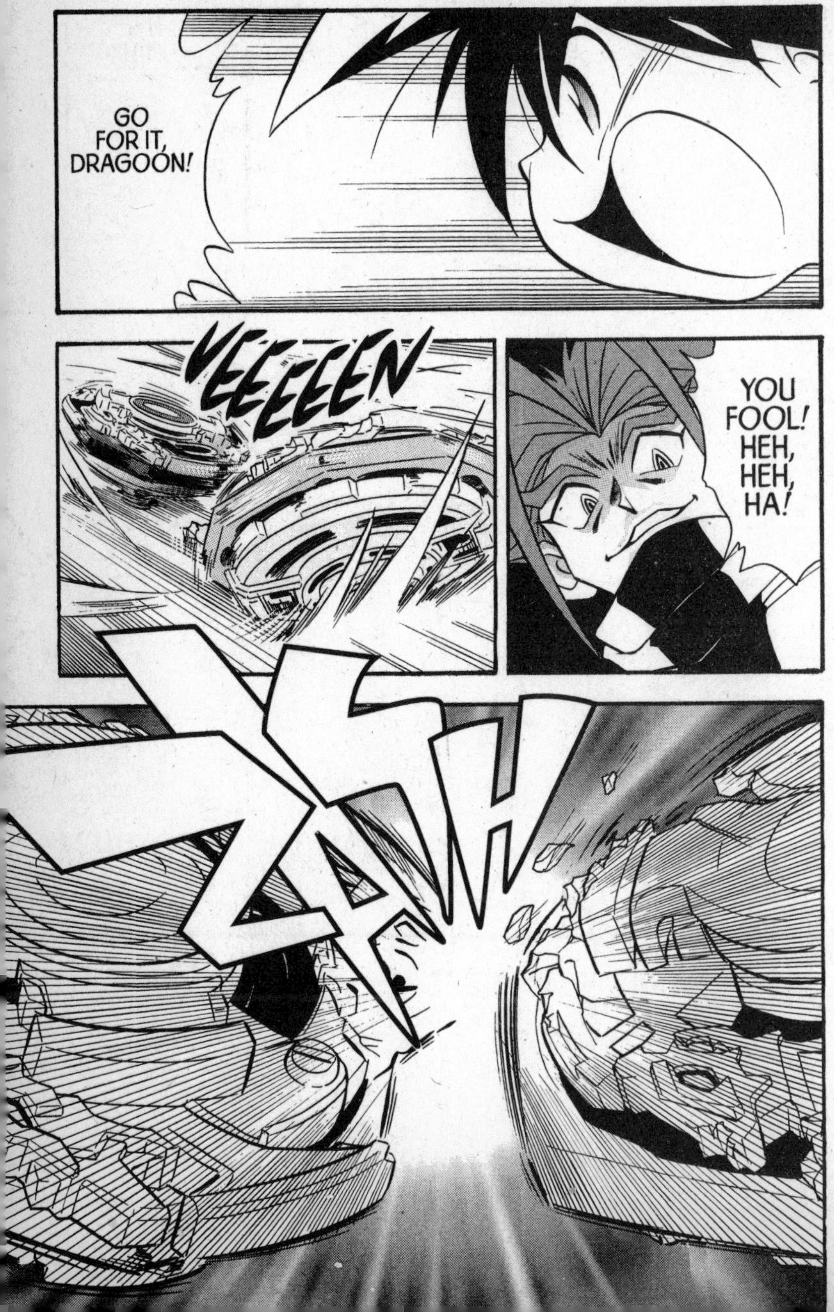
GO FOR IT, DRAGOON!
YOU FOOL! HEH, HEH, HA!
VEEEEEN
ZAAH

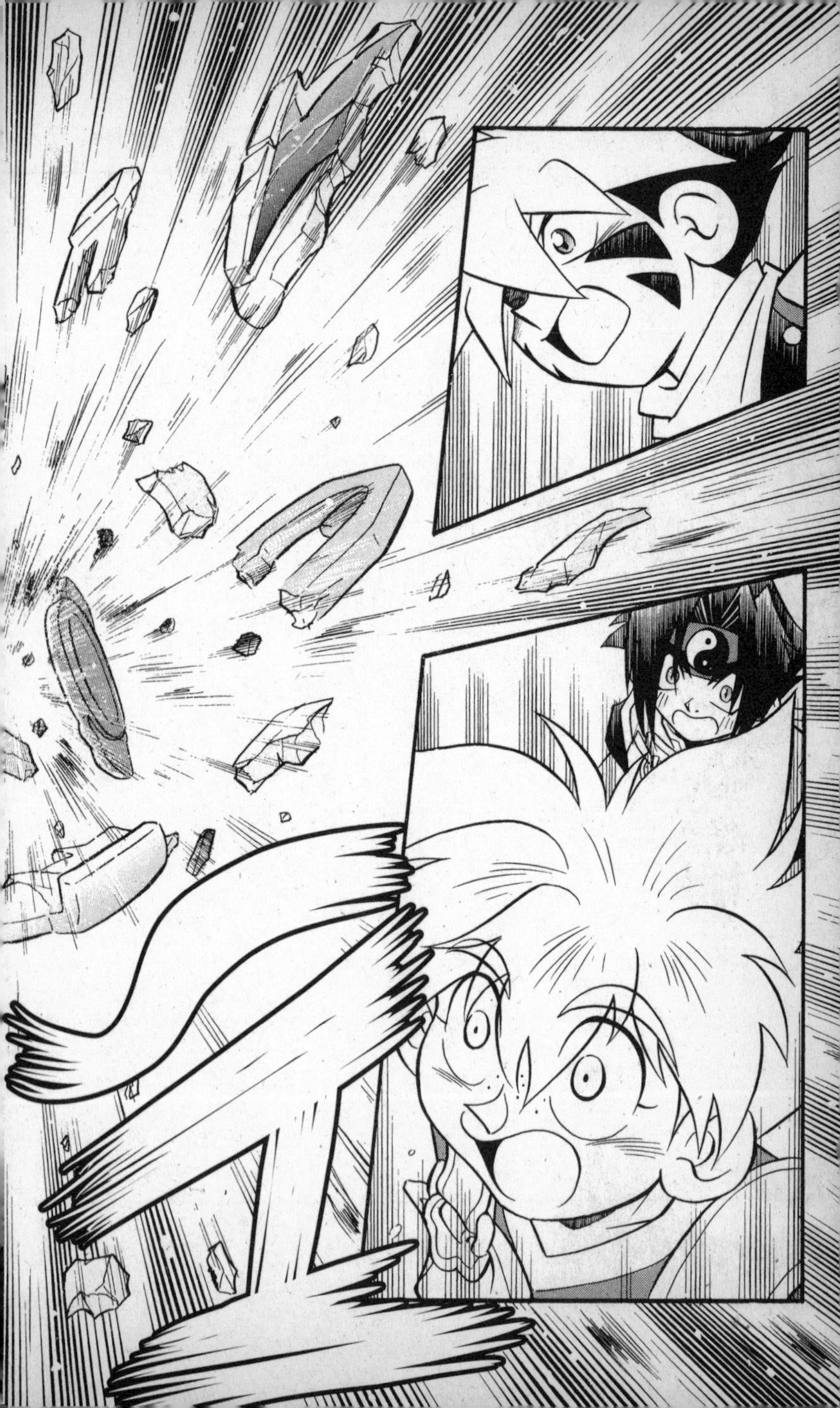

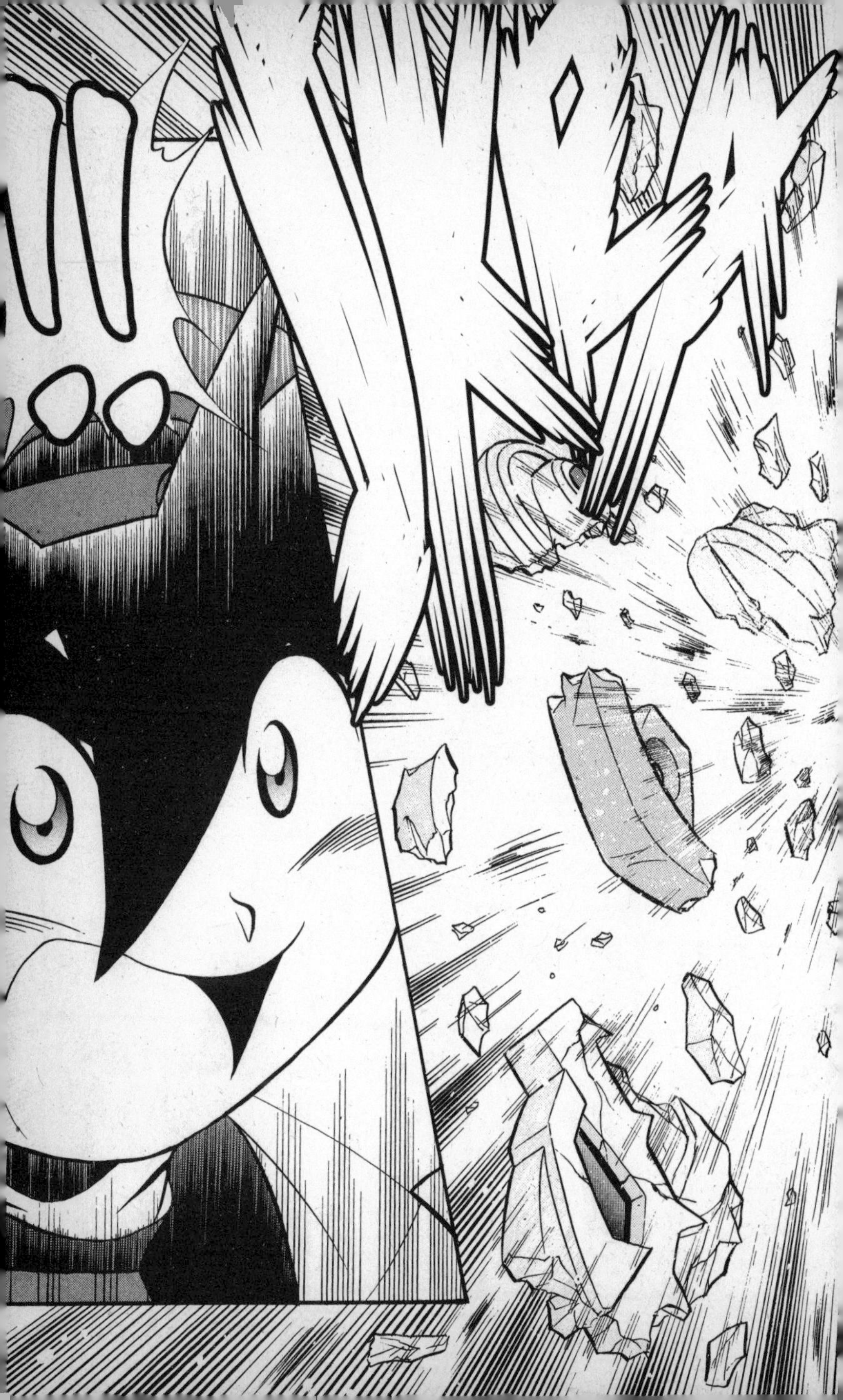

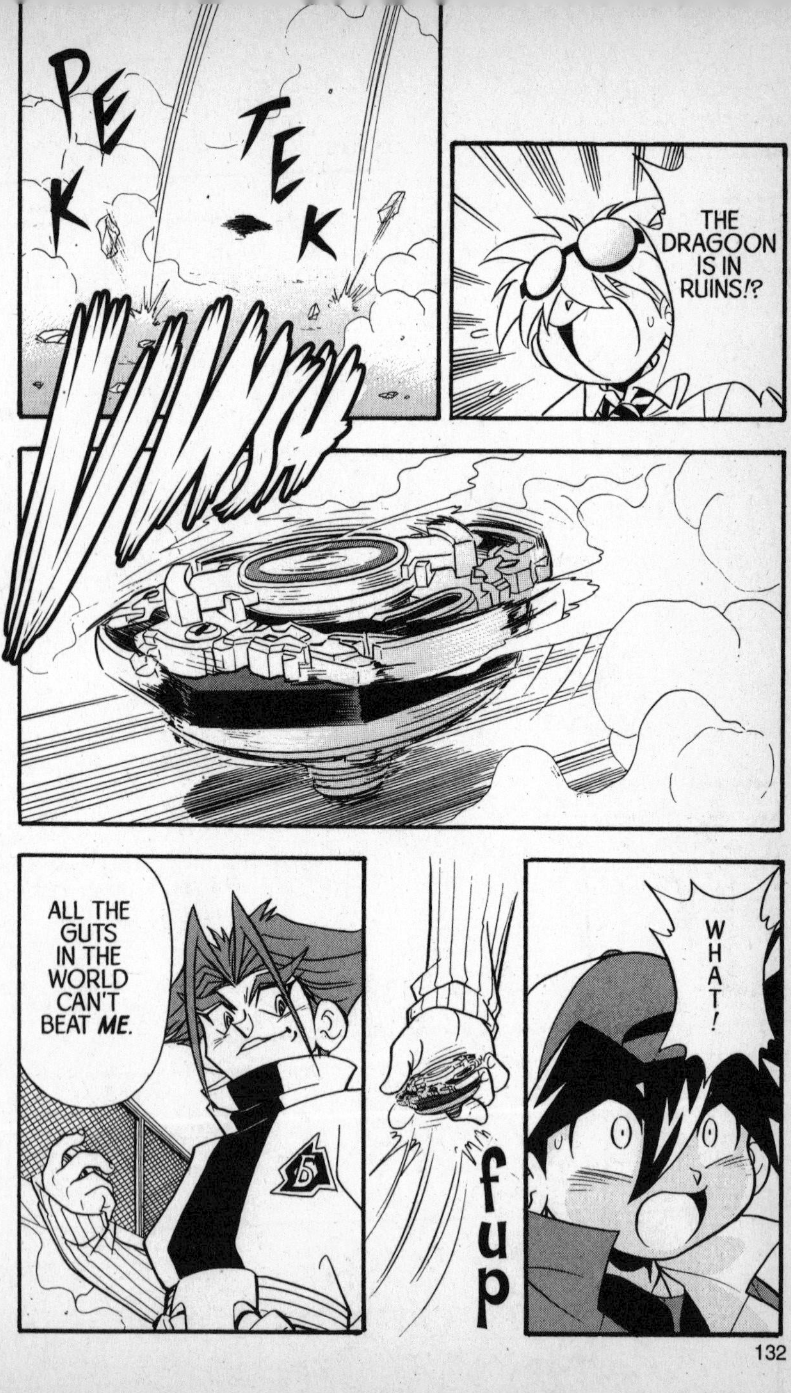
THE DRAGOON IS IN RUINS!?
PEK
TEK
WHAT!
fup
ALL THE GUTS IN THE WORLD CAN'T BEAT *ME*.

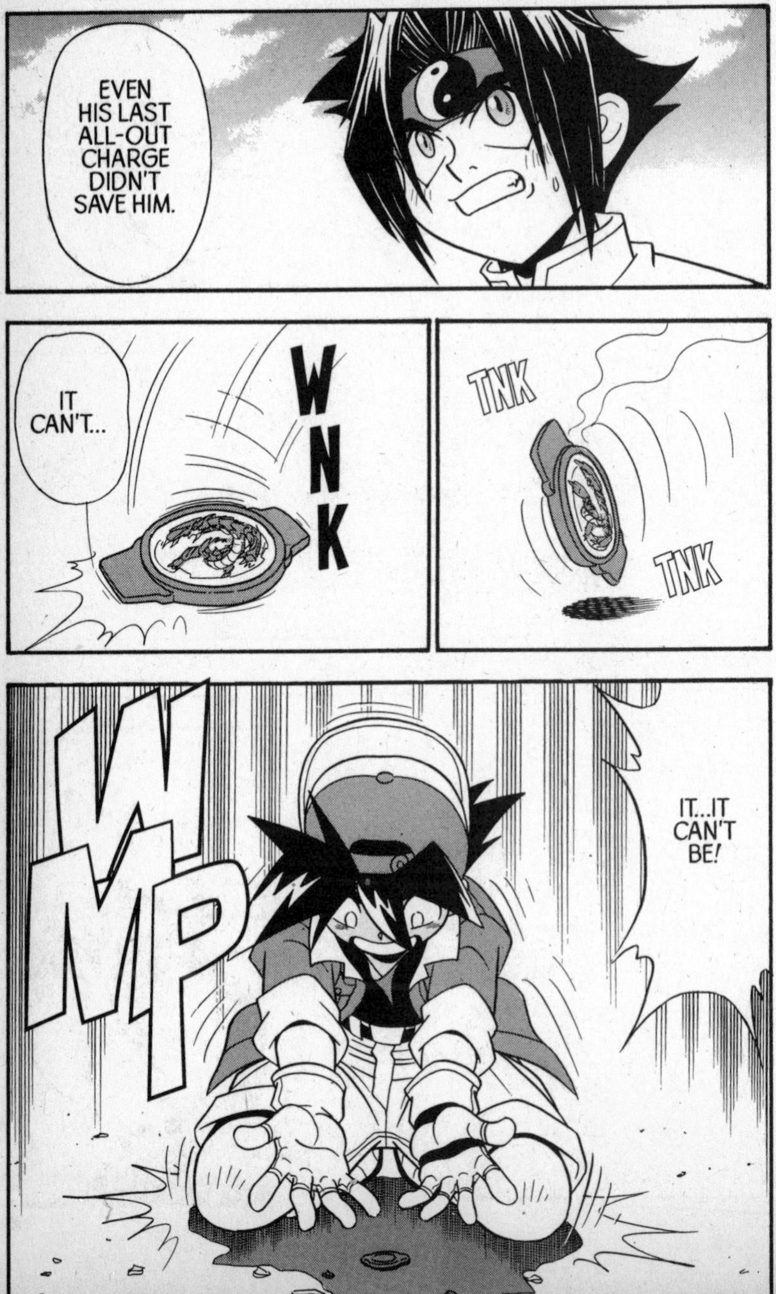
EVEN HIS LAST ALL-OUT CHARGE DIDN'T SAVE HIM.
TNK
TNK
WNK
IT CAN'T...
WMP
IT...IT CAN'T BE!

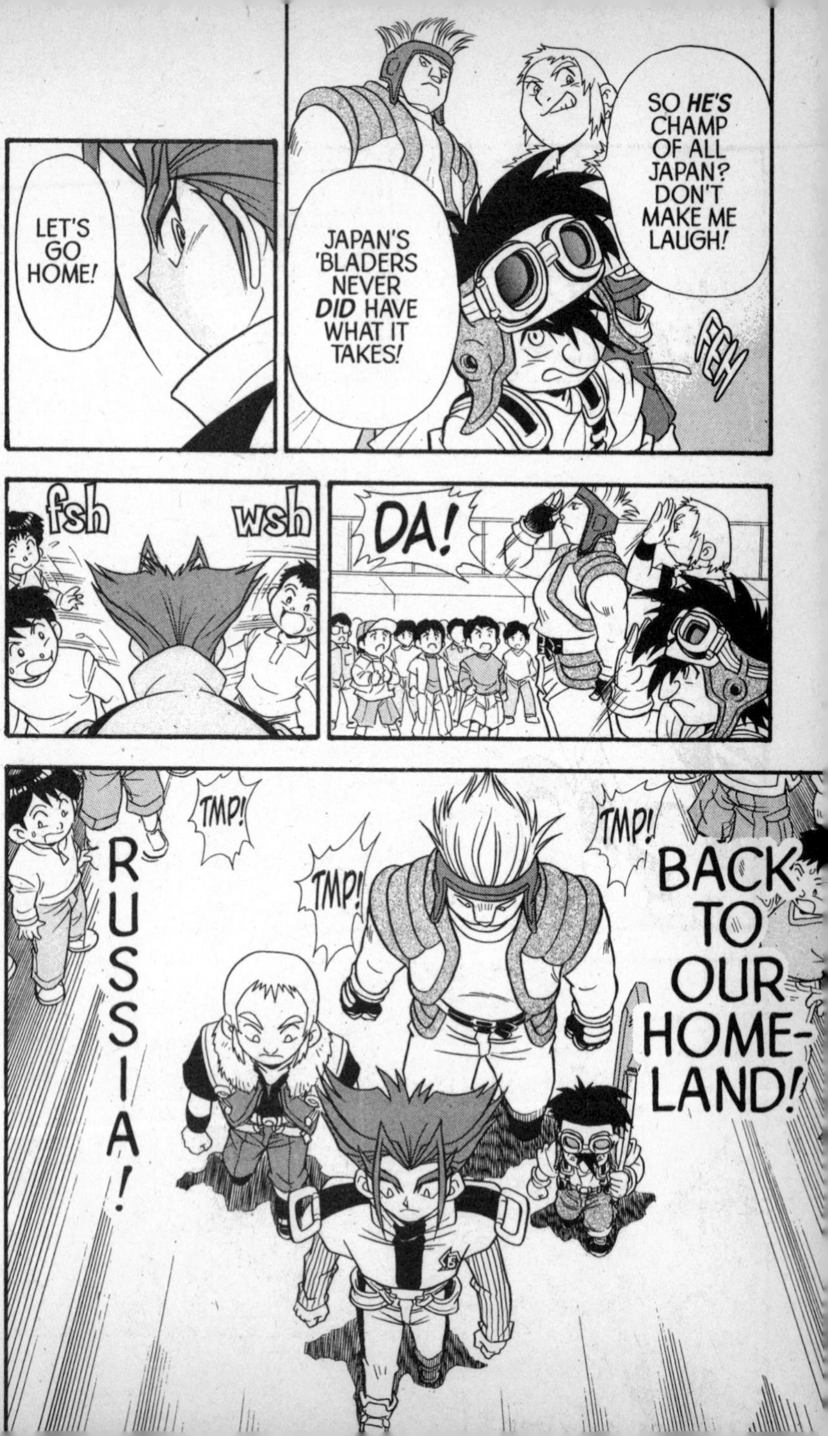
SO HE'S CHAMP OF ALL JAPAN? DON'T MAKE ME LAUGH!
FEH
JAPAN'S 'BLADERS NEVER DID HAVE WHAT IT TAKES!
LET'S GO HOME!
DA!
wsh
fsh
TMP!
TMP!
TMP!
BACK TO OUR HOME-LAND!
RUSSIA!

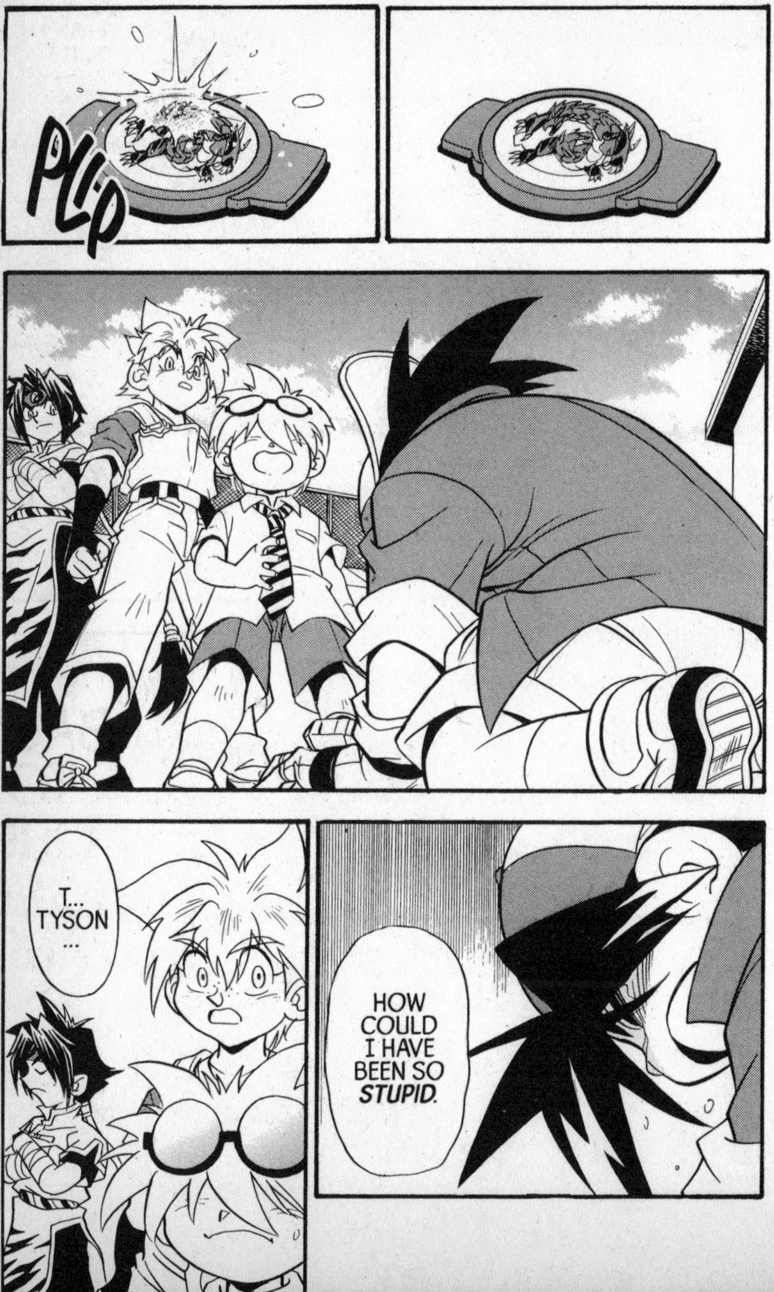
PLIP
HOW COULD I HAVE BEEN SO *STUPID*.
T... TYSON ...

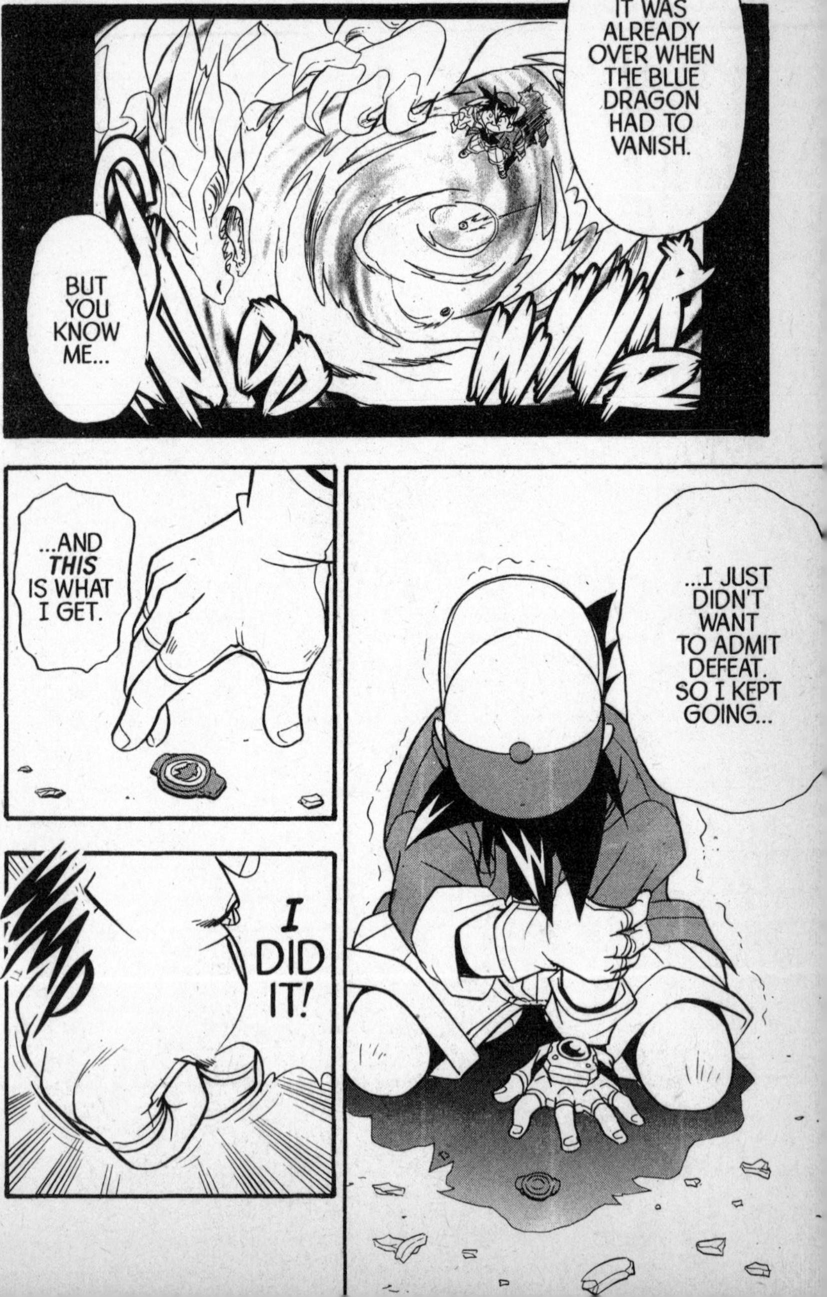
IT WAS ALREADY OVER WHEN THE BLUE DRAGON HAD TO VANISH.
BUT YOU KNOW ME...
...I JUST DIDN'T WANT TO ADMIT DEFEAT. SO I KEPT GOING...
...AND *THIS* IS WHAT I GET.
I DID IT!

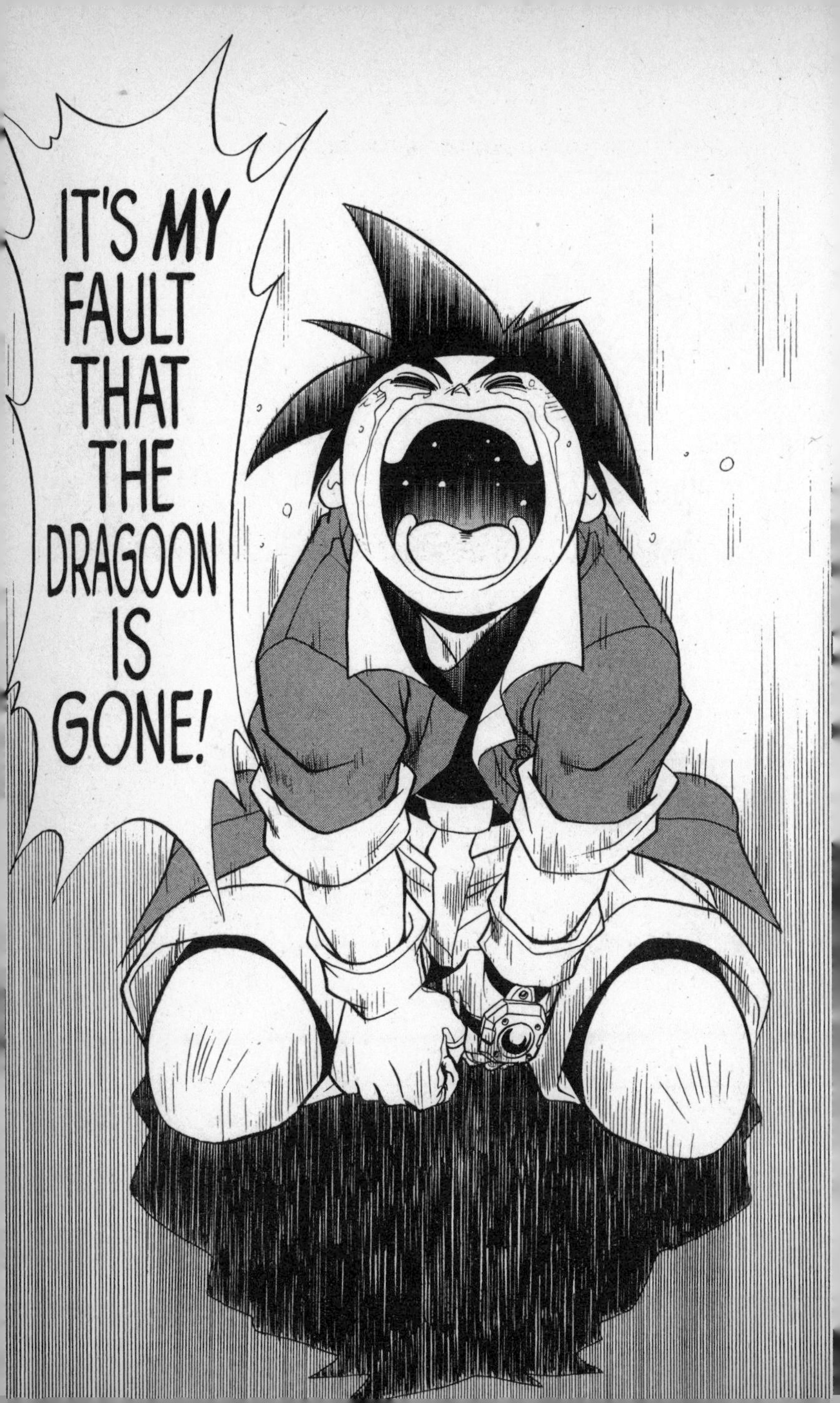
IT'S MY FAULT THAT THE DRAGOON IS GONE!

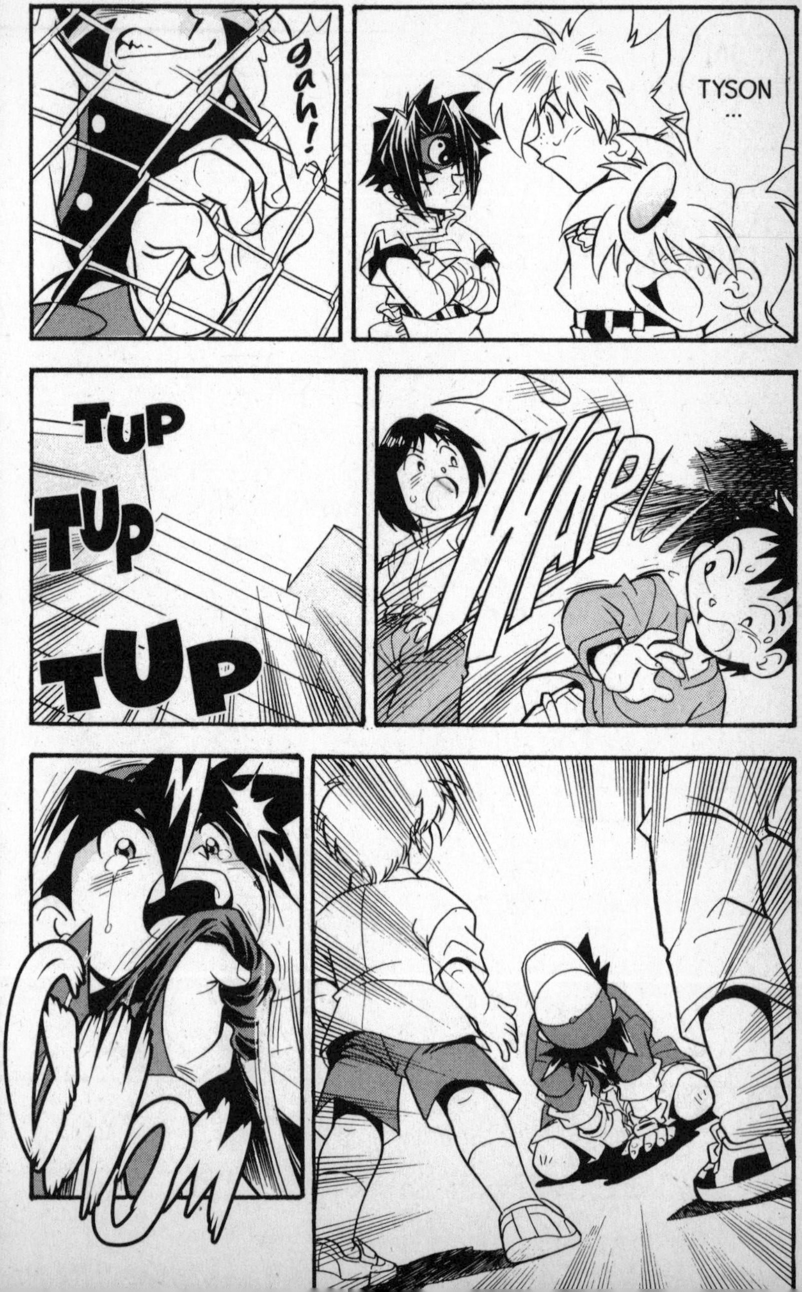
TYSON
...
gah!
WAP!
TUP
TUP
TUP

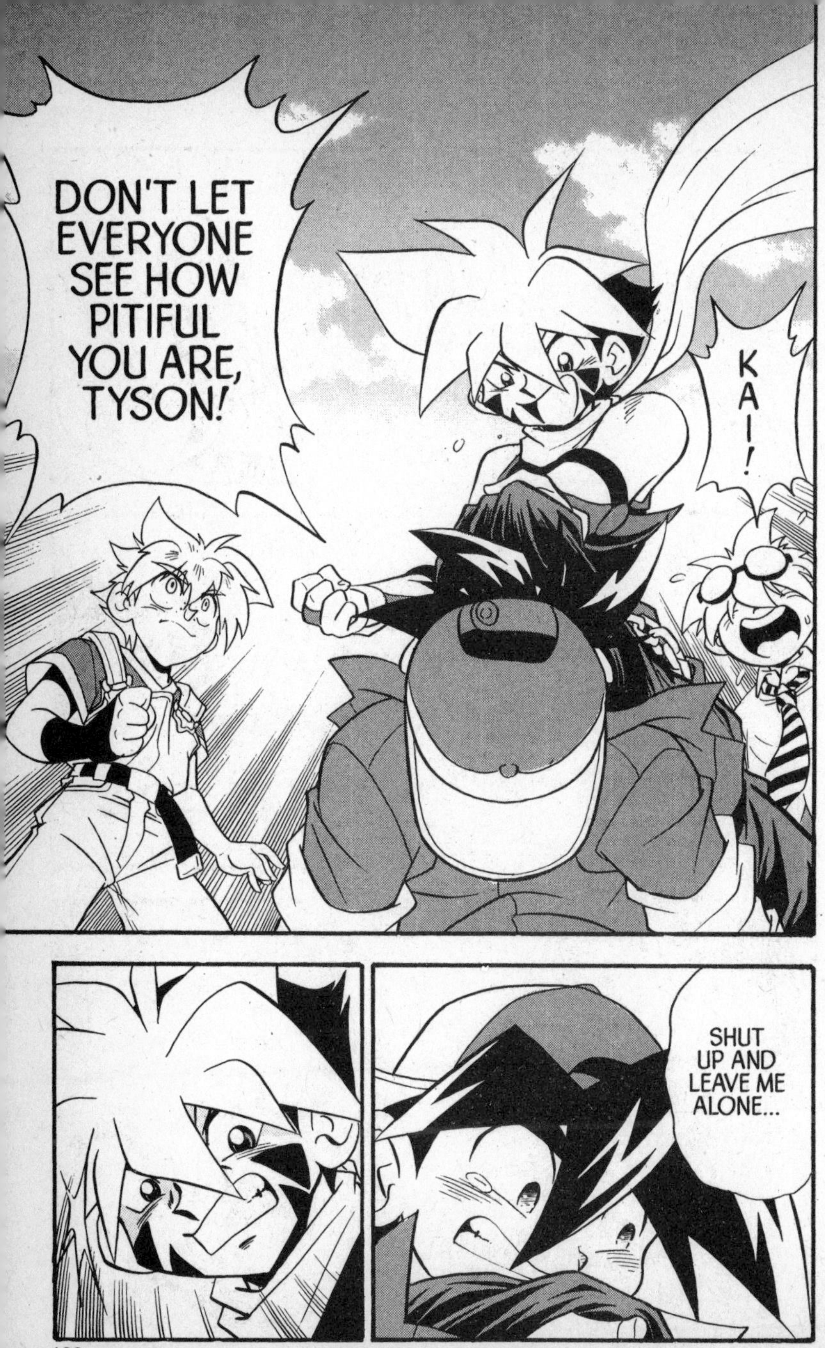
DON'T LET EVERYONE SEE HOW PITIFUL YOU ARE, TYSON!
KAI!
SHUT UP AND LEAVE ME ALONE...

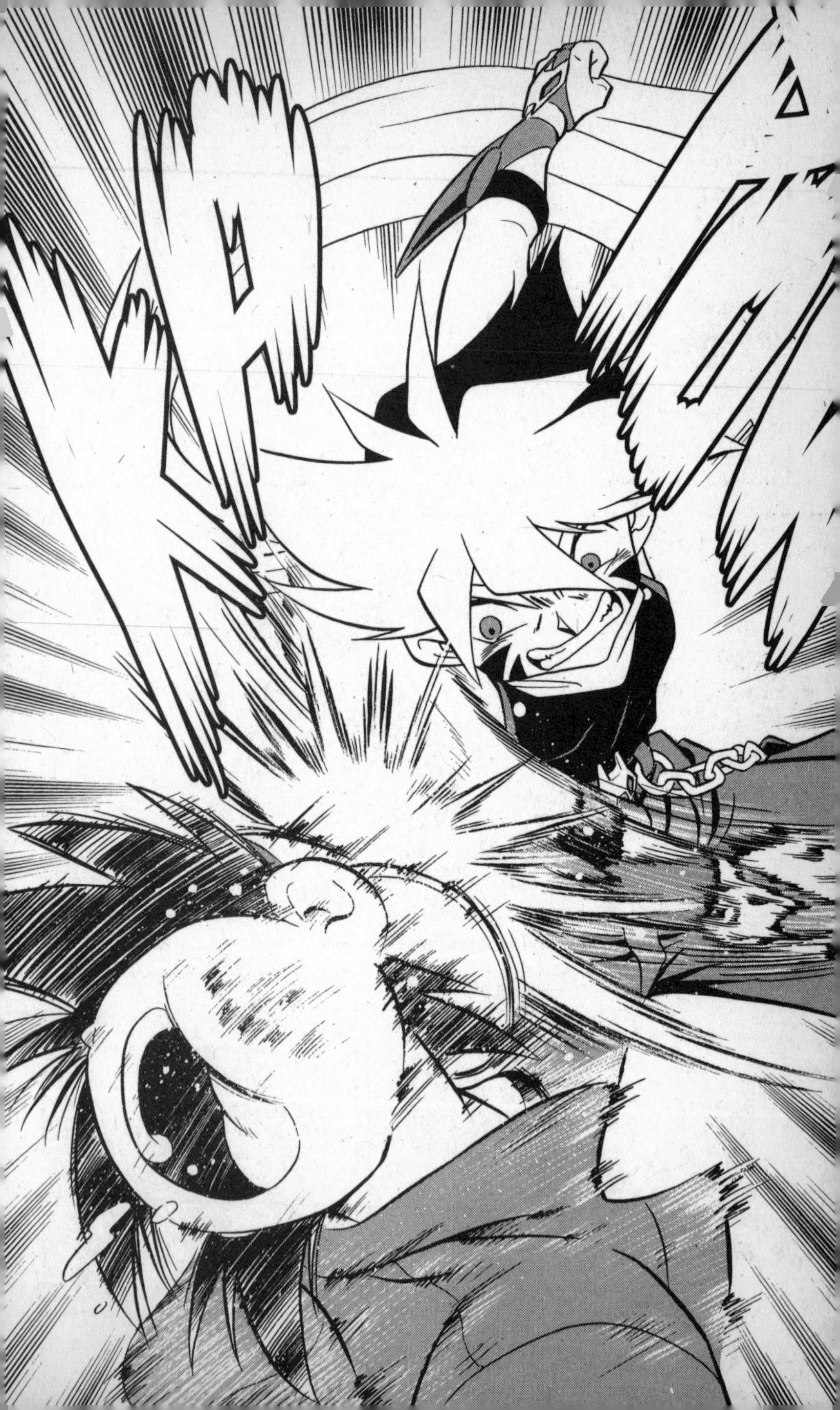

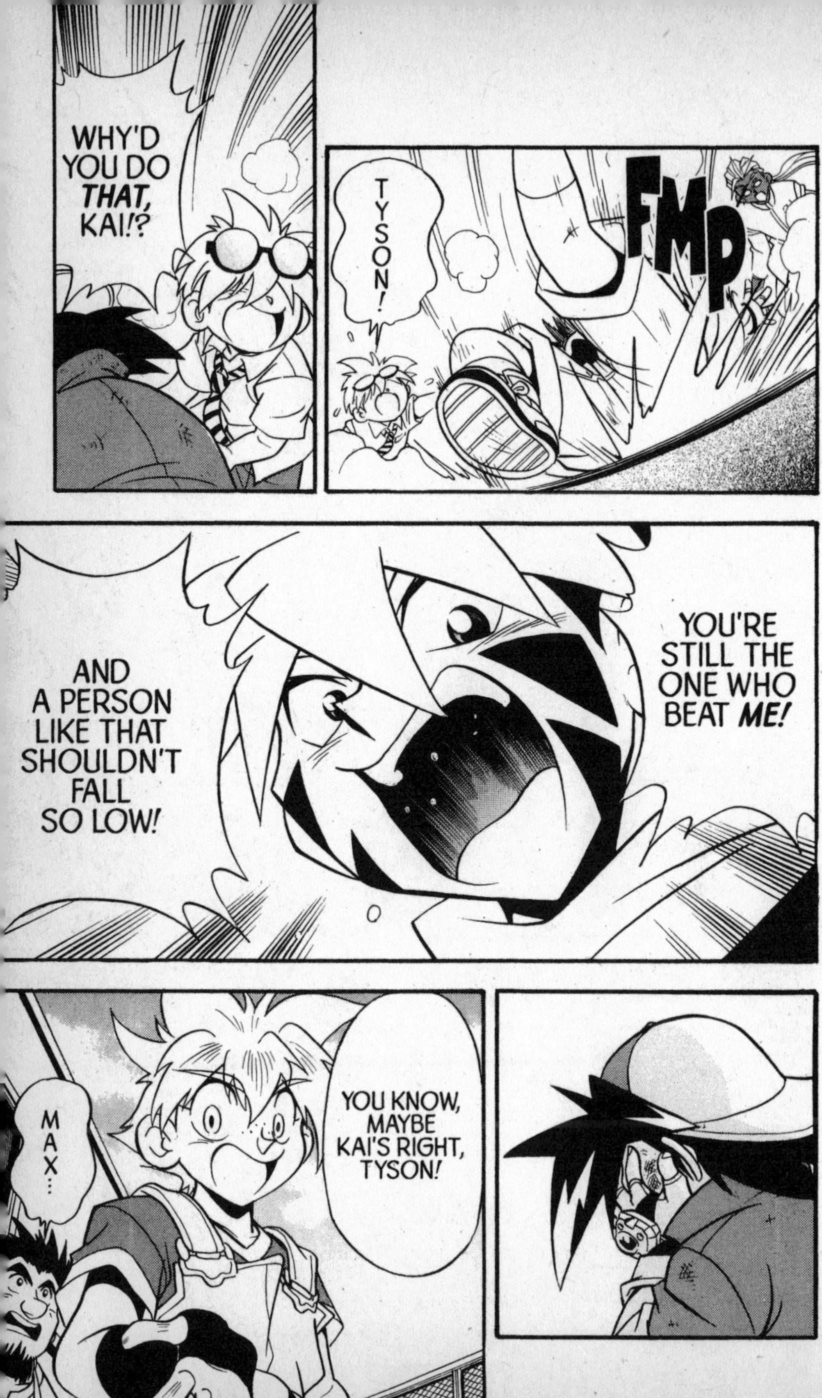
TYSON!
FMP
WHY'D YOU DO *THAT,* KAI!?
YOU'RE STILL THE ONE WHO BEAT *ME!*
AND A PERSON LIKE THAT SHOULDN'T FALL SO LOW!
YOU KNOW, MAYBE KAI'S RIGHT, TYSON!
MAX...

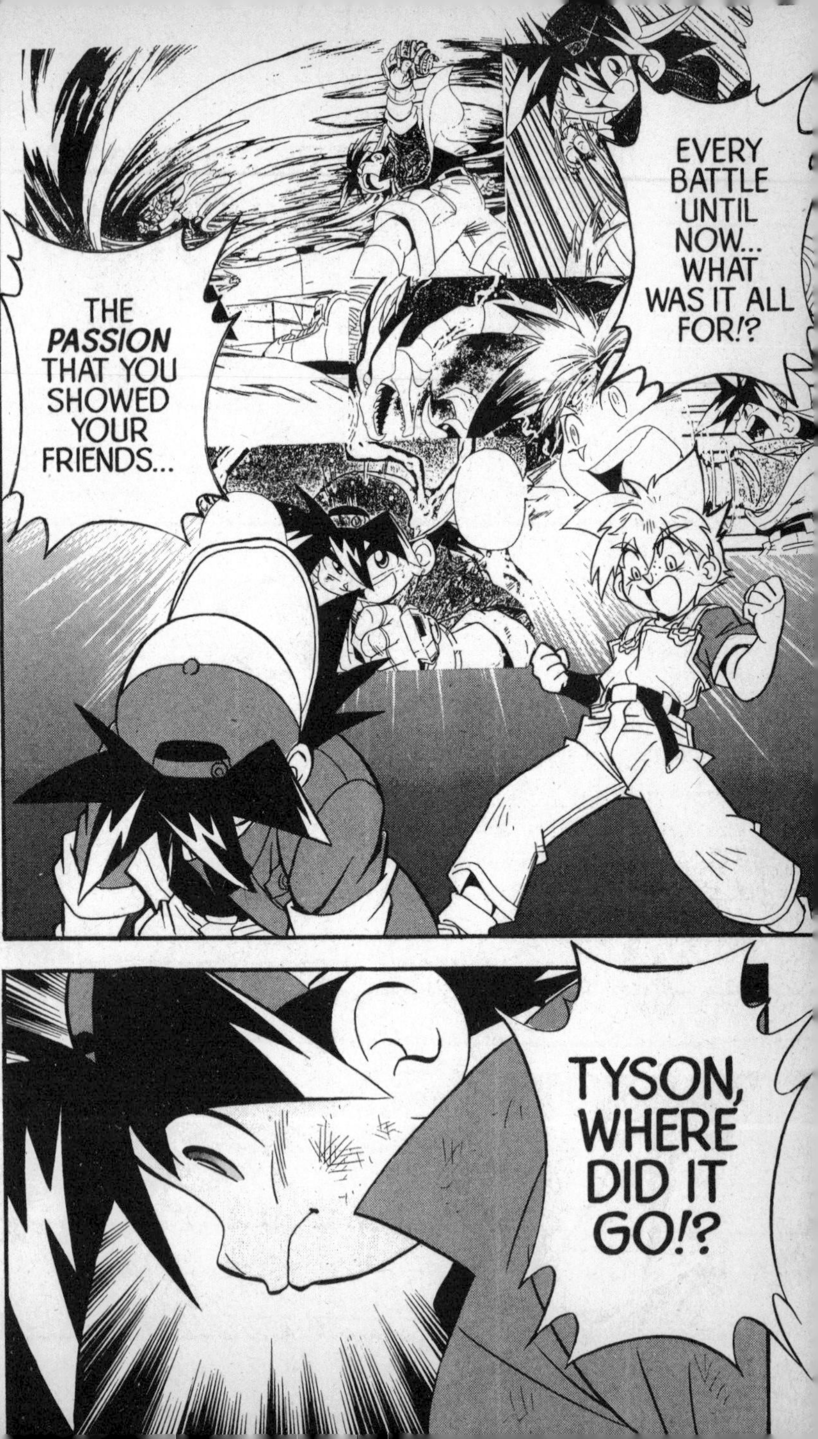
EVERY BATTLE UNTIL NOW... WHAT WAS IT ALL FOR!?
THE *PASSION* THAT YOU SHOWED YOUR FRIENDS...
TYSON, WHERE DID IT GO!?

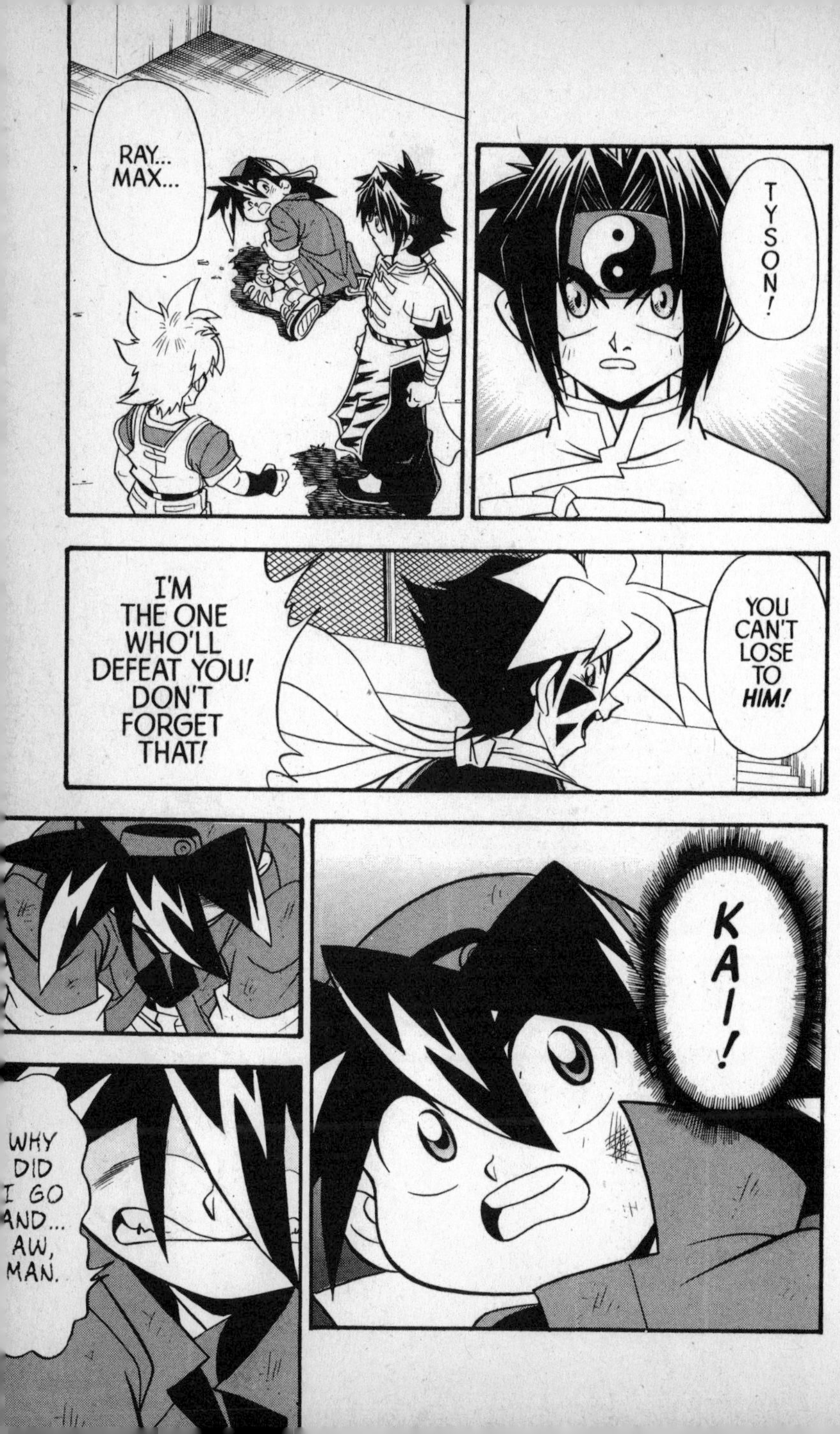
RAY... MAX...
TYSON!
I'M THE ONE WHO'LL DEFEAT YOU! DON'T FORGET THAT!
YOU CAN'T LOSE TO *HIM!*
WHY DID I GO AND... AW, MAN.
KAI!!

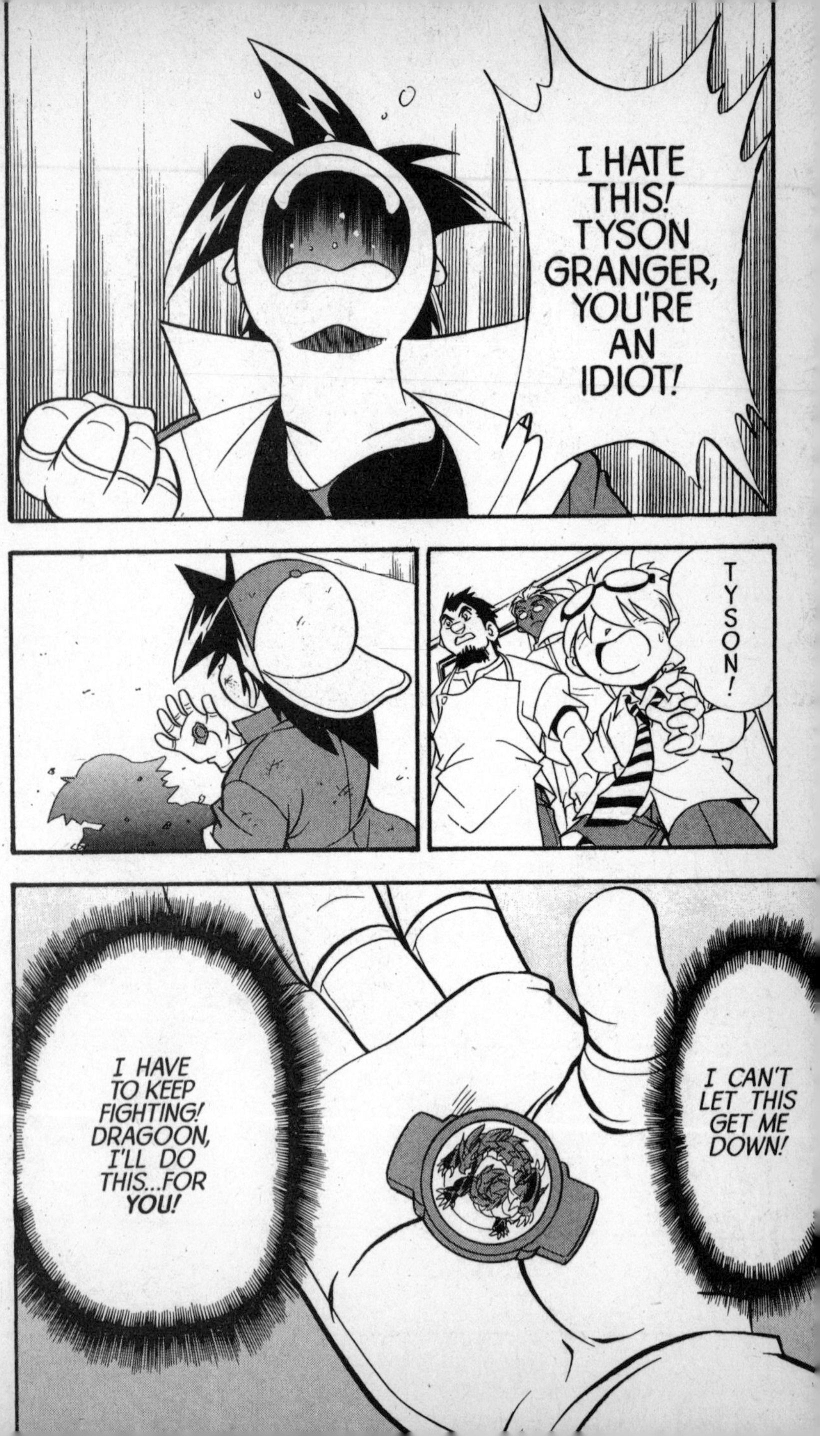
I HATE THIS! TYSON GRANGER, YOU'RE AN IDIOT!
TYSON!
I CAN'T LET THIS GET ME DOWN!
I HAVE TO KEEP FIGHTING! DRAGOON, I'LL DO THIS...FOR YOU!

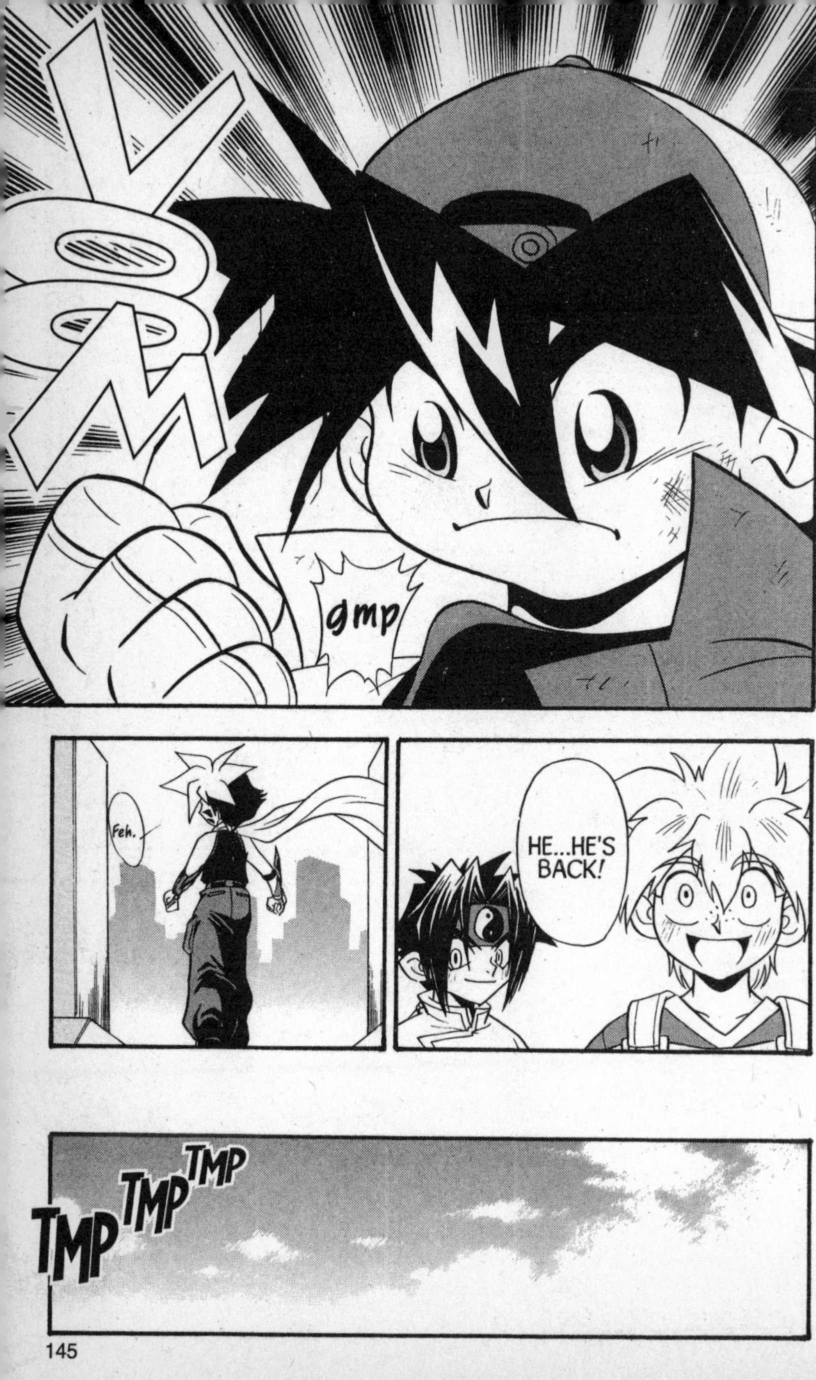
gmp
HE...HE'S BACK!
Feh.
TMP TMP TMP

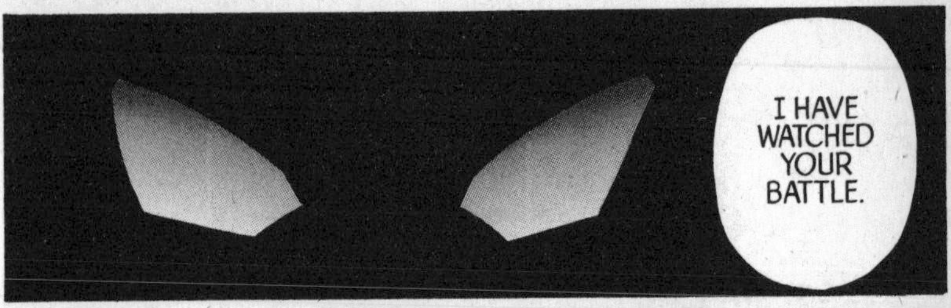
I HAVE WATCHED YOUR BATTLE.

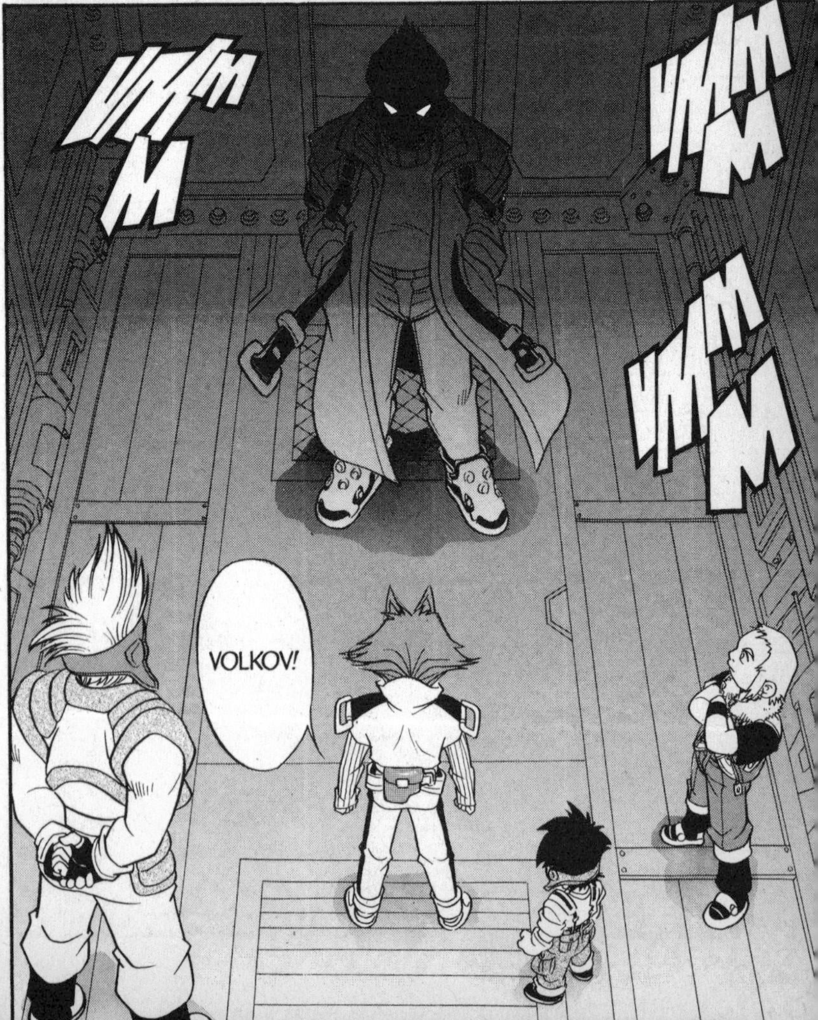
VOLKOV!

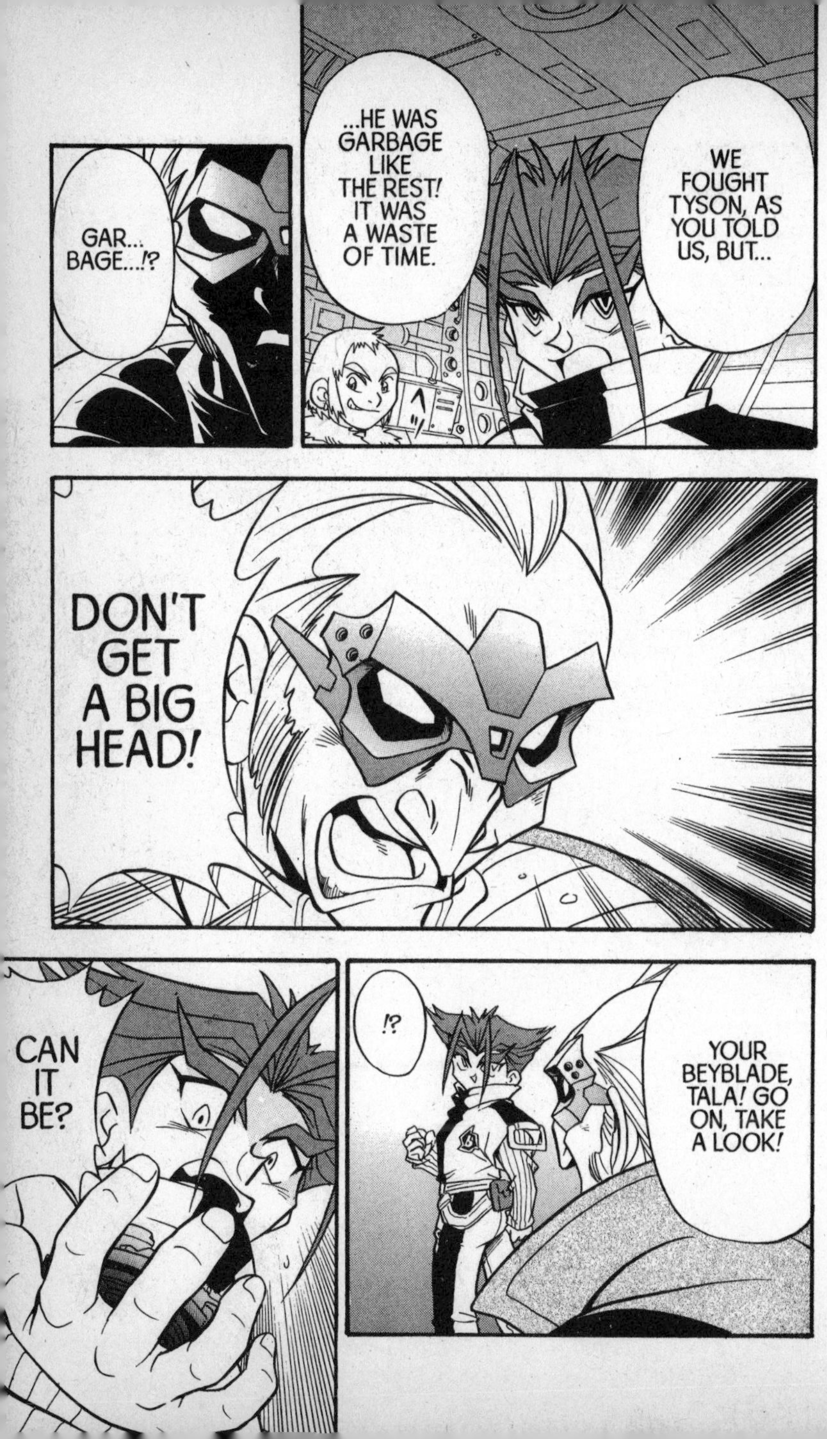
WE FOUGHT TYSON, AS YOU TOLD US, BUT...
...HE WAS GARBAGE LIKE THE REST! IT WAS A WASTE OF TIME.
GAR... BAGE...!?
DON'T GET A BIG HEAD!
YOUR BEYBLADE, TALA! GO ON, TAKE A LOOK!
!?
CAN IT BE?

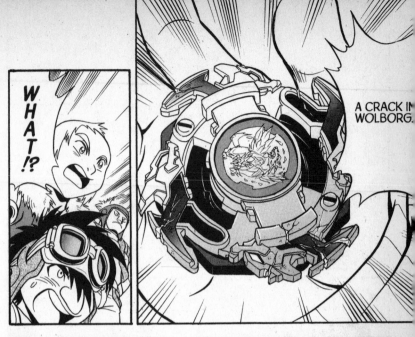

WHAT!?

A CRACK IN WOLBORG.

IT MUST HAVE BEEN FROM THE LAST BLOW!

TYSON WAS ABLE TO INFLICT *THIS* MUCH DAMAGE-- ON THE VERY VERGE OF DEFEAT!?

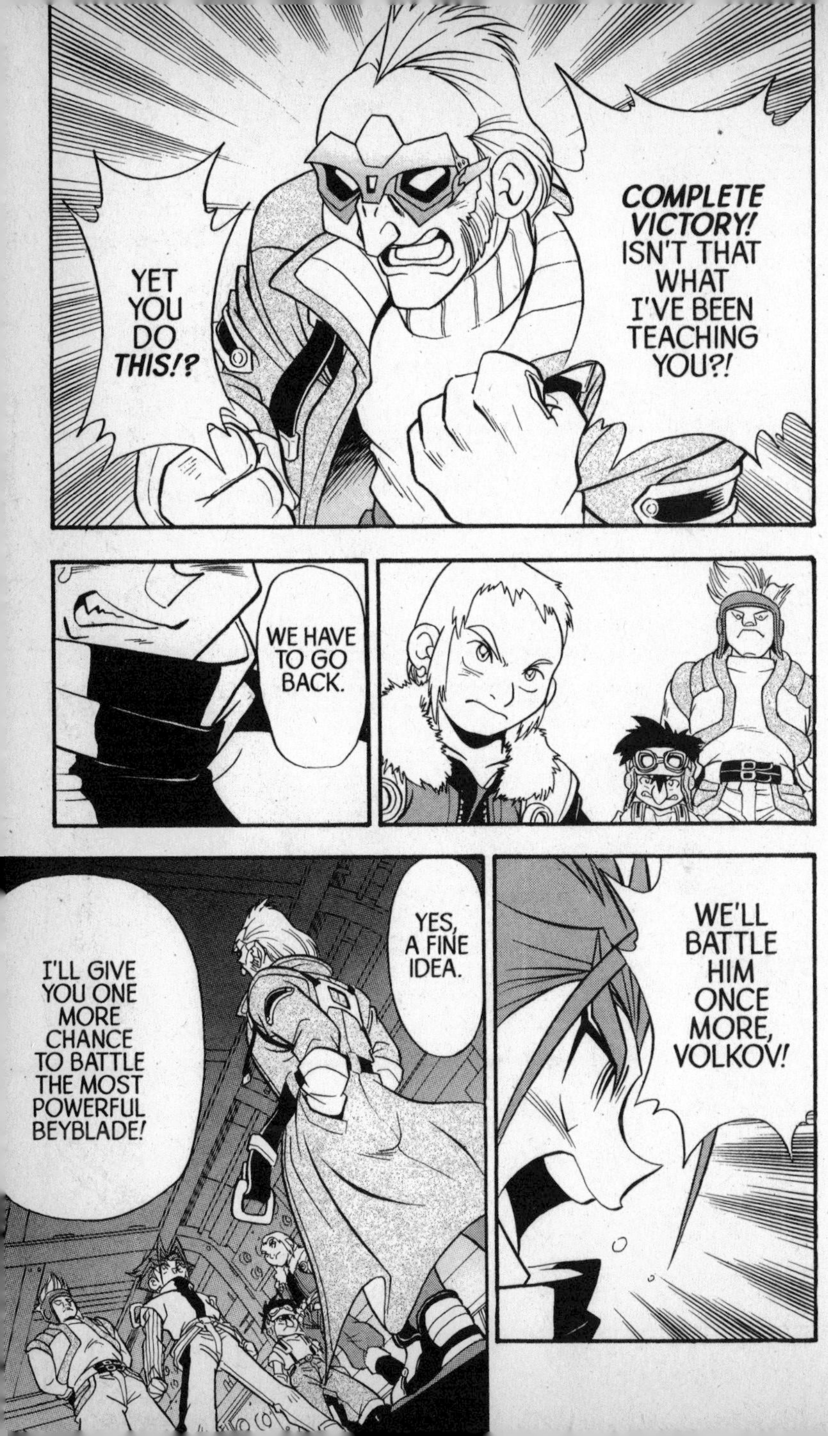
COMPLETE VICTORY! ISN'T THAT WHAT I'VE BEEN TEACHING YOU?!
YET YOU DO THIS!?
WE HAVE TO GO BACK.
WE'LL BATTLE HIM ONCE MORE, VOLKOV!
YES, A FINE IDEA.
I'LL GIVE YOU ONE MORE CHANCE TO BATTLE THE MOST POWERFUL BEYBLADE!

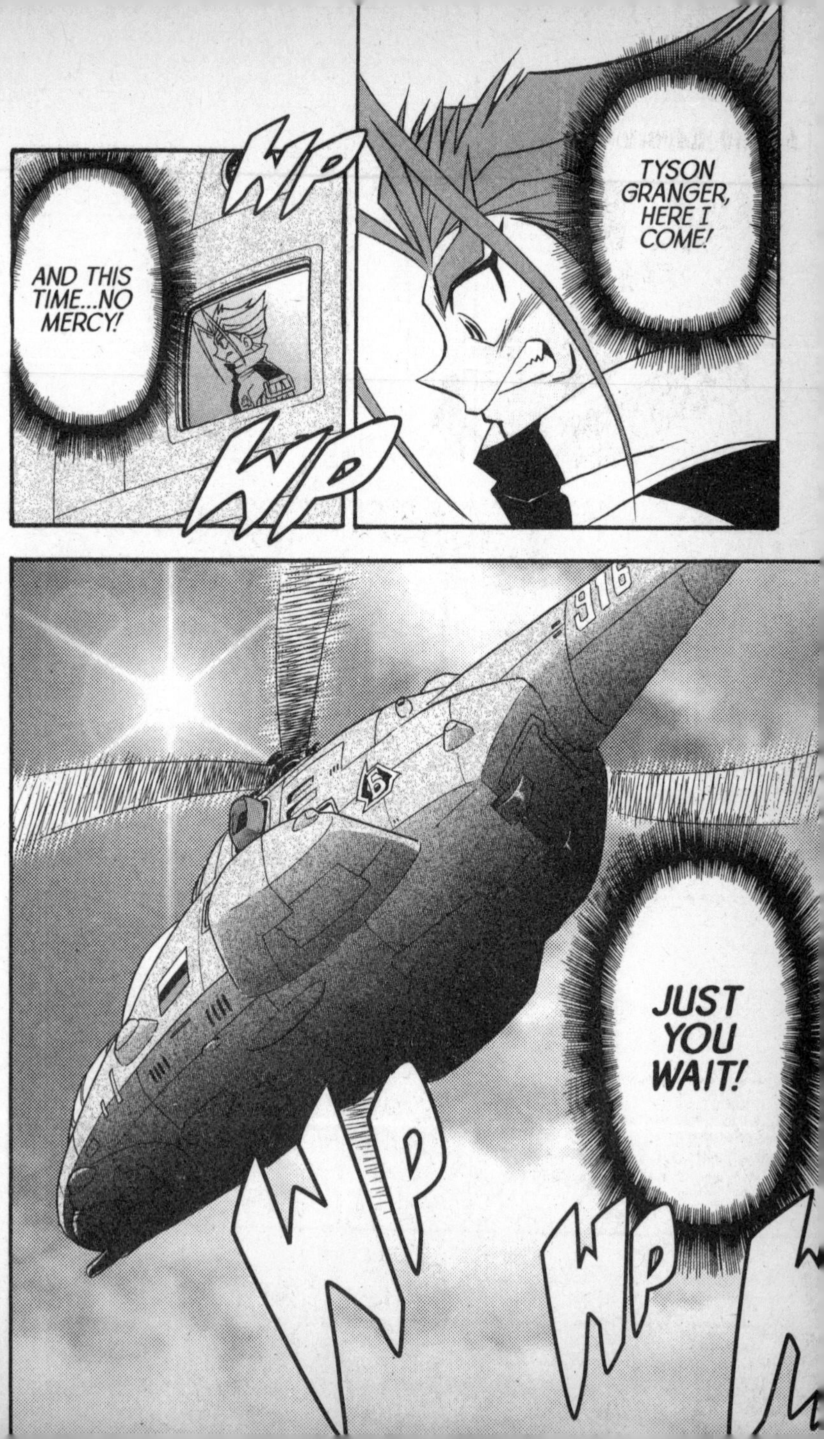
TYSON GRANGER, HERE I COME!
WP
AND THIS TIME...NO MERCY!
WP
JUST YOU WAIT!
WP
WP
WP

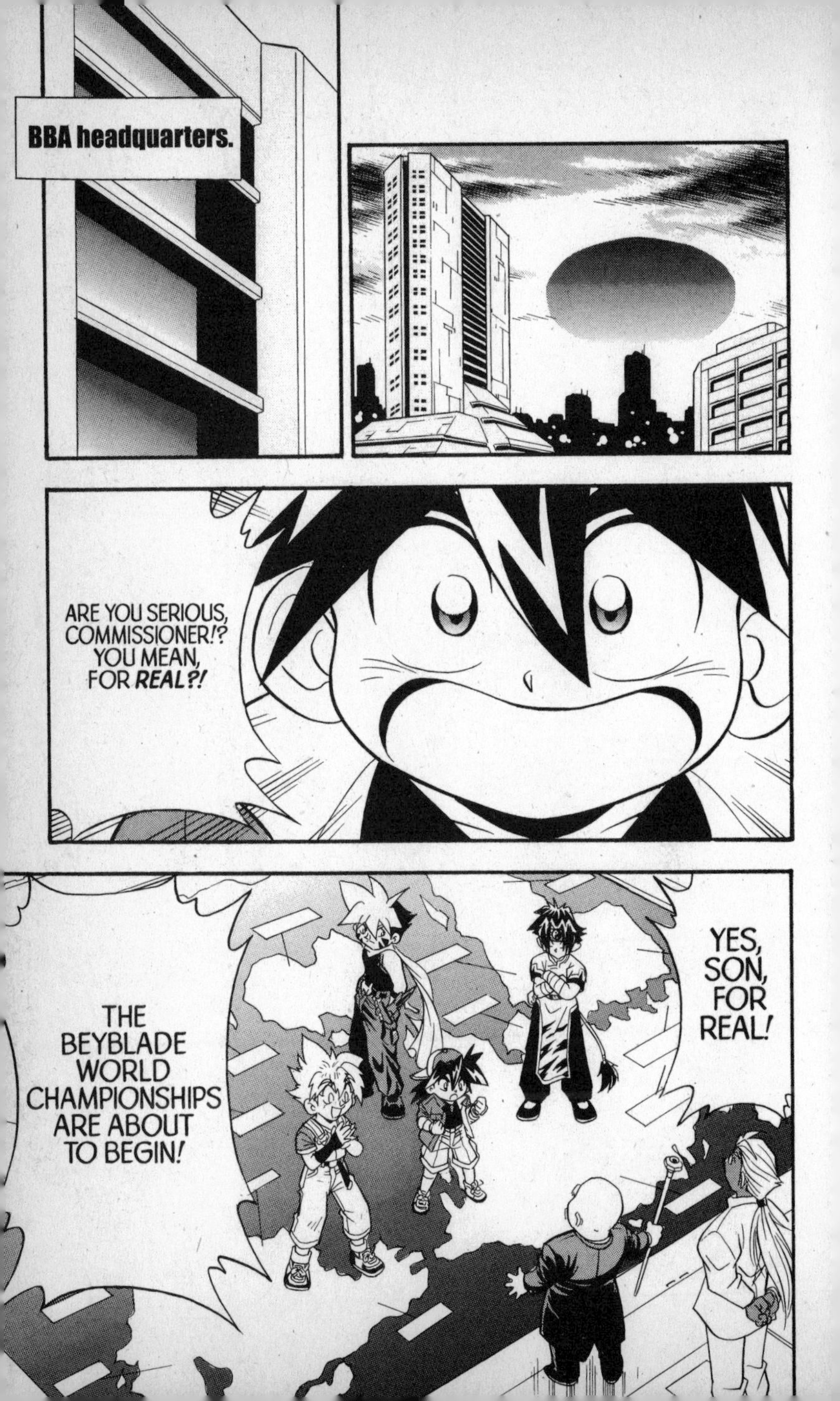
BBA headquarters.
ARE YOU SERIOUS, COMMISSIONER!? YOU MEAN, FOR REAL?!
YES, SON, FOR REAL!
THE BEYBLADE WORLD CHAMPIONSHIPS ARE ABOUT TO BEGIN!

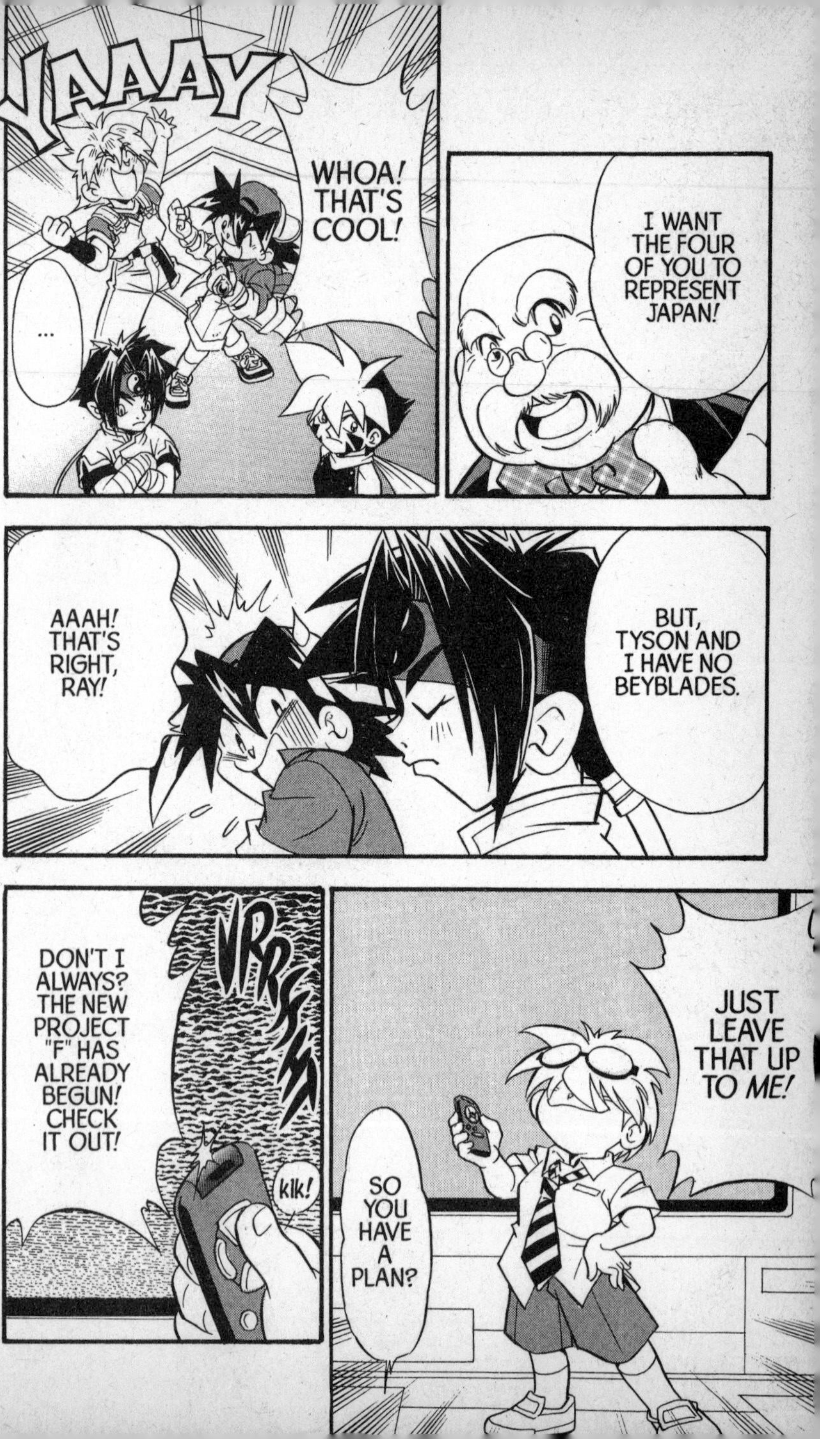
I WANT THE FOUR OF YOU TO REPRESENT JAPAN!
YAAAY
WHOA! THAT'S COOL!
...
BUT, TYSON AND I HAVE NO BEYBLADES.
AAAH! THAT'S RIGHT, RAY!
JUST LEAVE THAT UP TO ME!
SO YOU HAVE A PLAN?
DON'T I ALWAYS? THE NEW PROJECT "F" HAS ALREADY BEGUN! CHECK IT OUT!
VRRSSHH
klk!

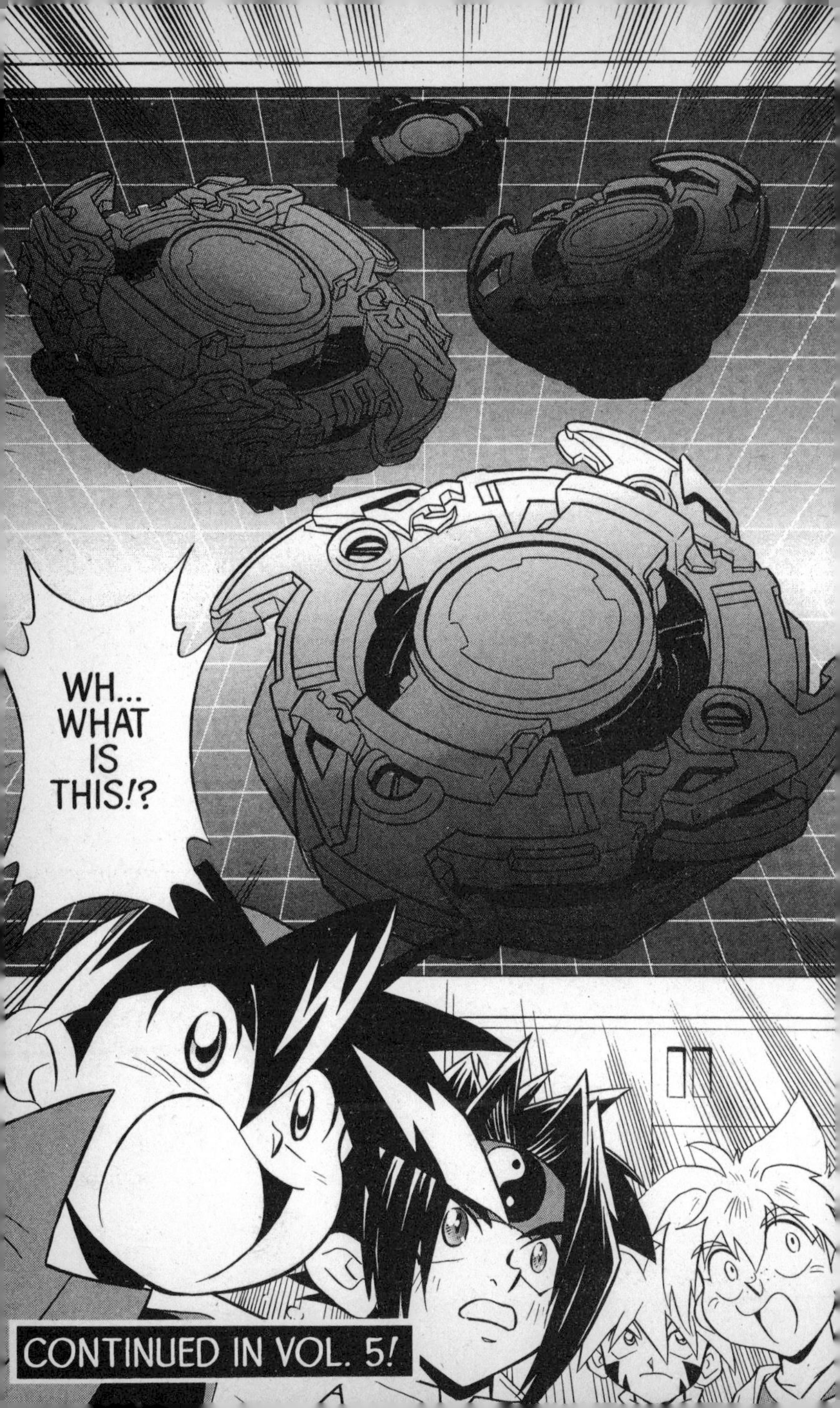
WH... WHAT IS THIS!?
CONTINUED IN VOL. 5!

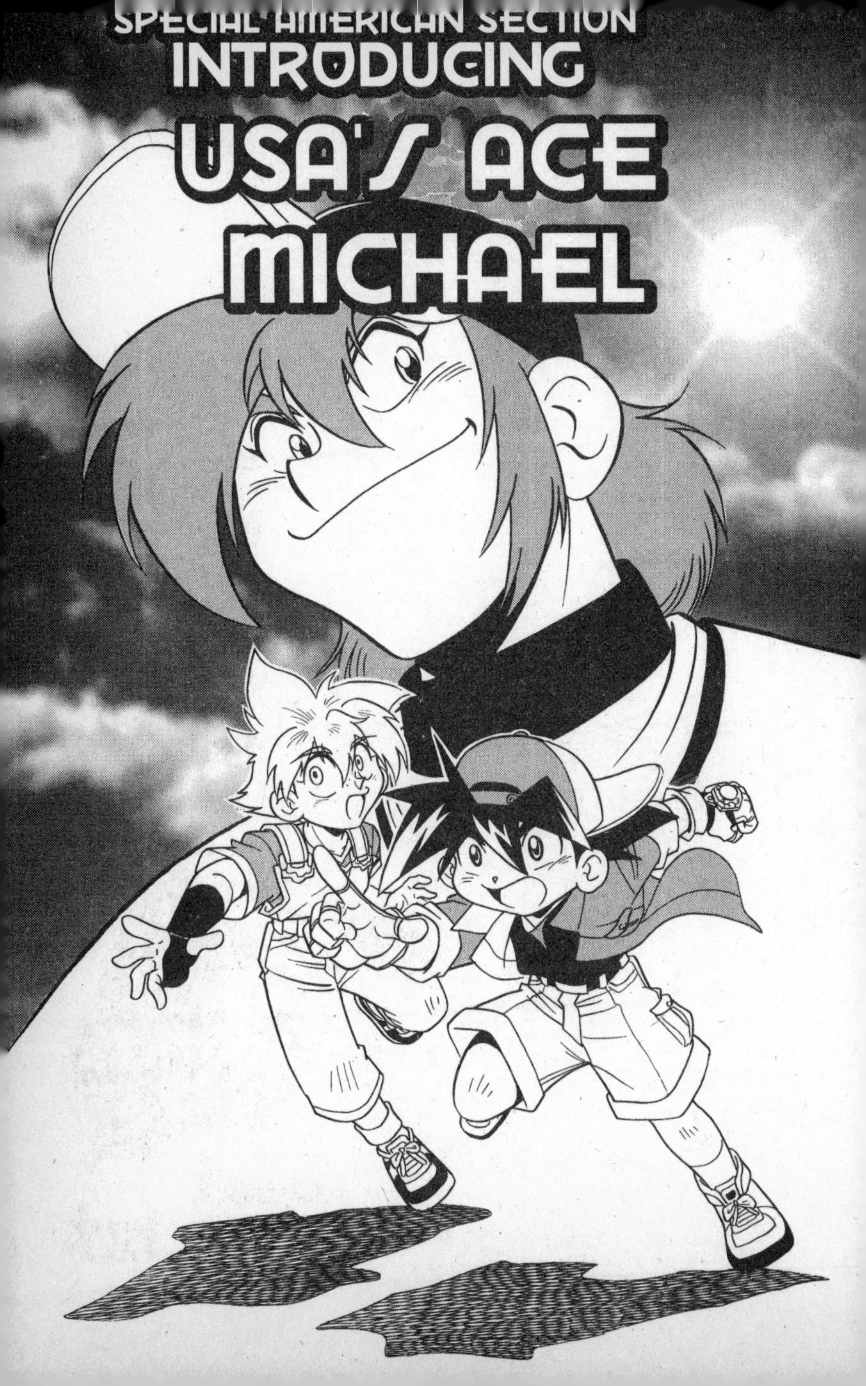
SPECIAL AMERICAN SECTION
INTRODUCING
USA'S ACE
MICHAEL

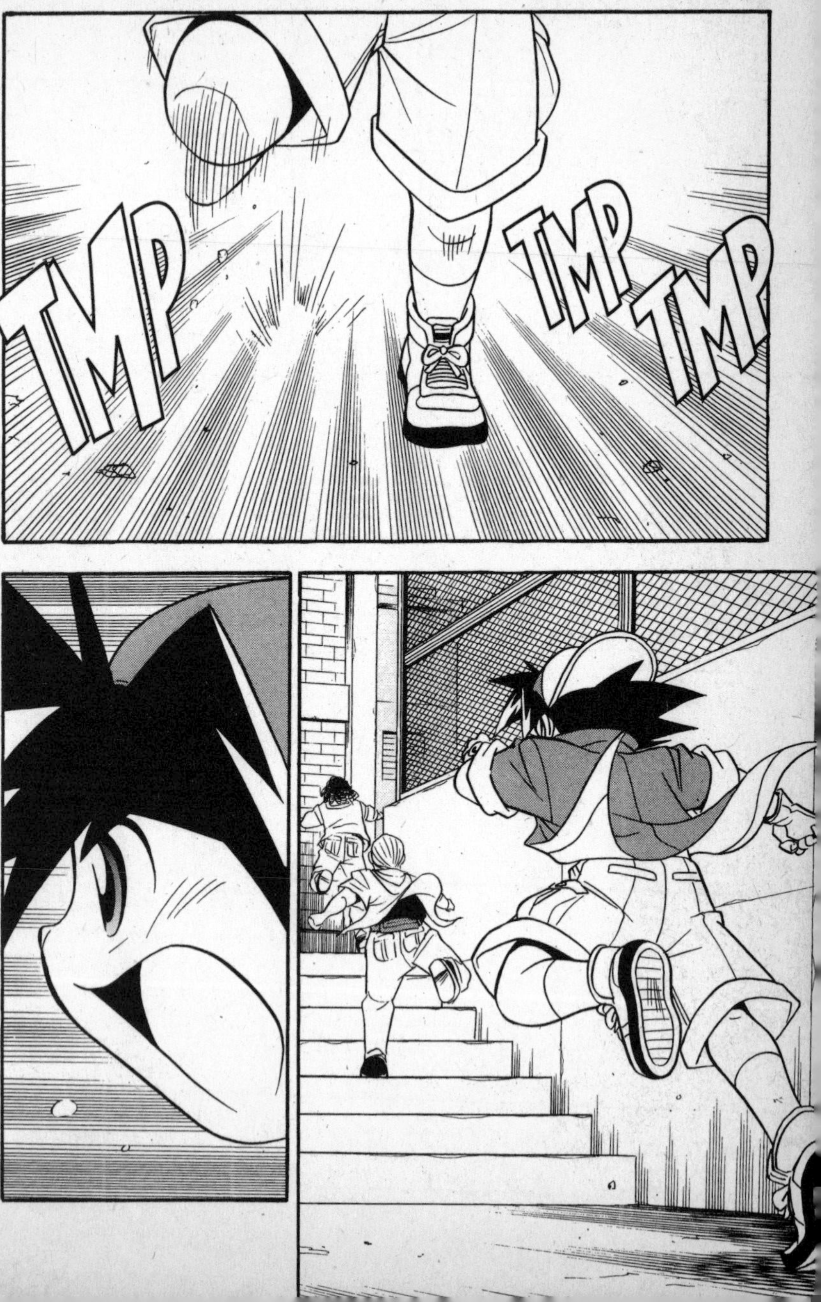
TMP
TMP
TMP

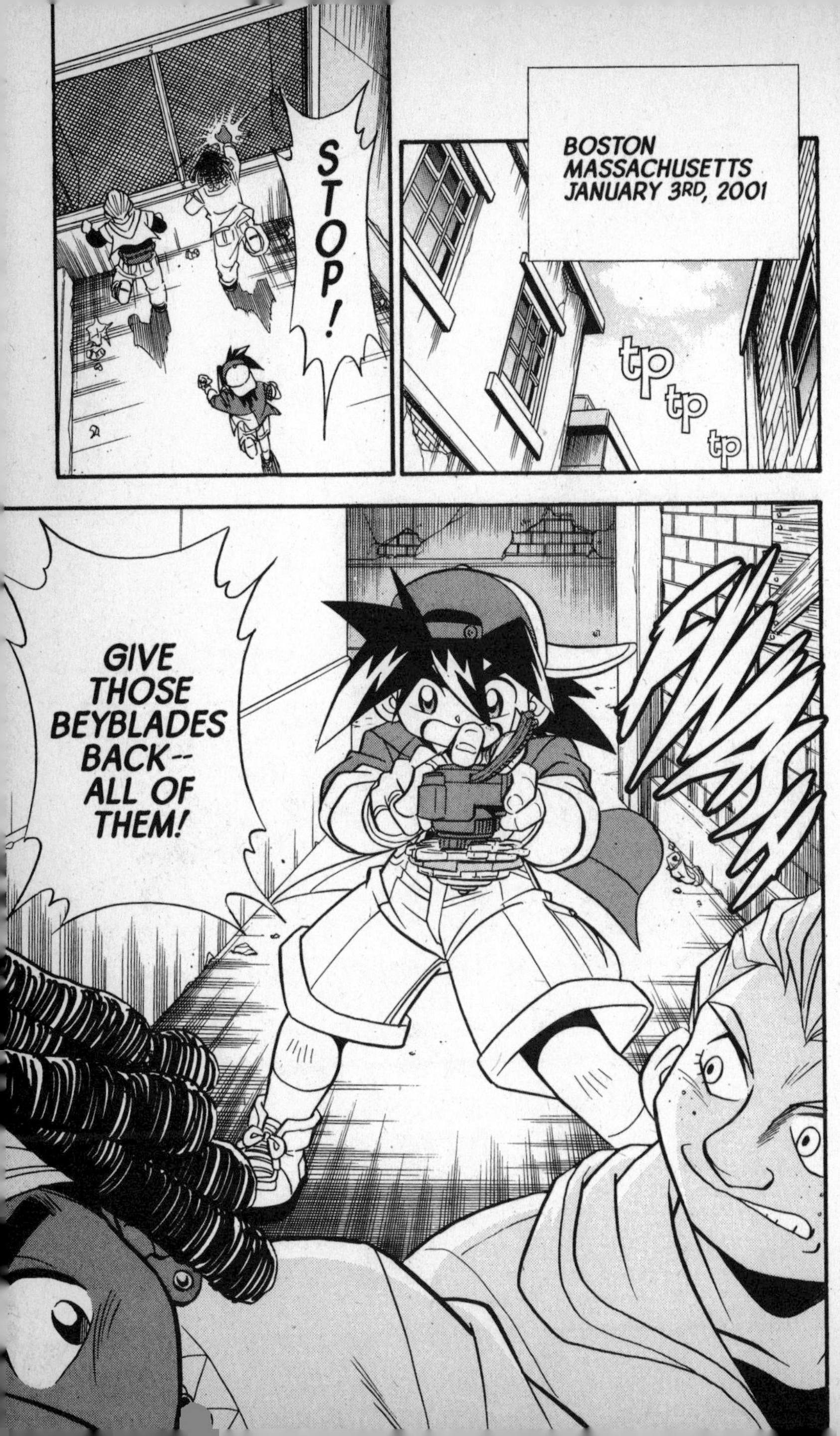
BOSTON
MASSACHUSETTS
JANUARY 3RD, 2001
tp tp tp
STOP!
GIVE THOSE BEYBLADES BACK-- ALL OF THEM!

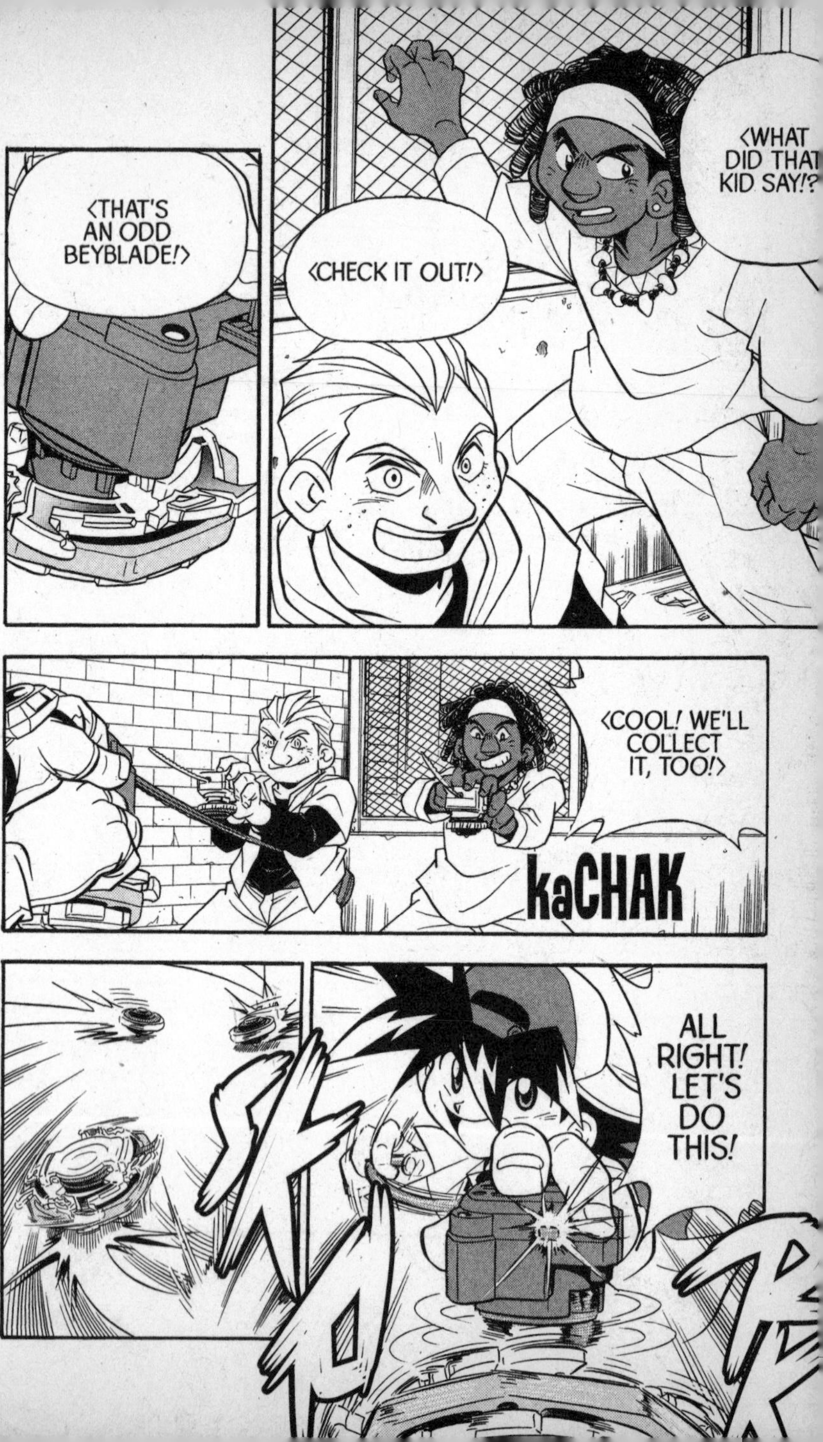
<WHAT DID THAT KID SAY!?
<CHECK IT OUT!>
<THAT'S AN ODD BEYBLADE!>
<COOL! WE'LL COLLECT IT, TOO!>
kaCHAK
ALL RIGHT! LET'S DO THIS!

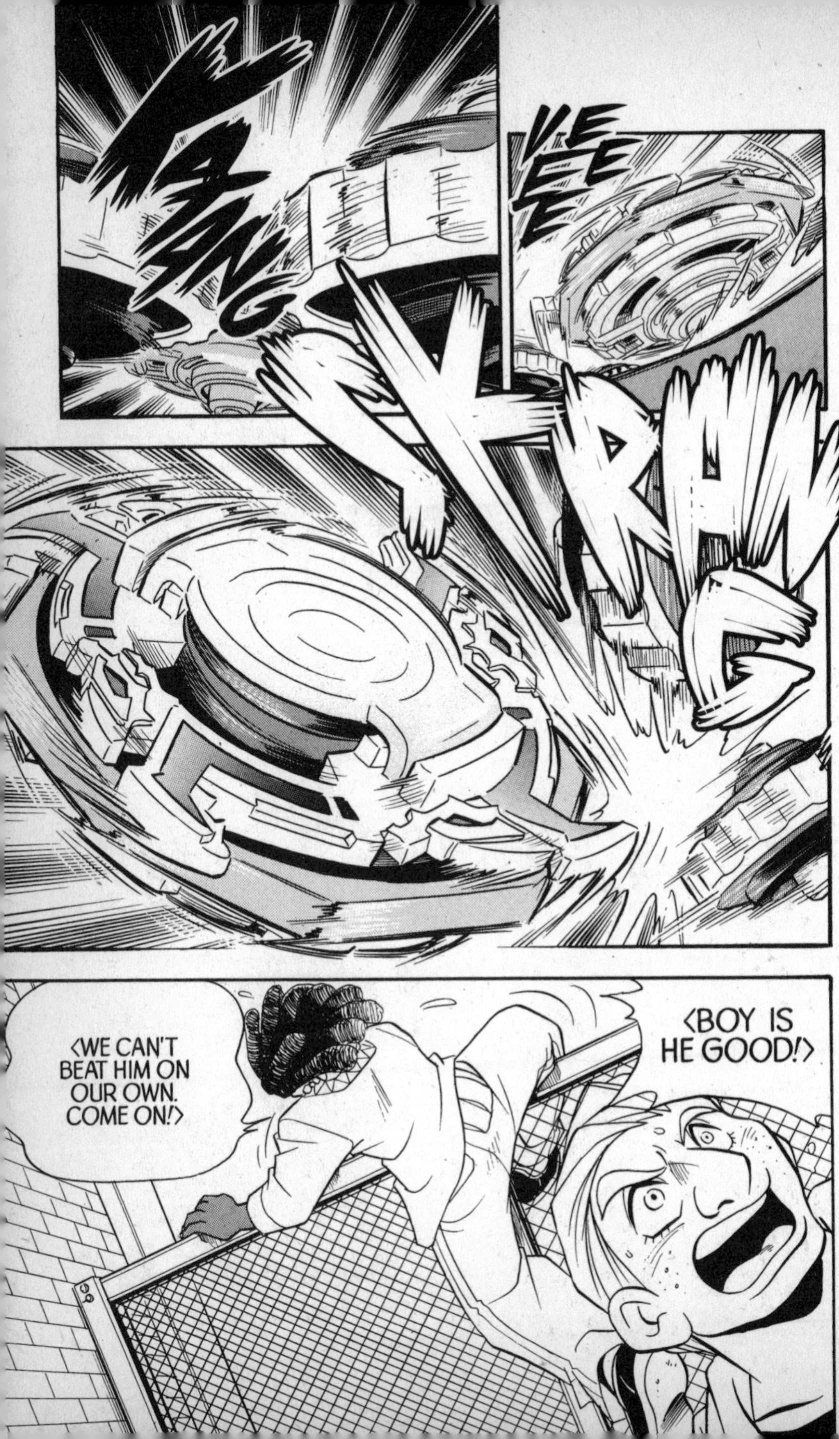
VEEEE
BANG
KRAK
‹BOY IS HE GOOD!›
‹WE CAN'T BEAT HIM ON OUR OWN. COME ON!›

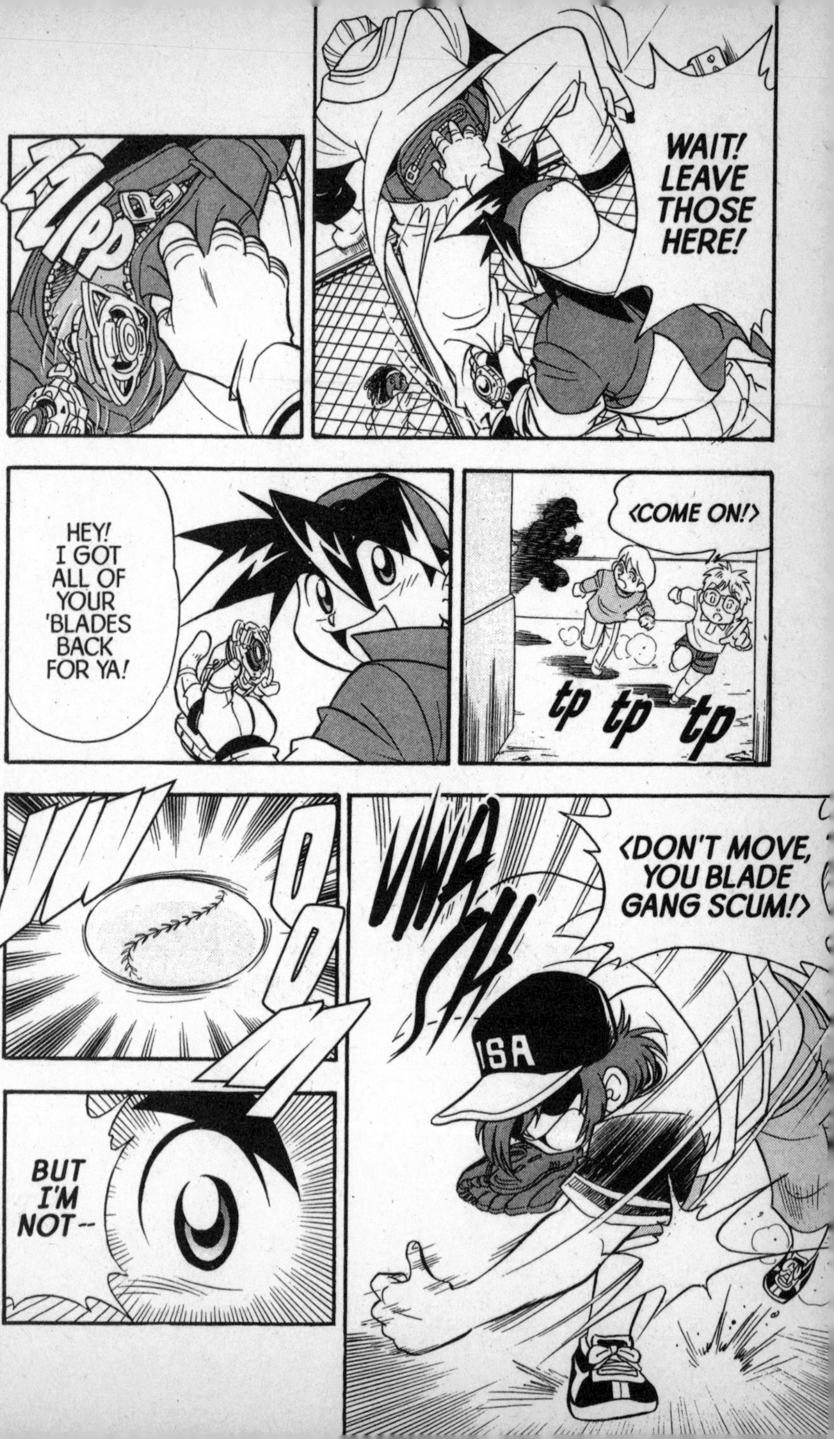
WAIT! LEAVE THOSE HERE!
ZIPP
<COME ON!>
tp tp tp
HEY! I GOT ALL OF YOUR 'BLADES BACK FOR YA!
<DON'T MOVE, YOU BLADE GANG SCUM!>
BUT I'M NOT--

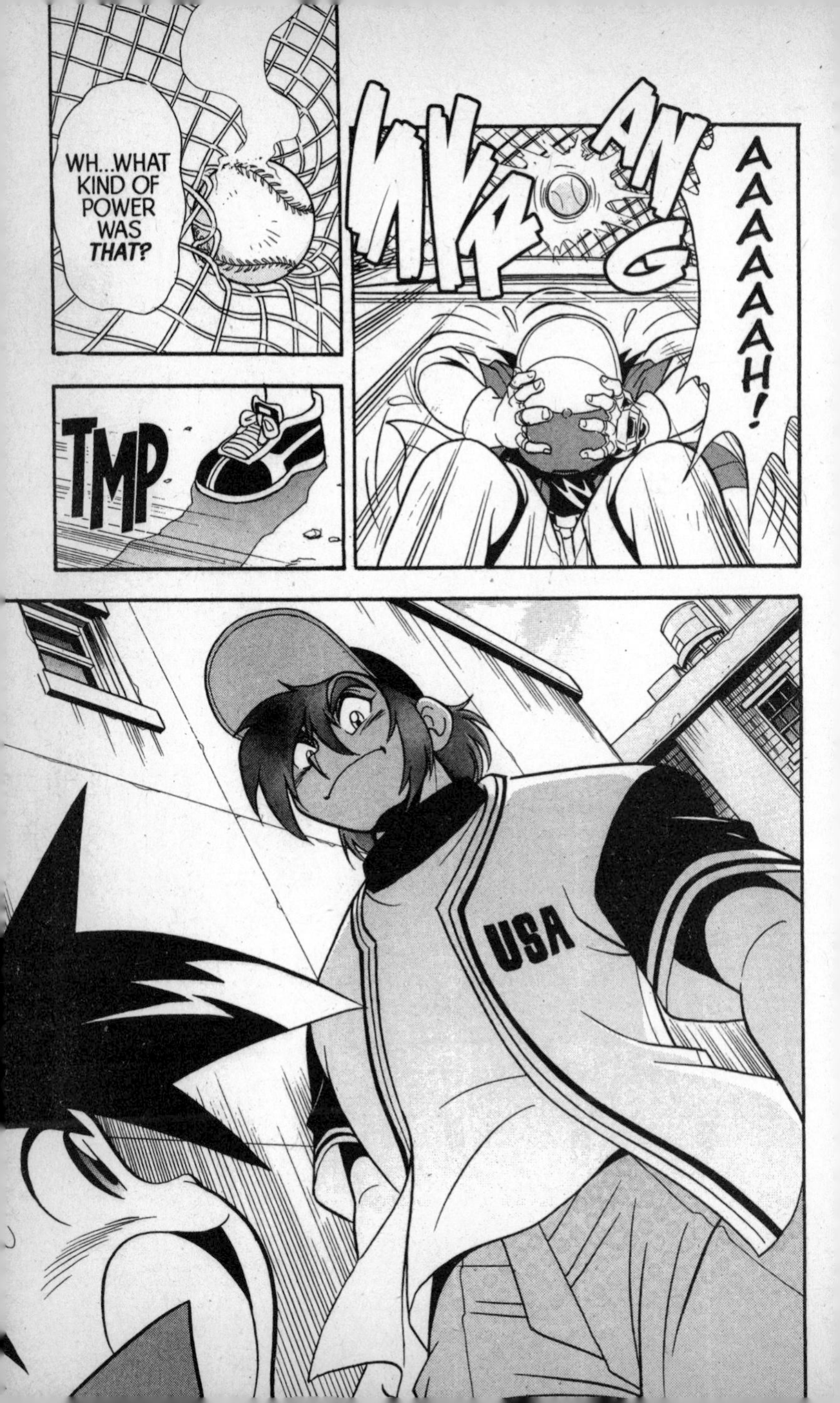
KWANG
AAAAAAH!
WH...WHAT KIND OF POWER WAS *THAT?*
TMP
USA

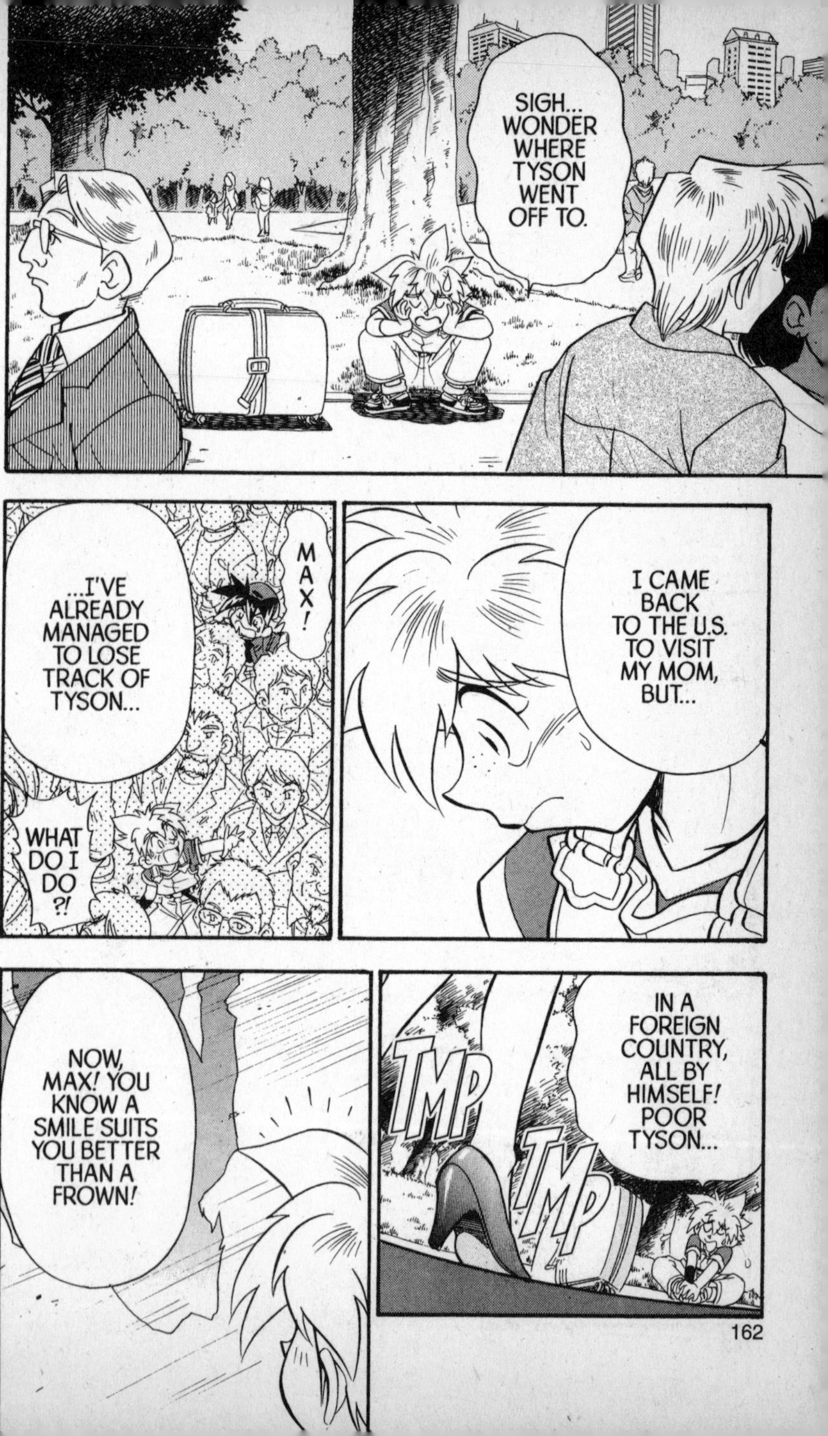
SIGH... WONDER WHERE TYSON WENT OFF TO.
I CAME BACK TO THE U.S. TO VISIT MY MOM, BUT...
MAX!
...I'VE ALREADY MANAGED TO LOSE TRACK OF TYSON...
WHAT DO I DO ?!
IN A FOREIGN COUNTRY, ALL BY HIMSELF! POOR TYSON...
TMP
TMP
NOW, MAX! YOU KNOW A SMILE SUITS YOU BETTER THAN A FROWN!

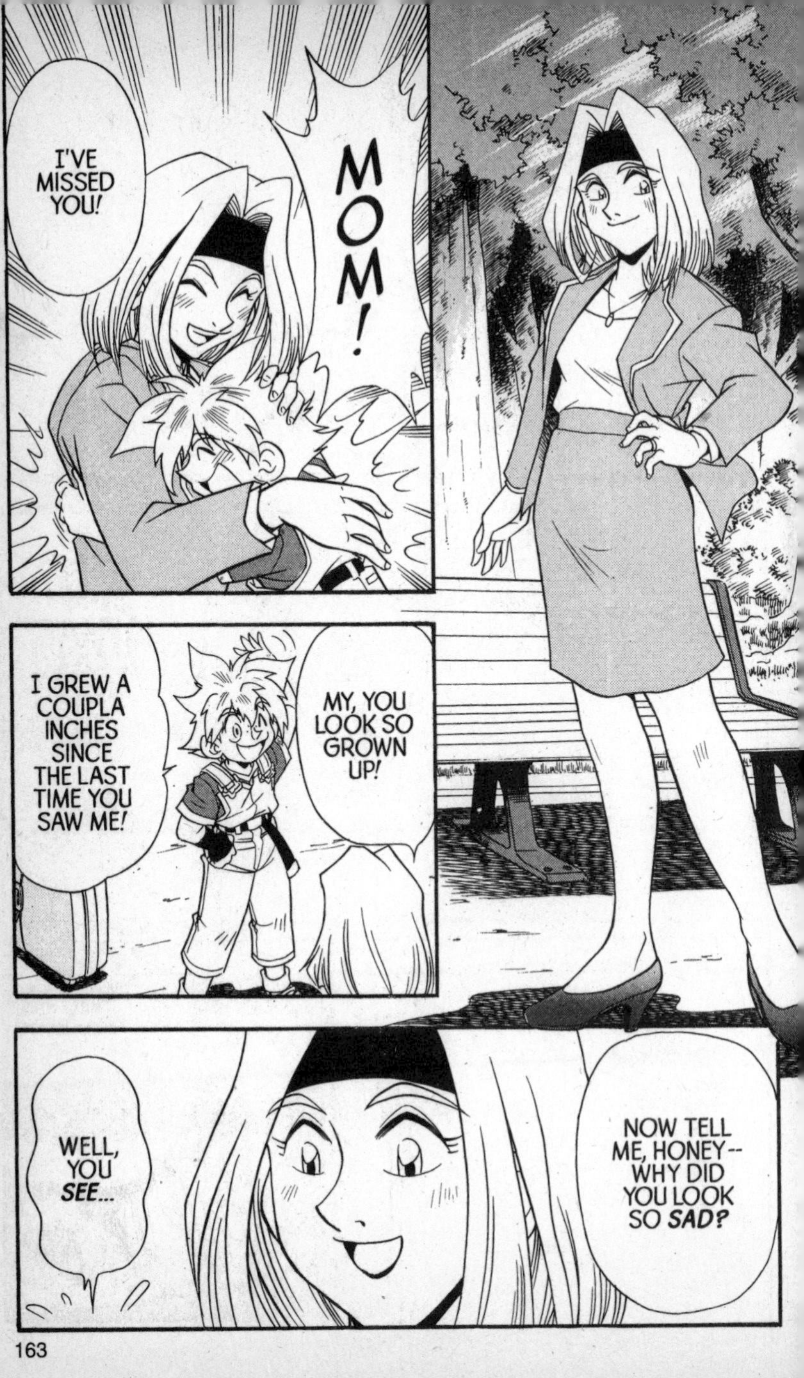
MOM!
I'VE MISSED YOU!
MY, YOU LOOK SO GROWN UP!
I GREW A COUPLA INCHES SINCE THE LAST TIME YOU SAW ME!
NOW TELL ME, HONEY-- WHY DID YOU LOOK SO *SAD?*
WELL, YOU *SEE...*

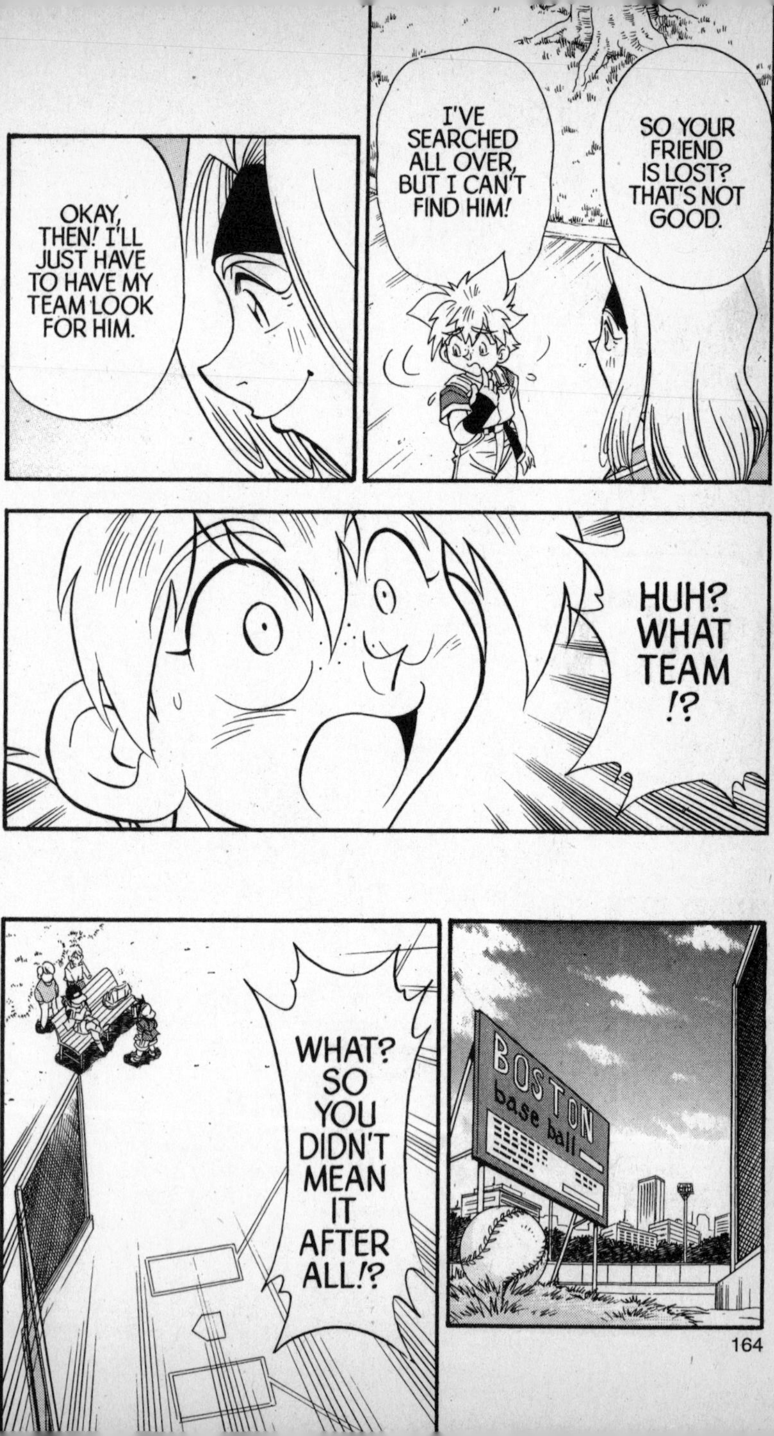
SO YOUR FRIEND IS LOST? THAT'S NOT GOOD.
I'VE SEARCHED ALL OVER, BUT I CAN'T FIND HIM!
OKAY, THEN! I'LL JUST HAVE TO HAVE MY TEAM LOOK FOR HIM.
HUH? WHAT TEAM!?
BOSTON
base ball
WHAT? SO YOU DIDN'T MEAN IT AFTER ALL!?

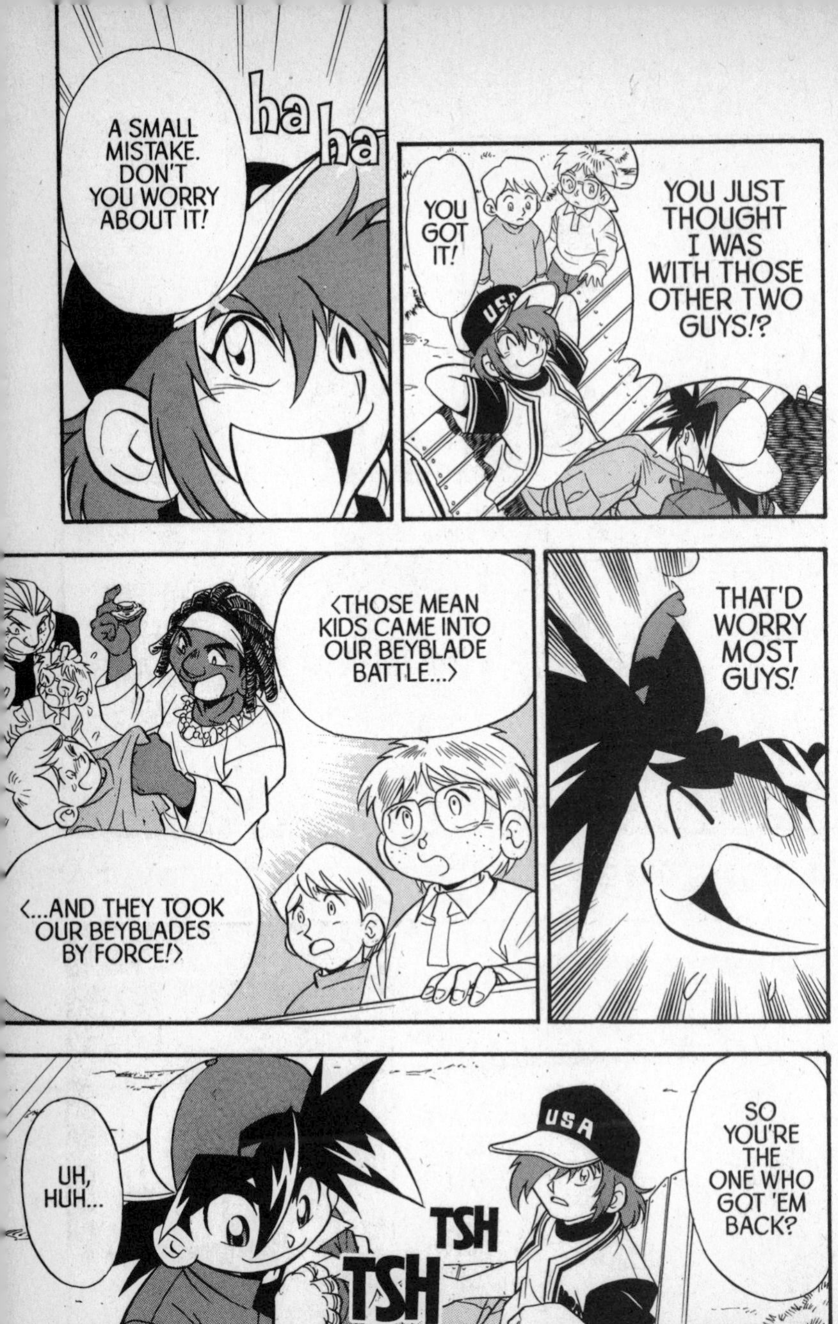
YOU JUST THOUGHT I WAS WITH THOSE OTHER TWO GUYS!?
YOU GOT IT!
ha ha
A SMALL MISTAKE. DON'T YOU WORRY ABOUT IT!
THAT'D WORRY MOST GUYS!
<THOSE MEAN KIDS CAME INTO OUR BEYBLADE BATTLE...>
<...AND THEY TOOK OUR BEYBLADES BY FORCE!>
SO YOU'RE THE ONE WHO GOT 'EM BACK?
TSH TSH
UH, HUH...

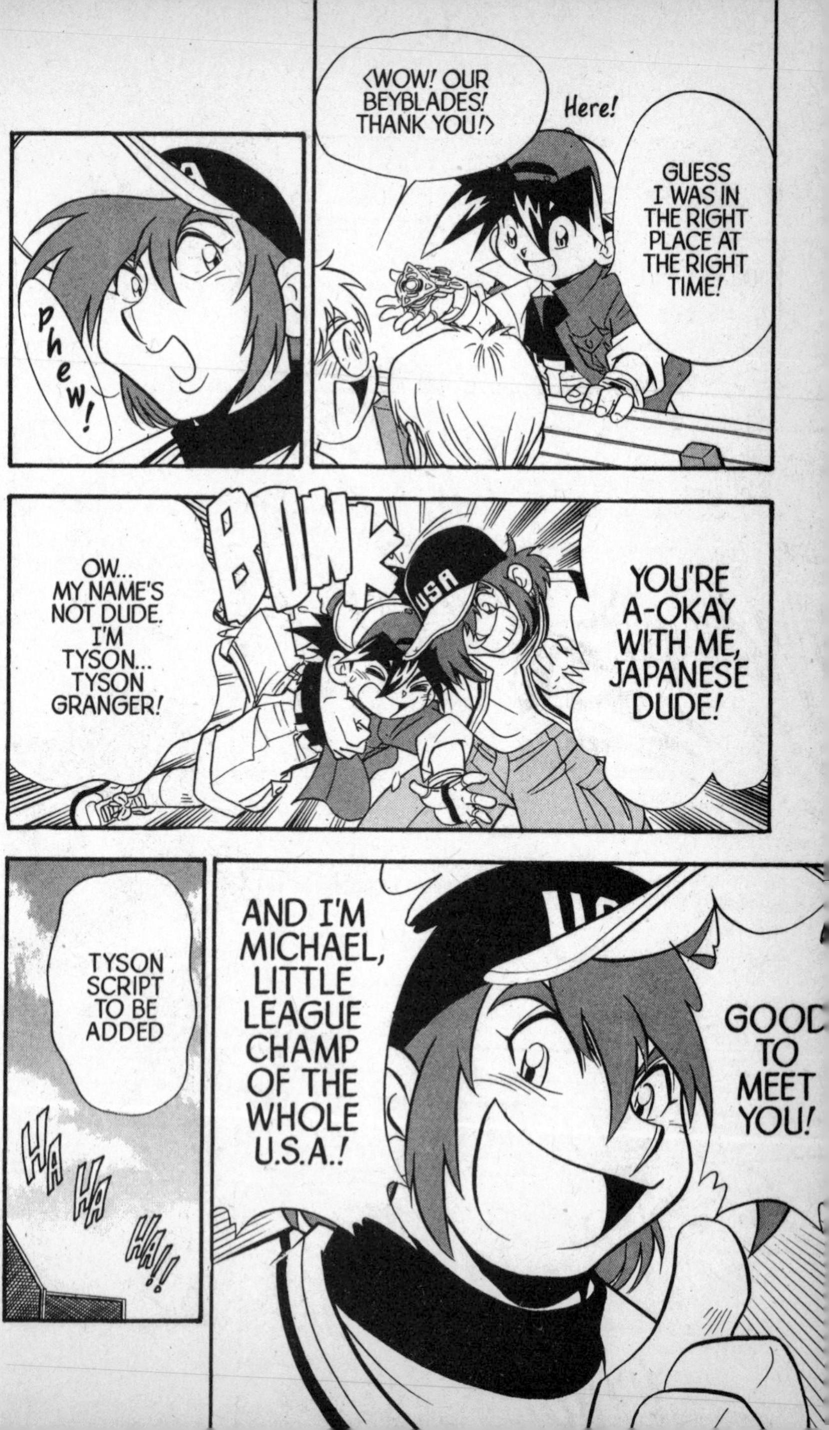

<WOW! OUR BEYBLADES! THANK YOU!>
Here!
GUESS I WAS IN THE RIGHT PLACE AT THE RIGHT TIME!
phew!
YOU'RE A-OKAY WITH ME, JAPANESE DUDE!
BONK
OW... MY NAME'S NOT DUDE. I'M TYSON... TYSON GRANGER!
AND I'M MICHAEL, LITTLE LEAGUE CHAMP OF THE WHOLE U.S.A.!
GOOD TO MEET YOU!
TYSON SCRIPT TO BE ADDED
HA HA HA!!

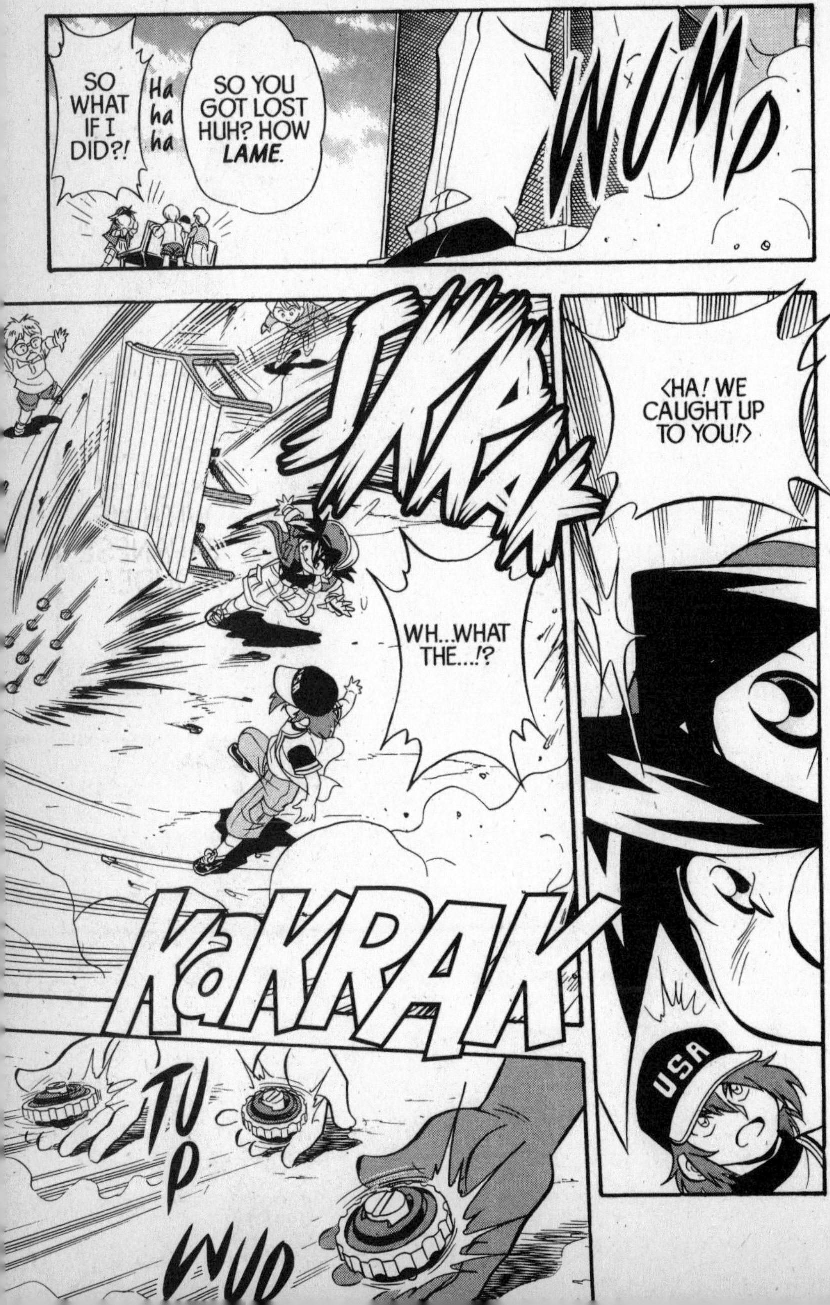
WUMP
SO YOU GOT LOST HUH? HOW LAME.
Ha ha ha
SO WHAT IF I DID?!
<HA! WE CAUGHT UP TO YOU!>
WH...WHAT THE...!?
KaKRAK
TUP

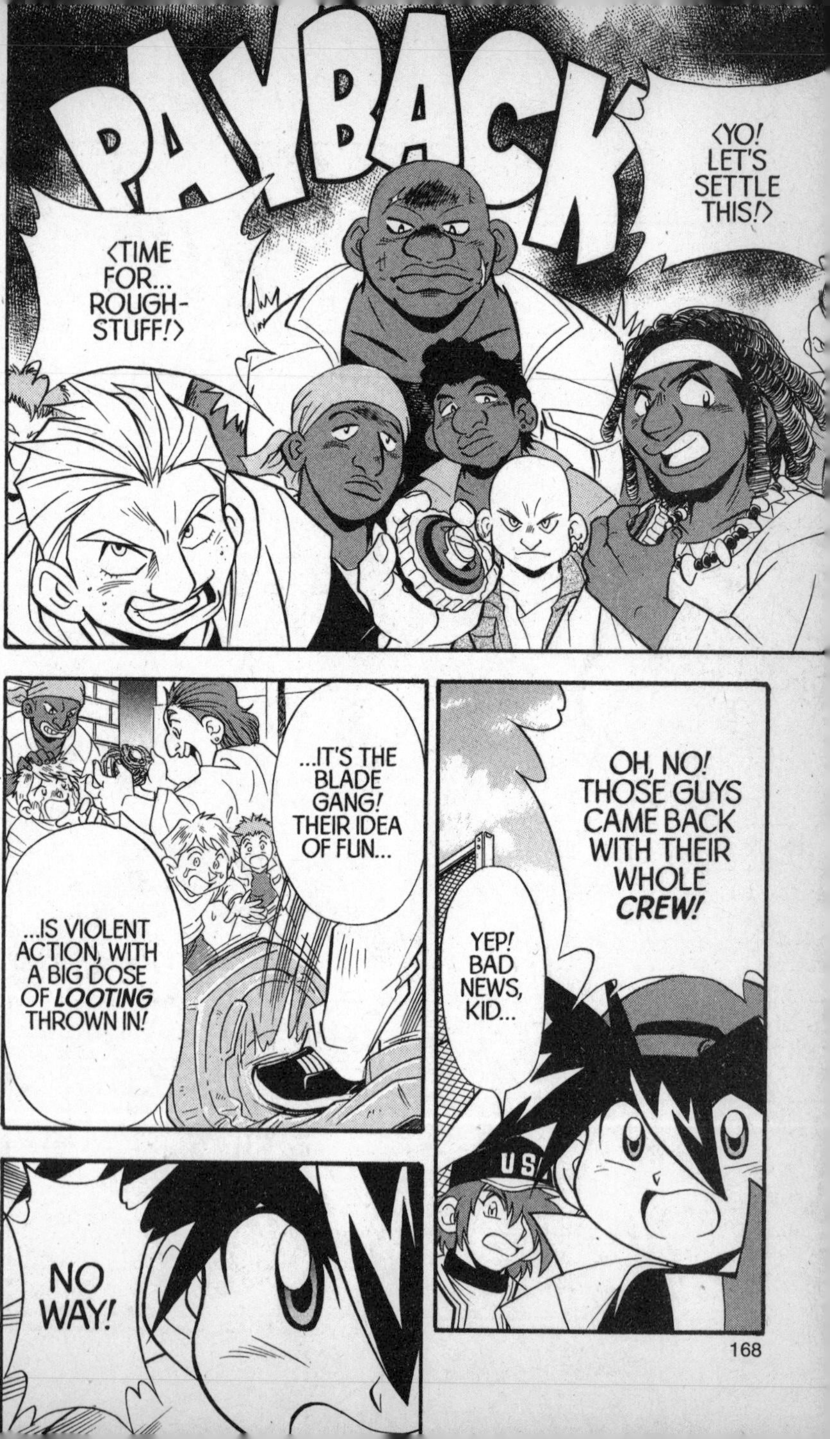
PAYBACK
<YO! LET'S SETTLE THIS!>
<TIME FOR... ROUGH-STUFF!>
OH, NO! THOSE GUYS CAME BACK WITH THEIR WHOLE *CREW!*
YEP! BAD NEWS, KID...
...IT'S THE BLADE GANG! THEIR IDEA OF FUN...
...IS VIOLENT ACTION, WITH A BIG DOSE OF *LOOTING* THROWN IN!
NO WAY!

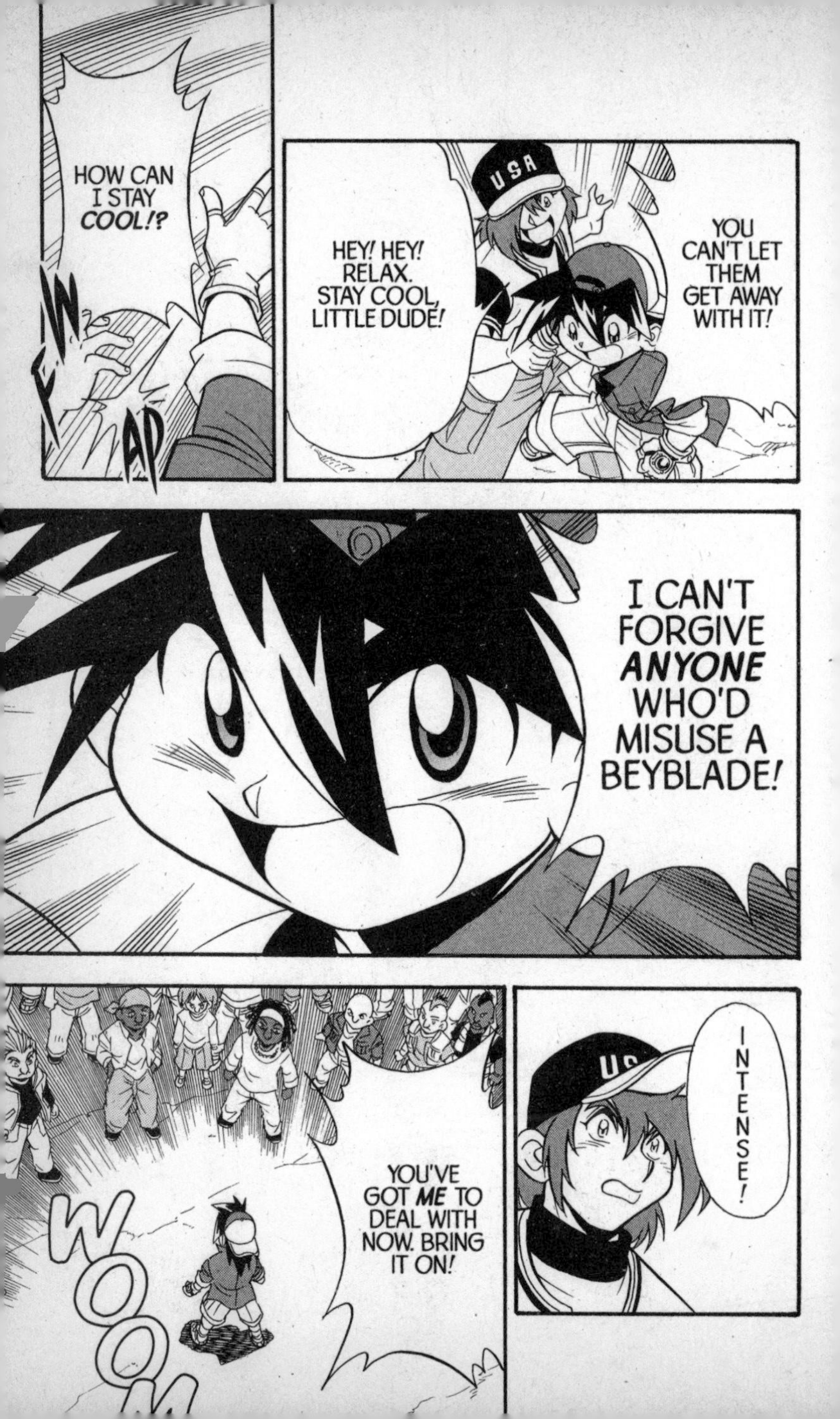
YOU CAN'T LET THEM GET AWAY WITH IT!
HEY! HEY! RELAX. STAY COOL, LITTLE DUDE!
HOW CAN I STAY *COOL!?*
FWAP
I CAN'T FORGIVE ***ANYONE*** WHO'D MISUSE A BEYBLADE!
INTENSE!
YOU'VE GOT ***ME*** TO DEAL WITH NOW. BRING IT ON!
WOOM

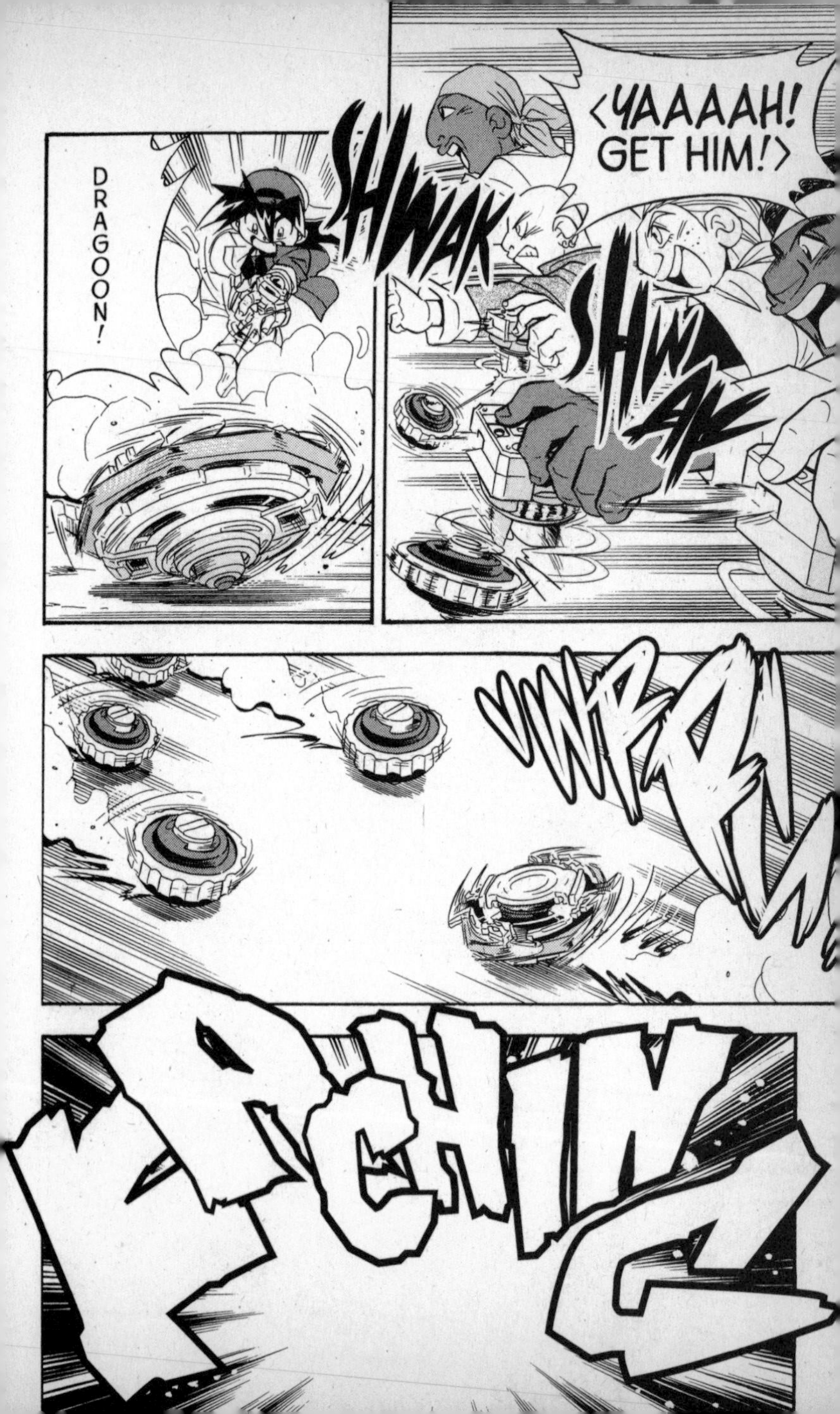
<YAAAAH! GET HIM!>
SHWAK
SHWAK
DRAGOON!

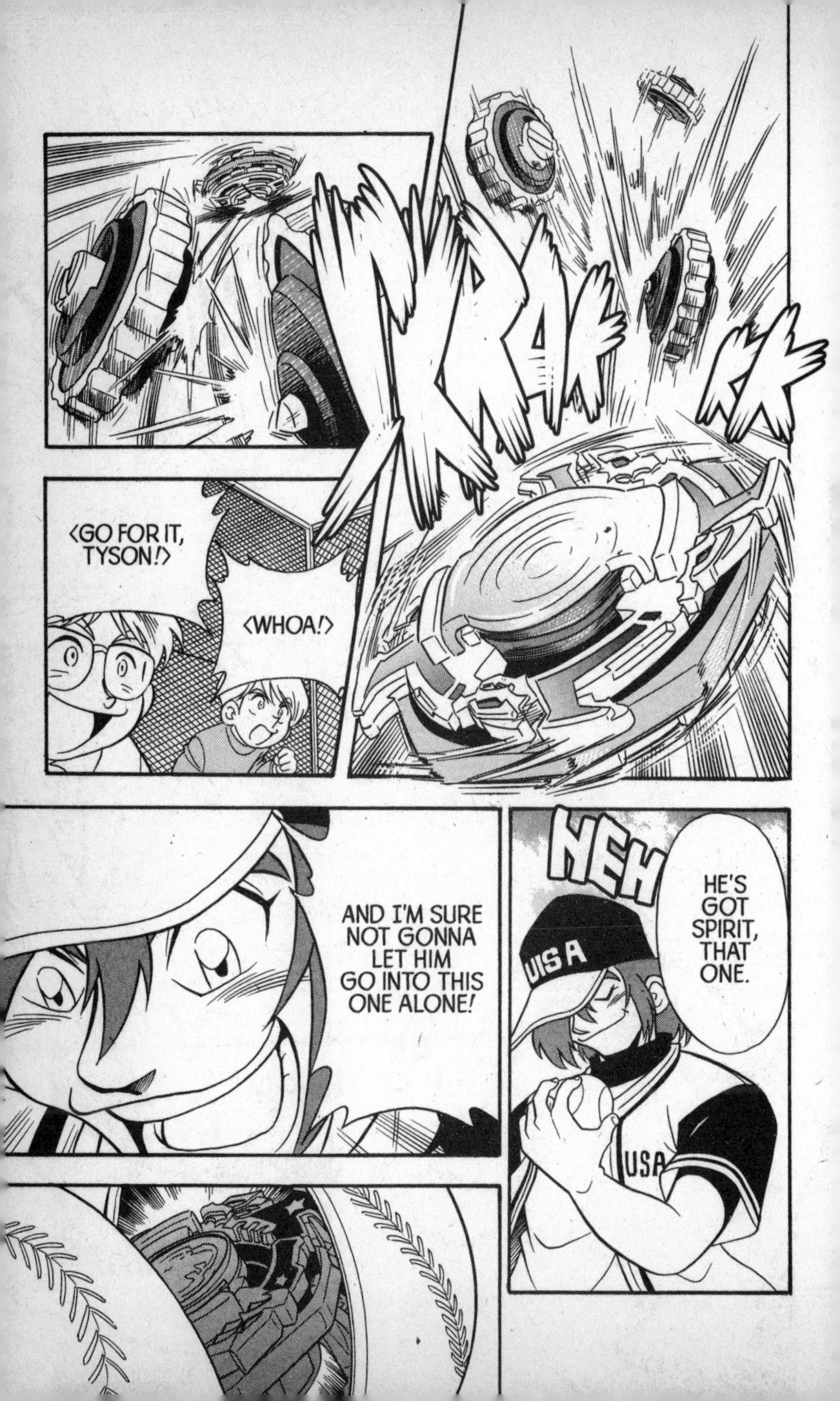
‹GO FOR IT, TYSON!›
‹WHOA!›
NEH
HE'S GOT SPIRIT, THAT ONE.
AND I'M SURE NOT GONNA LET HIM GO INTO THIS ONE ALONE!

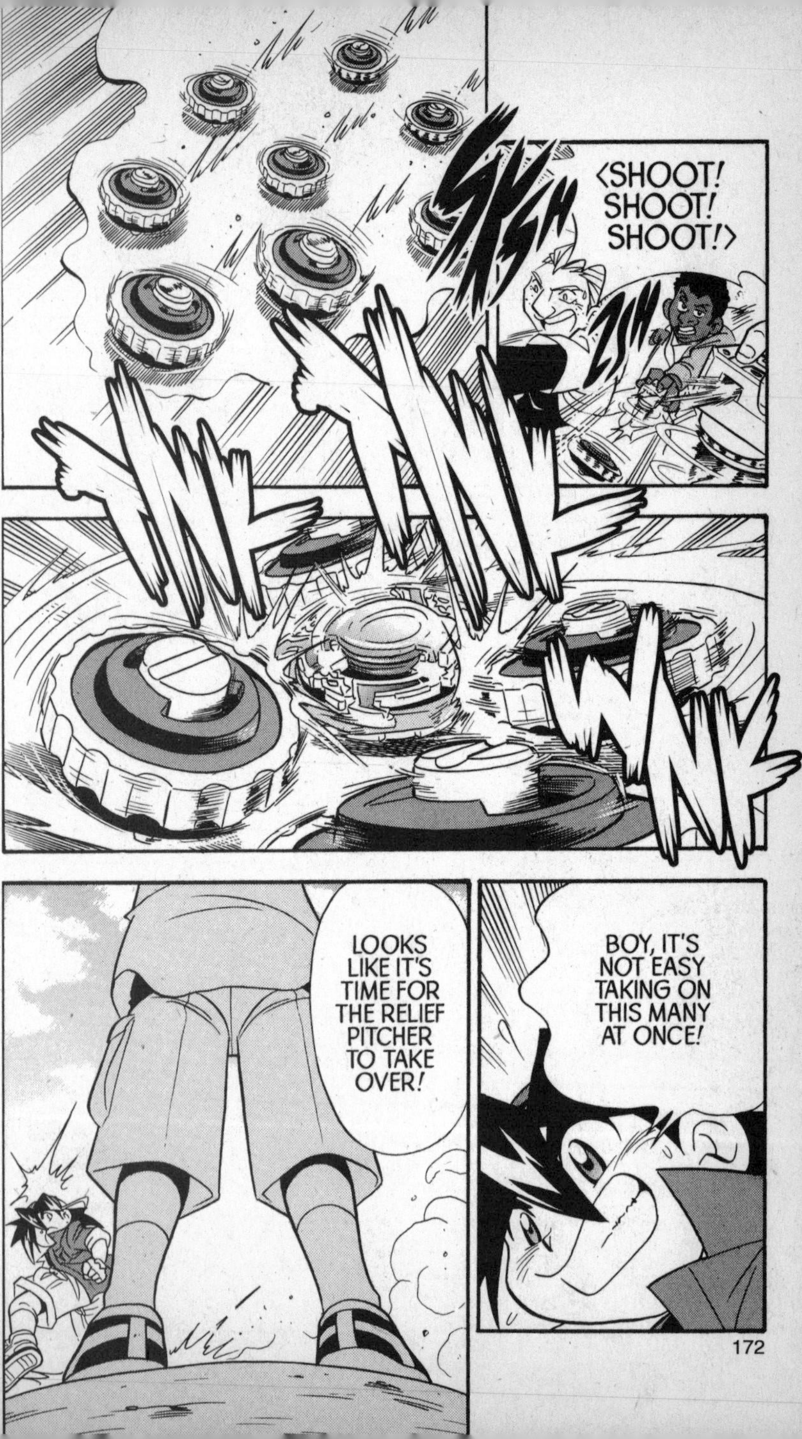

SHSH
<SHOOT! SHOOT! SHOOT!>
ZSH
TINK
TANK
WINK
BOY, IT'S NOT EASY TAKING ON THIS MANY AT ONCE!
LOOKS LIKE IT'S TIME FOR THE RELIEF PITCHER TO TAKE OVER!

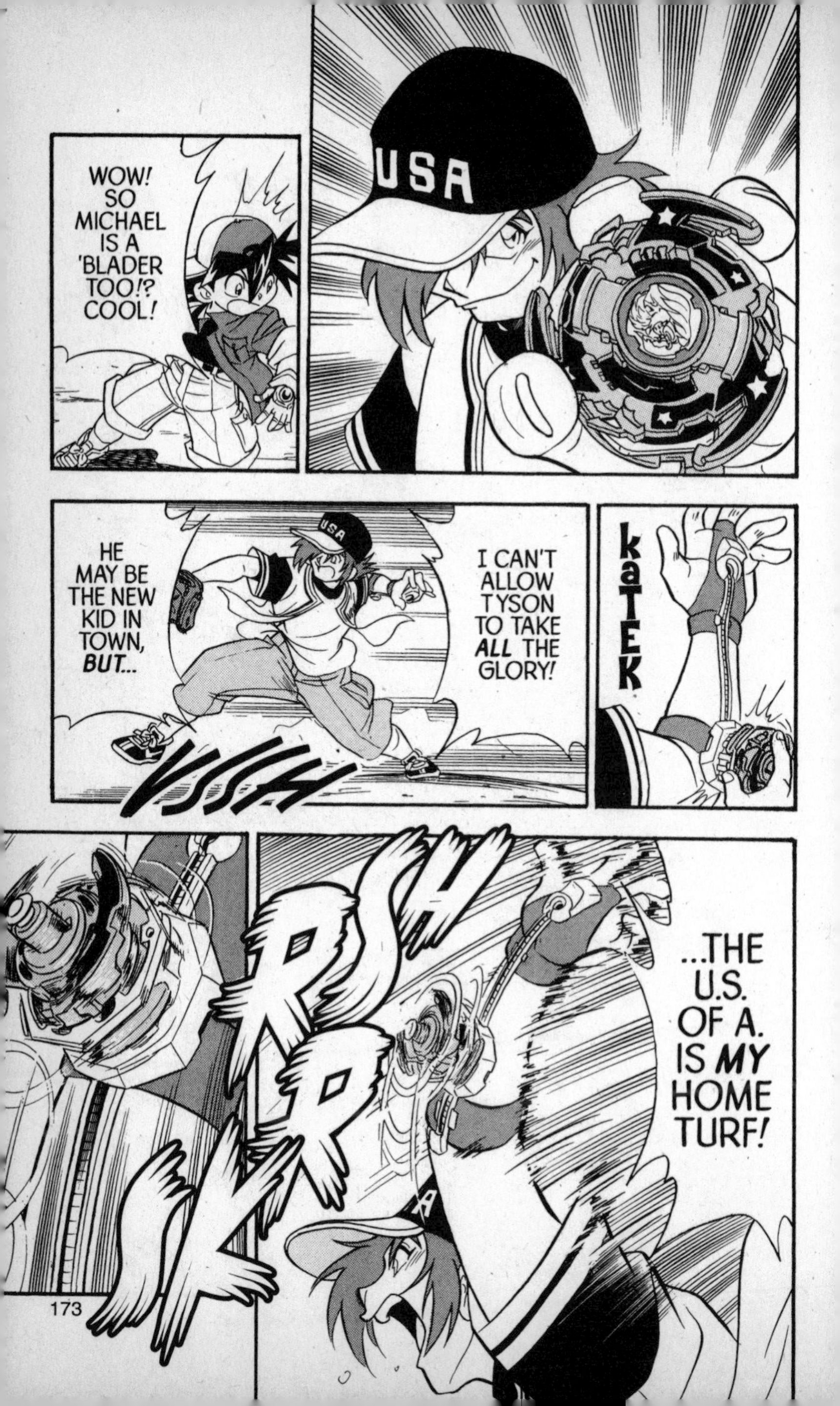
WOW! SO MICHAEL IS A 'BLADER TOO!? COOL!
kaTEK
I CAN'T ALLOW TYSON TO TAKE ALL THE GLORY!
HE MAY BE THE NEW KID IN TOWN, BUT...
VSSH
...THE U.S. OF A. IS MY HOME TURF!

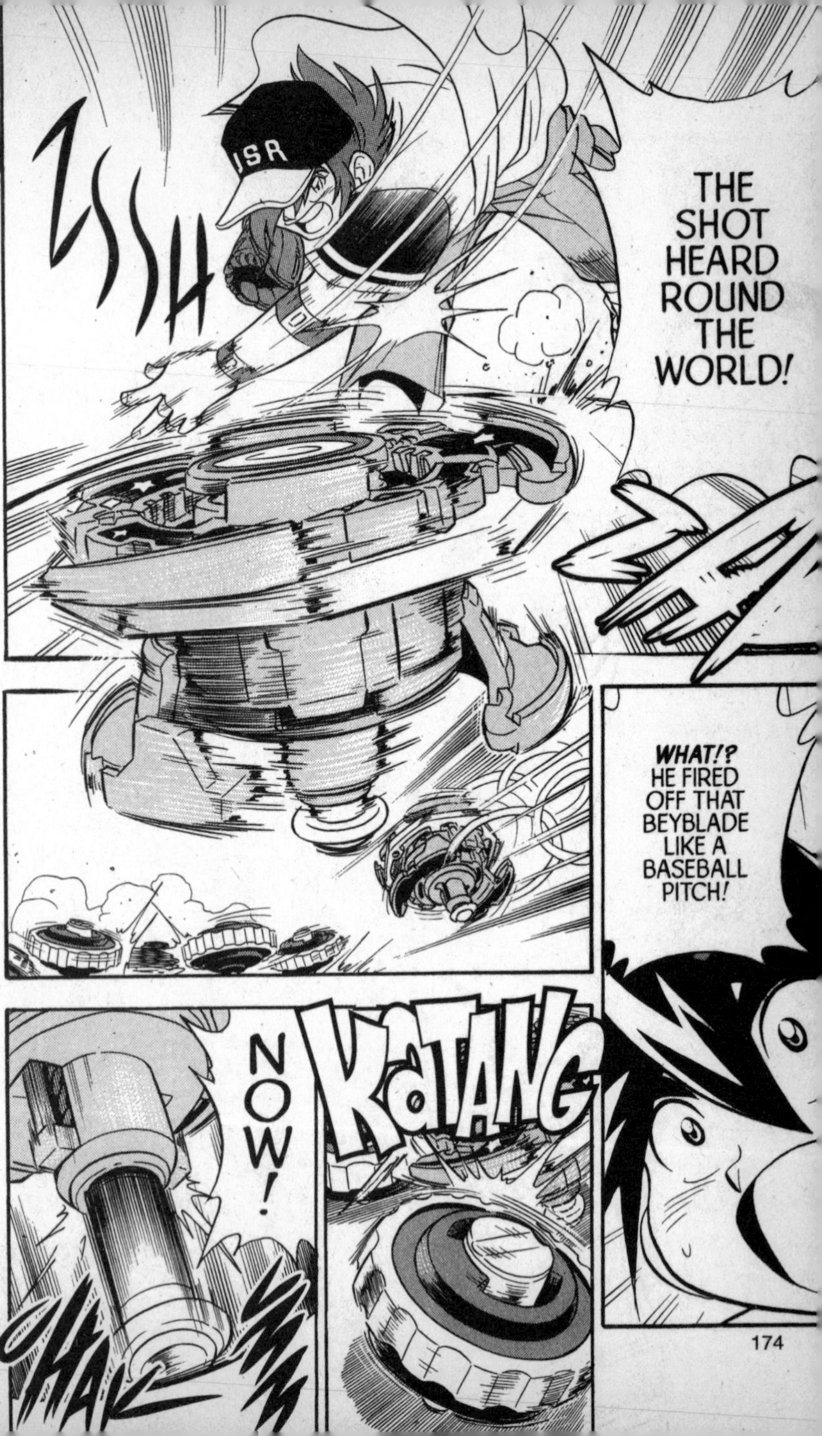
THE SHOT HEARD ROUND THE WORLD!
ZSSH
USR
WHAT!? HE FIRED OFF THAT BEYBLADE LIKE A BASEBALL PITCH!
KATANG
NOW!

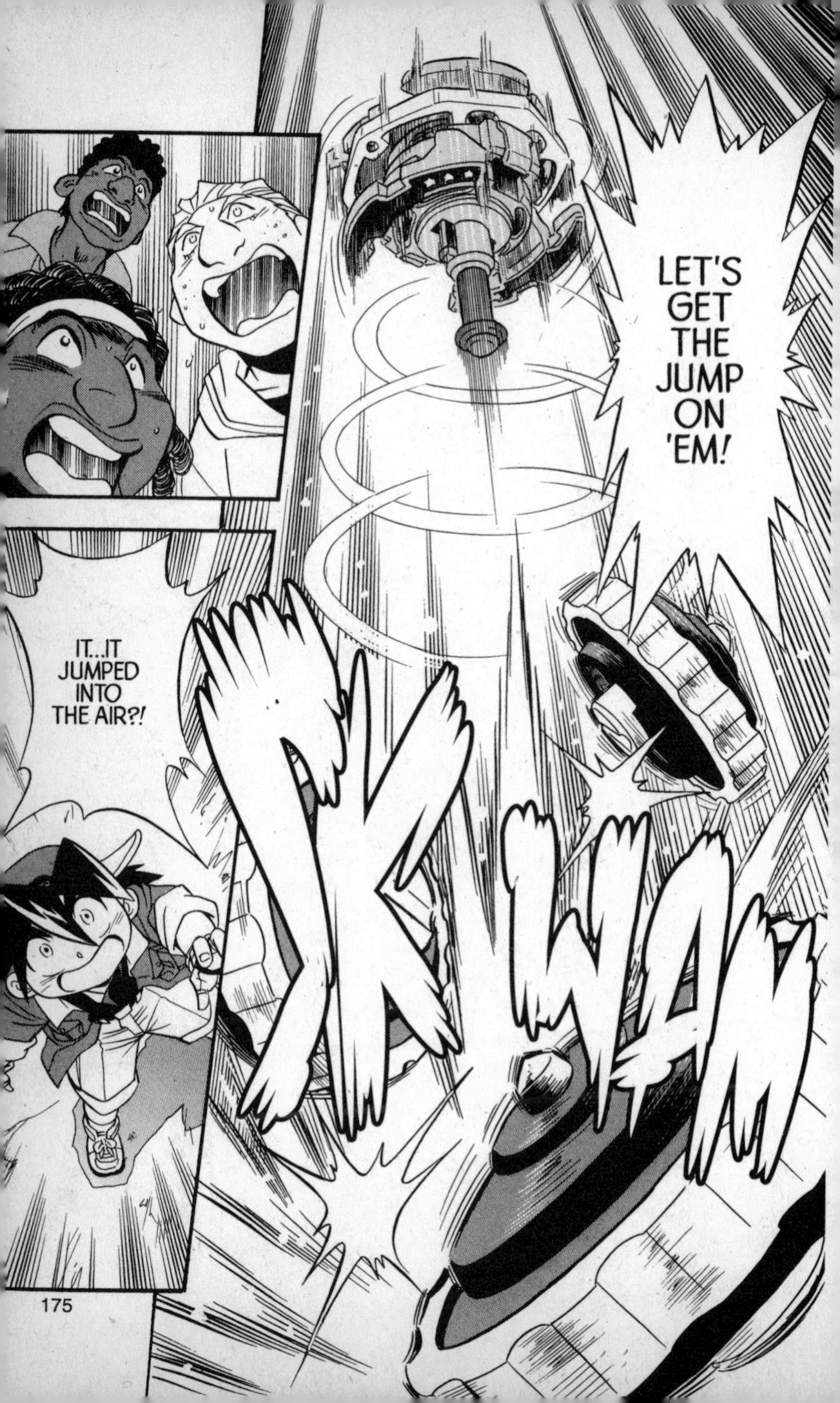
LET'S GET THE JUMP ON 'EM!
IT...IT JUMPED INTO THE AIR?!

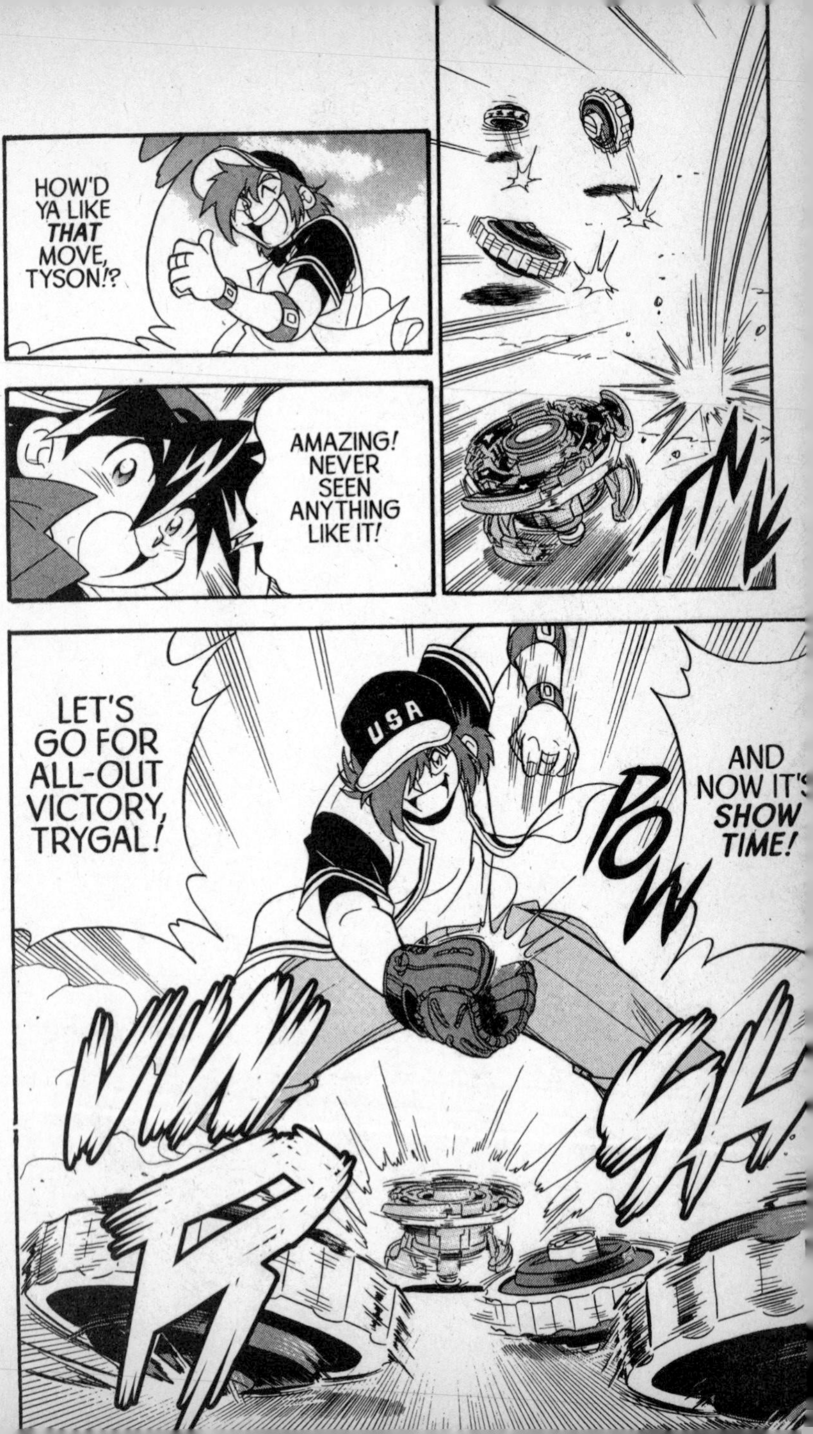
HOW'D YA LIKE THAT MOVE, TYSON!?
AMAZING! NEVER SEEN ANYTHING LIKE IT!
AND NOW IT'S SHOW TIME!
POW
LET'S GO FOR ALL-OUT VICTORY, TRYGAL!

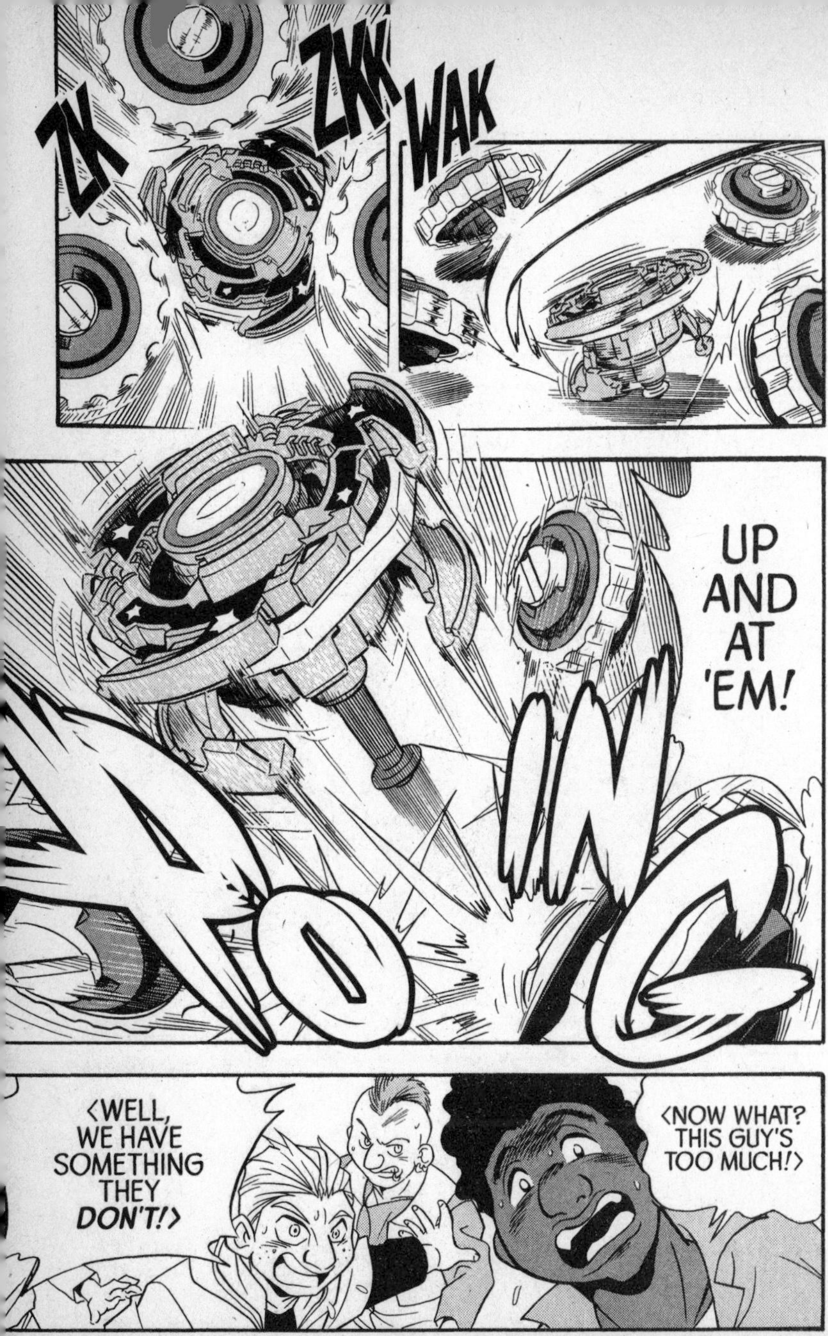
WAK
ZK
ZKK
UP AND AT 'EM!
<NOW WHAT? THIS GUY'S TOO MUCH!>
<WELL, WE HAVE SOMETHING THEY *DON'T!*>

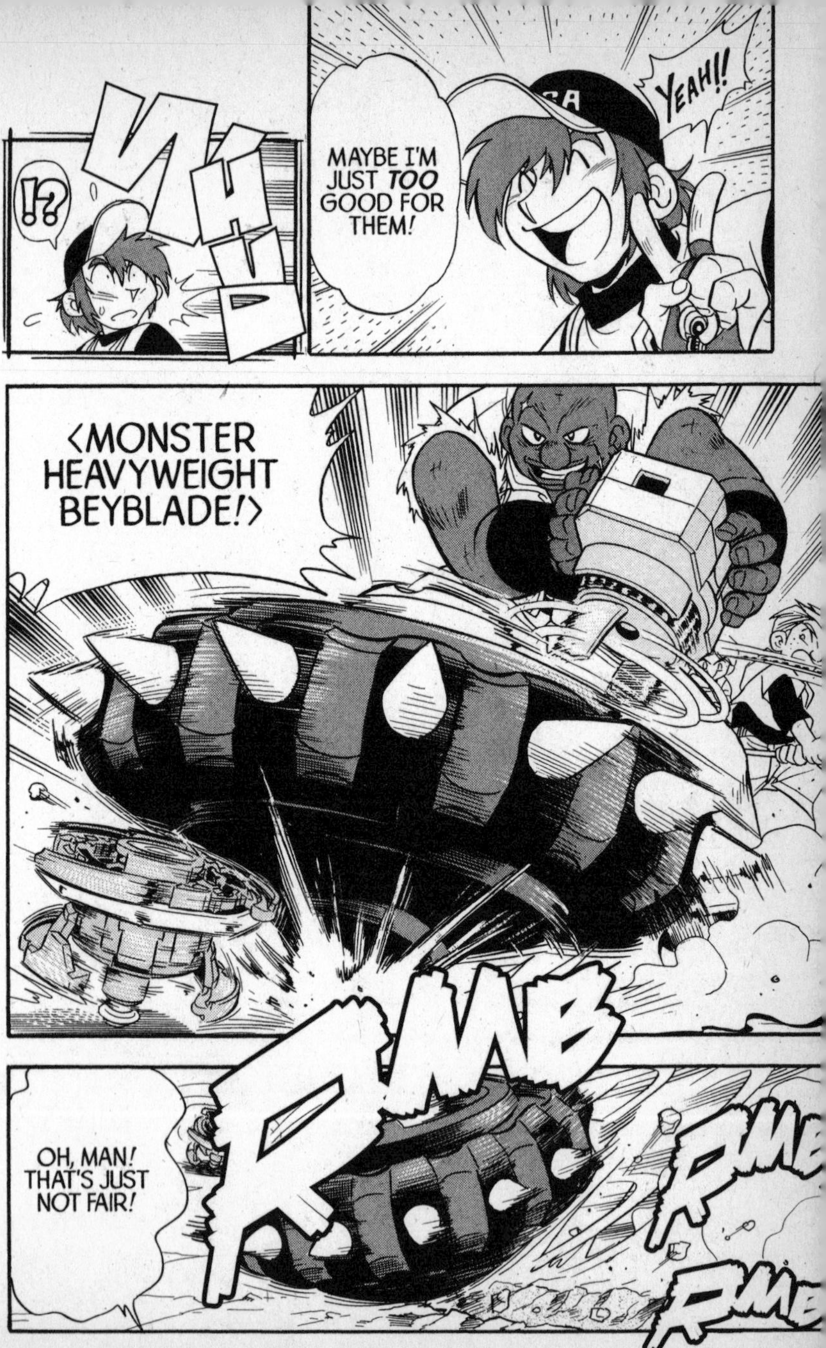
YEAH!!
MAYBE I'M JUST *TOO* GOOD FOR THEM!
!?
<MONSTER HEAVYWEIGHT BEYBLADE!>
OH, MAN! THAT'S JUST NOT FAIR!

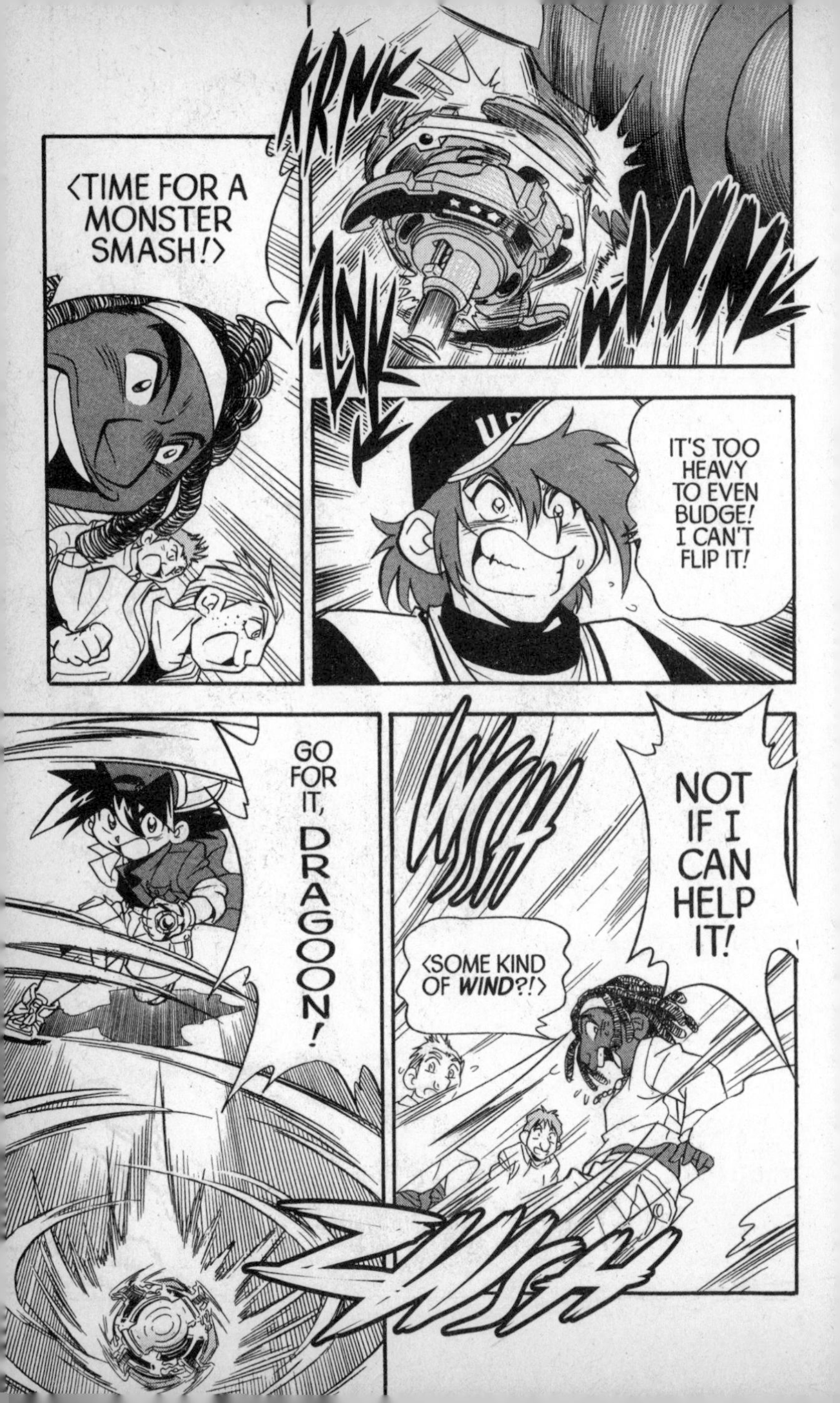
KRNK
IT'S TOO HEAVY TO EVEN BUDGE! I CAN'T FLIP IT!
<TIME FOR A MONSTER SMASH!>
NOT IF I CAN HELP IT!
<SOME KIND OF *WIND*?!>
GO FOR IT, DRAGOOON!

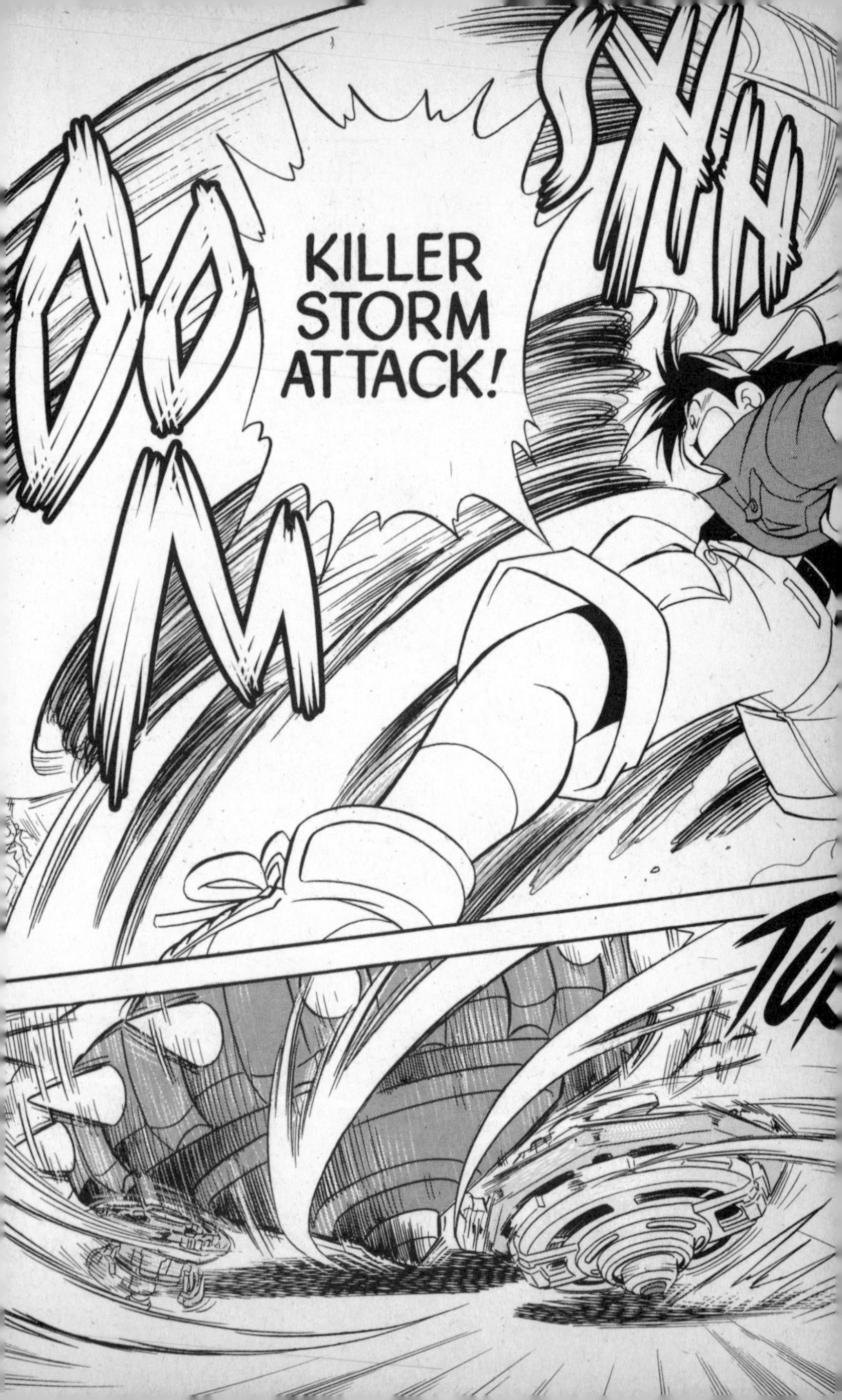
SHH
KILLER STORM ATTACK!

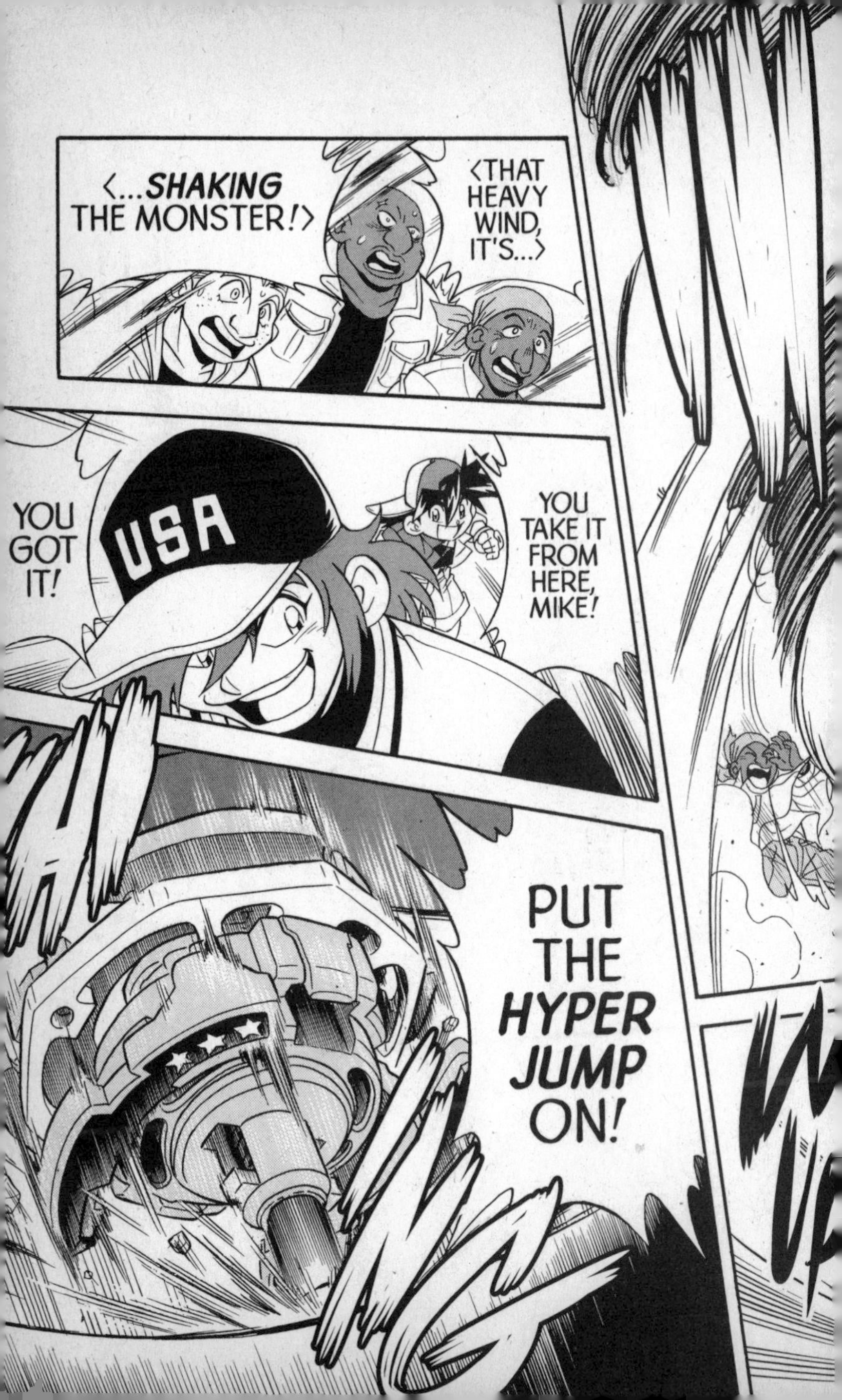
<THAT HEAVY WIND, IT'S...>
<...SHAKING THE MONSTER!>
YOU TAKE IT FROM HERE, MIKE!
YOU GOT IT!
USA
PUT THE HYPER JUMP ON!

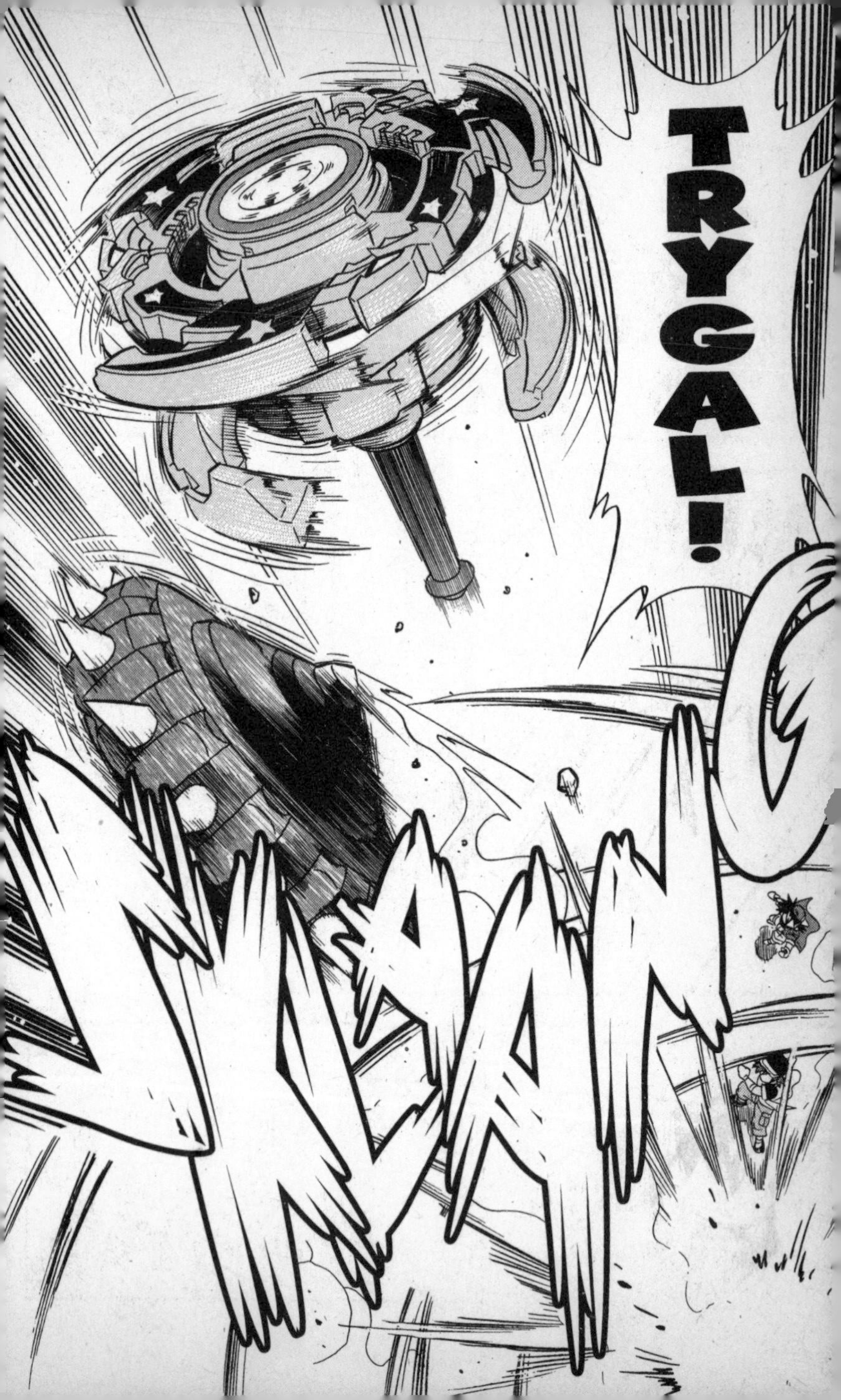
TRYGAL!

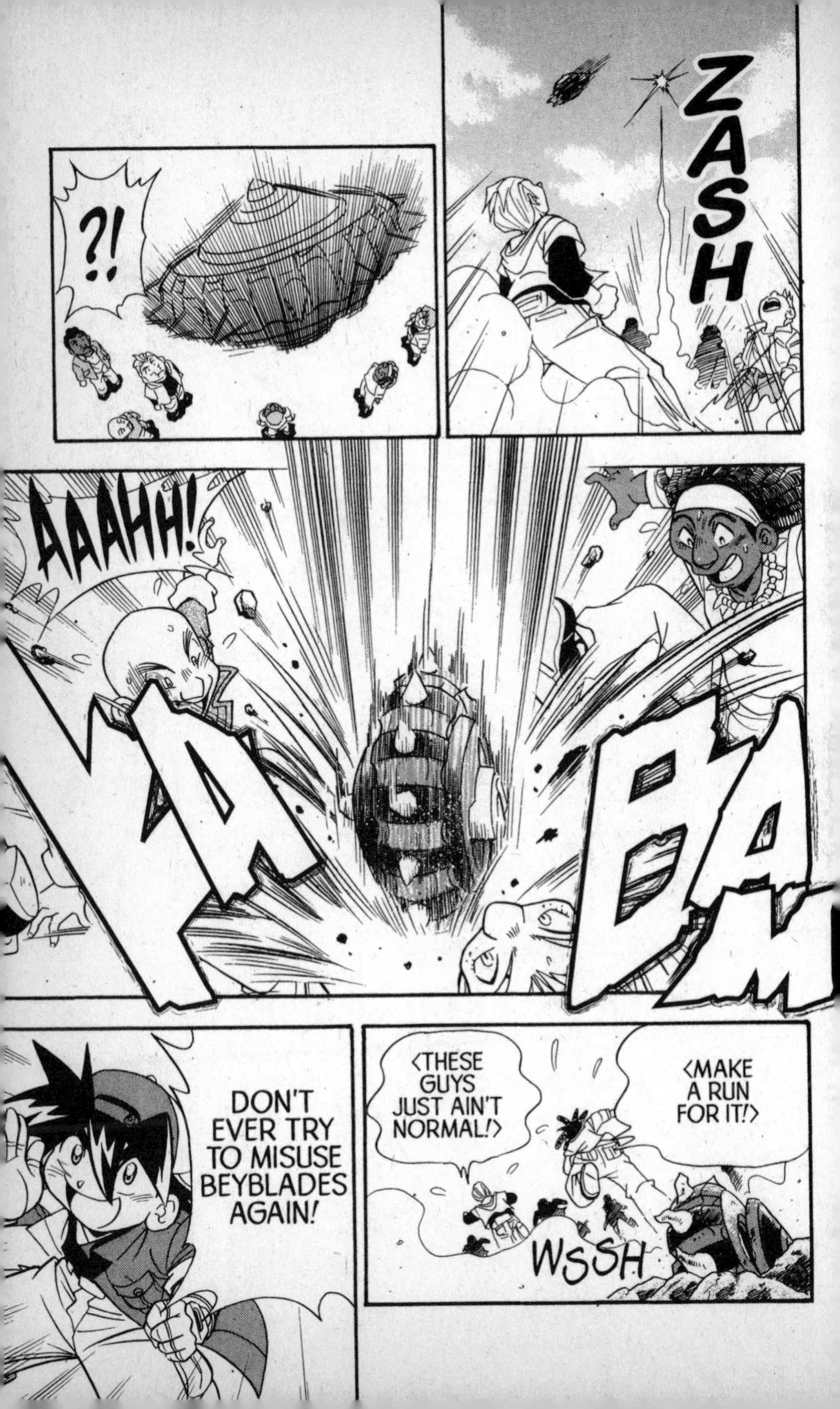
ZASH
?!
AAAHH!
KA BAM
<MAKE A RUN FOR IT!>
<THESE GUYS JUST AIN'T NORMAL!>
WSSH
DON'T EVER TRY TO MISUSE BEYBLADES AGAIN!

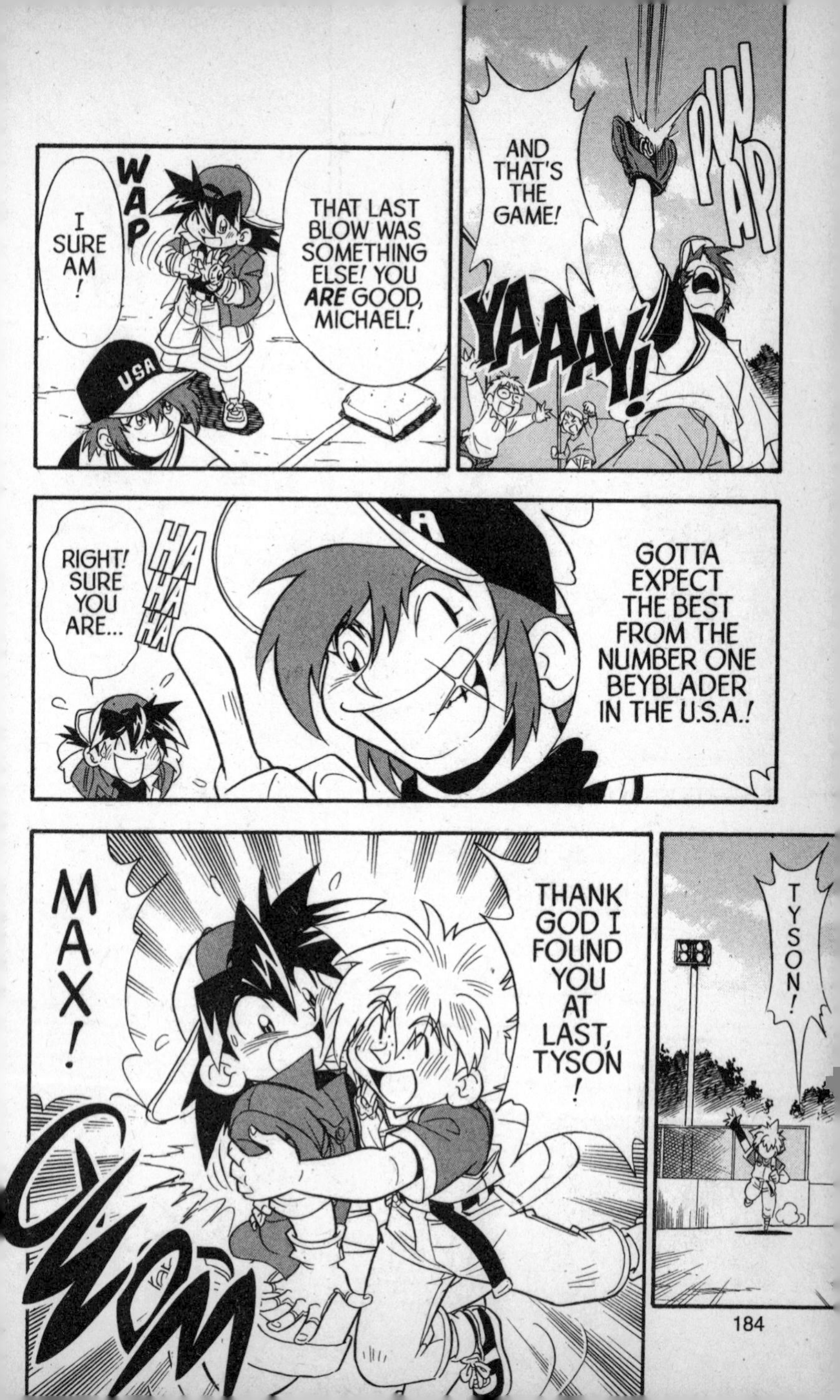
AND THAT'S THE GAME!
PWAP
YAAAY!
THAT LAST BLOW WAS SOMETHING ELSE! YOU ARE GOOD, MICHAEL!
WAP
I SURE AM!
USA
GOTTA EXPECT THE BEST FROM THE NUMBER ONE BEYBLADER IN THE U.S.A.!
HA HA HA
RIGHT! SURE YOU ARE...
TYSON!
THANK GOD I FOUND YOU AT LAST, TYSON!
MAX!

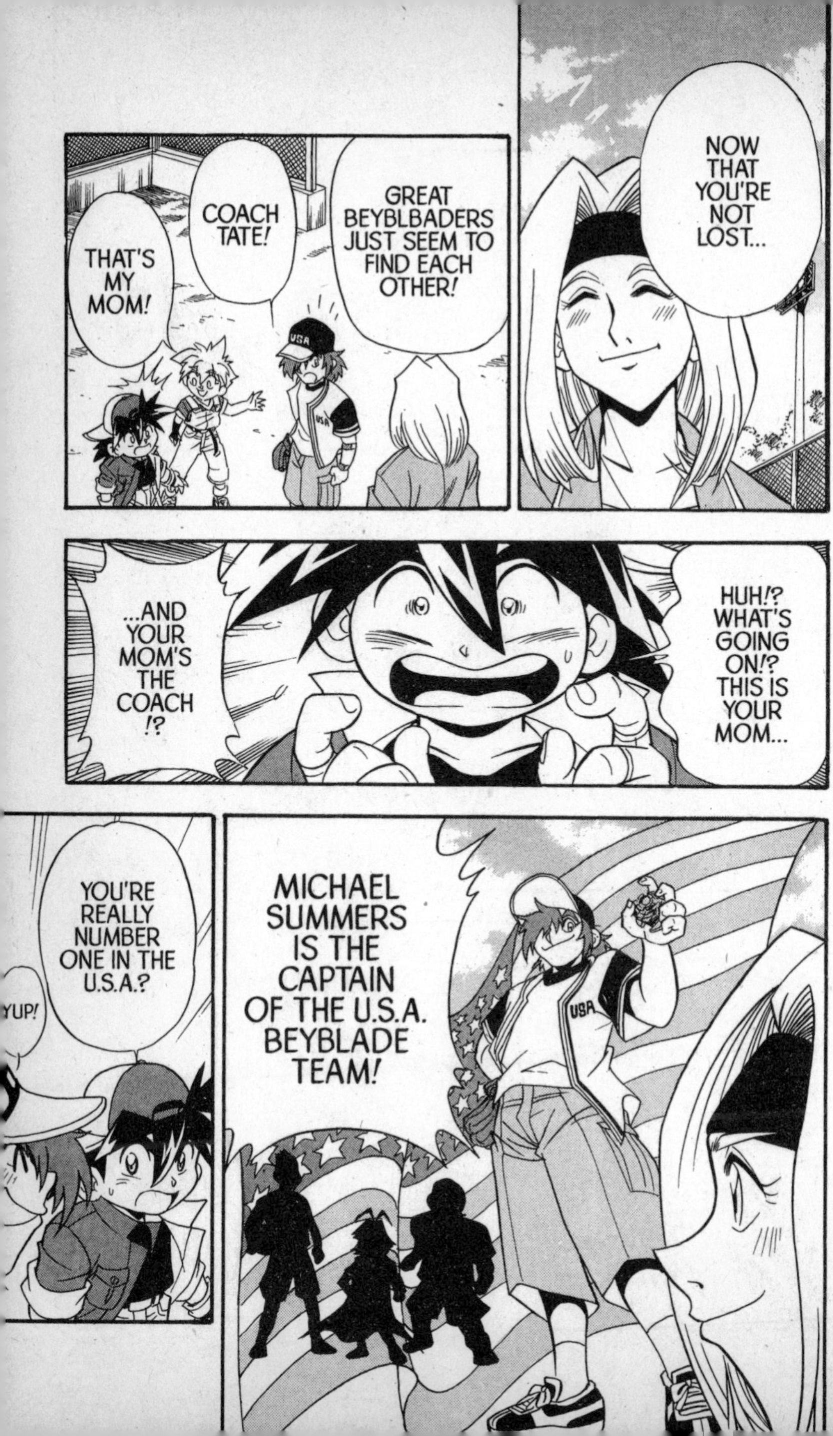
NOW THAT YOU'RE NOT LOST...
GREAT BEYBLBADERS JUST SEEM TO FIND EACH OTHER!
COACH TATE!
THAT'S MY MOM!
HUH!? WHAT'S GOING ON!? THIS IS YOUR MOM...
...AND YOUR MOM'S THE COACH!?
MICHAEL SUMMERS IS THE CAPTAIN OF THE U.S.A. BEYBLADE TEAM!
YOU'RE REALLY NUMBER ONE IN THE U.S.A.?
YUP!

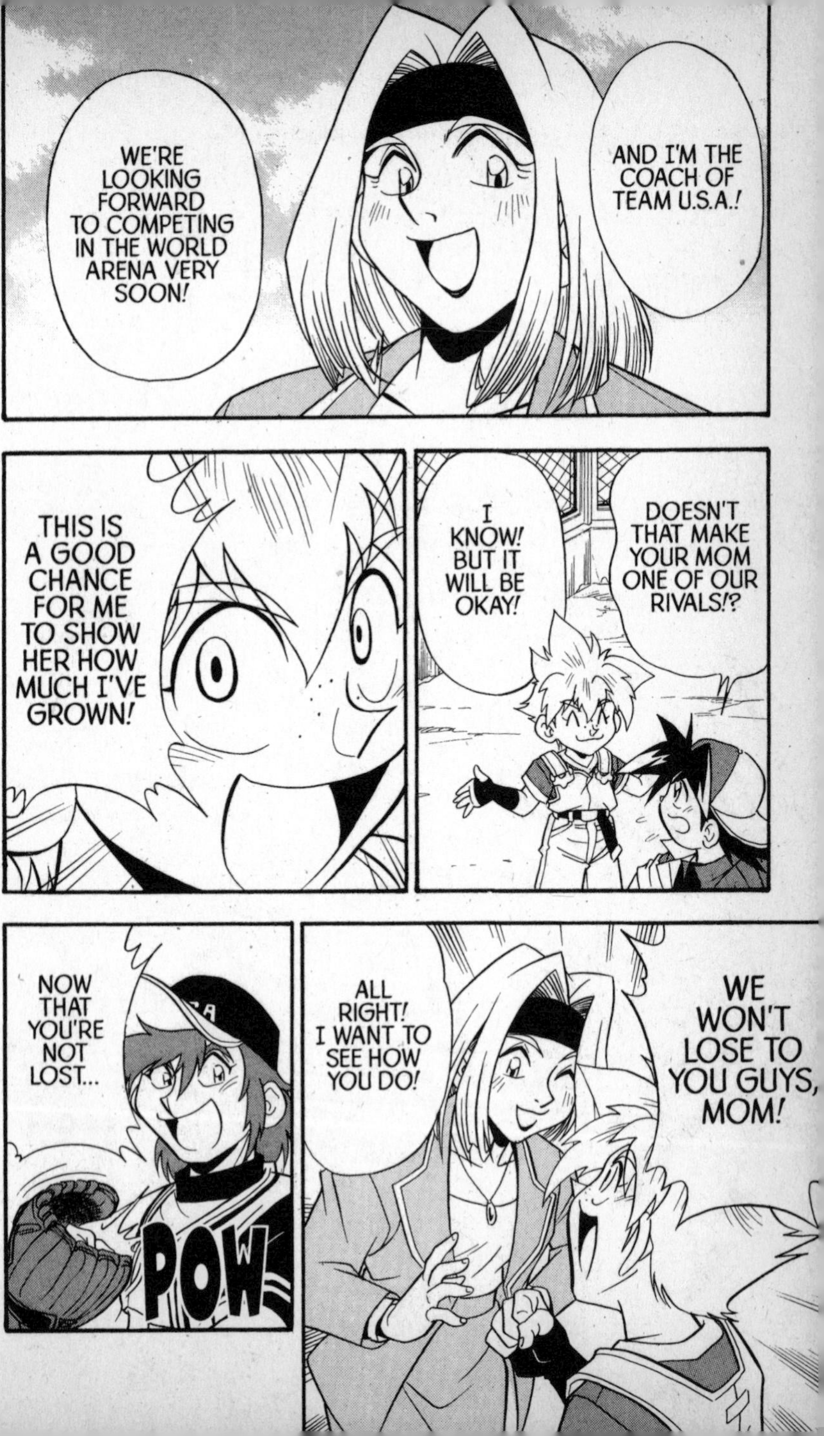
AND I'M THE COACH OF TEAM U.S.A.!
WE'RE LOOKING FORWARD TO COMPETING IN THE WORLD ARENA VERY SOON!
DOESN'T THAT MAKE YOUR MOM ONE OF OUR RIVALS!?
I KNOW! BUT IT WILL BE OKAY!
THIS IS A GOOD CHANCE FOR ME TO SHOW HER HOW MUCH I'VE GROWN!
WE WON'T LOSE TO YOU GUYS, MOM!
ALL RIGHT! I WANT TO SEE HOW YOU DO!
NOW THAT YOU'RE NOT LOST...
POW

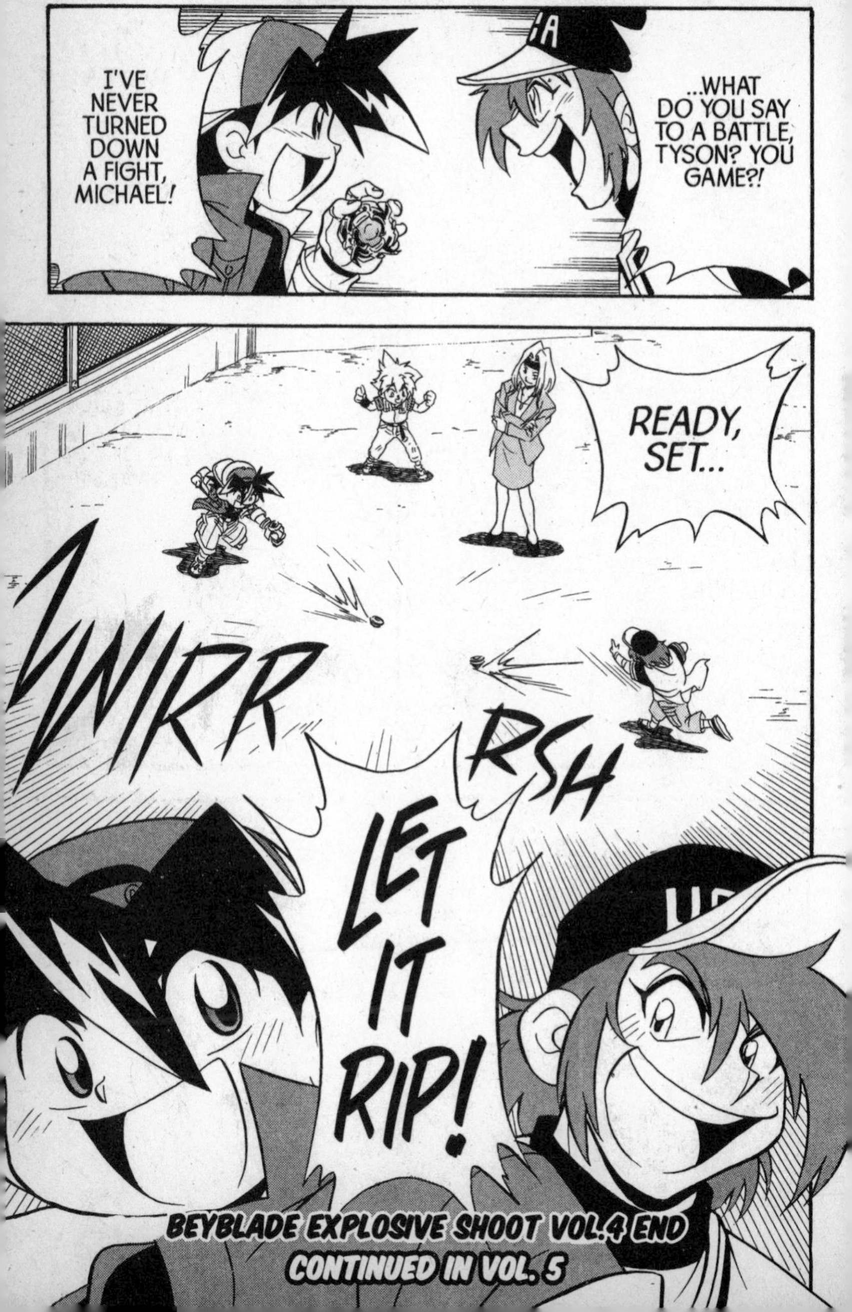
...WHAT DO YOU SAY TO A BATTLE, TYSON? YOU GAME?!
I'VE NEVER TURNED DOWN A FIGHT, MICHAEL!
READY, SET...
WHIRR
RSH
LET IT RIP!
BEYBLADE EXPLOSIVE SHOOT VOL.4 END
CONTINUED IN VOL. 5

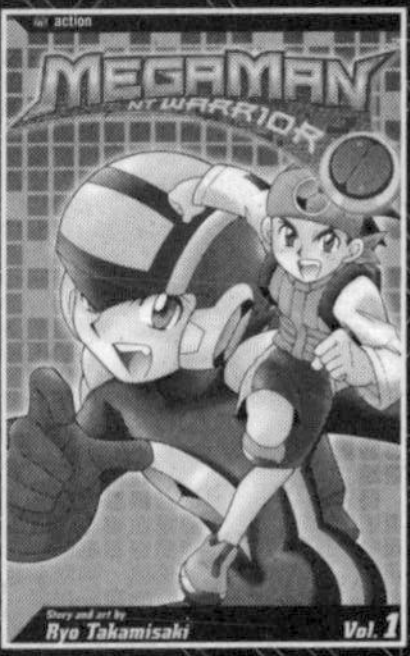

action
MEGAMAN
NT WARRIOR
Story and art by
Ryo Takamisaki
Vol. 1

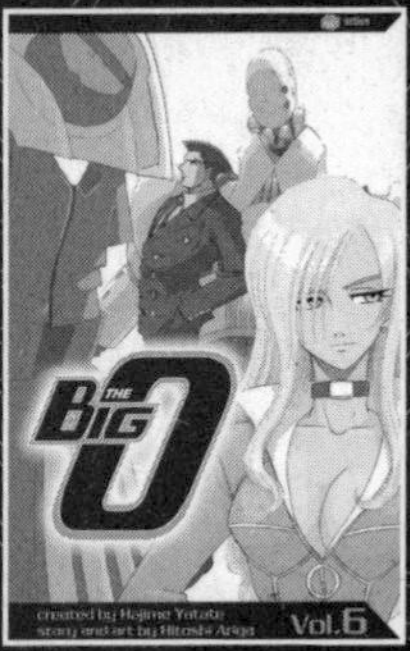

THE BIG O
Vol.6

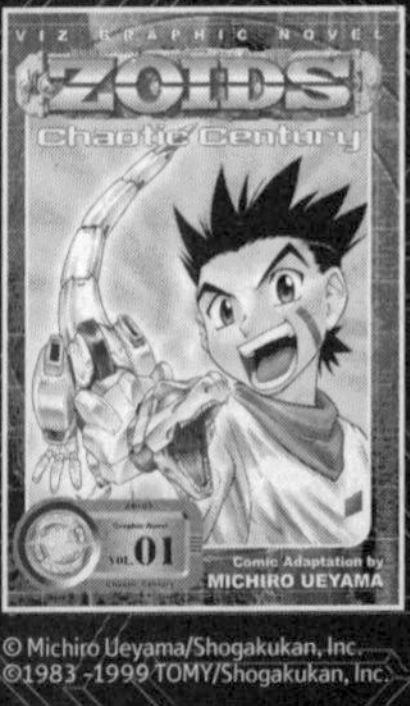

VIZ GRAPHIC NOVEL
ZOIDS
Chaotic Century
VOL.01
Comic Adaptation by
MICHIRO UEYAMA

EDITOR'S RECOMMENDATIONS

If you enjoyed this volume of ***Beyblade*** then here's some more manga you might be interested in.

MEGAMAN : NT Warrior

By Ryo Takamisaki. Our hero, Lan Hikari, synchronizes with *MEGAMAN* and becomes a super-charged dynamo. In and outside of the computer world they do their best to thwart the evil organization, World Three, from taking over the world.

THE BIG O

Created by Hajime Yatate with story and art by Hitoshi Ariga. More than a straight adaptation of the hit Cartoon Network series, the manga includes the prequel to events in *THE BIG O* anime, plus many completely new stories.

ZOIDS: CHAOTIC CENTURY

By Michiro Ueyama. Together, boy and machine fight for peace on Planet Zi. The anime was great. You'll love this series from VIZ, as well.

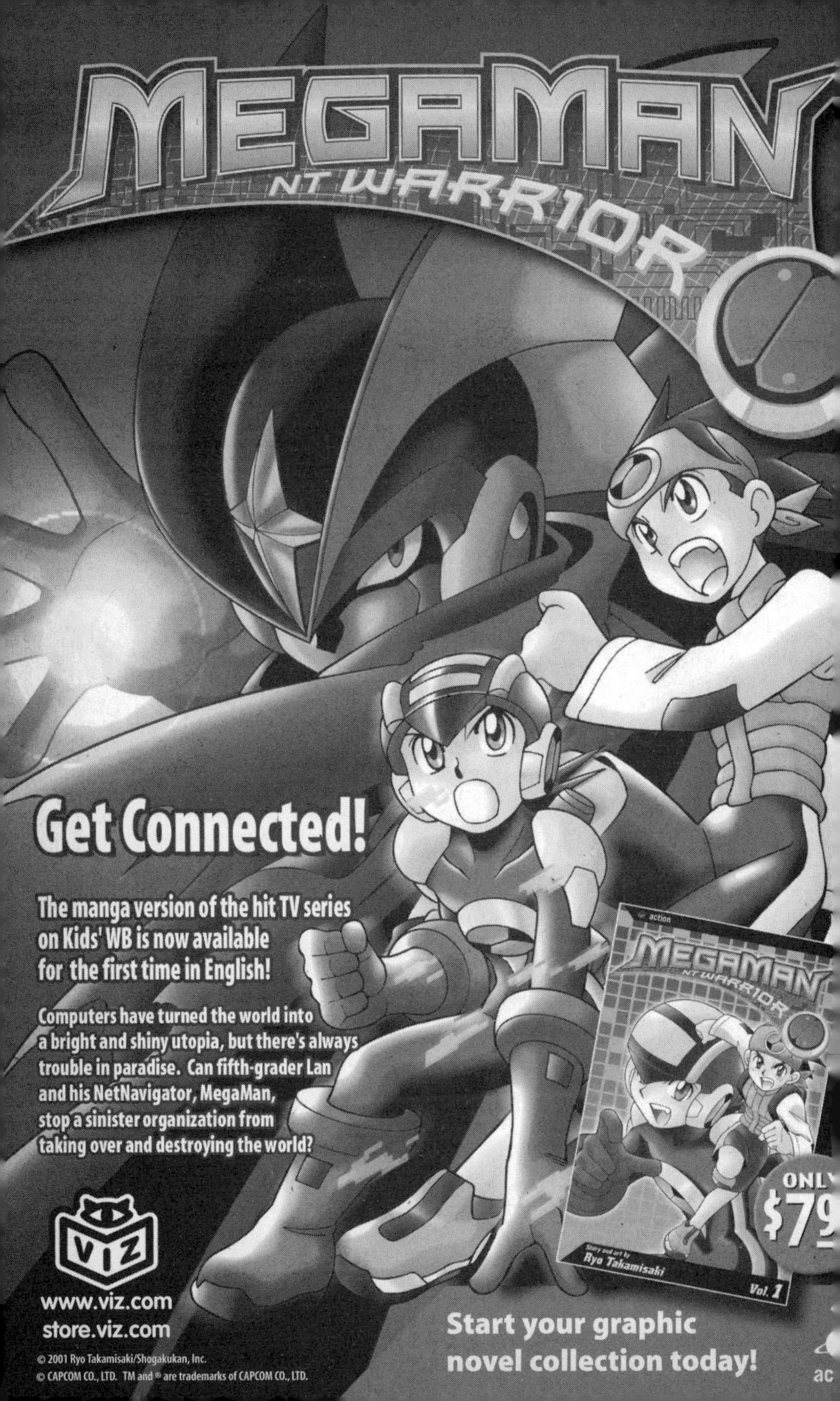
MEGAMAN
NT WARRIOR
Get Connected!
The manga version of the hit TV series on Kids' WB is now available for the first time in English!
Computers have turned the world into a bright and shiny utopia, but there's always trouble in paradise. Can fifth-grader Lan and his NetNavigator, MegaMan, stop a sinister organization from taking over and destroying the world?
action
MEGAMAN
NT WARRIOR
Story and art by
Ryo Takamisaki
Vol. 1
VIZ
www.viz.com
store.viz.com
Start your graphic novel collection today!
© 2001 Ryo Takamisaki/Shogakukan, Inc.
© CAPCOM CO., LTD. TM and ® are trademarks of CAPCOM CO., LTD.

COMPLETE OUR SURVEY AND LET US KNOW WHAT YOU THINK!

☐ Please do NOT send me information about VIZ products, news and events, special offers, or other information.

☐ Please do NOT send me information from VIZ's trusted business partners.

Name: _____

Address: _____

City: _____ **State:** _____ **Zip:** _____

E-mail: _____

☐ Male ☐ Female **Date of Birth** (mm/dd/yyyy): ___ / ___ / ___ (Under 13? Parental consent required)

What race/ethnicity do you consider yourself? (please check one)

☐ Asian/Pacific Islander ☐ Black/African American ☐ Hispanic/Latino

☐ Native American/Alaskan Native ☐ White/Caucasian ☐ Other: _____

What VIZ product did you purchase? (check all that apply and indicate title purchased)

☐ DVD/VHS _____

☐ Graphic Novel _____

☐ Magazines _____

☐ Merchandise _____

Reason for purchase: (check all that apply)

☐ Special offer ☐ Favorite title ☐ Gift

☐ Recommendation ☐ Other _____

Where did you make your purchase? (please check one)

☐ Comic store ☐ Bookstore ☐ Mass/Grocery Store

☐ Newsstand ☐ Video/Video Game Store ☐ Other: _____

☐ Online (site: _____)

What other VIZ properties have you purchased/own? _____

_____

How many anime and/or manga titles have you purchased in the last year? How many were VIZ titles? **(please check one from each column)**

ANIME	MANGA	VIZ
☐ None	☐ None	☐ None
☐ 1-4	☐ 1-4	☐ 1-4
☐ 5-10	☐ 5-10	☐ 5-10
☐ 11+	☐ 11+	☐ 11+

I find the pricing of VIZ products to be: **(please check one)**

☐ Cheap ☐ Reasonable ☐ Expensive

What genre of manga and anime would you like to see from VIZ? **(please check two)**

☐ Adventure ☐ Comic Strip ☐ Science Fiction ☐ Fighting

☐ Horror ☐ Romance ☐ Fantasy ☐ Sports

What do you think of VIZ's new look?

☐ Love It ☐ It's OK ☐ Hate It ☐ Didn't Notice ☐ No Opinion

Which do you prefer? **(please check one)**

☐ Reading right-to-left

☐ Reading left-to-right

Which do you prefer? **(please check one)**

☐ Sound effects in English

☐ Sound effects in Japanese with English captions

☐ Sound effects in Japanese only with a glossary at the back

THANK YOU! Please send the completed form to:

VIZ Survey
42 Catharine St.
Poughkeepsie, NY 12601

All information provided will be used for internal purposes only. We promise not to sell or otherwise divulge your information.